MEMOIRS 1897-1948

Through Diplomacy
to Politics

by

THE RIGHT HONOURABLE
LESTER B. PEARSON
PC, CC, OM, OBE, MA, LLD

With a Foreword by
BARBARA WARD

LONDON
VICTOR GOLLANCZ LTD
1973

First published in Canada under the title *Mike*

© University of Toronto Press 1972

ISBN 0 575 01709 0

Printed in Great Britain by
The Camelot Press Ltd, London and Southampton

to my wife

CONTENTS

❧❧

ILLUSTRATIONS

Following page 146

PREFACE

In his autobiography, Benvenuto Cellini wrote:

All men of whatsoever quality they be who have done anything of excellence or which may properly resemble excellence ought, if they are persons of truth and honesty, to describe their life with their own hand, but they ought not to attempt so fine an enterprise till they have passed the age of forty.

Whether I have done anything of excellence or properly resembling it is not for me to determine. I certainly have had many opportunities so to do. The years of my life have been filled with interest, variety, and excitement. Now that I am far beyond Cellini's age of forty, I venture to yield to his injunction and describe my life 'with my own hand.' This is the first of three volumes to that end.

They tell my own story and therefore, naturally, concentrate more on my association with certain events than with the events themselves. A large part of the first volume deals with my career as a civil servant in the Department of External Affairs. It was there I first played any discernible part in national and international events. At first that part was small, but there was compensation in having a fine view of the stage and its major actors. Later, I moved closer to the centre with appropriate changes in both role and view. The volume ends with my entry into politics as Minister of the department in which I had happily served for twenty years.

Volume 2 will cover my tenure as Secretary of State for External Affairs in the government of Mr Louis St Laurent from 1948 to 1957. The last volume will be concerned with my years as Prime Minister and

Leader of the Liberal party until my retirement from office in April 1968.

To examine and analyse all the relevant papers and documents available to me has been a monumental task. In undertaking it, I have had the invaluable and expert services of Professors John Munro and Alex Inglis. I owe them much, as I do the Canada Council and the Donner Foundation who made their assistance possible; my private secretary and friend, Annette Perron; and Mr A.A. Day, who read and criticized the manuscript. I also wish to acknowledge the skilled and untiring work of my staff in first deciphering and then typing my words. Most of all, I am indebted to my wife who has watched over my work with a constructively appraising eye.

Perhaps a word about the volume's title is in order. If Lester is my name, Mike is what I am usually called. This change goes back to World War I when I was training with the RFC. My Squadron Commander felt that Lester was no name for an aspiring fighter pilot and decided to call me Mike. It stuck, and I was glad to lose Lester.

LBP

᳕

FOREWORD

LESTER PEARSON'S LIFE presents a paradox. He spent most of his career – as a diplomat, as Minister of External Affairs and finally as Prime Minister – in areas strewn with the land-mines of prejudice, bitterness, jealousy and misunderstanding.

The chief task of Canadian diplomacy between 1920 and 1947 – the years during which Pearson rose from a junior officer to the permanent head of the Ministry – was to disengage the country from a 'colonial' relationship with Britain, define its role in the world in the midst of a total war and find a working partnership with its economically overwhelming and amiably indifferent American neighbour. To these complexities Pearson added, when he entered politics as Minister for External Affairs, a successful intervention in one of the great boneyards of diplomatic reputation – the Arab–Israeli dispute – for which he received the Nobel Peace Prize. Then for ten years he led the Liberal Party through the rigours of opposition, election and minority government – all activities calculated to bring out any latent strains of aggression, thwarted ambition or personal ungenerosity, either in the leader or the led.

But here is the paradox. After a life of such total exposure, it is probably more true of Lester Pearson – of 'Mike' as he was universally known – than of any other public figure of our time that he had virtually no enemies and that he was sincerely loved and profoundly mourned by a planet full of friends.

Perhaps there is no accounting for the love of friends. As Montaigne said of La Boëtie: 'I loved him because he was he and I was I.' Yet for a man to go through life in areas of high strain and competition, to be exposed to the most enflamed public issues, to be compelled by position and leadership to take sides and decisions and yet to end universally beloved, this surely is a phenomenon for which some explanation is required. And the fascination of the Pearson Memoirs is that they do begin to suggest an answer.

He was, of·course, a child of good fortune. It was good fortune to be born into a loving, harmonious and deeply religious home in which the twenty-four hours of each day were not long enough for the work and fun and interests of beloved parents and three vigorous, sports-loving sons. It was good fortune in the first World War to be neither killed nor maimed – although a lesser man might not have found such wry humour in the situation of being knocked out of the war by being run over by a bus. It was good fortune to have an excellent mind that could pass the examinations needed for a Fellowship at Oxford or for entry, at the top of the list, to the expanding Foreign Service. It was supreme good fortune – and good sense – to marry a wife of high intelligence and capacity who gave him lifelong domestic happiness but spared him a great man's most insidious risk – domestic idolatry. It was Maryon Pearson who invented the aphorism, delightedly repeated by her husband, that 'behind every successful man stands a surprised woman'.

It must perhaps also be counted good fortune that he happened to be, time and again, at the place where the action was taking place and where it most suited his gifts – in London, for instance, as Hitler's war drew nearer, in Washington when the centre of gravity of allied decision-making moved there, in Ottawa when the 'middle powers' possibility of effective international action depended upon a certain independence from the larger power centres.

But at this point, clearly, it is no longer a matter of fortune. Pearson was in these posts at those times not by chance but by superb use of his very great abilities. Of course they included a capacity to draft well and clearly under pressure, to work a fourteen hour day for weeks on end, to forget nothing and run an orderly office. Such gifts have taken many men to the administrative headship of great offices of State. But the extra gifts Pearson possessed took him further. His drafts were not only clear. They were creative. The hours of work were not routine. They produced a remarkable ability to turn colleagues into confident friends, to see other people's point of view, to keep all properly interested parties informed, to seek formulae that accepted the need for diversity and compromise, to achieve not triumphs, but agreements. It was not only the details he remembered. His mind was disciplined to see the widest interests of his own community, and, beyond it, the plight of all humanity and the desperate need to create an international order in which the horror of two World Wars would not lead to the ultimate horror of nuclear extinction. In his own words, his final aim – in hours of numbing committee work, in an overload of documents and resolutions, often in what must have seemed sheer, heartbreaking waste of time – was a world society sufficiently orderly and rational 'to end the savage tradition that the strong do what they can and the weak suffer what they must'.

A fortunate man, an able man, a good man – is this the explanation of the hosts of friends, the bright trajectory of affection and admiration, the universal mourning at the end? They are part of it but they are not enough. They still leave out the man himself who was all these things, yet carried his fortune and his virtues with a gaiety, a wit, a joyous self-depreciation and a sense of life's ironies that make him, in retrospect, the most humorous and least pompous world leader this or any generation is likely to know. In how many Prime Ministers and Nobel Prize winners would we spontaneously see 'a fellow of infinite jest, of most excellent fancy'? Yet anyone who reads the Pearson Memoirs will find, on almost every page, that crafty understatement, that happy self-debunking, that spontaneous joy in the oddities of the human condition that sprang from Mike's profound lack of sense of his own importance and his equally profound sense of everyone else's interest and value.

He writes of Mackenzie King bumbling through an after dinner speech: 'You would think of him on these occasions as merely a kind, simple old man and you could hardly be more mistaken'; of his own intention to write the definitive history of the United Empire Loyalists: 'Ultimately we collected a large mass of material, still waiting to be transformed by me into a Canadian classic'; of the work of a conference, 'much of which, as is always the case, was done behind the scenes and even in constructing scenes behind which to do it'. One could quote from every page. 'The tone makes the man' – funny, loving, understanding, temperate and wise. The mystery is not the number of his friends. It would have been a mystery if he had made fewer or left behind any less poignant sense of loss among those who were lucky enough to know and love him.

New York   BARBARA WARD
March 1973

MEMOIRS

BACKGROUND AND BOYHOOD

God was in His heaven and Queen Victoria on her throne. All was well. The Empire, on which a sun never dared to set, was being made mightier yet; Canada was about to enter the century that belonged to her. In these optimistic and comfortable – but now so distant – times I was born, on 23 April 1897, at the Methodist parsonage in Newtonbrook, then a village on Yonge Street north of Toronto and now engulfed in that city.

My immediate forbears were good, sturdy, God-fearing, and hardworking people. In the strong and sober fabric of their lives, however, there appeared occasionally a colourful thread of dissidence or eccentricity. My mother's family, the Bowles, came originally from Yorkshire but went to Ireland with Cromwell during the civil wars of the seventeenth century and took root in Tipperary. There they remained, Protestant, puritan, but, in time, completely Irish, until they came to Canada in the 1830s. The Reverend Dr R.P. Bowles, the family chronicler, has written: 'Their English blood had become at least eighty per cent Irish. They were no longer cold-blooded, calculating, rational folk. They had become warm-hearted, hospitable, sociable, highly emotionalized, a bit irresponsible, impetuous, hilarious and blessed with a high disregard of consequences ... in disposition and temperament, not to mention the persisting brogue of their speech, thoroughly Irish.'

Of this clan, I should mention first my grandfather, Thomas Bowles, born in 1830 and died in 1911. He added to my Irish blood by marrying

in 1857 Jane Lester, a girl possessing in generous and appealing
measure those Irish qualities I have just outlined. She always made me
feel, when I was a small boy, that there was no generation gap between
us, even though she was seventy years older. I loved to be with her,
more, I confess, than with my grandfather, a somewhat remote and
much sterner figure. Grandfather Bowles was elected reeve of his
township, Chinguacousy, for ten consecutive terms, and three times
warden of his county. He was a provincial Liberal candidate twice, and
a federal candidate once; and, although defeated each time by his Tory
opponent, it was never by more than one hundred votes. His services,
ability, and character were recognized when the Premier of Ontario in
1881 appointed him as first sheriff of the new Dufferin County. When
in impressive uniform donned for some judicial decision, cocked hat
and all, he was occasionally driven in his carriage from the solid Victorian, red-brick house in Orangeville, he then appeared to his grand-
son as on the very summit of official dignity and position, an impression strengthened by his stately manner and austere bearing. The
frailties of old age never removed the feeling of awe that he inspired in
me. The only one in his family to desert the farm for other activities,
business and politics, he was a highly regarded figure in Dufferin and
Peel counties for many years. Along with his two brothers, both remarkable men in their own ways, he had learned much with little
formal education. He was a Methodist local preacher, a pillar of that
church and of the Liberal party. When he died in 1911, the Toronto
Globe, which to the Bowles clan ranked only below the Bible as the
source of all truth and wisdom, wrote that 'he was a man of fine
presence and splendid physical and mental qualities; of the most un-
impeachable integrity and recognized rectitude and of a most obliging
disposition.'

Moving to the other side of my heredity, the Pearsons were also of
Irish stock and Methodist religion, and seem to have been more prosperous in Dublin than were the Bowles in Tipperary. My great-grand-
father was a linen draper, apparently of some substance. When he
came to Toronto, some years after the Bowles had begun homesteading
in the bush north of that city, he opened a small drygoods store on
Yonge Street. My grandfather, however, decided that the Methodist
ministry, and not merchandizing, was his calling. He became one of
that church's most distinguished divines at a time when Ontario pul-
pits were powerful with great preachers. He was a godly but cheerful
man with a zest for life and a great love of games and outdoor activity.
There was little of awe in my feeling for him, but an abundance of
affection and camaraderie.

Grandfather Pearson had a particular passion for baseball, a passion inherited by his son, my father, and his grandsons. My last outing with him was on Dominion day in 1913. He had retired from the ministry; he was frail, aging, and his eyesight almost gone. The Toronto baseball team, in the old International League, was to play two games, morning and afternoon, on that holiday at the Ball Park at Hanlan's Point, across Toronto Bay. Grandfather was determined to go, and his son, my uncle Harold, with whom he was then living, agreed, on condition that he was suitably escorted and that he return home right after the morning game, before the crowd began to gather for the afternoon. I was the happy and excited escort. I remember we had good seats. Equally important, they were free because the owner of the club, a Jewish gentleman, welcomed ministers of the Christian faith as his guests. It was an exciting game and my grandfather, who could barely see the players, let alone the ball, enjoyed it as much as I did. In fact, he suggested after it was over that we shamelessly disobey our instructions, get something to eat at a refreshment stand, and watch the afternoon game. So we stayed, and when we reached home that evening, the two happy, if guilty, companions shared the cold disapproval that met them. It was our last time together, for my grandfather died not long afterwards.

Grandfather Pearson ensured that my heritage should not be entirely Irish by marrying Hetty Marsh, a kindly lady who came from the village of Consecon in Prince Edward County, at the other end of Lake Ontario. Grandma Pearson was not interested in baseball but she insisted that I become a great pianist one day. She was of solid New England Quaker stock, on her mother's side a Whittier, and she provided a sober and redeeming balance to so much Irish blood in my inheritance.

If I later acquired any talent for diplomacy and ability to get along with people, its source must have been largely my Pearson grandfather. His last charge was Strathroy. He had been there three years and he was not certain that he would be invited for the fourth since he had reached the age of retirement. But he had no wish to retire. I am indebted to his former student assistant, the Reverend Mr Hone, for this story of how he managed to ensure·that he did not:

At that time in the Methodist church the pastoral term was three years, but upon a special invitation of the officials the term might be extended to four years. It was the custom for the Official Board to give a yearly invitation, usually at the February meeting. Your grandfather had been minister for three years, and would like to remain a fourth. The people liked him very well, but the officials thought they would bid for a younger man.

The February meeting came around with your grandfather in the chair. He grew very anxious as the usual routine business was gone through and no mention made of an invitation for the minister. Two or three times he asked if an important item of business was not being overlooked, but no one took the hint.

Finally, there was nothing for it but to ask the officials to rise for the benediction. They did. The astute old war horse cleared his throat and said: 'Brethren, there is a most pressing item of business which you have inadvertently overlooked. It is the matter of securing a pulpit supply for next year. All those in favour of inviting the present minister to remain for another year please remain standing. The rest may sit down.'

The officials looked at one another, and someone snickered. Before anyone could sit down your grandfather said, 'Thank you for this unanimous invitation to remain. We will be dismissed.' And he pronounced the benediction.

I should not end these references to my Pearson grandparents without adding that, in contrast to the Bowles, they all seemed to be Tories: loyal but not intolerant members of the Orange Order. My grandfather once agreed in a family discussion that if a Liberal candidate were honest, God-fearing, a good Methodist, and a prohibitionist, while the Tory was a rascally, hard-drinking Episcopalian, he would be morally obliged to vote for the foe, if he voted at all. He refused, however, to admit that such a situation could arise.

𝕿

If I owe much to my grandparents and their heritage, I have been doubly and deeply blessed in my own parents. There is nothing but joy and thanksgiving in my memory of two fine, saintly characters. It is not possible to assess, though it is to acknowledge, how much I owe to them.

My father, one of a family of five, three boys and two girls, inherited the warm personality of his own father. He was an outgoing, friendly, easy-going man. Indeed, my mother used to think that he was rather too easy-going and too loyal to his favourite philosophy, 'Live and let live.' He got along well with almost everyone and was considered to be an almost ideal pastor for his Methodist flocks; a better pastor, perhaps, than preacher. He worked hard on his sermons, spending hours in his study, composing and committing them to memory while he walked to and fro on the carpet. This was a time for three small boys to keep quiet or take our noise and high spirits beyond hearing distance of the study. My father was not an intellectual. He did not read widely, and his library was largely theological. He had little of the Irish eloquence that my grandparents had, preferring to reason and explain. He was a modest minister, not an embattled evangelist, and he led his flock rather than harried it. But his goodness and his sincerity shone through his words, and his congregations were respectful and impressed – as I well remember from sitting in the minister's family pew every Sunday for many years. With him, the man was the message. His life was one of service to his God and his fellow men.

He inherited from his father, as I did from him, a strong liking for games of all kind and he was good at them. This predilection for games was at the time unusual and, to the more rigid, no doubt, somewhat suspect for a minister of the Methodist church. Prayer meetings and ninth inning rallies were not regarded as a wholesome or acceptable ministerial mix. In his younger days he loved to play cricket and lacrosse, but baseball more than either. That love persisted over the years. At Sunday School picnics he would prefer to play first base in a pick-up game than to superintend the arrangements. As he grew older, and until his death, he curled and lawn-bowled. I remember how triumphant he felt when once a rink of parsons, the 'Sky Pilots' as they were called, won an Ontario bowling tournament.

When Father was given an honorary doctorate of divinity from Victoria College in 1927, the tribute to him included these words: 'Always well-informed, with a well-balanced mind, with sanity of judgment and with a warmth of heart which reveals itself in a genial and winning personality. He seems to us to be in very many respects the ideal Christian Minister.' He was proud to have his church recognize his ministry, but he was the least prideful man I have ever met; tolerant, modest, and humane. His children learned from him that rank and riches count for little among the higher values; that a man was indeed 'a man for a' that'; that sincerity and simplicity were good, pomp and pretence suspect; above all, that one's religion went beyond church-going and formal profession although these were very much a part of his life and of ours.

My mother made this partnership complete. She had been brought up in a comfortable home, with a good education befitting a young lady of her time. She was only a girl when she married a young minister with three country churches for his parish, a large brick house for a parsonage, and a few hundred dollars a year supplemented by contributions in kind for an income. She soon had to take care of three babies, all boys (of whom I was the second), though she would have dearly loved a daughter. She also cheerfully did all the parish duties of a minister's wife in the way expected by parishioners. Life was not easy for mother; there was cooking, including bread-baking; soap-making and washing in the backyard; pumping water from the well or even, at one parsonage, pulling it up by a bucket; serving for the family; making do and, also, making ends meet. Things were easier later on, but those first years for her must have been hard. If they were, they were also happy; certainly, for her children, they were very happy. We lacked nothing that was important, although I longed for a bicycle, a boy scout uniform, and a pair of genuine tube hockey skates.

We were a closely knit family group. We did things together and when, as in our school work, we had to depend on ourselves, mother and father were as interested in the results, and in helping to achieve them, as we were. Mother, who worked so hard and was often unwell, was the centre of our little group, its soul and its solace. She surrounded her children with a sense of security and love that had its greatest reward in their growth and their successes. She never failed us. She was ambitious that we succeed in what we undertook, but not at any price. Her advice to me, then and all through the years, might be summed up: 'Be a good boy' and 'Keep your feet dry.' She sent me off to war and into politics with these injunctions. I am not sure in which occupation it was the more difficult to abide by them. Like my father, she was unimpressed by pomp and position and heartily agreed with him when he once advised me to be kind and understanding to people I passed on the way up, since I would no doubt meet them again on the way down.

My father died when he was sixty-three. He was strong and healthy and might have lived for many more years if a ruptured appendix had not been wrongly diagnosed. Mother, who in middle age had often been ill and was supposed to be frail, lived to be ninety-four. After father's death, she kept house in Toronto for my bachelor brother and was active and alert until the end which came suddenly as she was dressing to go to a tea party.

As a child of an itinerant Methodist minister I moved every three years or so from one place to another, one brick parsonage to another brick parsonage; from school to school and church to church, always in southern Ontario. From Newtonbrook to Davisville (also now within Metropolitan Toronto); then up Yonge Street for a few miles to Aurora; back to Centennial Church in Toronto and the parsonage next to it on Dovercourt Road. Then followed a move to Peterborough (how we loved that city) and on to Hamilton and Chatham. World War I began while Father was the pastor at Park Street Church in Chatham, and when I returned from the war, we were living in Guelph. By then, domestically, I was on my own, and later parental homes in Windsor and London were for me only places to visit.

To a boy, there were advantages and disadvantages in moving

around so much. There was hardly time to take root or become attached to a house and community. But against this there were new scenes, new people, new experiences. I was fortunate in being able to adjust easily, and make new friends. The Ontario school system was always very much the same wherever we lived. So were the church and the parsonage, at least to the children of the family. Home was always warm and secure.

Parsonage life in those early days was simple and reasonably serene; a cycle of home, church, and school. Home, the parsonage, was usually a big house, with trees, a lawn, and a backyard for vegetables and games. It was the centre of our life, growth, and training. The air was pure and the skies clear and blue. We did our own work, and made our own fun, together. The pace of life was less hurried, and we lived more closely with nature. No one we knew suffered from tensions. We did know some very old people, our parents, of course, were old to us, but we had to wait for half a century to learn that there was a generation gap with something sinister about it. We did not need movies, radio, or television to help us pass the time, for we never had enough time for all the things we wished to do. Nor were we exposed to bold and shrill urgings to buy all sorts of things to make us splendid. We had little money, but our greatest pleasures cost us nothing.

We were shielded from such temptations as did exist by our small income and the religious teaching and convictions which formed so great a part of our lives. There was little occasion for tears or rebellion, for our parents combined the godly with the happy and humane, both in precept and example. Our household was religious, without being stuffy or sanctimonious. If we prayed before eating, we played afterwards. But not 'cards': that was wicked because it meant gambling – almost as bad as tobacco and strong drink. Against these we took pledges at Sunday School. Dancing was somehow wrong, too – at least for us. The children of a Methodist parsonage had to set an example and we were always under careful scrutiny. Even movies, when they entered into our lives, were 'off limits' until Father discovered that the owner of one movie house not far from our home attended church and did not ignore the collection plate. So this diversion, if not to be encouraged, became respectable. Our only problem was to find the five cents which got us in to a flickering version of *Ali Baba and the Forty Thieves* complete with a local pianist. Afterwards, I recall, we acted the exciting drama all over again in the school yard, and fought over who was to be Ali Baba.

There was not, as I remember, much intellectual or artistic stimulus in our home life. Church politics were discussed more than national, at least in front of the children. School and games, and my older brother's precocious interest in girls, were the main subjects of our chatter. Our school homework was conscientiously done; if we wanted to play, it had to be. Reading, of a kind at least to improve the mind and form an appreciation of good literature, was limited. All I learned of Shakespeare in those early days was from *Lamb's Tales*. I read through much of Dickens, however, some of Thackeray and some Scott. Redpath's *History of the World*, with wonderful illustrations, almost exclusively of battles, made a great impression on me.

The Sunday School library encouraged similar interests. From its shelves I learned of life and adventure through Horatio Alger, G.A. Henty, and similar heroic books. Henty was, I must admit, the author whom I knew best among all English writers until I went to college. His exciting stories based on history's more romantic episodes stirred my imagination mightily and, I suspect, had much to do with my liking for and concentration on history in my educational progress. When years later I travelled extensively abroad as Canada's Secretary of State for External Affairs, there was hardly a place I visited which I had not known through that prolific but now almost forgotten writer of adventure stories for boys.

The church was almost as close to us as home; so close that it became at times almost oppressive, at least on Sunday: Junior League at ten, morning service at eleven, Sunday School at half-past two, and Evening Service at seven. Voluntary service in those days, rather than conscription, might have made me a more faithful attendant in later life. But no minister's son had any choice.

I was spared Wednesday night prayer meetings but I have been to those, too; and to old-fashioned Methodist class meetings where, moved by the spirit, the faithful often called emotionally on the Lord. Once I was in disgrace for going to sleep on my knees; when all the others rose, I remained down. For a moment, this was taken as proof of an exceptional and deep spirituality in one so young, until it was clear that it was a sign only of weariness. Revival meetings too I remember, and the feeling of mild guilt I always experienced when I did not signal with others that I wished to be saved and walk to the front. Frankly, I was aware of no condition from which saving was required. Religion, if not very relevant to the Pearson boys in an evangelical sense, was ours by instinct, part of our being. Why, then, did we have to be converted? Signing the pledge to avoid like the plague all intoxicating liquors was different. That was a precise and accepted duty. I knew what drunkenness meant and how evil it was, something to be crushed. So I sang vigorously in Sunday School that 'We'll turn down our glasses [repeated three times] when filled with red wine,' only mildly wondering how you would clean up the ensuing mess. I even won a prize once for a Sunday School composition on 'Abolish the Bar.'

My first memories include somewhat uncertainly a pottery across the road from our house in Davisville; a barrel-organ making me cry with fear since the music came from nowhere; nightmares which seemed to occur often and from which I was always rescued by solicitous parents; the celebration of the relief of Mafeking. These recollections are now, of course, a bit shadowy, but my first day at kindergarten in Aurora, in 1901, at the age of four, is still vivid. Miss Lois Webster, my teacher, held my hand to show me how to write, or rather trace the word, 'cat'! We exchanged views about that sixty-five years later when she was persuaded to join me on the platform at a political meeting in Aurora, although she was ninety or so and I was Liberal leader.

In Aurora during my kindergarten days I first became a demonstrator, a public dissident, when I tagged along with the bigger boys and girls as they marched away from, instead of into, school because the authorities refused to dismiss us and give us a holiday on the Queen's birthday. Vivid, also, is the memory of the evening when, with a greater display of imperial patriotism, the whole village went down to the station to cheer and to pay their respects to the Duke of York, soon to be heir to the throne, and his Duchess whose train was to slow up as it came to Aurora en route from Toronto to the West. I was hoisted on my father's shoulders, to the disgust of my brothers who accused me of pushing ahead, and became, I thought, a prominent figure in the crowd. More than half a century later, as a minister of the crown, I found myself seated beside Queen Mary, that earlier duchess, at a dinner at Buckingham Palace. I reminded her of that great occasion at the Aurora station in 1902 at which I had been present. 'Oh, my husband and I always had such happy memories of that visit to Canada', she replied. 'I remember quite distinctly leaving Toronto station for the West and also, I think, slowing down so that we could greet the friendly people of, what did you say it was, of yes, Aurora. But you know, I haven't the faintest recollection of seeing you on your father's shoulders. I'm so sorry.'

From the Aurora kindergarten I graduated to Dewson Street Public School in Toronto. Fifty years later, when visiting there, I learned (the records having been carefully examined) that the eldest Pearson boy was among a group suspected of writing rude words on the walls in the school basement. Compensating for this threat to the good repute of the family name must be placed on the credit side that I did well in my exams; my elder brother, the suspected sinner, was a star on the school soccer team; while my younger brother ran races for Dewson against neighbouring schools.

My next school was Peterborough and this was a lucky change for me. I came under the tutelage of Mr R.F. Downey at Central Public School. His appearance was tall, gaunt, and awkward, but his personality was warm and kindly. His teaching inspired me; he first awakened my intellectual curiosity, and made me feel that school was good, not merely a compulsory limitation on freedom. I shall always be grateful to him and in later life was privileged to see him occasionally and acknowledge that gratitude. I had similar good fortune in high school in Hamilton with a teacher named 'Mike' McGarvin who encouraged me to develop a special interest in his subject, history. He had a strong influence on my scholastic ambitions. I kept in touch with him also in later years, but our friendship was severely tested when I became a Liberal politician, for he was a very staunch Tory. But before he died – like Mr Downey he lived to a very old age – he forgave me.

These two men made learning live for me during my school days, at least the kind of learning that had nothing to do with mathematics or science. In those subjects I was mentally retarded and only the most concentrated application made it possible for me to pass any examinations in them.

The combination of Mr Downey's teaching and my parents' interest, which was great but without pressure, and no doubt some quality within myself, resulted in an eager desire on my part to do well at school, to work hard and seek honours in the examinations. When I was able to do so, it was largely due to a fortunate facility for remembering what I had been taught. I was successful enough, then and later, in school examinations to have incurred the risk of unpopularity as a book-worm and prize-seeker, but was saved from this by a parallel, perhaps even a greater, interest in sports and a fondness for extra-curricular activities generally. I even gave proof of normality by showing a mild interest in girls, once I reached the age for such things.

Thus, growing was for me a healthy, happy, and relatively untroubled process. It was a good combination of work and play with a normal amount of youthful disappointments and perplexities. In due course at Hamilton Collegiate Institute in 1913, at the age of sixteen, I passed with honours my senior matriculation. I was now, if not ready, at least eligible for college and a new life away from the shelter of the family.

There are other memories, other links in the chain of growth. Very early in life I learned how to help at home and, when the time came, to do odd jobs outside, that enabled me, with my brothers, to add to the family income. Naturally, I sold papers. This, along with having been born in a log cabin, which I was not, is supposedly an important qualification for political acceptability. How fortunate, then, that in Hamilton I had a morning paper route for the old *Toronto World* which enabled me in later years to paint a very moving picture of an ambitious young Canadian on the job every morning at 6 am so that he could earn a few dollars for the family budget and help pay his way later through college. I did earn a few dollars, put them in the bank, and then saw them disappear as my father yielded to the well-meant, but ill-judged, advice of one of his wealthier parishioners to withdraw my fortune and invest it in an asbestos mine, which was the last he or I ever saw of it. My father laid up for himself, I know, much treasure in heaven, but he was singularly inept, as no doubt a minister of the Gospel should be, in making two dollars out of one dollar on earth .

In long summer vacations I had another kind of work, and play, to occupy me. From my earliest years, with my brothers, I was packed off the day after school closed to a Bowles' farm in Chingacousy Township and to other relatives in Orangeville where we remained until school reopened. I was a working, if not a paying, guest, as my farmer uncles and aunts always found things for a healthy youngster from the city to do. One aunt, who was too proud of her lawn, offended my sense of the fitness of things one summer by giving me the responsibility for keeping the grass not only short but free from the droppings of hens which wandered freely over it. I learned a lot about more adult aspects of farm life, and had many an argument with my country cousins as to the comparative importance of the 'city bug' and the 'country bug' in national development.

In Orangeville I also got my first taste of the thrill and excitement of electoral success. An uncle owned a general store there and one year Uncle Marshall was elected mayor. We were at his home when the town band, with many citizens, came to serenade him after the results were announced. This was true glory and I concluded then and there to become a politician, so I could be a mayor and have a band play outside my house.

The summer of 1913 was the last of my carefree farm holidays; the

responsibilities of being sixteen and of going to college were ahead.
The previous year I had already proudly graduated to my first long
pants. A blue serge suit and, of all things, a bowler hat were to be
delivered one Saturday evening so that I could wear them next morning
to church, and show the congregation that the minister's boy was now
a man. The hours went by; the suit didn't come; the sensation I was to
create next morning as I walked up the aisle was vanishing. Then, very
late, the doorbell rang and the beautiful suit arrived. I could sleep
peacefully.

I was also making good progress with the piano, advancing from
Sunday School concert duets with my brother, Duke (when we used to
battle for the right to operate the pedal), to more difficult classical
music. When we left Hamilton I was ready for an intermediate Con-
servatory examination. Here also I had been fortunate in my teachers;
one in Peterborough had the impressive name of Wilhelmina Gumph-
richt, while in Hamilton Miss Nellie Hamm was making the most of
what talent I had.

$$\mathcal{T}$$

It was taken for granted that I would go to Victoria College in the
University of Toronto, a Methodist foundation. My older brother Duke
was already there. It was assumed that his guidance and the strict rules
of conduct at the new students' residence, Burwash Hall, would shield
me from the temptations of life in the big city. My parents, for some
reason or other, hoped that I, of the three sons, would continue the
ministerial tradition in the family. I may have said my prayers more
loudly, or was more silent in church. Certainly I was less troublesome
than my older brother who occasionally caused crises by his belligerent
conduct, once even challenging and defeating the son of the Sunday
School superintendent in 'fisticuffs. I was more of a pacifier than a
pugilist. Perhaps for this reason and because I was somewhat more
studious than my brothers, my parents singled me out for theology
after a BA in honours history. They were to be disappointed. In this
respect I let them down. But while I was academically qualified to become a university freshman in October 1913, I was still intellectually
too young to benefit very much from my new and, as I wrongly saw it,
adult status. I was a young sixteen, with an absorbing rather than a
questioning mind and a rather superficial approach to life. I had escaped
most of the maturing tribulations of adolescence. I had, indeed, begun
to look at girls, even at one or two particularly. If not so glamorous as
Big League baseball players, at least they were worthy of cultivation,

a cultivation which, of course, excluded even dancing and could only be described as very cautious and correct by modern standards.

The world I left was a limited one in many ways, and did not, in fact, broaden much during my first college year. Indeed, to transpose John Wesley, the parish was my world, geographically and in other ways. The parish was an area of not more than fifty miles around Toronto. Quebec was virtually a foreign part which we read about in our school-books in terms of Madeleine de Verchères and the Battle of the Plains of Abraham. As for the rest of the world, I thought about it, and this was normal for the times, largely in terms of the British Empire which was looking after the 'lesser breeds' and keeping the French and Germans under control. Canadian nationalism hardly touched us in those days since our teaching was concentrated on Canada as part of an empire. I recall faint stirrings of interest as a boy over the threat from the Kaiser to Britain's naval supremacy and what Canada should do to help meet that threat. I remember my first political meeting in 1911 when Sir George Foster spoke eloquently, and to my father's approving 'hear, hear's,' against reciprocity in the Hamilton YMCA. I was startled when one or two members of the audience heckled him but not aroused into any great interest in the election or its issues. It was much the same at college in 1913. We students, or most of us, were unconcerned about the strength of the forces then gathering to shatter our country and our world. We talked about such things as little in the common room at Gate House in Burwash as we had in the living room at home. It was a far cry from the politically conscious and involved students of today.

My first year, however, was full of happy activity. It was a new life and I was kept busy between work and sport and college doings. I shared a room in residence with my brother, and we got on well together, though I was careful to recognize his superior status as a third-year man. The dean of residence was Vincent Massey. Thus was initiated a long and, for me, rewarding association, that evolved from Burwash Hall to Rideau Hall half a century later.

Mr Massey was a lecturer in history, and this was for me another point of contact. He had just returned from Balliol College, Oxford, and was concerned with introducing the manners and mores of that venerable institution into Burwash Hall. Our hall, however, was built in 1912, not 1412, and housed Canadian town and country boys who were not graduates of Eton or Harrow or from the stately homes of England. The dons of the other houses in Burwash, chosen I suppose by Mr Massey, were also graduates of Oxford and very English indeed. But the residence, built by Mr Massey's family, remained rowdily Cana-

dian, successfully resisting, in spite of disciplinary action, even the
demand that we should wear gowns at meals in hall. Traditions have
very real value and importance in a college, as in a nation, and there are
no better traditions, as I was to learn later, than those at Oxford. But
they took centuries to develop. Burwash was only a month or two old,
and would have to create and foster its own traditions.

The first year was soon over. I had played on some college teams,
made new and good friends. By the spring I was beginning, at least, to
appreciate the wisdom and wit of teachers such as Bell, De Witt, Pel-
ham Edgar, Alfred De Lury. Indeed, Dr Bell gave me a new incentive
to pursue Latin. When reading Catullus and some other Latin poets to
our class he would say, on occasion, 'We will now skip the next four
lines.' I would then hasten to the library afterwards to make sure I got
a precise translation and the full meaning of those lines. Obviously I
was maturing. Then came the first year examinations. My gift for
answering questions – except in mathematics and science – stood me in
good stead and, to my delight, I was first in the modern history course.

That summer I was to spend working in Hamilton where father had
secured me a job as timekeeper for gangs on civic works programmes.
I also played baseball in the City League. Things were going along
smoothly when in July we moved to a new church, Park Street Methodist, in Chatham. Only my older brother stayed behind to work in
Hamilton for the rest of the summer. I and my younger brother,
Vaughan, then at high school, went to Chatham. I had just settled into
another parsonage, looked over a new congregation and a new Sunday
School, begun to play second base for the Regiment Baseball Team in
the City League (Chatham was a great baseball town) when my world
ended, though I did not know it for some months, by the declaration of
war against Germany.

After 4 August life went on as usual, although the Armouries became
active in ways other than as the home of a baseball team. Chatham recruited a company for the First Battalion of the First Division and one
or two of my friends joined up. But I was only seventeen, the war was
far away, and would be over soon with a Charge of the Light Brigade
and a Battle of Trafalgar. It could not affect me or my family.

I went back to college, now a lordly sophomore. The autumn was as
before. But I was now more interested in my studies. I also won second
prize in the college oratorical contest against unfair competition since
the winner was a much older theological student who had already
preached for three years and had an Irish brogue. I played on the college

football team and lost the Mulock Cup for them by dropping a punt behind our line which allowed 'Meds' to beat us in the playoffs. It was a nightmare mistake which haunted me for ages. At Christmas we were all together, at home. Little did we realize that it would be the last time for many years.

After Christmas I returned to Toronto and Burwash Hall, but nothing was the same. The war had settled down to a bloody and lengthening struggle. A Canadian regiment was in the front lines and a division was training in England. Propaganda had already begun to prove that the first casualty of war is truth and I was stirred to hate and anger by stories of 'Hun' atrocities which I accepted without question. My college friends began to enlist and, as each did, he would have a farewell party in the common room and auction off his civilian effects; great fun. Then one day in March my brother joined the 25th Battery, Canadian Field Artillery, recruited from University of Toronto students. He went off to war, short in size but magnificent in riding breeches, a bandolier giving panache to his khaki tunic. I missed him terribly and the double room was very lonely.

I began to feel that I too must go. My motives were mixed and not particularly noble. I had a normal patriotic instinct – more British, I suppose, at this time than Canadian – and based on conventional impressions from the kind of history I had been taught. War was still a romantic adventure. Our views were not yet contaminated by revelations of prewar political manœuvring by the European governments in the pursuit of power rather than principle. We had no realization yet of the carnage that would follow the use of modern mechanical instruments of destruction. I believed, of course, in the justice of our cause, but, above all, I was young and adventurous, anxious not to be left out of the response of youth to such a challenge, or to lag behind the others and have a white feather pinned on me.

So I wondered what I should do. My parents, sensing this, told me to be sensible, to realize that I was not yet eighteen and that the war was not for boys. I should be content to wear a uniform in the University Officers Training Corps, to drill and march in Toronto, but not to think about overseas service yet.

Beginning on 1 January 1915 I had started a diary which lasted longer than any subsequent effort on my part to record my daily affairs. I kept it indeed until 4 July 1915 when it died with the words, 'nothing new.' That diary reflected my growing uneasiness about remaining at college while the war was on. Its insertions were short, to the point, and of a sameness: 'study ... hockey ... singing in common room after supper, *must* get more work done ... basketball ... church, a very good sermon ... studied all day, must do more of this.'

After February, however, the references to college activities lessened and those to the war increased: '10 March wrote home about enlisting in Eaton Machine Gun Battery ... 15 March Duke enlisted, also Art Brown. Room is deserted and everything seems broken up ... 16 March first time in uniform of OTC; drilled.' Then in April the decisive item: 'enlisted today; very sudden. Phoned home and got consent.'

2

TOUCHED BY WAR

That April day in 1915 I was in the college library studying for examinations. I was struggling, without much concentration and with some distaste, to read two Latin authors, Plautus and Terence, when the librarian told me I was wanted on the telephone. It was a call from a college friend at the Armouries on University Avenue. Pierce Congdon had enlisted a few weeks before with the University of Toronto Hospital Unit and had already achieved the dizzy heights of orderly room sergeant. In this capacity he had learned that there was a vacancy because somebody, for some reason, had been discharged. If I hurried down, I might be taken on. He would use his influence with the Adjutant. What a chance, as it seemed to me; especially as Pierce had told me orders to go overseas were expected any day. I rushed down to the Armouries and was duly enlisted (subject to later agreement by my parents) as Private Pearson, #1059, Canadian Army Medical Corps. Then and there I was put into an ill-fitting uniform and went back to the library to pick up my books. I created quite a stir among the other students by this sudden and surprising transformation into khaki.

That evening I called my parents and secured a reluctant consent. I impressed them, no doubt, by my argument that, if I did not go now in a noncombatant unit, I would certainly enlist as soon as they would take me in some 'suicide squad.' My father and mother came to Toronto, gave me their blessing, and saw me off to the wars, from which I was not to return for more than three years. As the unit was to sail in a fortnight, I was allowed to remain in residence, drilling each day as a stretcher-bearer and, more important, learning how to salute officers, keep in step, and other things that were of no help to me whatsoever later on.

I was excited and pleased that some of my college friends were in the same unit, most of them medical students. One of these, Billy Dafoe, became my closest companion and a life-long friend. There were others, too, who made things much easier, after the first excitement died away and I later found myself, a lonely youth, suddenly exposed to a life rawer than anything I had ever experienced or even contemplated.

On a fine spring morning we left Toronto by train for Montreal. The emotion of departure was soon forgotten in the knowledge that we were on our way to the great, unknown adventure, which for me began with by far the longest railway journey I had ever taken. That night we reached Montreal and marched on a troop ship. The *Corinthian* was an unimpressive-looking ship of seven or eight thousand tons. It was not my idea at all of a great ocean liner. It was over-packed with troops and the conditions, at least for the private soldiers, were horrible; especially for a boy not yet hardened to military life, only a few weeks away from civilian comforts. We were not only steerage passengers, we were down in the hold, right on the keel. We were jammed together, living, eating, sleeping side by side on boards almost touching each other. Each soldier had a straw palliasse and a blanket. From this black dungeon we could ascend by ladder-steps to the deck for fresh air, drill, loitering, and bewailing our lot. My diary told it all in four words: 'We live like cattle.'

The voyage down the river and through the Gulf was not bad, but when we reached the open sea there followed the worst week I had ever experienced. For sheer misery, nothing was to equal it during all my years of military service. I was homesick. I was seasick as no other human being had ever been. Never again was I to look on the sea – even from a prime ministerial suite on a luxury liner – with anything but fear and distaste. I could, of course, eat nothing. But even if I had been well and hungry, as I was when we approached land, I would have spurned what we were offered. The favourite dish was an offensive-looking boiled tripe which, the sailors told us, had been carefully saved from the surplus acquired in carrying troops to the South African war for use in the next one.

In time these horrors vanished. The sea was smoother, the land was nearer, and, as rumours had it, so were the submarines. I had not yet been sufficiently exposed to army rumours to have learned that they are never to be credited, but were to be considered only as an escape from monotony and ignorance. So I passed from worrying that I would not die, to worrying that I would. I survived. There were no submarines. One glorious, sunny May morning we entered Plymouth Harbour – Drake, bowls, the Armada and all that – with the green beauty of Devon as a backdrop.

Then to camp at Shorncliffe, near Dover, now crowded with Canadians. My spirits had reached a new high and my body regained its normal interest and energy. Two entries in my diary tell of the change: 'nearing land and in danger – worried.' Then my first day's entry at the new camp: 'unpacked, getting settled in our hut. Spent the rest of the day eating at different canteens.'

The next two or so months passed quickly. They were full of new sights, new activities, new experiences, and new revelations. One of these latter related to my own role in the war. I had no doubt it would be infinitesimal, but I thought it might be exciting. In my innocence and from my impressions of G.A. Henty and other war stories for boys, I expected to be sent quickly to the trenches, rescuing the wounded in no man's land with that calm courage that warranted, even if it did not receive, a Victoria Cross. The reality was very different: I became a night orderly at the camp hospital.

One midnight, while trying with incomplete success to stay awake while on duty in accord with His Majesty's Military Rules and Regulations, my first Canadian mail was delivered. There were two letters. One was from my aunt in Orangeville: 'I can see you now, a ministering angel to the poor men on the battlefield, helping them midst shot and shell.' At that point of reading, I was summoned by a rough and unsympathetic sergeant who had lumbago and ordered to minister to his bodily needs; ministering angel to a wounded hero, indeed! The other letter was an announcement from Victoria College that I had won the Regent's Prize for the best English essay in the second year by my contribution to a better understanding of Tennyson's view, 'Tis better to have loved and lost than never to have loved at all.' Since I was seventeen years young when I wrote this masterpiece, my success was a triumph of imagination over experience.

The weeks sped by with work and drill and fun; evenings in Folkstone, an exciting landing leave in London, and a glorious embarkation leave later in Scotland. I had not a single friend or acquaintance in the British Isles, but my soldier comrades made up for that. We had our own group, most of us had known each other at college, and I have met no better men or truer friends in all the years that followed. It was sad to see them disappear later; but during these early days we were close together in a comradeship that did much to fill the void of family and home.

One memorable summer day I learned that my brother, Duke, had arrived with his battery at Camp Otterpool, five miles or so away. We spent as much time together as we could in the following days, until one rainy evening in September our unit was paraded in full marching order. We were obviously going somewhere. After the normal delays due to military muddling, we found ourselves on the *Minnewaska* sailing out of Plymouth to set up a field hospital, so ran the scuttlebutt, on Gallipoli, or on an off-shore island.

The voyage was not unpleasant. The ship was infinitely better than the *Corinthian* of evil memory. We had clean hammocks and edible food. I was seasick, of course, but only for a few rough days. I was somewhat tougher and better conditioned to a soldier's life. There was much of interest in the voyage; through the Straits of Gibraltar, into the Mediterranean, and to Malta. There for three days we lay in harbour for no reason apparent to us. The officers were allowed on shore to explore that island which we could view only from the deck of a troop ship. I began to hate class distinction more than ever.

There was only one misadventure and that was of our own making. Orders were issued for the troops, in groups of thirty or forty, to be washed down on the deck by hoses. They were to parade naked for that purpose at the appointed time. The weather was hot and sticky and the baths available were needed for officers and ncos. Hence the hosing parade. The 'Imperials' made no difficulty over this iniquitous display of discrimination in methods to ensure cleanliness. But to the small company of Canadians on board, the order was humiliating and not to be obeyed. Some of us simply didn't turn up when our time for washing down arrived. We hoped that, perhaps, we would not be missed, but missed we were. Shortly afterwards we were paraded, as prisoners, before the ship's commanding officer. He was an officer of the regular army who looked and talked like one. We were not, as I recall, much disturbed by his tongue-lashing until he reminded us that once we had boarded this ship we were on active service in a theatre of war, legally at the front. Then he read, with intimidating deliberation, the relevant passages from the King's Rules and Regulations dealing with 'disobedience of an order in the face of the enemy,' even though the nearest enemy face was, on this occasion, some hundreds of miles away. At the end of each regulation he would look up, glare at us, and solemnly intone, 'The punishment for this offence is death' (long pause) 'or such less punishment as in this Act mentioned.' We were

rather shaken at the end, wondering whether our physical fastidious-
ness and our sturdy blow against discrimination had not been ill-timed.
We got off, however, with a loss of pay and some unpleasant duties
when we reached our destination a day or so later at Camp Gabarri, in
the desert a few miles outside Alexandria. The camp was on the way
to a village, Alamein, which was to become famous some years later in
another war after we had failed to save peace and democracy the first
time round.

We were at this camp only a short time, but long enough for me to
see something of life in an Egyptian city, then over-run by the traditional 'brutal and licentious soldiery,' at this period mostly Australians.
I was still relatively young and innocent and was shocked, though I
tried to conceal it, by what I saw and even more by what I learned.

By this time we sensed that we would not be going to Gallipoli since
all rumours about that campaign suggested an early withdrawal. But
where were we bound? Surely we were not to spend the rest of the war
at a military hospital in Egypt. Our destination was still uncertain until
one night in October we embarked on the *Carisbrooke Castle* sailing, as
it turned out, for Salonica in Macedonia.

It was a stirring moment when, after a calm and pleasant voyage, we
entered the harbour and knew we were about to land. But what were
the conditions and how were we to operate? Was our landing to be
resisted? Naturally, as soldiers we knew little about that. Ours not to
reason why. We might have been more worried had we known what
was actually happening. Serbia was being overrun by Austrian, German, and Bulgarian forces. Resistance was brave but hopeless. The
Allies, who were about to complete the evacuation of Gallipoli, decided
to open up a new front in the Balkans to save Serbia and defeat the
common enemy. British and French troops were therefore to land at
Salonica and press forward to join the Serbs. It is true that Greece was
neutral; but this was not Belgium and the Allies were not Germans.
Therefore, though Greek territory would be used for operations against
the enemy, Greece itself would not be occupied. In this sense her neutrality would be respected. We hoped that the Greeks would recognize
these fine distinctions when our small part of this expeditionary force
landed on the harbour quay and noticed the fierce-looking, fully armed
Greek soldiers drawn up. Were they there to welcome us or attack us?
It was a nervous situation, but we were too busy unloading supplies to
worry about it. Worrying in a different way, though we knew nothing

about this at the time, was the fact that while the British and French
had found it necessary to violate the substance of neutrality, they were
careful to observe its forms. As a result, in addition to Greek soldiers
on the waterfront German, Austrian, Bulgarian, and Turkish consu-
lates were also there and still open. During the landing, they were
busily telegraphing or telephoning information on military details to
enemy headquarters not too many miles away. It was, to say the least,
a rather strange way to begin a campaign.

When I returned to Canada some years later, in 1918, I reconstructed
those first trying weeks from the letters I had regularly written home
and which my parents had kept. All I had to do, while the memory was
still fresh, was to add a few details that the military censor would not
have passed. From this account I include here a few paragraphs.

In the morning, after reaching Salonica, I was put down in the forward hold
unloading supplies. After being in that dreary place all day with a few minutes off for a cup of tea and a biscuit, we were ordered to help loading lorries
on the dock. By this time it was quite dark, pouring rain and a stiff wind had
arisen which was becoming colder. I spent a very disagreeable night out in the
wet and cold and when everything was finished, about 4.00 am, Billy, Walt,
Charlie, and I, dead tired, climbed back into the ship, stole some blankets
and dropped off into a deep sleep. We must have slumbered all of fifteen
minutes when the dear old Sergeant Major roused us and told us to get into
marching order again. Tired and wet as we were, we pulled on our packs,
formed up and shuffled off into the wind and rain. Through the narrow evil-
smelling lanes of the sleeping city we made our way till finally after some
terrible miles of mud we halted by the side of the Monastir road. We had
reached a long rolling plain at the base of the hills. Some piles of supplies and
a tent or two signified that this was to be our home. The field was a sea of
mud and a dismal place to establish a field hospital. But we had received word
that the wounded would be coming in at once and our 'job' was to be ready
for them. We were given a few minutes to eat some 'bully' beef, drink some
tea, and then we started to work again, putting up tents, and so on. Billy and
I worked all that day and far into the next night. Finally we could stand no
more; we had been at it now for forty-two hours, so we both just dropped on
some bales and slept the sleep of the just, in spite of wind and rain. It was
morning before some spying NCO routed us out.

I think we established something of a record at this time. Forty-eight hours
from the time we left the ship, we had a tent hospital equipped and ready;
and we were already bringing in sick and wounded. It was rather a rough and
ready affair, of course, because we had neither the time nor the facilities for
anything else, but there was a real emergency and our quick, if rough, work
met it. Within five days we were looking after three hundred patients and
they were still arriving.

My impressions of those first few days are of a vast muddy plain with our
half dozen tents the only sign of human habitation; of ceaseless rain and
fierce winds; of horse ambulances coming down the road with their loads of

human agony; of the bugle blowing the convoy call; of the boom of guns; of struggling in the mire with wounded soldiers of the Tenth Division slung over our shoulders – we had no stretchers as yet. How wonderful those Tommies were! They had been undergoing terrible experiences up in the hills. The weather was below freezing, but through official mismanagement, they had only tropical clothing. Practically all of them were frostbitten and some in addition badly wounded, but not one complained.

It was little enough we could do for them. We pitched our tents, spread straw over the mud and laid the casualties down on that, till there would be forty or fifty in a tent. Then the medical officer would come around with his lantern, the dead and dying would be moved to one side, the dangerous cases would be attended to at once and the less serious ones simply cheered up. All the while the wind whistled over the Macedonian plain and the sleet beat against the canvas. Nightmare days when we all worked till we dropped, when we ate as we worked; but the chance for real service, the goal of our months of training.

In a few weeks the retreat had ended and the front was stabilized. An entrenched camp had been formed around Salonica. Each day we expected the Austrians and Bulgarians and Germans, who so greatly outnumbered our forces, to attack and drive us into the sea or a prison camp. But they never came. It seems – though we had then no knowledge of this comforting development – that there was a very real difference of opinion among the enemy governments, including the Turkish, over what should be done with the conquered territory. To complicate matters there were also the Greeks who had refused to join the Allies and had to be considered.

We were the beneficiaries of these complications and so were spared from a fate that was even worse than remaining at Salonica. But that at the time seemed bad enough. The elements became our worst enemy. We were still in summer uniforms. Someone in the War Office must have thought Salonica was a tropical Mediterranean resort. But those Macedonian plains and hills in the winter of 1915 were cold, wet, and windy; often below freezing; with mud and slush, rain and sleet. Then in November came the worst blizzard the area had ever experienced. As the fighting lulled, the wounded were soon outnumbered by the frostbitten and the sick. Pneumonia, dysentery, typhus, blackwater fever, became more deadly than bullets. War in all its hideousness was revealed, and my last illusions of its adventure and its romance were destroyed.

When off duty, there was little to make us forget where we were. The amenities of a later war contrived to entertain and distract the troops were nonexistent. But we had our own all-male concert parties; we had our sports, too, with fierce and morale-boosting games of soccer and

later ground hockey among ourselves or with other units. When we
had a day off, we could do nothing better than explore the Macedonian
countryside. A weekend pass to Salonica, one every three months or so
for a private, was very heaven because it meant a dinner at the White
Tower restaurant and a room at the Spendid Palace Hotel which was
luxury indeed. Some of my more mature friends, who had not my parsonage background, were more adventurous. There was, of course, no
such thing as leave that would bring you back to London or Paris;
certainly not for a Canadian. To secure this, you had to be invalided out
and while about half of our unit eventually succeeded in accomplishing
this, it was far too high a price for most of them. In any event, I remained invincibly healthy. In my earlier teens I had acquired chronic
bronchitis which used to plague me during the winter. I remember
Mother telling me the army would find out about this the first time I
got my feet wet, and would send me home. My feet were soaked much
of the time that winter, and my body often chilled, but I never then, or
during the rest of my sojourn in the Balkans, suffered from a sniffle,
let alone malaria, typhus, or any of the fevers that plagued that front.

By 1916 the war on this forgotten front had settled down to a stale-
mate which, with sporadic and unsuccessful forays, was to last for
many long months. The British troops had moved out of the entrenched
camp toward the Serbian and Bulgarian borders. They could not get
very far so they settled down and made themselves as comfortable as
possible. Only the Serbs – the remnants of those tough and valiant
fighting men who had survived the terrible retreat to the coast through
Albania, had refitted at Corfu, and joined the forces at Salonica – only
they were determined, whatever the results, to come to grips whenever
possible, even in isolated attacks, with their hereditary enemies and
temporary conquerors. No long-distance gun duels interested them;
only close, bloody, hand-to-hand combat.

There was no continuous front line of trenches, only a series of out-
posts and positions. In certain sectors there were miles between the
contending forces, patrolled by cavalry. Two of my friends and I
learned this by personal experience one day in the spring of 1916. We
had the day off, hopped a lorry going up to what we thought was the
line, and when the lorry stopped we got out and started walking to have
a look at what was going on. After trudging along a path for some time,
we ran into a patrol of the Lothian and Border Horse. The officer
stopped us and wanted to know where we were going. 'Up to the line to
see if there is any excitement' was our jaunty reply. This seemed to
cause the Scots great amusement. The only line, they told us, was that

of the entrenched camp miles behind us. This was open country for patrols only. If we went on for another mile or so, we would certainly find some excitement, that of being captured by Bulgarians, either to be shot by them as spies because they had never heard of Canadians, or to be put in a prison camp (they were very unpleasant in Bulgaria) for the duration or as much of it as we survived. My military, perhaps my whole, career nearly came to an end right there. We did an about-turn, smartly, doubled in the other direction toward the road we had left, and looked for transport going back. As they rode off the Scots no doubt muttered 'crazy Canadians!' That was, of course, the Tommies' stock expression for a Canadian soldier when he did something incomprehensible, such as spending money lavishly, as we could with our $1.10 a day, or feeling easy and acting normally in the presence of an officer, or showing some interest in the war in the Balkans.

Then came the hot summer of 1916 and malaria, so all-pervading that at any one time about half the troops were down with it. From the frozen, wind-swept hills of the winter of 1915 to the steaming, swampy, malarial Struma valley to which a High Command had moved most of the British troops in May and June was a shocking change. The soldiers felt it and were without the excitement of action to take their minds off disease.

We drank pints of quinine to make ourselves so sour and poisonous that a mosquito would fall back dead before he could bite. Notwithstanding these heroic measures, practically everybody had malaria in a serious or mild way, at one time or another. I was one of the small minority. If I were disappointed, it was because by now it seemed that only malaria would get me out of this place and its dismal kind of service. So an attack of malaria, mild enough to be permanently curable but strong enough to return me to Blighty, seemed the answer to my discontent. I must have shared this feeling with many thousands, not including those, however, who had already had their fill of fighting on Gallipoli or in France.

I personally was faring well and thriving physically. My incompetence in giving first aid, or later care, to a sick or wounded soldier, had been recognized. Through friendly relations, going back to prewar days with a few senior officers and, more important, with some sergeants, I was given a cushy job in the quartermaster stores. This was a happy change for me and gave my two brothers in combat service an excuse to address me in their infrequent communications as 'Dear Fighting Grocer'. In this honourable military post I gave service far beyond the call of duty, for I wanted to make sure that I would not lose my new post. As long as I was with a hospital unit, I knew where I was most qualified to operate. It certainly was not in an operating tent. I had already been exposed to that possibility and muffed my opportunity by fainting dead away at the first gruesome incision. That was no way to win a medal for gallantry.

The army could not advance and win the war. It would not withdraw and get us out of that particular war, out of disease, boredom, and mounting frustration. This growing malaise was not cured by my own fortunate personal lot, by the comradeship of good friends, by the games we played and the fun we had off duty. It was increased to the point of being intolerable by the fact that my college friends were falling in France, while I was safe and comfortable among my quartermaster stores. My older brother, soon to be severely wounded, was with his battery on the Somme; my younger brother was soon to arrive in England as a gunner. So I must get back and join the fighting services. Moreover, I was now nineteen years old, so my parents could no longer use the argument of infancy. What to do?

My first choice was the Royal Flying Corps. That ambition was born of what I had already read and seen, but, as I had never liked heights, I felt that I would not realize it, or perhaps should not try. Then one day in February 1916 that hesitation was quickly swept away. A French squadron had its airfield not far from our hospital camp; indeed, it was close enough on one side and an ammunition dump close enough on the other to make our big Red Cross signs on the tents a good target for the bombs that, it could be argued, hit the hospital by mistake.

One or two of us had struck up an acquaintance with a young pilot of this French squadron and we visited him occasionally when off duty. To watch the flying gave us some vicarious excitement. On one visit it ceased for me to be vicarious. As we arrived my friend, getting ready for a flight, asked me if I would like to come along; there was room for one passenger. So I left my heart and courage on the ground and he took the rest of me up into the air. After the first spasm of fear passed, I found that I liked flying. I had no fear of the height, and felt only a pleasurable excitement at the experience. My pilot friend may have sensed this for he gave me more flying than I expected, heading his machine, a Voisin monoplane, all canvas and string and wooden struts and a 90 hp engine, northwards to where the enemy were. When he indicated that he was going to do a little reconnoitring of the Bulgarian positions, my exhilaration diminished; and my relief at a safe return later was not too well concealed from my companions who were waiting to greet me, I hoped, with admiration and awe. For a few days I was the company hero. I certainly should have been, on the strength of my tale of flying over the enemy lines. I have always claimed since that I was the only man in the history of military aviation whose first flight was over enemy territory.

At that time, however, I got nowhere in my hope for a commission in the Royal Flying Corps. Salonica was a long way from the Air Ministry in London; there was apparently no shortage of air cadets, and I had to stay where I was. Meanwhile, I had begun the process of securing a commission in the Canadian infantry. I applied through proper channels, which meant my Commanding Officer, to Canadian Military Headquarters in London. But, again, there seemed to be no great desire on the part of those in authority to move me to a post where I could win the war or, more likely, lose my life.

By the autumn of 1916, however, I had learned quite a lot about pulling strings in a good cause. So I decided to short-circuit all these channels. My father knew Sam Hughes; more than that he had played lacrosse and, I think, gone to Sunday School with him. General Hughes was now the Minister of Militia in Canada and had already gained a well-deserved reputation for cutting through red tape and, indeed, for unorthodox behaviour generally. So I wrote my father a long letter, which I posted one day when I was in Salonica, thereby avoiding the military censor. I told him to go to work on the Minister and persuade General Hughes to order Pte Pearson back from Salonica to a Canadian cadet battalion in England for an infantry commission. That letter took quite a long time to get to Chatham, Ontario, but it did so eventually. The reply was a shorter one from my father and mother telling me not to be rash, to think things over carefully, but if, after doing so, I still wanted a transfer, he would do what he could.

Time was passing, and none of it was needed for second thought. Indeed, so anxious was I to expedite matters that, finding myself in Salonica again a few days later, I went into a civilian cable office (the minor proprieties of neutrality were still being inexplicably observed) and sent a message for immediate delivery to my father which read: 'Commission decidedly immediately. Love.' It was dated 31 September 1916. I had enough drachmae to pay for it. It was delivered the next day to our home in Chatham at midnight. I learned later that its receipt caused a spasm of fear in my parents' hearts. Telegrams from overseas in those days usually carried dread news. I found this telegram, and many other messages from overseas, years later among father's papers.

He went to work – and it was effective. General Hughes was delighted to help and would see that Pte Pearson became a Canadian officer. He was even better than his word. He ordered the Canadian military authorities in London to request the War Office to order the Headquarters of the Mediterranean Expeditionary Force to order their Headquarters in Salonica to send Pte Pearson back to England at once and no nonsense. But even with this kind of high level expediting, 'immediately' meant some weeks. One day in January 1917 I was paraded before my colonel who told me that the army authorities at the base were furious at this gross interference with proper military procedure and had it been anyone but a Canadian soldier and a minister of the Crown they would not have tolerated it. But they did tolerate it and I was to hold myself in readiness for departure as soon as transport could be arranged. He wished me good luck, kindly added that I would be missed, and, as evidence of this, proposed to make me an acting corporal. This meant two stripes, no extra pay, but exemption from fatigues on the voyage back. Things were at last happening with a vengeance. As an acting corporal, I could now command a private soldier, except that I wouldn't know how to do this as I had been commanded myself for so long. I had begun the dizzy military ascent to field marshal or, for the moment, to lieutenant. A few more weeks remained, but one day early in March 1917 I was told that I would be leaving in forty-eight hours.

The last day was one I remember well. I shared in a victory far more important than an acting military promotion. It was in the field of sport. A week or so before, I had been chosen, with one or two other Canadians, to play for the army against the navy in a ground hockey match. We lost, 5–2. In our own unit, however, several first-class ice hockey players formed the nucleus of a ground hockey team which had managed to win every game it played within a month or two of learning how to play at all. Only a few of us had been chosen to take part in the army-navy game, but we were confident that our Canadian team could beat the victorious sailors. We persuaded the navy to play us and, on my last day, I helped our team win the hockey championship of Macedonia. A spectacular finish to my service in that theatre of war. I was very happy to leave but, as I faced a future that was surely uncertain and possibly short, there was real regret at cutting ties that had become so close.

The Mediterranean was a dangerous place for Allied shipping in March 1917. Submarines were very active and we saw some of the results of that activity as we put into Crete, to escape them, so we were told. Then, after three or four days, we continued to Marseilles, where the soldiers on board were transferred to several rather primitive troop trains. For two or three days we meandered across France, stopping and going, locked up in our crowded hard compartments, with beans and bread tossed in for meals. I was in high spirits. I was going to England and, I hoped, the delights of a long leave.

We eventually reached Le Havre on a cold, rainy night. Then, instead of marching to the harbour and our cross-channel ship, we moved off into the night in the opposite direction. The scuttlebutt had it that the Germans had broken through after heavy fighting and every soldier available was needed. We struggled through a mile or two of a muddy country road. My spirits had sunk to zero after the buoyancy of a few hours earlier. It seemed that we must have got somewhere near the western front, when we turned into a 'rest camp' in the countryside. By then I had become depressed and exhausted enough to throw away some cherished souvenirs, a small piece of ancient Macedonian pottery (so I had been assured) and two Bulgarian horse pistols! I was too tired to carry them further and anyway we were going in the wrong direction.

As it happened, we were only five or six miles out of Le Havre. The next morning we marched off in the right direction, and at eight that evening I was discharged at Victoria Station in London, amidst a milling crowd of soldiers, their families and friends. I seemed to be the sole military stranger in the lot. I spent one night at the only hotel I knew, the Regent Palace, and the next day I reported, as instructed, to the Canadian Army Medical Corps depot at Shorncliffe for further orders.

☞

I was overjoyed to find my brother Vaughan at Shorncliffe. He had missed going to France with his artillery draft, waylaid, of all things, by mumps. He was now impatiently awaiting the day he would rejoin his friends. From him, I learned that my older brother was at a convalescent home a few miles away recovering from his wounds. We went to visit him. For one hour, the first and last time in the war, the three Pearson boys were together. We crowded a lot of talk into that hour, none of it about the future.

The next day I went on my long-awaited leave – supposedly of two weeks. I found several Canadian friends also on leave, and was beginning to revel in the forgotten comforts of hotel-living and other pleasures available to a soldier with a large amount of accumulated pay at his disposal, when a telegram, curtly and without apology, ordered

me to report at once to D Company, No 4 Officer Cadet Battalion, at
Wadham College, Oxford, where I would begin the process of becoming an officer and 'temporary gentleman.'

My anger over this unfair treatment was not diminished by the
realization that the fighting in France had been hard, the Canadian
casualties high, and the need for infantry subalterns great. They might
at least have given me a week. But the course began the day after I
received my telegram and I was to be there. There was, however, a
major compensation. I was to live at an Oxford college, something I
had always dreamed I might do as an undergraduate. Four months as a
military student would at least be something.

So I turned up on 30 March 1917 and reported to my company commander, a timid-looking, very English, donnish type, Captain Morrell,
of a wealthy brewing family. I lost my corporal's stripes and my Red
Cross armband, but instead got infantry equipment and a white band
around my cap to show to all the world that I was now an officer cadet.
Then began the best four months, by far, of my war service. It was
April in Oxford, the city of spreading gardens and dreaming spires, of
a beauty and peacefulness almost unnatural after Macedonia and no
doubt quite incredible to cadets back from the trenches in France.

Our company consisted of three platoons. Two of them were filled
by English boys, just out of public school; the third, in contrast, com-
prised colonial non-commissioned officers, who had already served at
the front for some time; one or two of whom, sergeant-majors, were
old enough to be the fathers of the younger cadets. In that platoon
were Australians, New Zealanders, South Africans, and Canadians –
the Afcananzacs, as we proudly called ourselves, all overjoyed at this
reprieve from slaughter and determined to make the most of it in fun
and games. We were a rough and rowdy bunch, of whom I was the
youngest and the most innocent; no great distinction in such company.

Our platoon officer was Robert Graves, of the Royal Welch Fusiliers,
to become famous later as a poet and writer. He had been shell-shocked
in France and sent back for this kind of duty to help his recovery, the
military authorities no doubt hoped, from a deep and sickening revul-
sion against his experiences as an infantry subaltern. He was an unlikely choice to manage our unruly and high-spirited 'colonial' platoon.
He had, however, enough good sense to give us our heads, and to
accept our somewhat unconventional ideas of spit-and-polish and military discipline, so we got along well together. For me, it was the
beginning of a friendship continued after the war and extended to
other members of a remarkable family.

We trained steadily, we attended lectures, we got ourselves fit and ready to become casualties, when one day in July we were told that we had all passed the examinations. No one was allowed to fail and repeat. We were dismissed to be gazetted to our regiments. It had been a very happy four months and, if I did not distinguish myself in military tactics or musketry, I won the prize for throwing the cricket ball at the battalion sports and even got a mention for this in the London *Times*. Apparently I had broken a record.

After three days in London to celebrate my new dignity, to be fitted with my first officers' uniform, and to get my first salute, I reported for duty to the 4th Canadian Reserve Battalion at Bramshot Camp to await inclusion in a draft for the First Battalion in France. To my delight, I found that my brother Duke was there also and in the company to which I was posted. As a gunner, he had been recommended for a commission in the artillery but had been sent to an infantry cadet school. He assumed that this mistake would soon be discovered and he would be transferred to an artillery school. If this meant a few weeks longer in England, well, who would begrudge that to one who had already been in France for a long time and, more important, had just become engaged to the very attractive young Scottish nurse who had taken care of him in hospital. Incidentally, it was the best thing he did in the war. For him, however, things did not work out as he hoped. He had begun as an infantry cadet, and an infantry cadet he would remain; a decision of higher authority that was bound to infuriate a gunner. So there he was at the 4th Reserve Battalion, with his young brother, the former 'fighting grocer' from the Balkans.

More drilling, more training; a gas course, a musketry course, while we waited. Dignitaries visited and inspected us; it invariably rained when they came and invariably they kept us waiting. Once General Currie turned up and gave those of us who were on the draft list a word of hope and encouragement. At least I assume it was meant to be that, but he spoiled its effect by reminding us two or three times: 'Some of you will not come back.' Each time he used these unfortunate words he seemed to be looking straight at me.

General Currie had nothing to do with it, but shortly afterwards, I was withdrawn from the list of those who were to be sent across the Channel. The Allies were having a difficult time in the air. The Germans had achieved temporary superiority and British pilots were being shot down at an alarming rate. An appeal was made to base units for those who were found suitable to transfer to the Royal Flying Corps or the Royal Naval Air Service. This was my brother's chance to avoid the indignity of remaining with the infantry. It was also my chance to resume where I left off in February 1916 with that flight in Macedonia. We both applied for transfers and, after a very cursory examination indeed, were told to report for training. I was sent to join the Royal Flying Corps and my brother to the Royal Naval Air Service.

My own experience is some indication of how great was the need for pilots. After three weeks at Reading I had completed my ground training; engines, wireless, theory of flight, navigation, and the rest. I had known nothing about any of these things and had very little aptitude for them. I really didn't know much more after twenty-one days but I was sent off none the less for flying training to Hendon, on the outskirts of London, and after one hour and forty minutes of dual instruction on a primitive Graham White 'pusher,' properly known as a box kite, I was told suddenly one afternoon as the instructor jumped out, that I was on my own: 'Take-off,' he barked at me.

It was a good tactic, for, before I had time to be afraid, I was off and on my own; not into the azure blue as a 'knight of the air,' to use Lloyd George's phrase, but into London's foggy sky, lumbering around in circles a couple of thousand feet up. I liked it. It was easy. I was obviously meant to be a flyer. Then I saw signals below, to come down. This was different. I was safe in the air, but getting down was something else. So I continued to fly until the dreadful possibility of running out of gas drove me down. I made it safely but crudely: levelling off too soon, with a series of diminishing bumps during which, luckily, the under-carriage did not collapse.

The weather was bad, naturally, at that time of the year, but our flying training was under pressure and we had to fly every moment we could. In consequence, there were too many training casualties, including my room-mate who had also transferred from the Canadian infantry.

The King and Queen inspected us one dark and misty morning. I had not seen them since that day in Aurora in 1901. The Queen, unaware of that earlier encounter, stopped to give me a royal and friendly greeting. She saw my 'Canada' shoulder badge and opined that I was a long way from home and, more controversially, that I was very young to become a pilot. A veteran now, if not yet grizzled, with nearly three years in uniform, I did not welcome this commentary on my boyish appearance.

A short time later I confirmed the old saying that 'pride goeth before a fall.' I fell, but with more damage to the plane than to myself. My engine had let me down (or more likely I had let it down) when banking

before coming in to land. I was exempted from flying for a few days to
make sure my scratches and bruises were not fatal. That exemption
almost proved my permanent undoing. Restless and eager for diversion, forgetting my confinement to the station while remembering that
I was only a bus ride from Piccadilly, I yielded to temptation and sallied
carefully forth for an evening on the town. I ran into two Canadian
kindred spirits at the Regent Palace Hotel, and we were enjoying ourselves hugely over a good dinner at the Trocadero, when an air raid
warning was announced. Raids were not very serious affairs in 1917
(that was to come a quarter of a century later), but I thought I should
hurry back to Hendon. My presence was not required to drive back the
raiders, but my absence might be noticed by the orderly officer with
regrettable results for the reputation of the Canadian Officer Corps
for strict obedience to orders.

Hence I found myself rolling along the Edgeware Road on a bus
going too fast, especially as both the bus lights and the street lights
were off. A bomb exploded all of half a mile or more away. The driver
had had enough. He stopped and told his few passengers to get out, as
he proposed to do, until the all-clear sounded. I obeyed, walked behind
my bus to cross the road, and stepped in front of another coming fast
in the other direction. A London omnibus is no mean battering ram,
and it must be accounted as something of a miracle that my short and
uneventful career did not end then and there.

The next twelve hours were hazy and unpleasant. My memory of
them is based partly on recollection, partly on what the driver and the
doctor told me later. The ambulance that was presumably summoned
turned out to be a species of push-cart with two policemen in charge.
On coming to, I found myself on this contraption under a blanket. The
street lights were on again. It was Saturday night at a busy corner, with
people milling around. I recall some bystanders gazing at me with one
remarking, ' 'E 'as had too much to drink.' This was almost as much of
a shock to me as being hit by the bus. Up to that point of time, and in
spite of all incentives and pressures, I had not only never tasted
alcohol, either rum ration or canteen beer, but I had never even
smoked. In these matters, I was probably the purest soldier in all the
allied or enemy forces! So naturally this insulting reflection on my
sobriety sent me back into unconsciousness. When I came to again I
was in what appeared to be the surgery of a doctor's house. He had
sewed up a gash in my leg, done some repairs to another in my head,
and was now asking for two pounds sterling. I indicated that he might
find it in my wallet some place in my torn uniform.

I was still a mile or so from the air station and eventually was deposited in my room in the officers' quarters some time after midnight. My arrival must have been noticed, if without great concern, since the orderly officer honoured me with a visit at breakfast time. He saw that I was neither drunk nor disorderly, but in some distress, as my leg wound had begun to fester and was very painful. So at last, about ten in the morning, having been hit by the bus at ten o'clock the evening before, I found myself in a bed in the Westminster Infirmary, close to Hendon airfield, in a room with two other officers. My active service, though I didn't know it then, had ended, and ingloriously. The two other officers and I were occasionally visited by those dear old souls whose war work was to comfort wounded heroes. If not heroes, we were wounded; certainly two of us looked wounded, swathed in bandages. But an examination of the medical records would have disclosed that one of us had been hit by a bus; one had been kicked in the head by a mule in France; and the third had a bad case of asthma, caused, he said, by high flying.

For me the first few weeks were not easy, but by Christmas I was well enough to be carried out on a stretcher which was fastened to the top of a motor car (where *were* those ambulances? There were plenty of them in Salonica) and driven to the home of an American family in Regent's Park, the Cabells, who had been wonderfully kind to all three Pearson boys overseas, and were to continue their kindness until we all left for home. I was soon well enough to be sent to a convalescent home and, later, was given leave until a medical board and the RFC decided what to do with me. This took time and I had six weeks of freedom from military life. It was a time I shall never forget. It was then that I became an adult. I began to think of things beyond the pleasures and excitements, the troubles and fears of the moment. I began to think, for the first time, about the war in its deeper significance and to realize its full horrors and gruesome stupidities, culminating in the bloody and pointless sacrifice of Passchendaele. My brother was there now. My other brother was flying a Camel. I would meet friends in London on leave from France and learn a few weeks later that they had gone for good. I spent much of that sick leave with a Canadian friend, Clifford Hames, who had just finished his abbreviated flying training and was on leave before going to France. We spent hours trying to get some understanding of what we were being asked to do; to bring some reason to the senseless slaughter. For what? King and country? Freedom and democracy? These words sounded hollow now in 1918 and we increasingly rebelled against their hypocrisy. Cliff Hames and I came closer together in that short time than I have ever been with any person since, outside my family. He knew where he was bound within a few days. He could not know that it was to his death within the month. I did not know what was to happen to me. I hoped that I would be sent home to Canada to finish my convalescence and my training, but hardly expected it and gave it little thought.

We both assumed that our generation was lost. The war was going badly in France. The great German March offensive was about to begin. The fighting would go on and on and on. We, who were trapped in it, would also go on and on until we joined the others already its victims. All this had to be accepted. It never occurred to us that we could do anything about it. We might as well make the best of it, getting what pleasure we could.

That was our despairing philosophy as we talked and talked. Then, for me, everything changed with one telegram: Report to Headquarters at the Hotel Cecil. I did, and was told that I would be leaving for Canada on the first ship. I was to stand by. All my despair was swept away. I was going home, if only for a short time. The Germans were smashing through on the Western front, and casualties were heavy. But I was going home.

ॐ

I arrived at Saint John on 6 April. The train journey to Toronto seemed to take only a few minutes, until I was amidst a welcoming crowd at the old Union Station. Reunion with my mother and father was the happiest emotional moment of my twenty-one years; for three of them I had been overseas.

I reported, as instructed, to the Royal Air Force Headquarters in Toronto and was sent to a medical board, the chairman of which had been one of our doctors at Salonica. Next day I reported to the RAF commanding officer, a prissy, immaculate little regular army colonel named Cruickshank. He had my report in his hand, looked at me severely, almost accusingly, and said that I had been recommended for discharge on medical grounds, not merely from flying duties but from all further service. Therefore he had no alternative but to return me to the Canadian army who would presumably restore me to civilian life.

I was even more surprised than he. I expressed my astonishment and the Colonel then seemed somewhat more agreeable. He asked me if I wished to leave the service; I said no. He then asked me whether, if the medical board would reconsider and agree, and he could find something for me to do, I would join the staff of No 4 School of Aeronautics at the university, as a ground instructor, pending a later return to flying duties which he thought he could arrange. I thought that would be fine. Then came the question of what I could teach. 'What do you know about engines, wireless, rigging, theory of flight, to enable you to teach others?' asked Colonel Cruickshank. I confessed to a deep and basic ignorance of these things apart from what I had learned at Reading a few months before. 'Well,' he sighed, 'we will have to make you an instructor in aerial navigation.' All of this was shortly put in hand. Aerial navigation was somewhat rudimentary in those days but not more so than my teaching of it.

Life was pleasant and the going was easy. I was living again in Burwash Hall where I had been a student long years ago. Our officers' mess consisted of air force veterans. It was the happiest and most congenial group of officers I had yet encountered. The war seemed far away, but there was nothing I could do about that, for the moment.

The summer of 1918 brought the turning of the tide in France. The end was approaching, and everything seemed in suspense. It was obvious by September that I was not going to be transferred to flying duties or to anything else. My war was, in effect, at its end. Indeed, it was only a few weeks until the whole ghastly business was over, and it was 'all quiet on the Western Front.' That never-to-be-forgotten day, 11 November 1918, saved the rest of my generation and gave the world, not peace, but a reprieve. 1939 was only twenty years away; we did not keep faith with those who died; the torch was not held high. But we could at least rejoice at that time in the almost incredible relief of the present. Those autumn days were full of idealism and hope; full of resolve, too, on the part of those who had been spared to see that it would never happen again.

3

FINDING A FUTURE

My own problem now was merely to start again where I had left off in the spring of 1915 and to finish my university course. The air force co-operated by keeping me in the service and on leave from December 1918 until April 1919, so my pay took care of college expenses. After a happy Christmas reunion at home (now Guelph), the first since 1914, I joined the class of 1919 at the University of Toronto. Having passed my second year examinations in 1915 when in uniform, and having been given my third year for overseas service, I now found myself in the last half of the fourth year of my honours history course, with graduation examinations confronting me in four months.

After so long a period away from my books, it seemed hopeless to catch up. But I went to work; I was now in good physical and mental condition. Indeed, I played senior football that autumn with the air force team, and hockey during the winter with Victoria College. This kept me fit for the long hours of study. Then, on 5 June 1919, I got my Bachelor of Arts degree, with honours. I shall always believe, however, that this was due in part to a generous understanding by my examiner of the difficulties of a young veteran away so long from school.

Now I was ready – or was I? – to face the postwar civilian world. The course of least resistance seemed to be to study law at Osgoode Hall. This meant 'articling' with a law firm. To this end, I waited on McLaughlin, Johnson, Moorehead and Sinclair to see whether they would take me. I had good reason for applying there, since my father had done so many years before, when he wished to become a lawyer.

He left after a few months when he felt the call to the ministry. Mr McLaughlin, the senior partner, remembered my father's brief association with the firm and hoped that mine would be longer. But it was not. I was duly articled, paid some fees, and began to study as instructed Anson's *Law of Contract*. This was the dullest book which I had ever read and I was told I would have to read many more like it. After four years away from books, followed by a four-months crash course of reading for my degree, the prospect of another two or three years of lectures, clerical work in a law office, and Anson on contracts became abhorrent. It occurred to me that I had no wish to become a man of law. In less than a week the Supreme Court was deprived of a potential chief justice.

What, then, to do? I was restless, unsettled, and had no answers. But it was early summer and I loved baseball. I went to Guelph, the home not only of my parents but also of a team in the Inter-County League, a very good semi-professional organization. I knew one or two of the players, turned up at the ball park, was taken on. To preserve my formal amateur standing I was put on the payroll of the Partridge Tire and Rubber Company, where I punched the clock and did odd jobs when not playing baseball.

A week or so later brother Vaughan, now also back from the war, came home and joined the team. He was a much better player than I and could have been a Big Leaguer, I am convinced, had he wanted to follow that profession. He went back to college in the autumn but played baseball in his summer holidays in the Senior City League in Toronto where he was a star. Later, when I had become a public figure, references were occasionally made to my love of and proficiency in baseball. As to my love, there is no question, but I fear that my proficiency was often confused with my brother's. I used to point this out on occasion but perhaps not so emphatically as I should have. My brother never held it against me; he understood the exigencies of politics.

Naturally, I could not stay at home, play baseball or even wrap up tires forever. But I had had some weeks to consider the future and make a decision. My mind went back to a talk I had with my older brother one evening in Bramshot camp in August 1917. We were wondering what we should do in the event, which seemed then an unlikely one, that we would survive the war. He had his degree and for him it was to be law school, as he had always planned. I was uncertain, but decided to write to an uncle in Chicago who worked with Armour and Company, the huge meat packing corporation, to see whether there was an opening there for a bright and eager young veteran. I received in return a very encouraging reply, urging me not to worry about the future, but just win the war, in which the United States had now joined. Uncle Edson would see that I had a job with the company if later I wished one.

As it turned out, it was the oldest of the Pearson brothers who first turned up in Chicago. He had married overseas, a baby was coming, so for him it was not law school, but the Armour Leather Company and a salary. The tannery was not exactly the executive office but he seemed happy and hopeful for the future. I decided that I too, would join the world of business and make my fortune in Chicago with Armour and Company, of which my uncle was now the president. Indeed, that may have had something to do with my choice of meat-packing and Chicago for my fortune hunting! My uncle was informed of my desire; he remembered, and kept his promise, though not, perhaps, in exactly the way I had hoped. He told me to report to their Canadian subsidiary, the Fowler Packing Company in Hamilton. This I did, rather expecting that I would be assisting the manager there briefly before my transfer as a rising young executive to the president's office in Chicago.

I reported to the manager in Hamilton one fine September morning and was told to start work next day at eight AM in the sausage department. If I was startled, I hope I concealed it. The next morning found me undergoing instruction from my foreman into the intricacies of turning on a compressed air tap, I think it was, which shot the sausage meat into the sausage casing until it was filled. Failure to turn off the tap at the exact right moment would have dire consequences. I was now a skilled workman, or at least I became one in a few weeks, and have had a great liking for sausages ever since. This was a new life for me, and I had enough sense to realize that I had better be good at my work or I would never move up the ladder in the best tradition of Horatio Alger. Moreover, I enjoyed the company of my fellow workers. The company had a good hockey team in the Hamilton City League, and I became favourably known in the plant as a hockey player if not as a sausage stuffer.

It was not until the beginning of February that Chicago took notice of me and I was transferred. But the president still felt he did not need me: I was asked to join the fertilizer branch of the company as a clerk. This, I was assured, was a real promotion, from working in sausages to clerking in fertilizer. I was not exactly thrilled but tried to be a competent clerk and in time was given some sales responsibilities. I was forging ahead, doing my best to think that the world revolved around our Big Crop brands, and that I was a benefactor to humanity in trying to get them into the hands of farmers.

Quite apart from the Armour Fertilizer works, this was a stirring time to be in Chicago. It was the era of Mayor 'Big Bill' Thompson who was more concerned with 'punching King George on the snout' than in doing anything effective about corruption and crime and Al Capone. There never was a time when the contrasts of good and evil in an American city were more startling. Chicago was the stockyard, slums, vice, crime and graft; but Chicago was also the university, the opera, the symphony orchestra, the world's finest collection of French modern paintings, and a most imaginative plan for city development. It was throbbing with energy and full of excitement. It was the new industrial frontier with all the vigour and crudity of a pioneering community.

I had some opportunity to see both aspects of Chicago. I lived in a YMCA on the south side – the stockyards area – and saw some rough and even frightening sides of life. I also spent weekends and holidays at my uncle's farm estate at Lake Forest, as rich a country-club suburb as any American city possessed, where I met good as well as gilded people. Through my relatives, I also experienced much more of Chicago's cultural and social life than a clerk at $200 a month could normally expect to enjoy. My aunt and uncle, Mr and Mrs Edson White, and their three children treated me as a member of the family, with a kindness and warmth that made me feel ever after indebted to them. My aunt was truly a second mother to me. Indeed, all the people I met in Chicago were generous and friendly, whether of my own generation or older, whether at my work in the Loop or at play at Onwentsia Country Club. When Chicago is sneered at as a crude, violent, and barbarous city, as it often is, I think of the kindness I received there, the people whom I met, and the fine friends I made in those years.

I was homesick only for a few months, but soon it became clear that I had no wish to remain in business, however successful I might become; nor did I want to live in Chicago or indeed in any part of the United States for the rest of my life. In short, I wanted to remain a Canadian in Canada, to finish my education, for I now realized I had not done so in spite of my degree, and then teach history or political science at a university. During the winter of 1921, I knew, for the first time, what I really wanted to do with the years ahead.

But how? It seemed very ungrateful to my uncle casually to throw aside the opportunity he had given me, especially as I seemed to be making enough progress to satisfy him. Moreover, how could I finance the postgraduate studies essential for an academic post?

I first wrote to my parents about my plans to get their blessing and their advice. They were, I think, surprised, but they gave me encouragement and the assurance that they would do everything possible to help. Heartened, I then approached my aunt. She was comforting and approving. 'Where did I want to study?' 'Oxford University, but how can I possibly arrange that? Toronto will certainly be all I can manage and I will have to find outside work if I am to spend two years there for a Master's degree.' My aunt was a gracious lady of infinite faith, a devout Christian Scientist. There was no problem. 'If you wish to go to Oxford, as you should, and it is right to do so, as it is, the Lord will provide. So you go ahead. Have you told your Uncle Edson?'

I had not, nor did I relish the prospect. He was not a Christian Scientist and was likely to think that I was an ungrateful and foolish young man to desert Armour in order to go back to school. When he felt so inclined, Uncle Edson could express himself in strong and straightforward language. My aunt brushed aside my unworthy timidity telling me to go for a walk with my uncle that evening after dinner and to let him know my plans and hopes. This I did. He looked at me in an enquiring but friendly manner (my aunt must have softened him up) and said he was glad that I had decided to do something so important as teaching. Whether to salve his business pride or because he had been observing me more carefully over the months than I thought, he added: 'I don't think you are cut out for business anyway.'

☞

I came home to Canada in the spring of 1921, the path ahead clear, at last. But how was I to get started on it? That is to say, how could I get a scholarship? They were not nearly so numerous in those days as now. A Rhodes scholarship would, of course, be the best road to Oxford but, even had I the qualifications, I was ineligible as a graduate of two years standing. Then I learned of the Massey Foundation Fellowship which enabled the holder to do postgraduate work at any university of his choice. I applied, wrote some papers, and appeared before Vincent Massey, my old don of prewar days at Burwash Hall, for an interview. He was kind to me, impressed, I believe, by my desire to forsake the fleshpots of Chicago for the educational opportunities of Oxford. However this may be, a few weeks later I was informed that I had been awarded a fellowship and I proceeded to prepare for the realization of a dream long held. I applied for admission to St John's College. An army friend and fraternity brother at Toronto, Bartlet Brebner, later to become professor of history at Columbia, had just come down from

Oxford. He gave St John's high marks and promised to put in a good word for me with the college authorities. Later in the summer, I learned that I was accepted and sailed for England, full of happy anticipation.

Oxford University, and St John's in particular, turned out to be all that I had hoped and dreamed. Seldom are expectations so completely fulfilled as were those of my two years at Oxford. I loved it all, from the day I reported at the porter's lodge to the celebration with friends at the Mitre after we wrote our last examination at 'schools.' I was now old enough, and my life since 1915 had given me a wide enough range of experience, to savour to the full the incomparable charm and stimulus of life at Oxford.

My arrival, however, was not propitious. I had been given much helpful advice by Brebner before leaving Toronto on how to comport myself at an Oxford college so as to respect its social as well as its academic traditions and conventions. I was told to keep in check some of my plebeian North American social impulses, at least until I had achieved a status which would make unrestrained behaviour acceptable; in other words I should adapt myself to the dignity and disciplines of the society of an Oxford college. St John's was not Burwash Hall: I would, for example, have a college servant called a 'scout' but I was not to slap him on the back or offer him a drink. The most important man in college, apart from the president and the senior tutor, was the head porter with whom I should get on good terms, but again, by convincing him that, while a colonial, I was a well-bred and cultivated one. Above all, I must not be mistaken for an American.

When I turned up then, a very new boy, at the porter's lodge, and seeing a man there who looked like the porter (he certainly dressed like one), I had no hesitation in addressing him with that mixture of hauteur and kindliness that was apparently appropriate. 'Henry,' I said (I had learned that his name was Henry and that he was to be called by it), 'I'm Pearson, from Toronto. I sent a message about my arrival. I would like to go to my rooms and have somebody bring up my bags, which are outside.' The tone and even the English was, I flattered myself, just about right.

The reply, however, was disturbing. 'Oh yes, Pearson,' said my porter in an unmistakable Oxford academic accent, 'we were expecting you. I'll show you to your room. However, first let me introduce myself. I'm Powell, the Senior Tutor.' I soon recovered from this initiation, but the Senior Tutor never did. He was a very distinguished classical scholar, of national reputation, but he was also a dear old man with a keen sense of humour and his account of our first meeting became one of his most cherished stories.

He scored a point of his own a few weeks later in telling me that they were going to move me from the top cell in Staircase 4, which was considered to be too small for one of my age and experience, and to place me in an attractive four-hundred-year-old suite, a panelled 'sitter' and two 'bedders,' with another American. I protested that I was a Canadian, not 'another American,' but 'Jup,' as we called the Senior Tutor in the best Oxford manner, was vague about North American developments since George III, or perhaps was anticipating history. In any event he judged that no change of plan was necessary. Nor was it. My room-mate was Conrad Chapman, BA Harvard, and son of the famous editor and essayist, John Jay Chapman. He was a perfect room-mate, quiet and studious, not interested in games or parties. He was very good for me. His very presence urged me to study more. He was also generous. He once gave me ten pounds as a Christmas present since I was going to the continent with the hockey team and he knew that I was short of money, as always.

I needed little time to feel very much at home at St John's, to love its beauty and its peace, and to value the introduction it gave me to a new kind of education and, indeed, of living. Even the mediaeval discomforts (a hundred yards to a bath-house, only an ancient fireplace against the Oxford winter) seemed in keeping with the setting. For most of the academic year that fireplace was indeed the focus of our lives. In front of it we had breakfast and lunch, and huddled close to study and write; our tea-time discussions were brightened by its glow.

The teaching practices of Oxford gave me particular pleasure. Here was no frantic scramble from one formal and compulsory lecture to the next; here no hastily scribbled notes for bemused recall, with luck, against the grim reckoning of examination day. There were, of course, university lectures, listed for our information. We went to those that seemed of interest to us, or were recommended by more knowledgeable friends, or we did not go at all. In my two years, I went to very few.

My work was in the Honours School of Modern History. To get my degree I knew what I had to learn, and it was up to me to learn it under the guidance of a college tutor whom I used to see once or twice a week or oftener by agreement. For him I produced an essay on a subject he had given me. We discussed the essay and anything more or less related to it, sitting comfortably by his fireside, while he smoked at me. Then I left for further reading and writing until our next assignment.

My first tutor, for only one term, was a mediaevalist, whose cloistered manner seemed to reveal a mild embarrassment at my rather bustling North American approach to my work. I am not sure that he was not almost relieved when each tutorial was over. He was not born to impart ideas or to foster inspiration, a scholar rather than a teacher. My next tutor was W.C. Costin, lately an army officer of my own generation, with a background and interest not unlike my own. He was a fine teacher and became a fast friend. Some years later he became President of St. John's. Our friendship was to endure, and I used to see him on later visits to England whenever I could. I spent a happy day with him in the summer of 1970. He had retired from the college which was his life and only love. On that summer afternoon we discussed the halcyon days of long ago. He died a few weeks later.

Costin took a special interest in overseas students and in Canadians particularly. He was inordinately proud when one of his 'boys' achieved distinction in later life. I recall now the telegram I received from him when I became prime minister: 'With Dean Rusk (St John's) Secretary of State in Washington, Michael Stewart (St John's) Foreign Secretary in London, and Mike Pearson (St John's) Prime Minister in Canada, all's well with the world.'

Each student at St John's had also a second tutor whose duty presumably was to look after the moral aspect of his personal development. From this spiritual control, however, I was exempt. The college authorities, perhaps the Bodger himself, that legendary, unseen, ancient presidential figure, had decreed, by some strange process of involuted reasoning, that a veteran of the Great War had no need either of a moral tutor or of compulsory chapel.

A good deal of our education at St John's was acquired by rubbing minds with our companions. We even had college clubs for that purpose, as well as others for more mundane social purposes. Two of these latter were of limited membership and thought to be exclusive. Both of them, the Archery and the King Charles, were centuries old and had developed their own dress, traditions, and elegant formalities. The King Charles was a dining club, and was founded by Prince Rupert during his sojourn at the college three centuries earlier. Its monthly dinners were elaborate in ceremonial and generous in libations. A toast had to be proposed by the vice president at the end of each dinner in these terms: 'Mr President, I give you King Charles for his bounteous graciousness in sending Prince Rupert to dwell amongst us.' At the end of a King Charles dinner, it was no mean feat for a vice president to get through these words clearly, even if he had no lisp. If he failed, the punishment was swift and original. I know; I was once the vice president.

A part of my Oxford life that gave me particular pleasure was collegiate sport. For this there were ample facilities and opportunities. Each college, however small (St John's had only about three hundred

students), had its own playing field for intercollege competitions. I
certainly took full advantage of every opportunity. I tried out for almost everything except rowing, the most famous of all major sports at
Oxford. As an oarsman, you could do little or nothing else in sports,
and I like variety. So my rowing activities were restricted to cheering
on the college crews in 'bumping' races and to joining wholeheartedly
in the celebrations when we made enough bumps to warrant them. I
played rugger and hockey and lacrosse. The first sport was new to me,
but I got to love its speed and spontaneity. In my second year I was
given a varsity trial at full-back without, however, making the team
against Cambridge, the one game that qualified for a Blue. I was more
fortunate in hockey and lacrosse where the competition was less keen
and where Canadians predominated.

I played twice against Cambridge at lacrosse where we won easily
and I was on the Oxford team which won the South of England Lacrosse
championship for the first time in the century. I was surprised to see
how much lacrosse was played in England in those days, especially in
the north, and I admired the speed of the game and the calibre of the
players. I was chosen in 1922 to play for the South of England against
the North, and thereby became the possessor of that highly regarded
piece of athletic attire called an 'international cap.' The match was not
international since no European countries played lacrosse, so England
was divided for 'cap' purposes into two countries, north and south.

In the Easter vacation of 1922 a combined Oxford-Cambridge lacrosse team toured eastern US colleges, playing fourteen games in thirty
days, with only three substitutes. That was no mean physical achievement since our training had been of the rather easy-going Oxford
variety, and we played, as was the custom in England, without pads or
protection against squads of well-trained, hard-hitting, heavily-pro-
tected American athletes. Our style made us speedier, no doubt. But we
were a battered and bruised, if still cheerful, group that sailed back to
Oxford on 1 May. We had won most of our matches, and were rather
proud of our record and of ourselves.

How did we manage a tour like this when we had no manager, no
coach, no money? It was easy, and in the true but long-gone spirit of
amateurism. Our captain, H.O. Hopkins, an Australian, was our coach;
another player, F.L. Neylan, a Canadian, was our manager. An American agent organized our tour, looked after arrangements, and advanced
us enough money to cover our expenses. What he did with the cash he
received above that amount was his business, so, naturally, he hoped
for large crowds. One way he tried to ensure this was imaginative if

unorthodox. He decided to make one of our players a peer of the realm. For that purpose he picked out the name in our list that sounded most aristocratic and made its owner Lord Wansbrough. He was fortunate that 'Wanny' was an Englishman, since the majority of our members were overseas students, most of them Canadians. A transatlantic accent would have given the show away at once.

'Lord Wansbrough,' who was begged to go along with the 'gag,' became the centre of attention wherever we appeared, often to his acute embarrassment. I do not know how many spectators paid their admissions to watch the local players, in the inelegant words of one sports reporter, 'crack the nobleman's dome' but the total attendance was enough to cover our sponsor's guarantee and leave something over. Indeed, we had something over ourselves. We could not, of course, divide the surplus among the players. That would have been a shocking violation of Oxford's 1922 amateur code which insisted, among other things, that we pay for our own uniforms, and, while in England, our own travelling expenses. We therefore gave ourselves a magnificent banquet on our return at which our captain presented a silver cup, commemorating the tour, to each of us.

Hockey also gave me many good times. We had to call it ice hockey at Oxford to distinguish it from the ground variety which for climatic reasons was naturally much more widely played. Indeed, to choose the Oxford team from the Canadian and American students who were interested, we had our trials in one of the two or three artificial ice rinks then existing, mainly for figure skating. This one was in Manchester. In that year, 1921–2, we happened to have enough players who had played senior college hockey in Canada, and one, Mac Bacon, who had been captain of Harvard the previous year, to ensure a respectable team by any standards. By European and Cambridge standards, which were modest, we were magnificent and indeed unbeatable. Swiss and other European teams were eager but not very skilful, as yet, while Cambridge had, of course, no Rhodes scholars. The varsity match which was played at Mürren in Switzerland was in consequence very one-sided, so much so that it was called off at the end of the second period with Oxford ahead 27–0. Our matches with the European clubs were also easy victories, so we thought, naturally, that we were better than we actually were by Canadian standards.

That first tour of Swiss winter resorts was a dazzling experience for us. The next Christmas vacation the experience was repeated with a similar unbeaten record. This time, no doubt, I dishonoured my university and my country by becoming a member of a Swiss hockey club

at Davos so that I could play for Switzerland in the European championships. The eligibility rules for international competition were very
elastic in those early years, at least in hockey. Indeed, in 1923 I was
asked to play for England in the Olympic winter games the next year
at Chamonix. By that time, however, I was back teaching in Toronto.

My tutor, Costin, took these sporting diversions with equanimity,
and even some pride, during my first year. But in my second, he became
worried. Playing rugby, lacrosse, and tennis for the college in term time
was quite legitimate and indeed I was to be congratulated on my energy
and ambition. But spending vacations meant for reading and study in
fun and games in foreign parts was something else. I worked at my
books, therefore, during the long summer vacation of 1922, assuring
Costin that I would stick to them faithfully during the next academic
year, except for the one Christmas hockey trip to Switzerland.

Vacations, instead of being a time for money-earning as in North
America, were money-consuming for the homeless Oxford student. So
two of my friends and I decided to combine the broadening experience
of continental living in a university atmosphere with the necessity for
economy by going to Heidelberg in Germany. It was as romantic and
beautiful a place as one could wish and for the visitor there was the
added attraction, though it was a tragedy for the inhabitants, of gallop-
ing inflation. By changing our money into plunging marks a few shillings at a time we were able to live comfortably for the entire summer on
ten pounds sterling. Indeed when the time came to return, the cost of a
first-class railway ticket to the Belgian border, three or four hours away,
came to about a hundred million marks – on that particular day, about
sixpence.

Many years later as I was being welcomed officially by the Burgo-
master of Heidelberg, I told him that his city must have done something
special for three Canadian students who spent the summer of 1922
there because one, Dick Bonnycastle, became the Mayor of Metropolitan Winnipeg; another, Lester Pearson, became Prime Minister of
Canada, and the third, Roland Michener, became Governor General of
Canada. They also, incidentally, all played together on the Oxford
hockey team.

My second year at St John's was as happy as the first although, as it
progressed, the approach of 'schools' threw a shadow over that happiness. 'Schools' are the final examinations and they are, in my view, a
weakness in the educational system of the university. The examinations
for degrees are all crowded into a single period. You write them one
after another, morning and afternoon, day after day, until the frightful

ordeal, physical as well as mental, ends. This is surely not a valid test of educational progress and achievement, since, in those days at least, a 'first' required not only knowledge but a gift for clever and arresting writing to display that knowledge.

My tutor told me that I had given too much time to extra-curricular activities to expect a first after two years. He thought that if I stayed another year, which my fellowship permitted, I might make it, even though he had some doubts whether I was a 'first' type. By this time, however, I had been approached by the head of the history department at the University of Toronto, the respected dean of Canadian historians, Professor G.M. Wrong, on one of his visits to Oxford. He told me that he had been examining my record, which was quite good. He then added to the panic of my mind at the imminence of 'schools' by telling me that if I got a first there would be a place for me in the history department at Toronto.

I decided to do my best that year, and if I did not get the first I would at least have an honours degree from Oxford and could spend my third year there seeking a graduate degree. So I wrote my examinations, had my oral afterwards, and made a second class, near enough to a first to persuade Professor Wrong to renew his offer. By September I had an appointment as a lecturer in modern history at the University of Toronto, to the delight of my family and myself, with an awe-inspiring salary of $2000 a year. I was at last anchored in the harbour of my choice. I was now twenty-six years old, reasonably mature both physically and intellectually, even emotionally, and I expected to spend at least the next quarter century teaching history to the students of my old university, with forays into related activities. I knew that I would never become a cloistered scholar, but I did not know where one of these forays was to lead me.

I was fairly well prepared to join the university world. Two years in Chicago and two at Oxford had certainly been exposure to contrasting conditions. My factory and office experience had been short, but it had taught me much through working with men in a packing house and in a corporation office in a great city. I was grateful for that experience. Then for two years I was immersed in the intellectual and social life of an ancient university. It may be true that the tranquillity of Oxford seemed in many respects far remote from the life and problems of England. But the postwar ferment was working. Social and political developments were beginning to change the face and the soul of Britain. There was some impact of these changes on Oxford students, but I had no desire as an overseas scholar to become concerned with British social change or political activity; all the same, I had a normal interest in what

was going on in the world, with many a midnight discussion with college friends over the follies of politics that led to war but neglected the
evils of poverty and injustice.

I should add that I had also to concentrate on living on my scholarship, on the few dollars I had borrowed, and on the equally few I had
earned by writing an occasional article at, as I recall, ten dollars per
piece for *The Christian Guardian*, the magazine of the Methodist
Church in Canada. Oxford was an expensive university for overseas
students with no home to go to for the holidays and no parents near at
hand for emergencies. At St John's we received a bill at the end of each
term for tuition, living, and miscellaneous expenses. The bill was
called 'Battels,' for no reason that anyone knew. Oxford colleges take
pride in these meaningless but ancient terms. The obvious explanation
for 'Battels' is that the college had to fight so hard to get the bills paid.
But this could not be true: no college would demean itself by 'dunning,'
just as no young gentleman would be so common as to pay his bills at
once.

I have been looking at my 'Battels' for the winter term of 1922. They
came to £45, the irreducible minimum. My laundry expenses for those
eight weeks I kept down to £3 6s; my coal and wood to £1 7s, and my
baths, though I swear I remained clean, to five shillings. I fear that I
was a shade more extravagant as I became a senior student, and certain
additional expenditures became absolutely unavoidable; such as 'Barge
teas and other entertainments' in the glorious summer term: 'eight
pounds.' My total expense for each academic year in college, three terms
of eight weeks each, was £150, or about $725. As my scholarship was
$1000, and it had to cover the other twenty-eight weeks of vacation, I
had little chance to lead an extravagant life of pleasure and luxury,
even if I had wished to.

When I reached Toronto, I had learned to look after my affairs and
to live on what I had. By autumn 1923 I was not only a lecturer in history but a don at Middle House in my old undergraduate home, Burwash Hall. This meant a free and comfortable apartment, with inexpensive meals at high table. So with my lecturer's salary, I now felt
financially secure.

☞

The Toronto history department in 1923 was small and our group was
most congenial. Professor Wrong was in his last year as chairman, and
was soon to be succeeded by Professor Chester Martin from Manitoba.
The age of research and scholarly production as the first requirement
for prestige and promotion had not yet descended on us, and we were

encouraged to concentrate on teaching and on giving good lectures. Of course, we juniors (there were only three or four of us) were also expected to become so interested in the subjects allocated to us that we would in time publish learned articles and a book or two about them. But we were not plagued by this necessity. It was never even suggested to me that I must get a PHD quickly or depart. Thus in my first year I was able to concentrate on teaching and lecturing. So far as teaching was concerned, the student body was still small enough to work with discussion groups of not more than eight. This made teaching through personal contact and immediate exchange of views possible, even though we could not match the Oxford luxury of a single student sitting with his tutor in front of the fireplace. As for lectures, they were usually given to large numbers of students who dutifully wrote down what we had struggled to prepare, trusting that they would remember enough of it at the critical examination time to pass.

I greatly enjoyed teaching and found it stimulating. Lecturing was something else. It was less personal and more remote, though there was always the possibility of saying something that might provoke thinking or intellectual curiosity among the listeners. There was also the temptation to try to be witty as well as wise, usually with mixed results.

The undergraduates had not changed much since my own days, whether in their high spirits or their general indifference to matters outside their academic, social, or athletic interests. They were not normally involved in extra-curricular activities other than these or persuaded that they had to take over control of the university or even the country. They were concerned with preparing for the professional, commercial, or other careers which required an education. There were always exceptions, of course, earnest, impatient, social and political radicals, but they were not encouraged by the assurance that they could arrange for television coverage whenever they wished to express their dissent; providing, of course, that they could guarantee a demonstration or a confrontation likely to result in a clash. Only by today's standards were our students passive.

In my study groups and in the contacts I had with the men in Middle House as their don, I found the undergraduates far from lifeless and no part of my experience at the university was more rewarding than the association and the discussions I had with them. This was the aspect of teaching I liked best. Among the faculty I made new and life-long friends, including Hume Wrong, who later became one of my closest colleagues for many years in the Department of External Affairs.

The courses I was asked to give (we taught more hours then than is normal now) included European history from 1815 to 1914, which covered events leading up to the Great War; the development of the British Commonwealth of Nations; British constitutional history; England under the Stuarts; and the Reformation and Renaissance. Of some of these subjects my knowledge, to begin with, was scanty enough and it kept me busy to keep one lecture ahead of my class.

The absence of any Canadian content is noticeable and, for me, was regrettable; but my European history courses aroused my interest in diplomatic matters, in international affairs, and especially in the tragic, almost automatic developments that led up to 1914. I became more and more concerned about a recurrence of this catastrophe, about the necessity of international action for peace, and about my country's responsibilities in international as well as national affairs. I decided that those responsibilities could not be discharged until Canada had full control of her own policies.

My interest in Canadian politics had previously been spasmodic and superficial, largely because of my years of absence from Canada at the time when normally I would have been increasingly concerned. If anything, I was a British-Canadian conservative, but with no party allegiance. From 1923, however, I was becoming more and more liberal and nationalist, though far from a radical in my views.

My interest in sport remained unabated, but began to turn now toward coaching as well as playing. Tennis and squash gave me plenty of exercise and competition. I am the proud possessor of a squash cup, and I once had the great honour of getting to the second round in the Canadian national tennis championships, paired with my old Oxford friend, Roland Michener. We were eliminated by a Davis Cup pair who eventually won the title. Many years later I had to correct the Governor General publicly at a banquet when he said that we had been put out in the first round. It was the second; we had a bye in the first round.

Those were days at the university when the coaches were all amateurs, though a change was soon to come. I was on the athletic association board and found myself becoming actively engaged in teaching football and hockey as well as history. During my first year I coached the Victoria College football team to the interfaculty championship, and helped during the winter with the hockey and basketball teams.

Then, in the next year, I moved over to university teams, both in football and hockey. I loved doing this. It took up only two or three hours a day, and I had some talent in getting the most out of my players; working them hard but keeping the fun in playing, without all the pressures that now have become common in competitive sport. The hours I spent coaching and travelling with Varsity hockey and football teams, and in the spring as playing coach of the lacrosse team on their postseason American tours, are among my happiest memories of those years. They also helped me in my academic work by bringing me closer to many students than would otherwise have been possible. As a footnote I should add that, while no contract or salary was even considered, the athletic association decided to recognize my enjoyment of coaching by presenting me with a modest gift of furniture at the end of each season and in my last year something more substantial, in the form of a small honorarium for football and another for hockey. I needed it because I married in 1925, and by the end of 1927 was the proud father of a son.

My marriage was naturally by far the most important event of my years at Toronto, or indeed of all my years since 1897. I must tell how it came about.

☞

Although I had reached an age well beyond the average for matrimony, and although I had the normal young man's interest in girls, having established that fact to my own satisfaction in Chicago and Oxford, I was a contented bachelor when I came to Toronto in the autumn of 1923. Here, however, I was vulnerable. Perhaps half my history students were young ladies. Some of them I had to face each week in those small groups mentioned earlier. They seemed to me to be almost uniformly attractive. But one group of fourth-year girls in my European history course seemed even more attractive than the others. In that particular group, one pretty dark-haired girl with a clear and enquiring mind (which, as a professor, was what I was supposed to be solely concerned with) was by far the most attractive of the eight, however beautiful the others. She has remained so ever since. In March 1924, with final examinations approaching, Miss Maryon Moody decided that, while it might not be necessary, an easy way to ensure that she would get her degree was to become engaged to her teacher. It worked. She did well in her examinations, but I did far, far better in linking my life with one who since that day has meant more to me than I could ever begin to acknowledge. Without her love and help, her cheerful and wise acceptance of more than half the burden of our partnership, I would never have reached a position where I would be writing this story.

The next year, on 22 August 1925 in Winnipeg, she married, as she thought, a professor, to live the tranquil life on a university campus which most appealed to her. She is now the wife of a retired prime minister, who has after forty-three years returned to the civilized privacy of a professor's home. In between there has been a variety of experience that would have amazed us both if we could have seen the future in 1925. My wife once questioned the validity of the old cliché that behind every successful man there is a good woman. She claims it should go, 'Behind every successful man there is a surprised woman.' I certainly gave her much cause for surprise. I hope I have given her half as much happiness as she has given me.

Our wedding in Winnipeg was a double affair, for her sister, Grace Moody, married Norman Young on the same day. My father was there to guide me through the ceremony, and my mother was almost as happy as I was. There was also my new family by marriage. I could not have been more fortunate. My wife's father, Dr A.W. Moody, was the personification of all that is fine and generous and unselfish in the family doctor. My new brother-in-law, however, did not conduct himself very well on this occasion as my best man. At one moment in the ceremony when I was already nervous enough, he saw fit to hiss at me, 'Mike, I couldn't find your going-away pants to pack.' This conjured up a frightening vision of a deplorable beginning to my married life. My own behaviour, however, was by no means exemplary. At the wedding reception, Norman Young spoke first since he was marrying the elder sister. He was eloquent and witty, and he thanked all present for their kindness. My new wife, with that candid and loving frankness which I had already learned to appreciate, said that my speech was the worst ever made by a bridegroom. It certainly was the shortest; little more than 'Me too.' There were occasions in later years, however, listening to me for the two-hundredth time on an election campaign, when she doubtless would have considered two words to be the perfect speech.

The autumn found us back in Toronto, an old married couple by now, installed in a flat on the top floor of a solid Victorian house at 12 Admiral Road, not far from the university The academic year went quickly, and pleasantly, and I was feeling more than ever that I had found a permanent and most satisfying vocation, as well as a permanent and even more satisfying domestic ménage from which to practise it.

During the next summer we went to Ottawa, where fate first began to change my plans for permanence in the academic life of Toronto. At the time, I was concerned only with research at the archives for a book I had decided to write on the United Empire Loyalists. It was a subject which had not been carefully or comprehensively explored by our historians, so I thought, and what had been done had been influenced too much by British Tory emotion or patriotic hostility to the United States. I decided, therefore, to correct all this. I thought also that the time had come when I should learn more about Canadian history, particularly the effect of the Loyalist tradition on its interpretation. My wife and I worked diligently much of the summer on papers and documents in the Ottawa archives. Ultimately we collected a large mass of material, still waiting to be transformed by me into a Canadian classic.

At that time, Ottawa was an unplanned, rather ragged national capital but beautifully situated, with rivers and lakes and the Gatineau hills surrounding it; a lovely place in which to live and bring up a family. There was also Parliament. I spent some evenings that June in the gallery of the House of Commons during the highly dramatic parliamentary discussions that led to the election of 1926. For the first time I sensed the excitement of political and parliamentary life and the privilege of being close to stirring events by living in the capital. That feeling was increased by meeting some men during the summer who were active on the political or official side of our national life. One of these was Dr O.D. Skelton, who had been chosen by Prime Minister King to be deputy minister of External Affairs with a mandate to build up the department so that it would be capable of administering Canadian foreign policy and diplomatic relations, responsibility for which Mr King had decided should be transferred from Downing Street to Ottawa.

All of this gave me a new interest in the Canadian capital and in political affairs. But when we returned to Toronto and the new academic year began, I had no thought of changing either my occupation or my residence, all the more so because in the autumn of 1926 I was promoted from lecturer to assistant professor, now with the stupendous salary of $3000.

At that time, however, everything else in life became secondary to the realization that our first-born was coming. We were as exhilarated and as apprehensive as most young couples are in such circumstances. My wife went into hospital during the afternoon of 24 December and, in the best marital tradition, I was far more nervous than she was. I was, however, comforted by knowing that the obstetrician was Dr W.A. Dafoe, one of the best in Toronto and my old Salonica friend, of whom I had seen much in Toronto. I had, after all, introduced him to his wife by a letter from the Balkans, so the least he could do for an old comrade was to look after my wife during these trying hours.

The event was not completely successful. On the medical side all was perfect, but my close relationship with the obstetrician led to an unexpected misadventure. The doctor had come to tell me in the waiting room at the earliest possible moment that I was the father of a fine healthy son and that the mother was fine. The time was just before midnight on Christmas eve. I suddenly realized how much I might save over the years ahead if my son's birthday and Christmas celebrations could be one. Billy Dafoe agreed to mark the birth certificate 12:02 instead of 11:58, a minor and pardonable slip. So far, so good! My doctor friend then asked me if I would like to go into the delivery room to greet my wife. I was a little dubious about this since I was not exactly at home in delivery rooms and thought that it might be better if I waited for a few moments until my wife was wheeled to her own room. But I did not wish to appear timid or, more important, hesitant about seeing my wife at the very first moment possible. So I followed the doctor. It was a mistake. My wife seemed to be still under the anaesthetic, so Dr Dafoe led me to the side of the room with our backs, as we thought, to the still unconscious young mother. He offered me a cup of coffee and a ham sandwich and began to discuss with me the forthcoming Christmas trip of the university hockey team to play Yale, Harvard, and Princeton. It was a subject of great interest to me because I was the coach, and to Dr Dafoe because he had been the coach the previous year.

My wife awakened and instead of a proud and loving husband leaning over to thank her for the gift of a son and heir, she saw him turned away from her, munching a sandwich, and eagerly discussing hockey with the doctor! I have never been allowed to forget this mismanagement of the arrival of Geoffrey Arthur Holland Pearson.

Our baby, naturally, added a new and happy dimension to our lives, our hopes – and our worries. The latter stemmed in part from the disciplinary school of pediatrics, which was then fashionable; an infant from the first breath should be put on a rigid routine from which there must be no swerving. However long and violently the child cried, and ours was a specialist in this exercise, he must be given no soothing care lest he be ruined for life. If he was to be fed in the morning at six and clamoured for his breakfast at five, no notice was to be taken of his noisy tactics to advertise his hunger. It was often nerve-racking, but we were foolishly determined to follow the book, if it killed us; and at times it nearly did! We knew better with Geoffrey's sister who was reared on flexible principles of feeding and on shameless demonstrations of affection on any or no occasion, with satisfactory results for all concerned.

A family man now, I worked even harder. There were extra-mural lectures, a summer school, some addresses on international affairs and on a foreign policy for Canada, a subject in which I was becoming more and more interested. I even criticized in public the government of the day for its waffling attitude toward its obligations under the League covenant and to the newly signed Treaty of Locarno, on which great if unfounded hopes for the peace of Europe were built. I must have begun, however, even in those early academic days, to learn the ambiguous language of diplomacy. An address I gave on Locarno to the Annual Convention of the Ontario Educational Association was headlined in one Toronto paper: 'Must Rely on British Navy to Avoid War' says Professor L.B. Pearson; and in another 'Must Break Away from British Empire to Avoid War.'

ॐ

It was during the winter of 1927 that I first heard that examinations for first and third secretaries in the Department of External Affairs were to be conducted by the Civil Service Commission in Ottawa. Dr Skelton had written me about them and suggested that I might like to be a candidate. The fact that entry into the new Foreign Service was now to be governed by competition rather than by patronage and that the British, rather than the American, system was to be adopted, appealed to me. This seemed to promise a career in a new and attractive branch of the Canadian public service which would be governed by merit and in which one could reasonably look forward, I was assured, to occupying the highest diplomatic posts without private income or political influence.

I felt no urge to leave my university life and work but, when application forms were sent to me in the spring, I decided to fill out that for first secretary, to write the examination, and to see what happened. I was quite certain by this time that Canada would soon take over full responsibility for the conduct of her own foreign relations. That was evident from the results of the Imperial Conference of 1926. Clearly, there would be a greatly expanded Department of External Affairs in Ottawa and, before long, diplomatic representation in many of the countries of the world. The diplomatic unity of the empire was to be succeeded by a commonwealth of independent co-operating national states, a development which I enthusiastically supported. About this I shall have more to write.

So in June of 1928 I wrote five examination papers to qualify for permanent appointment as first secretary in the Department of External

Affairs, with a starting salary away up in the stratosphere at $3900 and with good opportunity for promotion. I knew, however, that there were many candidates and only one appointment to be made. I did not think that I would be the one, but it would be no disappointment to return to the history department. If I *were* successful I could then decide whether to go to Ottawa or not.

There were papers on international affairs, modern history, and international law. There was a test in précis writing, and an essay on a subject to be chosen from a short list. I recall that I chose 'The Rise of Fascism.' There were no gimmicks or gadgets in 1928 to test one's IQ or one's skill at not putting square pegs in round holes. Surprisingly, there was no requirement, or even opportunity, to show any knowledge of French, the traditional language of diplomacy and of 30 per cent of all Canadians. There was also an oral examination in which the candidate, if he had secured the minimum passing mark on the written papers, was questioned by a board of five members set up by the Civil Service Commission. This oral examination, plus the candidate's education and experience, was given a weight of 40 per cent in the final result.

On each board there was a representative of the War Veterans' Association to ensure that the Veterans' Preference was observed. I recall vividly an exchange I had with this representative on my board. In the letters of reference which I had been asked to submit there was one from Professor W.P.M. Kennedy, a brilliant but somewhat mercurial colleague of mine at the university. In an effort to assist me to the maximum, he had written with imaginative Irish exaggeration: 'Mr. Pearson had a brilliant war record, not only on the battlefield but in the camp.' The protector of veterans on the board was naturally interested to get further details about my brilliant war record in the camp. I could tell him only about my skill at St Martin's Plain in picking up stray papers and refuse with a pointed stick and whisking them into a large sack so that everything would be clean for parade. There was also my home run at Bramshot Camp when I was playing third base for the 4th Reserve Battalion team. He was satisfied.

For some weeks I waited for word from Ottawa and began to assume that its absence meant that I had failed. This did not bother me and I kept busy with my summer school lectures. One course, I remember, was on the Reformation. This should not have caused me any particular worry, except that the first row of the class was occupied by nuns and I had some doubts about my ability to deal with this subject in a way completely acceptable to them. So I was relieved after the last lecture when one of them, on behalf of the group, came up to thank me and to assure me that for a Methodist minister's son I had been fair and objective.

Then one afternoon, on 10 August 1928, a telegram was delivered to me at Baldwin House, where the history department was located. Unfortunately, I had just returned from an oculist who had put some drops in my eyes which temporarily blurred my vision. I held the telegram up to the sun and against the shadows but it was no use; I could make nothing of it. There was no one in the building that afternoon to read it to me, so I walked across the campus to the library and, to her surprise, asked one of the librarians to read me the telegram. She must have thought this a strange request from a professor, or an original way to strike up an acquaintance – she was a pretty girl – until I explained.

The telegram read: 'Civil Service Commission report you first in competition for First Secretary post. Can you report at Department Monday.' My veteran's preference, especially my brilliant war record in the camp, must have been responsible.

Obeying my first instructions from a superior in the civil service, I reported for duty at once. In doing so, I had perforce to leave my wife behind to pack up and see to the moving. This has been a chore she has had to take on many times since, though I claim that it was invariably because of my insistence on obeying official instructions when they were in conflict with my domestic responsibilities. The first time it was not easy to convince her, or myself, that my hasty departure without her was necessary, for during my first two weeks in Ottawa no one seemed to be in any great need of my services – a frequent experience of public servants when ordered to move at a moment's notice.

There was, however, a compensation in my initial idleness, for the interval gave me time to look for a place to live. I was fortunate to secure the apartment of Jean Désy, counsellor in the department, who was being transferred to Paris. This apartment was adequate for a family of three, but our daughter was on the way. When she arrived on 9 March 1929 we looked for more room and a back yard – which meant a house. I have always been a great believer in the importance of a back yard, however modest, in bringing up a family. It was not easy to find a house we could afford, even to rent; but we succeeded, and in the late spring of 1929 moved, to 20 Russell Avenue. Patricia now made our little family complete. It has ever since meant more to me than anything else in the world.

It was, I think, a closely knit family. I know I was proud to be its head. I trust that I was a good one in the normal meaning of the word, but I confess to two great weaknesses. While I could undertake the roughest of domestic duties, I was quite helpless to fix or to make anything. I was a complete failure in any mechanical activity and the 'do it yourself' role in our ménage, as well as the business management role, was played, and well played, by my wife. I also had a tendency to spoil the children. My excuse in leaving so much of their discipline to their mother was that I was so often away from home on official duties. The pretext had just enough validity to ease my conscience.

Life in Ottawa, as in Toronto, was very agreeable, and we made many close and lasting friends, not all from official circles. However, I was now first secretary in an 'élite' department of government, as we, and others, may occasionally have been inclined to regard External Affairs and its diplomatic work. We thus had to live a rather more elaborate social life than in Toronto. Believe it or not, we were now invited to ministerial and diplomatic receptions, and even once to dinner at Rideau Hall. I had to learn, though the first attempt was a failure, how to make and serve a cocktail. I also bought my first dinner jacket – not prematurely since I was now some thirty years old – and our first car, a second-hand Ford. For exercise, I played tennis, where I had some modest success in local tournaments, and, in the winter, squash rackets.

Ottawa lived up to our earlier expectations that it would be a good place to live; and External Affairs turned out to be a good place to work. It also soon became clear that I had arrived at the right time, at the beginning of a growth which during my years of service was to lead the Department, in the scope and importance of its activities, to a respected place among the foreign offices of the world. It was a great privilege, and opportunity, to be there at the beginning of this expansion. That privilege was equalled only by the pleasure of working during this period with a group of civil servants of unexcelled quality.

I was tempted, however, to abandon this new career almost before it began. Within a few weeks of my arrival in Ottawa, I received an offer from the university, which I had just left, to return as director of athletics and head football coach, while retaining my rank as assistant professor of history with reduced teaching duties. It was October. The students were returning to the campus. The history department and the football stadium would be alive with activity. The academic year was beginning again and I loved all that it had meant for me, in work and in play. My income would be larger than in Ottawa and this did not lessen the temptation to return. We talked it over and thought of the future which, in Toronto, would now inevitably mean more emphasis on 'director of athletics' and less on 'professor of history.' I thought also of my increasing interest in international affairs, and the new responsibilities which Canada would be assuming in the great and new world of foreign relations. We decided to stay – a decision which I have never regretted.

4

INTO 'EXTERNAL'

The Department of External Affairs, with which I was to be associated as a member, a Minister, and a Prime Minister for the next forty years was, above all, new. It was also a department on the threshold of exciting growth.

It had been determined before I joined the department that the officers and the staff of the foreign service of Canada would be recruited neither through political affiliation nor influence, but through competitive examination. Moreover, the conditions for promotion were to make it possible for a member to move from the lowest to the highest rank, helped or hindered neither by party politics nor private means. It is, I believe, essential for the morale and maximum effectiveness of a foreign service that there should be this assurance. There is a danger, however, of professionalism becoming ingrown, too self-satisfied and exclusive. A third secretary who has read too many books of nineteenth-century ambassadorial reminiscences, or has been unduly impressed by his diplomatic passport, may feel that he is superior in some way to a civil servant of his own seniority and salary in the Post Office Department. There has been little of this in the Canadian foreign service. Diplomatic work still has a certain aura about it and there are certain perquisites attached to working and living away from home, often in countries where life is not only different but difficult. But the glamour of old has gone and the perquisites are today scrutinized very carefully by Treasury officers. Foreign service officers soon find out that theirs is a shirt-sleeve rather than a striped-pants job. When they do have to wear the latter at an official function or at a diplomatic cocktail party, this is often required duty, and they would usually prefer to be back in the office in shirt sleeves. In any event, striped pants are not so much an item of apparel as a state of mind, and you can find that in any government or other office.

The foreign service requires training and experience like any other profession. With the right qualities to begin with, such training and experience normally makes one more competent to take on increasing responsibility. It is foolish to think that a member of parliament's nephew will be a good third secretary merely because of that fortunate relationship, or that the MP himself qualifies as an ambassador because the party thinks he may lose his seat next time, or because he contributed a lot of money to the election chest last time.

Nevertheless, there will always be situations when a government will be wise to appoint as head of a mission someone from outside the foreign service. This may be due to the special position and competence of the person in question or because the current problems between Canada and a particular foreign country require at that post a man or woman with special skills and experience not found among the career officers. This practice of appointment from outside the service has been followed from time to time by Canadian governments, including appointments of officials from other government departments. The results, on the whole, have been good. This need may well increase as the nature of diplomatic relationships changes and becomes more technical and complex. In meeting it, Canada will, I hope, continue to follow a course between the British and the American practice. The former, until recently, has been overly concerned to keep *all* appointments within the Foreign Office; the latter has gone to the other extreme. The right course is surely to maintain high professional standards by competitive entrance and high morale by knowing it is possible to reach the top posts, but to avoid any feeling that the foreign service is a closed corporation limited to those who are able to pass an examination and who can take for granted promotion to the top. The things to be avoided are the pressures of politics and jealousies from outside, and the feelings of complacency and superiority inside. Canadians can take pride in the fact that the Canadian foreign service is considered to be one of the best in the world.

The transfer of control over Canadian foreign policy from London to Ottawa had not been completed when I arrived in the department in September 1928, but it was well under way. The substance of independence for Canada within the Commonwealth had been won, but some colonial forms and legalities remained; indeed, one or two remain by our own choice to this day. While public opinion generally approved national control over foreign relations – which was, in fact, inevitable with the transformation of empire to commonwealth – there remained an 'imperial' minority which watched the change with indignant reluctance and opposed some of its manifestations and implications. When we lament today the lack of a Canadian identity, of a strong sentiment of Canadian national pride, we should remember that we are not long removed from colonial subordination and that for us there has been only a relatively brief interval between the limitations of dependence on Great Britain and the fear of domination by the United States. Further, we achieved our political independence, our sovereignty, precisely at a time when, demonstrably, sovereignty and independence gave no assurance of security or of progress. We had to learn that the aspirations of independence often had to be reconciled with the necessities of interdependence. It was a difficult time to come of age, in foreign as well as in domestic affairs. If we do not understand this, we cannot understand the hesitations and apparent inconsistencies in so much of the conduct of Canadian foreign policy in the twenties and the thirties; or the changes that took place in that policy after World War II. With many of these changes I was myself concerned in one way or another, and so it may be useful to review briefly, as I saw it, our by no means consistent or continuous evolution from colony to nation in the field of foreign policy.

Until the First World War, Canadian relations with foreign countries were conducted as part of imperial relations and through a governor general who, until 1926, was the representative in Ottawa of the British government, as well as of the Crown. The channel of communication from the Canadian to a foreign government was through the governor general, to the Colonial Office in London, to the Foreign Office, to the British diplomatic mission abroad, and through this mission to the foreign government. This was awkward, time-consuming, and inefficient, especially as Canada's overseas business became more important. Therefore, on 1 June 1909, legislation had been passed in Ottawa setting up the Department of External Affairs. Its first budget was a modest $13,350 and its staff consisted of the under secretary of state, two chief clerks, and four other employees. Its quarters were over a barber shop on Bank Street. Its duties were largely those of a post office requiring no concern with, or even interest in, foreign policy. From 1912, the new department was placed under the prime minister which gave it new prestige, and its permanent head greater authority.

The development of the department and the growth of its responsibilities are illustrated by the changing nature of its annual reports. That, for instance, for 1915 dealt with no policy matters at all. As for the Great War, it was dismissed in the sentence: 'The war has increased our correspondence.' The 1917 report refers to the Imperial War Cabinet in a few words as merely a fresh development in the constitution of the British Empire. The only reference to the United States in these early reports is to boundary questions. The report for 1920 makes no reference to the separate position of Canada at the Peace Conference or in the League of Nations. One need only compare that report with the report for 1945, after the Second World War, to see the changes that have taken place in the size, nature, and scope of the work and responsibility of the department. In this 1945 report there are many pages about the postwar activities of the government and about new international organizations, about the San Francisco Conference, the birth of the United Nations and its specialized organizations, and about our relations with the United States. The report has thirty printed pages reflecting the growth of Canada's position in the world and the increasing importance of her international affairs.

That growth should be examined. In earlier years, Canadian governments could at most influence Empire foreign policy. They could advise, they could complain, they could even participate in negotiations, though only as a part of the British Empire. All decisions, however, were made in London, the centre of the Empire. When necessary, Canadian national interests were subordinated to imperial considerations and imperial requirements. Canadian objectives could only be realized through British action. While national feeling and the desire for complete self-government in all aspects of policy were growing in Canada, especially in Quebec, there was no evidence, up to 1914, that such feeling represented a majority view in the country as a whole, or that in any sense it meant imperial disunity or national separation.

Sir Wilfrid Laurier, for example, said in 1900 in the House of Commons: 'In future Canada shall be at liberty to act or not to act, to interfere or not to interfere, to do just as she pleases and that she shall reserve to herself the right to judge whether or not there is cause for her to act.' In saying this, however, he did not question the right of the British government to create by its own action a state of war which would be binding on Canada as on all of Her Majesty's dominions. He also assumed that Canadian public opinion as a whole would insist on coming to the help of the mother country in any life-and-death struggle, even though Canada might have had nothing whatever to do with the policies leading up to the struggle. Nor did Laurier ask for or desire Canadian responsibility for the formulation of imperial policies. His objective was more modest: that Canada should conduct her own relations with other countries in matters of direct concern to her, and make her own arrangements to that end.

By 1914, although the Canadian national picture was changing, the fundamental British loyalties of the majority of the population, and the very great majority of its English-speaking sector, remained the same. If self-government had been achieved in domestic affairs, colonialism ruled in foreign and defence policy and the diplomatic unity of the British Empire and the indivisibility of the Crown remained unchallenged. This was shown clearly enough on the outbreak of war. Again, as in the past, the king's proclamation of war automatically covered Canada. Again, while the nature and scale of Canadian participation would be decided by the Canadian Parliament and government, the great majority of Canadians insisted that the decision must be for combatant forces to serve overseas as part of an imperial army. They felt, with some important exceptions, however, that theirs was not to reason why, theirs was to volunteer and die; and many thousands did.

The Great War was a turning point. In the pride and sacrifice of combat, Canadian nationalism began to come of age, notwithstanding the bitter controversy in 1917 as to how this nationalism should express itself in the conduct of the war.

During the war, Canada sent representatives to the Imperial War Cabinet in London. The Canadian Prime Minister, Sir Robert Borden, insisted on at least being formally consulted on political and strategic direction. Lloyd George was only too glad to further such consultation and provide for machinery for it, because it could lead, he thought, to a postwar sharing of the burden of imperial defence, while not, he hoped, destroying the diplomatic unity of the Empire, or, indeed, the centralization of control and decision in Downing Street. So he agreed that the dominions should be represented, separately, at the Peace Conference at Paris, and sign, separately, the resulting peace treaties. Sir Robert Borden took the lead in insisting that this was the least that could be done to recognize their massive contribution in blood, effort, and treasure to the common victory. But the old constitutional formalities were also observed. Canadian ministers were at Paris, true, as members of a Canadian delegation with power to sign resulting agreements. But they were also there as representatives of the British Empire and received their credentials from an imperial sovereign.

Canada also became a full and separate member of the new League of Nations (indeed in 1927 she was chosen to be one of the non-permanent members of the League Council), but the British Empire was also a member of the League. This in effect meant the United Kingdom, but Canada was still part of that Empire. Therefore, though we had marched through blood and slaughter to the achievement of full self-government, with recognition accorded us as a new international personality, yet the constitutional situation remained confused and the hope still existed both in London and in some quarters in Canada that in resolving that confusion both imperial unity and separate national status could be recognized; control would be centralized in London but policy co-ordinated and burdens shared with the dominions. In short, unity with diversity.

The problem created by the facts of dominion self-government and the desire in London for imperial unity seemed to require the clarification, if not the reconciliation, of an imperial constitutional conference. Indeed, during the war, it had been agreed to hold such a conference after victory had been won. It was not held, because it soon became clear that any such conference would be more likely to confuse and divide than clarify and solve. It is easy to see why.

Lloyd George had said on 14 December 1921 in regard to the progress made by the dominions in acquiring an international position, 'You must act through one instrument. The instrument of the foreign policy of the Empire is the British Foreign Office.' Mr Mackenzie King, who had succeeded Mr Meighen, was not accepting any such doctrine, so Lloyd George's successors were wise enough not to pursue it. Its implications had been spelt out in the Chanak incident when a request was made by the British Prime Minister for immediate support from the dominions in a crisis with Turkey which appeared to be leading to war. The voice of the imperial past was heard in Mr Meighen's response (he was then leader of the opposition): 'Ready, aye, ready.' The voice of the Commonwealth's future was that of Prime Minister Mackenzie King – cautious and non-committal.

At the next Imperial Conference, in 1923, Lloyd George's single imperial policy was rejected by Mr King and the Prime Ministers of South Africa and the Irish Free State. At the 1926 Imperial Conference, new guide lines for relations between all the self-governing parts of the King's domains were laid down in the Balfour Declaration. The future was to be based on co-operation between free governments within a Commonwealth of Nations, rather than on a single, centrally administered, imperial policy reached after consultation and agreement between separate parts. The new principle of equality had been accepted. All that remained for Canada was to bring its laws and symbols into conformity with the principle. This was gradually accomplished over the years that followed, notably through the Statute of Westminster in 1931. The change was made, moreover, without destroying, or even weakening, the ties of friendship and the actuality of a special relationship between the United Kingdom and Canada. It is a development which will always be associated in Canadian history with two names: Robert Borden and Mackenzie King.

As a young member of the history department of the University of Toronto, lecturing on events leading up to the Great War, on the growth of the British constitution, and on the nature of the new British Commonwealth of Nations, I had earlier followed these developments with great interest. At first, I hoped that Canada's national progress from colonialism to complete control of her own affairs could be reconciled with a single, co-ordinated foreign policy for the Empire reached by consultation through imperial institutions. But I soon came to the conclusion that this would be impossible without a subordination of Canadian interests to those of the British Empire with its world responsibilities. So I watched with approval Mr King's insistence on complete Canadian control of her own affairs in a co-operating Commonwealth, though even then I thought that his fears and suspicions of British designs against our evolving independence were often exaggerated and that some of his measures to counter these alleged designs were unnecessary. The reason for his strategy became clearer to me later, even though I never could approve or even wholly understand some of his tactics, which seemed over-subtle to the point of mystification.

Mr King's purpose was to move steadily forward to full national freedom, and to avoid any external entanglements likely to complicate or impede this progress. This required a policy of great caution, avoiding commitments that would interfere with complete freedom of national decision and action. In a very real sense, Mr King was a 'Canada First' isolationist, notwithstanding all his emotional speeches on the mother country and the glory of our inherited parliamentary and monarchical institutions, and his equally emotional reflections on the brotherhood of all men and the internationalism implied by this brotherhood.

The source of this Canadianism was three-fold:

1 After World War I, Mr King was determined to do what he could to prevent a free, North American Canada from being dragged into the 'vortex of European militarism' as he once put it, which the war had not destroyed.

2 The greatest danger, as he saw it, stemmed from our association

with British Imperial policies, which he mistrusted. He viewed these policies as inevitably designed to protect and to advance Britain's world interests. He saw them in action at the League of Nations, an organization dominated by Britain and France and used by them, he was convinced, for their own purposes, which meant exploiting the strength of Canada and similar countries. The League would also be used to bind Canada to commitments designed to perpetuate long-standing injustices that should be remedied. It was all the more to be watched because the United States, our neighbour, had repudiated its own child in refusing to become a member. Canada, therefore, had to be especially cautious not to become committed to international policies, in Geneva or in London, which might divide the British and American governments from each other, thus forcing Canada to make the dreaded, indeed the impossible, choice between her North American and her Commonwealth destinies.

3 Finally and most important, every position taken by Canada on moving into the world as an independent state had to be related, Mr King was convinced, to its effect on Canadian national unity, ever his passionate and over-riding concern. He was certain that British traditions, British loyalties, British connections were still deeply and strongly felt by a majority of the Canadian people. But he was aware also of a growing Canadian nationalism centred in, but not restricted to, Quebec; a nationalism dreading involvement in another war; suspicious of British and European policies; sensing that if the price of association with Empire or Commonwealth was to be yet another holocaust across the Atlantic, such a price was far too high to pay. In brief, he believed that any decisions bringing into open conflict two irreconcilable policies, the national against the imperial, would be damaging, even fatal, to Canadian unity.

If he seemed oversuspicious of certain British policies, as I often thought he was in those years of the late twenties and early thirties, if he insisted on pushing his policies of caution and non-commitment at Geneva to the point of timid isolation, as he did, his abiding preoccupation with Canadian unity was behind every move – or, more accurately, every refusal to move. This I understand more clearly now, I admit, than at the time.

There were two further reasons for Mr King's preference for the cautious and unadventurous in the conduct of Canada's international relations. Although determined that Canada should take sole responsibility for every aspect of her affairs, whether domestic or international, he often seemed to mistrust our capability to do so, at least in foreign relations. We were new and inexperienced; we would not be able to hold our own against the wily diplomats and the specialized experts of older countries, especially the British whose skill in these matters he admired almost as much as he feared. His doubt of Canada's ability to develop and make effective a foreign policy of her own was unwarranted, as the sequel proved. But his misgivings persisted. His attitude reflected a prominent but unhappy Canadian characteristic, a persistent depreciation of our own capacities.

Finally, Mr King's temperament and instinct preferred the process of consultation and conciliation to immediate decisions leading to decisive results. Collective talking was preferable to collective action, since he believed it would lead to lasting agreement. No doubt there was much to be said for this negative attitude and policy at Geneva and elsewhere in the twenties when Canada took her first modest steps upon the international stage. In my view, however, there was nothing to be said for this stand after 1937.

☞

I soon fell into the routine of work for a new officer in a department now beginning to grow. At the beginning, the work was undemanding and uninspiring. I shared a room in the attic of the East Block with two new officers. There were bats beneath the roof and darkness in the corridor. In those early days there was nothing of the traditional foreign office glamour, either in our surroundings or in our work. My colleagues in the top floor were D'Arcy McGreer, Ken Kirkwood, Scott Macdonald, Hugh Keenleyside, and Norman Robertson, all of whom were to distinguish themselves later in the foreign service. My former colleague in the history department at the University of Toronto, Hume Wrong, had already joined the new Legation in Washington, together with another old friend, Tommy Stone. With Jean Désy and Pierre Dupuy in Paris and Laurent Beaudry in Washington, they were the nucleus of our future diplomatic corps.

In charge of us, and of the department, was the deputy minister, Dr O.D. Skelton. He, Hume Wrong, and Norman Robertson, were the main architects of our foreign service. They were a brilliant trio to whom Canada owes more than it may realize. Dr Skelton was a quiet, unobtrusive, retiring person. His somewhat shy, even distant, manner and his rather unimpressive appearance concealed a first-class, well-trained mind, and a relentless capacity for work. He was mild enough in expressing his views, but he held them firmly and pursued them with quiet determination. He felt strongly about Canadian nationalism and shared Mr King's suspicion of and opposition to foreign, and particularly imperial, entanglements. This, plus his Liberal predilections (he had been a biographer of Laurier), and the fact that his position as deputy minister for External Affairs brought him into close and continuous contact with the Prime Minister, made him in those days one of the half-dozen most powerful men in the country. But few Canadians ever heard of him. The power he possessed was never used for any personal or selfish purpose and his abhorrence of publicity was almost excessive. I never got close to him personally – few people did – but I greatly admired and respected him as a man of the highest principle. I learned much from him.

My first assignments were modest enough. I recall being asked to put together a brief on the position to be taken by Canada at a forthcoming League Conference on the nomenclature of causes of death. It seemed an odd introduction to my work in international affairs. I remember also being asked to look into the question of what imperial treaties, presumably going back to the Norman Conquest, applied to Canada, and of these which should be retained and which abrogated. Then I was asked to help the new legal adviser, John Read, who had come to the department from being Dean of Dalhousie Law School, in the famous rum-running case of the *I'm Alone*. The American Coast Guard had sunk this Canadian schooner in the open sea, claiming the right to do so under the doctrine of 'hot pursuit.' Working for Mr Read, who was to become one of External Affairs' most valuable and influential officers before he crowned his career by election to the International Court of Justice, I got my first, but far from my last, experience of protecting Canadian rights against American encroachment. Indeed at that time, as later, a great part of the work of the department was concerned with differences and problems with our neighbour.

I learned then, and had the lesson confirmed many times later, that while the power of the United States was always in the background in these differences, we were quite able to stand up for our own rights, to work out fair agreements, and to do so without destroying the specially close relationship advantageous to both countries. The picture of weak and timid Canadian negotiators being pushed around and browbeaten by American representatives into settlements that were 'sell-outs' is a false and distorted one. It is often painted, however, by Canadians who think that a sure way to get applause and support at home is to exploit our anxieties and exaggerate our suspicions over US power and policies. It is quite true that American negotiating procedures were sometimes insensitive and aggressive, with the heavy handedness that often accompanies the possession of superior power. But it is also true that we Canadians were on occasion too touchy and suspicious and not free of that self-righteousness, and its moral expression, that sometimes accompanies an inferiority in material strength.

Contrary to the popular belief that secret negotiations were evil and dangerous, especially for the weaker party, my own experience has been that Canada, in settling her differences and resolving her problems with the United States, usually did better through quiet, rather than through headline, diplomacy. Indeed the latter is not diplomacy at all, but international public relations. This has an important role to play, of course, in the relations between states, but it does not remove the necessity for quiet and confidential discussion as a prelude to equitable and agreed solutions. Indeed, the concentration of modern media on the immediate and the sensational makes off-the-record negotiation, with later public disclosure and decision by legislatures, more necessary than ever.

My practical education in our relationship with our neighbour, soon to become the most important part of our external policy, was broadened when I was sent to Washington to take charge of our legation in the summer of 1929.

In those spacious and leisurely days of government, the humid heat of Washington was considered unsuitable for diplomats, who moved with most of their staffs to more agreeable weather by the seaside, on the reasonable assumption that nothing much would happen in a Washington summer which could not be entrusted to a junior secretary left behind to hold the fort. As the staff of the Canadian legation was very small at that time and had no one to leave behind, I was sent down for that purpose. I had a most interesting and instructive first experience as a Canadian diplomatic representative abroad, with all the privileges and allowances appertaining thereto.

I made some warm friendships that summer with young officers in the State Department and with members of the Press Club that I was to appreciate even more later when we met again in Washington in senior and more responsible positions. I recall also with great appreciation the help and good-will I enjoyed from colleagues in the British embassy, and especially the kindness and courtesy of a very distinguished ambassador, Sir Esmé Howard, who practised the old diplomacy at its very best.

September found me back in Ottawa, soon to face new duties, new masters, and a depression. The new duties had something to do with the new masters, who, in turn, had everything to do with the election of 1930. It was the first election in which I had a personal, though not a partisan, interest. Naturally, as a civil servant in the Prime Minister's Department, I was interested in the fate of Mr King and his government. But like a good civil servant, I had no partisan involvement. I thought that the depression which was beginning, and the unemployment resulting from it, which Mr Bennett and the Conservatives were exploiting with vigour, would be too much for the government. And so it proved.

In consequence, one day in August 1930, Mr King said goodbye to the members of his department, for some of whom it was 'hail and farewell.' I found myself serving a new Prime Minister and Secretary of State for External Affairs, the Right Honourable R.B. Bennett. I have also, of course, more personal memories of those tragic years of the depression. As a permanent civil servant I had a secure position, but it was certainly not gilt-edged. If the 10 per cent cut that was imposed on civil servants made life a little more difficult and domestic economising even more necessary, we could still count our blessings and were very happy.

I got to know Mr Bennett better than I had known Mr King. I was, indeed, given assignments that brought me into direct contact with him. He was also an easier man to get to know. He was more out-going, more straight-forward than his more subtle and complex predecessor. Both his virtues and his defects were more obvious. His reaction to the defects of others, when he detected them, was frank and expressive. I once was accused by Mr Bennett of taking a decision as secretary of a Royal Commission on Grain Futures which resulted in the insertion into its report of a passage both inaccurate and misleading and, even worse, which got the government into trouble in the House of Commons. The Prime Minister gave me some stormy minutes in our discussion of the matter and let me know in no uncertain terms that I had not only exceeded my authority but had acted either stupidly or maliciously or both. When eventually I was allowed to get a word in, I was able to show that I was being most unfairly accused and that I was not responsible for the offending words and figures. Mr Bennett at once apologized and directed his wrath elsewhere. His storms were rough, but they were usually of short duration and often cleared the air.

I do not recall that Mr King ever stormed. When he felt that he had been badly used or not adequately or wisely served, the weather became sultry and overcast. For those around the presence at these times, a fan was more useful than an umbrella. Where, to change the metaphor, Mr Bennett would burst into flames, Mr King would smoulder. Where Mr. Bennett made a frontal attack, Mr King would exercise an outflanking movement; he would reproach himself in your presence for expecting too much of a young officer. That, of course, made a junior feel more unhappy than any outright criticism; especially when the insinuation was quite unfair. I had, however, no cause for complaint, but good reason for gratitude in serving these two prime ministers, both so different in nature but alike in their dedication to Canada. From them both I received much personal kindness and many opportunities for work of increasing responsibility and interest.

The change of government in 1930 tested the non-partisan character of the Department of External Affairs. The posts of high commissioner in London and Canadian minister in Washington were filled by political appointees of the new Conservative Prime Minister. Vincent Massey, who was about to be transferred to London by Mr King, would have been quite happy if that transfer had been carried out by Mr Bennett, thus confirming Massey's view that, as minister to Washington since 1927, he was a diplomatic and not a political officer of the government. The tradition, however, that the appointment to Canada House was solely political, to be held by a friend of the government in office, was too strong. Added to this was the fact that Mr Massey had for a short time been a member of Mr King's government in 1926 and was certainly no favourite of Mr Bennett. The result was Mr Massey's resignation and the appointment of the Honourable G. Howard Ferguson, a former Conservative premier of Ontario, as High Commissioner to the United Kingdom. Mr Ferguson would have been amused by the idea that this was anything but a temporary, political appointment, which would end, as it did, immediately on the defeat of a Conservative government in Ottawa.

Mr Massey was replaced in Washington by Mr Bennett's brother-in-law, William Herridge, who, while a highly successful and effective Canadian representative in the United States, was also active in formulating Conservative policies in Ottawa, along lines, indeed, often more progressive than conservative.

At this time, of course, there were few, if any, Foreign Service officers with enough seniority and experience to fill our two most important posts, London and Washington. But, as the department grew in maturity and in numbers, and as its officers acquired administrative skills and diplomatic expertise, these two key posts could be assigned to career officers.

Even more important, because of the precedent established, was the retention in 1930 by Mr Bennett of Dr Skelton in the top rank of Under Secretary of State for External Affairs. In view of the circumstances of his appointment, his ultra-nationalist views, and his close relationship with Mr King, it would not have been surprising had Dr Skelton been replaced. Indeed, many years later, when he had retired and was living in England, Mr Bennett told me that the replacement of Dr Skelton was one of the matters high on his agenda when he became prime minister. He neglected, however, to take action in the first few weeks, because of the press of other duties such as forming a Cabinet. By the time he got around to it, Dr Skelton's services to the new Secretary of State for External Affairs had become so valuable that Mr Bennett decided to postpone the change for a few more weeks. But Dr Skelton soon became as indispensable to the new Prime Minister as he had been to the old, and served him, as he had his predecessor, with complete loyalty and great ability. This incident was of importance in that it confirmed the non-political character of the department and of its members. Dr Skelton's replacement by a political appointee might well have resulted in the new foreign service developing along party lines as in the United States.

During Mr Bennett's regime I was given new and varied responsibilities; some of these took me to conferences overseas, in London, Geneva, and The Hague, and with them I shall deal later. In Ottawa, I played a part in two royal commissions that, apart from their immediate political importance, proved to be invaluable to scholars, so I am told, in making available for the first time data sufficient for a broad study of Canada's economic structure. The first was an assignment as secretary of the Royal Commission on Grain Futures, whose chairman, Sir Josiah Stamp, had been borrowed from England. He was one of the ablest men I have ever met. His handling of the Royal Commission hearings and the completion of its report were models of speed and efficiency not invariably characteristic of royal commissions. During our travels with this commission through the prairies, I made my first acquaintance with Western Canada. For the prairies, 1932 was a year of drought, dust, depression, and despair. I realized, as I had never before, how much more there was to my country than the industrial East and how dangerous it could be for our future if we concentrated our attention excessively on the Atlantic and European worlds.

Later, in 1934, I was asked to serve as secretary of another royal commission, on price spreads and mass buying, set up to examine certain abuses stemming from the concentration of corporate power revealed by the depression. As secretary, my responsibilities on this commission were heavy, in organizing its work, gathering an expert staff of economists and research specialists, and supervising and helping to write drafts of the report for the commissioners who were all members of parliament. Never, I believe, did I work harder than on this assignment. The report, with its appendices, was a thorough and penetrating survey of a crucial aspect of our economic life revealing the danger to healthy economic development stemming from excessive concentration of economic power. The preparation of the report, especially in the last few weeks, was a crash operation requiring twelve to fourteen hours of work every day. At the end I was completely exhausted.

A short time later Mr Bennett asked me to accompany him, as a secretary, on his visit to London to attend the Royal Jubilee and the Commonwealth talks that would be held at that time. We sailed on the French liner *Paris*, chosen perhaps because it was reputed to have the best cuisine on the Atlantic. Mr Bennett loved good food. I also found out on this voyage that he professed to be a connoisseur of wines; this was somewhat surprising since he was generally regarded as a total abstainer. The Prime Minister, however, was a man of wide-ranging interests, confident and catholic in his expertise.

Mr Bennett spent many hours on this voyage working on an honours list which he had restored after its abandonment by Mr King, and which he wished to submit to His Majesty on arrival in London. One night he asked me to go to his cabin. I was reluctant to do so as the sea was rough and, as usual, threatening my weak, rebellious stomach. A request from Mr Bennett, however, was a royal command. Praying for strength, I went. He showed me his honours list and flattered me by asking whether I had any comments to make thereon. I was going over the list at great speed, having decided that the quickest way to regain the refuge of my own cabin was to approve enthusiastically every name. To my surprise I came to my own name among the OBEs, an honourable award but a distinction not likely to be regarded by my descendants as an immortal tribute. This, however, did not worry me so much as the conviction that my chief, Dr Skelton, would be most disturbed if he saw the name of one of his officers on this list, especially without his knowledge. His reaction was certain to be violent as he had stronger and, I think, more sincerely held views on imperial awards, or indeed, on any awards, than even Mr King.

With no great interest in this particular recognition but anxious to preserve the good opinion of my deputy minister, I ventured to ask Mr Bennett why he had done me the honour of recognizing my services in this way. He replied that it was because of my valuable and arduous work as secretary of the Price Spreads Commission. I expressed my great appreciation of his kindness, as I had earlier when he had mentioned this in the House of Commons but, greatly daring, I suggested that he might perhaps alter the form of his recognition by reclassifying me in the civil service. This would increase my income, which would be exceedingly welcome, since, as I said politely to the Prime Minister, 'You can't raise a family on an OBE!' I was prepared for an explosion, but the Prime Minister took it calmly enough, merely grunting that if I made him change this list once again, not only would I not get an OBE, I would never get a promotion as long as he was Prime Minister. I said no more.

To complete the story of my induction into this order of chivalry, I was away at a conference and unable to be present at the investiture at Rideau Hall to receive my decoration. On my return, as I was playing tennis at the Rockcliffe Club one Saturday afternoon, a car stopped opposite our court and out stepped my friend, the secretary to the Governor General, Sir Alan Lascelles. He interrupted our game by saying that he had something important to show me. I strolled over to the wire fence, over which he then tossed a small case, with the words: 'Here's your OBE.' In such impressive ways are great deeds rewarded.

There were other interesting assignments. During the Imperial Economic Conference of 1932 at Ottawa, I was assistant to the minister in charge of press and information matters, Dr R.J. Manion. As the Prime Minister alone decided what should be given to the press and kept most of the information on Canadian policy to himself, Dr Manion's role at a press conference was an unenviable one, since he knew very little about what was going on. But Dr Manion was not only a cabinet minister, he was an attractive but very volatile Irishman and had no intention of being placed in any false position. He told me, therefore, to look after press conferences and press enquiries. I knew even less than Dr Manion, but Malcolm Macdonald, who was a friend, was my opposite number on the British side. They did things differently in that delegation. He was always well briefed and was kind enough to give me about as much confidential information as he gave to the British journalists. Therefore I was able to hold Canadian press briefings which were not entirely useless but certainly not entirely Canadian. During this conference, I got my first experience in making news bricks with a minimum of straw, and without dropping too many. It was a very valuable experience for one who was to have many occasions to 'meet the press' privately and publicly in later years.

At this 1932 conference, Mr Bennett did not allow his strong imperial feelings to interfere with his determination to protect Canadian trade and commercial interests. As chairman, he operated in a dictatorial and somewhat brow-beating fashion which greatly irritated the delegation from Mr Bennett's 'mother country,' headed by Stanley Baldwin, who was of a more equable and conciliatory temperament. I recall, after the last crisis had been resolved and the last agreement reached, motoring with Malcolm Macdonald to spend the weekend with friends in the country when he complained about Mr Bennett's policies and tactics, especially the tactics, and assured me that another imperial conference like this would end the Commonwealth. The British obviously preferred to play on their own home grounds where the rules and the atmosphere were of cricket rather than baseball.

Tactics apart, the protectionist character of so many of the trade arrangements made at this conference was no remedy for the depression now raging in Canada and throughout the world. For Canada, more trade, not higher or preferential tariffs, was needed. The situation was grim and there were many – I was one of them – who wondered whether fundamental changes in our economic thinking, indeed in our whole economic structure, were not necessary to avoid chaos and even revolution. Radical reform was in the air, as the breadlines lengthened and the governmental economic policies seemed futile. I remember giving a talk at this time at a church meeting where I spoke favourably to an eminently respectable group about Soviet Russia's Five Year Plan; no one protested or walked out. I was also intensely interested in President Roosevelt's New Deal in the United States and in the energetic and imaginative action being taken there about which we were getting enthusiastic reports from our Canadian minister in Washington. Indeed, Mr Herridge spent a good deal of time in Ottawa in those years trying to sell to Mr Bennett the idea of a Canadian new deal. I was on the outskirts of those discussions, some of the most vigorous of which used to take place at lunch in the cafeteria of the Chateau Laurier, which became a kind of poor man's Rideau Club, for threshing out radical ideas for a Conservative government in a deepening depression. I remember being asked to draft a speech for Mr Bennett to make on receiving an honorary degree at the Rensselaer Polytechnic Institute in New York State. I put into my draft some thoughts more likely to be popular with a socialist than with a Tory. I assumed that the Prime Minister would drop or alter them, but when I got on the train with him that night to ride to Rensselaer I found that he had not had time to go over my draft. Moreover, he was too tired to read it carefully so he gave it to his college audience next morning substantially as it was written, to the astonishment of his old friends. Astonished also must they have been over the broadcasts advocating social and economic changes which he gave in Ottawa at that time and which were largely the work of Bill Herridge.

Desperate times produce startling ideas, often in the hope of producing not only favourable economic, but favourable political results. No such good fortune attended Mr Bennett. He was doomed by the depression to defeat in 1935. Canada and other countries survived that economic depression not so much by radical new deals but by the old and dirty deal of war and preparation for war.

5

THE INTERNATIONAL STAGE

During this period, 1930–5, I attended my first international conferences. The most important of these were concerned with disarmament. My studies in this subject in Ottawa had deepened the concern I had formed in the twenties over the looming possibility of another war, and over what could be done to prevent it. At the university I could only read and discuss and lecture on these matters. Now, as an official of the Canadian government, I could, perhaps, in a small way, influence Canadian policies and the part we could play in the search for peace and security. Our special relationship with a major power, the United Kingdom, gave the government a good opportunity to bring its views to bear on those held in London. With Washington, in those days, we had no such relationship, but that was not so important then as the centre of crucial decisions had not yet moved to the United States.

The first of the series of disarmament meetings that I attended in the thirties was the Naval Conference which opened in London in January 1930 and did not formally close until 1936, though its failure had been registered long before this. The London Conference was to have been limited to the five big naval powers, the United Kingdom, the United States, Japan, France, and Italy. What was Canada, with a navy of only three or four small ships, doing in such company? The reason was to be found in the changed nature of the Commonwealth in which the dominions now had the full right of self-government, even though they all owed allegiance to the Crown and all their citizens were British subjects. Foreigners, understandably confused by the almost metaphysical nature of this free association, insisted that any British figures for tonnage adopted at a naval conference should be binding on the whole Empire. They were suspicious enough to think that otherwise the British might accept, for example, an upper limit of five battleships and then transfer one or two of them to the dominions; or might help finance the construction of naval vessels for a dominion which would be at the disposal of His Majesty, that is, of the British Admiralty, in time of war. This thesis, however, was not likely to commend itself to governments so sensitive about their new status as those of Canada, South Africa, and the Irish Free State.

So there we were, five dominions sitting around the council table in perfect, if somewhat perplexing, sovereign equality with the Big Powers. This meant that every time a speech of welcome or regret, refusal or acquiescence was made by one foreign delegate, there could be six speeches from the British Commonwealth, even though their naval forces, apart from those of the United Kingdom, were very small.

The Canadian delegate, Colonel Ralston, Minister of National Defence, did his best to reconcile theoretical equality with practical good sense by keeping his interventions very short and to the point. Our most helpful contribution to this Big Power naval conference, at least at its formal sessions, was to add only a few minutes to the time needed for talk.

In view of the circumstances that made Canadian representation at this conference necessary, it was only appropriate that the first issue confronting the Canadian delegation in London was not naval, but constitutional. Should Ramsay Macdonald, the British Prime Minister, introduce *all* the Commonwealth delegates to the King when, at the opening, His Majesty received the members of the conference at Buckingham Palace? Or should each chief delegate from a dominion introduce the members of his own delegation? The United Kingdom wished the first course to be followed; Colonel Ralston, the second. The Canadian view prevailed; dominion status was maintained.

Thus at the opening session of the conference, all members of the Commonwealth present made speeches, more in number if not in length, than all the other delegations together. The foreign powers, however, had insisted on the responsibility of the whole Commonwealth, so we made them listen to us separately, even if they were not impressed.

The same problem arose over informal meetings of the conference for the discussion of special issues. Were all six Commonwealth delegates to attend every meeting? We took a sensible view of this, but the

Irish and South Africans felt that, while conferences came and went, dominion status must be preserved for ever. Then came my first experience of the indispensable Canadian compromise. All dominions would be invited to every meeting, however informal, but only one would appear, chosen by the others as being most concerned with the particular matter under discussion.

The Irish were especially insistent, and their sensitivity could be understood, that there should be no suggestion, no appearance, of anything like a 'British Empire delegation.' They felt it necessary to carry their insistence on this score to extremes which must at times have seemed absurd to the foreign delegations. The Canadian delegation, as instructed by Mackenzie King, and the South Africans were also alert to maintain our constitutional purity. But when once our rights were acknowledged in theory, we were careful not to impose them on the conference unnecessarily in practice.

I received a specialized education in these constitutional subtleties of the Commonwealth at this conference. At times they made me impatient, but I soon began to realize that behind what might seem to be stubborn and unrealistic insistence on the recognition of equal status there was a very real principle – the right not to be bound by, or to appear to be bound by, a British decision which often had to be made because of considerations that were imperial far more than they were Canadian, Irish, or South African. The Australians and New Zealanders were not so worried as the other dominions. But they were, of course, more British, and their citizens in general concerned less with dominion status than with imperial unity, at least in foreign and defence policies.

I also began to observe, in a further essential stage of the diplomat's progress, that new problems stemming from dominion status were far less thorny than those which accompanied the pride and sensitivity of older sovereign states in their relations with one another, relations which carried with them the touchiness and temper not of constitutional adolescence but of aging historical experience. To these older sovereignties, protocol seems often to be as important as power. There were good examples of this at my first international conference, such as the dinner given by the Lord Mayor of London, staged with all the traditional pageantry, dignified display, and the medieval ceremony surrounding the Lord Mayor and his official functions. These rituals are beautifully and lavishly observed, as I was to appreciate even more fully many years later when I was myself the central figure honoured by being given the Freedom of the City. On this first occasion, however, I was an awe-struck neophyte in diplomatic life, fortunate enough to be included as an adviser on a delegation, with a seat for a gourmet banquet on gold plates at a table in the rear of the hall.

As the heads of the delegations arrived, each was given a welcoming fanfare of trumpets and escorted for presentation to the Lord Mayor by magnificent heralds. But through some tragic oversight, Count Grandi, the Foreign Minister of fascist Italy, one of the few whose appearance and manner seemed to fit perfectly into this kind of ceremony, arrived and walked up the red carpeted aisle without serenade or escort. Italian pride and honour had been insulted. There was consternation, almost panic, as the British realized what had happened. The future of the conference hung on a Latin thread – even worse, a fascist Latin thread. I could see an agonized group of officials making frantic gestures at the end of the aisle. How could the situation be restored? Would His Excellency retire, and re-enter, when he would get a ceremonial welcome unequalled since the day of Dick Whittington? His Excellency would do no such thing. He took this national rebuff with admirable aplomb and refused to leave either the dinner or the conference. Count Grandi was one of the most impressive figures at this conference, a wise and skilful representative of his dictator. It was an unhappy day for Europe and for peace when he had to leave the Foreign Office in Rome.

The Guildhall dinner was only one item of a too-crowded social calendar at this conference. Such glittering social affairs can be additional obstacles to agreement, though they are meant of course to be helpful. They use up a lot of energy. They can also reduce the mental alertness and the understanding patience needed for the next morning's session. Negotiation at times can be harder on the stomach than on the brain.

I recall my own experience at a conference some years later when my social and representational responsibilities were greater than in 1930. After four or five successive official dinners, I found myself once again in 'white tie and decorations,' about to be wined and dined – and bored. Seated next to an Asian foreign minister, I opened the conversation by a friendly sally, 'How is your constitution standing up to all this?' His English, unfortunately, was rudimentary but he did get the word 'constitution' and hung his reply on it: 'Oh, constitution; in my country we have an upper and a lower chamber.' My diplomatic and political experience has taught me that official entertainment is hard on the 'lower chamber' and often makes it more difficult for the upper one to operate effectively.

However, I loved the social side of this Naval Conference in the thirties, the more so, I suppose, because I had little worry and not too much work. It was my first international meeting, and the great men of the political and diplomatic world were there. My enjoyment of all this was enhanced by the fact that my wife was with me. It was as new and exciting for her as for me. The Department of External Affairs had made this possible. There were three advisers to the head of our delegation: Commodore Hose and Lt-Col. Georges Vanier from National Defence, and I from External. I was not put on 'expenses' but had a *per diem* allowance. The department had not yet acquired much experience with international conferences, or else I was a good advocate, since my allowance this time was more generous than on similar missions later. My wife and I did some calculating. With great care, with two in a small room at the hotel, one meal for two, we could manage, and we did; as also did Georges Vanier who had his wife with him We had a very happy and inexpensive time together. This was the beginning of a close and enduring friendship with the Vaniers, two of the deservedly best loved Canadians of my time and two of our country's most distinguished and devoted servants.

I seem to have written at length about this conference without mentioning its purpose, its work, or its results. This is no doubt because its purpose was obvious, its work unfinished, its results negligible.

The purpose was to improve and broaden the agreement reached at Washington in 1922 on naval limitation by the United States, the United Kingdom, Japan, France, and Italy. While much work was done in London, this purpose was not achieved; political differences proved, as is often the case, to be insuperable obstacles to technical progress. The conference adjourned later in 1930. It was resumed some years after, but by then naval limitation was a vanished illusion. Japan withdrew from the conference, ostensibly because the others had refused to accept a common upper limit of naval strength. By this time too, the other naval powers had a new fear: Nazi Germany was returning to the seas and a new dimension of dread and insecurity had been superimposed. So all that remained for the London Naval Conference to do in 1936 was to acknowledge the end of thirteen years of futile effort to limit naval armaments by international agreement. London and Washington could put the blame for the death on the Japanese, while fraternizing at the funeral and linking arms over the grave in Anglo-Saxon solidarity. This (not the death, but the linking) pleased Canada. Were we not the linchpin that made this link possible, as we have so often been told, or tell ourselves, in after-dinner speeches?

Those early days at this conference, however, remain vivid in my memory as an important stage in my own education. It was on 22 January 1930, for instance, that I first spoke for the Canadian government at an international meeting. It was not an important meeting; it was not even connected with the Naval Conference. The British government took advantage of the presence of dominion representatives in London to convene a meeting to discuss what the Commonwealth policy, or rather policies, should be in relation to the League of Nations draft treaty on financial assistance to victims of aggression, to which the Canadian government had some objections. I did not myself think much of these objections, which were based on our consistent policy to avoid League commitments that might imply participating in any arrangements for collective security. But I had my instructions. Therefore I compromised with my conscience, according to my notes made at the time, by speaking unemphatically. Very quiet diplomacy, as it were.

It might, perhaps, be appropriate here to complete my observations on disarmament in the thirties, including certain developments at Geneva which made a mockery of disarmament, and yet supplied an unanswerable argument for its need.

The London Naval Conference was limited both in representation and in scope. Long before it assembled the League of Nations had begun to concern itself with disarmament on a world-wide and all-inclusive scale. A preparatory commission had been established in 1925 for a world conference on the subject in which non-members, notably the United States, were to participate. It was decided that this first World Conference on Disarmament was to open in Geneva on 2 February 1932. This, it was hoped, would be the beginning of a new era in our progress toward peace.

One of my early assignments in External Affairs was to assist the deputy minister on the interdepartmental committee established to formulate policy recommendations to the government for the forthcoming conference. The committee included top-level officials and the chief of staff. This was my first experience of that indispensable piece of governmental machinery with which I was to become so familiar later, the interdepartmental committee. As government becomes more and more complex and specialized, as it covers more and more of the daily life and activity of the citizen, as it helps and hinders him from the cradle to the grave, it is not surprising that permanent officials, with their continuity of experience and their expertise, should become increasingly powerful, just as the cabinet, advised by them, gains power at the expense of the legislature. This concentration of official power is,

I think, inevitable and up to a point desirable, but it must be kept under parliamentary control if political and personal freedom is not to be intolerably diminished. This can only be done by responsible ministers and by a vigorous legislature of alert and informed members on both the government and opposition sides of the House of Commons.

Having served both in government and in the civil service, I believe that Canada has up to the present escaped the major danger to freedom and responsible government that can arise from a powerful, dominating bureaucracy. Our civil service has respected its position in the hierarchy of democracy. It has discharged its duty to recommend, to advocate, to argue, and try to influence, but it has recognized also that the responsibility for policy decision is ministerial, that when this decision has been made, it is the duty of the official to administer the policy with all the efficiency and energy he can muster; and that it is his duty also to serve the government in office with complete loyalty, whatever its party complexion. Canada has been fortunate in the acceptance and the practice of these principles by her civil service; just as she has been fortunate in the high quality of that service.

The interdepartmental committee on the deputy-minister level is usually composed of the busiest men in town. It is always necessary, therefore, to set up working sub-committees on lower levels whose members can give more time to the problem and then report back to the full committee. I was chairman of such a working sub-committee, made up of Norman Robertson and Lt-Col. H.D.G. Crerar. Robertson, of course, was my colleague in External Affairs, but Harry Crerar was a new associate. Our work together at this time began a valued and close friendship through all the following years when we both moved into positions of greater responsibility. Harry was serious, studious, clear-headed, with a great capacity for concentration on the problem at hand, and the industry and knowledge to make his concentration effective. As a result of the work done on the official level, the government delegates were well briefed when the first World Conference on Disarmament opened at Geneva in February 1932. The head of the Canadian delegation was the Secretary of State, Sir George Perley, with the Solicitor General, the Honourable Maurice Dupré, and Miss Winnifred Kydd, president of the National Council of Women, as the other delegates. The senior adviser was our permanent representative to the League of Nations, Dr W.A. Riddell. Our military advisers were General McNaughton and Colonel Crerar, and I was secretary to the delegation.

The appointment of Miss Kydd deserves special mention. Dr Skelton and I were in Mr Bennett's office one day when he was considering possible members for the delegation. He felt it should include a lady delegate, but whom? He had a brilliant idea – 'Let's appoint the president of the National Council of Women. After all, she is, in effect, the prime minister of the women of Canada.' So he sent for *Who's Who* to find out who the lady 'prime minister' was. She turned out to be a Miss Kydd who was also Dean of Women at Queen's University. 'Fine,' said Mr Bennett, 'phone and ask if she could see me tomorrow or the next day.'

Miss Kydd was no doubt surprised at this summons to Ottawa by the head of the government. But she could not have been more surprised than the Prime Minister when she arrived at his office. He naturally thought that the president of the National Council of Women and a dean of women to boot would be a lady of at least middle age with the maturity and even severity one might expect to attach to these two offices. Miss Kydd turned out to be a most attractive, smart, auburn-haired lady in her late twenties. I'm sure Mr Bennett's surprise turned at once to delight. Like Mr King, he was not unappreciative, except in the marrying sense, of feminine grace and charm. His undoubted pleasure at being able to ask Miss Kydd to represent Canada at this conference on disarmament was certainly shared by those who worked with her later on the delegation.

The head of our delegation, Sir George Perley, was an elderly veteran of the Conservative high command, having been High Commissioner in London during the First World War. He was a very serious, almost a dour, man and knew less about international affairs than about domestic politics or business. He was as insistent on an ordered routine as he was rigid in his views, by no means an extrovert, but conscientious and persistent in his work. Every morning after breakfast, I read to Sir George an impromptu translation of the editorial in the day's *Journal de Genève*, the Bible of the conference. Every evening at 8 PM, if there were no official engagements, I was also conscripted to make a fourth at bridge, which I do not enjoy. Precisely at 10 PM, regardless of score or anything else, the bridge ended and we were dismissed. Lady Perley was the exact opposite of Sir George in temperament; warm, sociable, bubbling over with good will and good humour. She was a great asset in maintaining Canadian morale and we were sad when she went off to Aix-la-Chapelle – as she often did – to take the waters.

Sir George was a man who liked his instructions to be carried out quickly and without question. I knew this, so I was the more disturbed one afternoon by an unusual order from him. We were sitting together at a plenary session listening to a speech. Sir George turned to me and asked if I knew the name of the League official sitting on the dais next to the Chairman. I did. It was Aghnides, head of the disarmament section of the Secretariat. 'Has he lived in Geneva long and do you think he knows the place?' asked Sir George. I told him that he had been with the League from the beginning and undoubtedly knew Geneva perfectly. My curiosity about Sir George's interest in Aghnides was then satisfied. 'I am having trouble with my teeth,' explained my querulous chief, 'so go up and ask him if he can give you the name of a good dentist.' I was rather startled by this. The assembly was very quiet, hanging on the words of what seemed at the time a very important speech. I would have to walk up the aisle, make my way to the platform, walk across it (by now the centre of attention), and ask a surprised Mr Aghnides for the name of a dentist. It seemed an unusual way, in the circumstances, to interrupt the attention being given to a speech on world disarmament. But an order was an order, especially from Sir George.

As it happened, I knew a way around the side of the hall to the platform. On the way, I met, fortunately, a Canadian friend who was on the Secretariat. From him I got the name and address of an excellent dentist. That was not enough, however. I had to be seen by Sir George getting that address from the man he had chosen for the purpose. So I moved up to and across the platform, in full view and with some embarrassment, and quietly asked Aghnides a perfectly normal question about the number of speakers on the list as the Canadian delegate *might* wish to speak. Sir George watched me, no doubt with interest, and was fully satisfied with the name and address of the dentist I gave to him when I rejoined the delegation. It was, if I do say so, a very skilful exercise on my part, indicating that I was beginning to learn something of the niceties of diplomatic manoeuvring!

The opening session of the Disarmament Conference on that cold and windy February morning in 1932 at the Salle de la Reformation was given over to the presentation of petitions for disarmament and peace from the plain and humble people of the world – those who suffer most when peace is lost. The Canadian petition alone had half a million signatures. The millions of names and the prayers for peace were deposited at the rostrum. The bearer of each country's message was a wounded veteran, a war widow, a 'silver cross' mother, or an orphaned child. It was an intensely moving occasion. The emotional atmosphere created was reflected in the opening speeches of the delegates, in their pleas for peace and international friendship. Our spirits were lifted in a way that for me was not to be repeated until the opening days of the San Francisco Conference, many years later, and after the slaughter of many more millions had testified to our failure in these earlier years to do more than talk.

After this inspirational beginning the conference got down to work and the spiritual lift declined rapidly. The basic difficulty, and this remains true of all disarmament discussions, arose out of the relationship between security and disarmament. The French maintained the position which they had consistently held in the twenties: no disarmament before security. If security could not be ensured by international action and agreement, then it could be ensured only by adequate armaments for national defence. Other delegations were reluctant to undertake new security commitments and insisted that the reduction of armaments would itself lead to a greater feeling of security.

There was no greater success at Geneva in 1932 than previously in reconciling these two points of view which were the result of national circumstances and experiences. By 1934 the United Kingdom, the United States, and Italy were willing to permit a measure of German rearmament without new security guarantees. But France remained adamantly opposed. Apart from this basic difference, there were other difficulties reflecting national policies and interests – which in practically every matter discussed were given precedence over international considerations.

The United States remained suspicious of European entanglements and cynical about European power policies. The British concern was primarily with naval and overseas interests. The Soviet Union, through Litvinoff, was able to make to other suspicious and cynical delegations all-embracing proposals for instant and complete disarmament. These were not taken seriously and, it could be argued, did not deserve to be by the way they were formulated. The Germans, now entering once more the Big Power club, were insistent that there must be equality of rights for all powers in disarmament. This meant that the special limitations of the Treaty of Versailles must be removed. If this were not done, and if the other Big Powers refused to reduce their strength to the German level, German armament in that event must go up to their level for her own protection. The British and Americans were sympathetic to this position; the French, not surprisingly, were not. The last representatives of democratic Germany argued eloquently and reasonably, but without result. Then in 1933 the arrogant spokesmen for Hitler and Nazism appeared on the scene to make their position unequivocally clear. When this was not accepted, they goose-stepped their way not only out of the conference but out of the League of Nations.

We know now that Hitler was happy to be given such a good opportunity to withdraw from Geneva and rearm from Berlin. Shortly afterwards, Japan, condemned by the League for her aggressive actions in China, also gave notice of her intention to withdraw. The last meeting of the general committee of the Disarmament Conference was held on 1 June 1934.

Before that, however, in the committees, after the great ones had returned to their capitals, we met and argued for week after week about techniques and priorities in armament reduction. I remember especially the debates over how to divide weapons into offensive and defensive categories. A warship with guns of ten inches was offensive and should be prohibited; one with six-inch guns was defensive, and could be retained. There is a café in Geneva, the 'Bavaria,' where some of us, younger and hence wiser than our seniors, used to gather for food and drink and talk. Those gatherings remain among my most pleasant memories of that time. We had no difficulty in deciding in a few minutes points which senior representatives had been arguing for days. We agreed at once, for instance, that there *was* a valid distinction between an offensive and a defensive weapon: if you were in front of it, it was offensive; if you were behind it, it was defensive.

There were other proposals, less complex but even less practicable politically, which we used to discuss with increasing scepticism as the conference proceeded.

The United Kingdom, whose draft proposals were the base for conference deliberation, proposed the abolition of all military and naval aircraft and all bombing from the air 'except' – and some of the other delegations regarded this exception as a good illustration of Anglo-Saxon hypocrisy – 'for police purposes in certain outlying regions.' (It is interesting, if idle, to speculate on what would happen to this kind of 'exception' at the United Nations now!) There was even a proposal at Geneva for an effective international control of all civil aviation, and a draft convention for the regulation óf the 'private manufacture of arms.' In those days, Zaharoffs, rather than governments, were thought to be the more dangerous 'merchants of death.' There was even a 'committee on moral disarmament' which probably occasioned some ironic amusement among Nazi, Fascist, Japanese, and Soviet delegations.

The great crisis for the Canadian delegation came when someone proposed in a naval sub-committee that the number of warships be reduced by one-half. This put us in an impossible position, politically and mathematically, since our naval strength at that time was three ships. Fortunately, at least for us, the proposal was not taken seriously.

It was not easy to keep one's idealism, sense of proportion, or even of humour, as the conference bogged down in sterile detail and in petty debating exchanges. For me, the effort ended when I came home to Ottawa in the summer of 1932. When I returned for a few weeks in 1933, the disintegration had begun of a conference which had opened on that February morning a year and a half earlier in such a moving atmosphere of noble purpose and of splendid hope. The failure of the Disarmament Conference and the successful defiance by Japan of the League's efforts to halt her aggression in China made it a depressing time for those who, like myself, had hoped that progress might be made toward peace and security by collective action through the League. National fears, national rivalries, national ambitions proved far stronger than any sense of international solidarity, or even co-operation.

☗

Worse was yet to come – the Italo-Ethiopian dispute. The problem began in 1935 while I was still in Ottawa and remained on the League agenda until 1938 when I had been stationed in London for three years. If I now go into this dispute in some detail, through its various stages of fear and exhilaration, hope and despair, it is because I believe it was the most important international crisis between the wars; because Canada played an active if not a proud part in the drama; and also, as I am writing about myself, because it confirmed my own conviction, which had been developing since I first began to teach history, that only by collective international action and by a consequent limitation of national sovereignty through the acceptance of international commitments, can peace and security be established and maintained, and human survival ensured.

The dispute, and the League's handling of it, will be better understood if we recall that, as a result of a Three Power Conference of the United Kingdom, France, and Italy at Stresa, the League Council created, on 15 April 1935, a Committee of Thirteen to examine how economic sanctions could best be applied against a violator of the peace in Europe. This committee, of which Canada was a member, was to restrict its examination of sanctions to Europe, owing, it was alleged, to a Franco-Italian deal by which Mussolini would have a free hand in Ethiopia in return for joining the United Kingdom to protect France against Nazi aggression in Europe. It is ironic that a League committee, under Italy's sponsorship, was discussing sanctions against aggression at the very time Italy was threatening aggression against another member of the League. Indeed, this danger had become so imminent that the Canadian delegate on the committee, Dr Riddell, whose instructions had been to emphasize that the League of Nations should be more concerned with conciliation and arbitration than with sanctions and collective action, was told to pursue this argument less vigorously as it might be exploited by the Italian government in its increasingly aggressive policies in Africa. He was permitted to be more 'constructive' in the discussion of sanctions in the committee and to point out (and this is particularly interesting in view of the immediate future) that economic sanctions should cover not merely the export to an aggressor of key products and raw materials, but also imports and credit facilities. To this broadening of sanctions, the Italian member of the committee was, of course, strongly opposed.

By August 1935 Italy's aggressive intentions toward Ethiopia were clear and fighting began. The League, while emphasizing the need for conciliation and peaceful settlement, took a strong position against Italy's right to use force in pursuing its claims. To determine the facts, the League established a committee of the Council on 3 October 1935, which reported two days later. In the discussion of this report the United Kingdom pressed for action against Italy under the Covenant. M. Laval, for France, was more hesitant. On 7 October, however, the Council, unanimous except for Italy, agreed that Rome's actions had brought about a state of war in violation of the Covenant. It then decided to co-ordinate action against Italy under Article xvi of the Covenant, the sanctions article. To this end, a meeting of the Assembly was called for 9 October.

I was appointed secretary and adviser to the Canadian delegation to this meeting, which took place during the last stages of an election campaign in Canada. The head of our delegation was the Honourable G. Howard Ferguson, High Commissioner in London, a politician in a diplomatic office, a kind and unpretentious chief. He spoke his views frankly and clearly, without verbal camouflage, but his friendly personality usually made it possible for him to express disagreement without giving offence. Moreover – and this turned out to be important in the days ahead – his political prestige in the Conservative party gave him direct access to the Prime Minister and ensured that his views would be listened to with respect.

The Assembly met in a tense atmosphere. The hour of decision had been reached. The Council had been firm. Would the Assembly, and especially its more powerful members, also remain firm and insist that the principles of the Covenant be upheld? Our hearts were lightened and our emotions stirred when His Majesty's Secretary of State for

Foreign Affairs, Sir Samuel Hoare, in a moving oration and to the surprise of many said at the very first meeting: 'In conformity with its precise and explicit obligations, the League stands, and my country stands with it, for the collective maintenance of the Covenant in its entirety and particularly for steady and collective resistance to all acts of unprovoked aggression.'

Hopes for effective collective action ran high. Laval, a shifty-eyed, rather sinister figure with drooping cigarette and white string tie, did not destroy these hopes by his speech which followed, though he certainly did not strengthen them. Mr Ferguson's statement for Canada was a firm and clear declaration of our willingness to 'join with the other members of the League in considering how by unanimous action peace can be maintained.' Indeed, this was the overwhelming feeling of the whole Assembly, with the natural exception of Fascist Italy. On the morning of the day set for the Assembly to decide the question of aggression, a telegram was received from Mr Bennett in Ottawa instructing Mr Ferguson to refrain from voting on such an important issue, since Parliament had been dissolved and a new one was to be elected the following Monday. The action of that new Parliament should not be anticipated in any way. This message caused consternation in the Canadian delegation. I could hardly eat my continental breakfast at the Hôtel de la Paix before rushing off to see Mr Ferguson.

We at once sent a reply to Ottawa pointing out that the vote was to be taken that day on the single and straight question that Italy had violated the Covenant; that there could be no doubt of this as war had already broken out. We also explained that a canvass of the Assembly showed that every member except Hungary, and possibly, though, for different reasons, Switzerland and Austria, would vote to declare Italy an aggressor. The specific question of sanctions was not involved in this vote. Under these conditions, Mr Ferguson argued 'Canada's abstention would without question be misinterpreted in Geneva and its importance magnified.'

There was, of course, little possibility of getting a reply to this cable before the Assembly opened that afternoon at 2:30 Geneva time. I asked Mr Ferguson what he was going to do. In his forthright way, he replied, 'Rather than abstain as instructed, and join that minority of one or two, I'll not go to the Assembly at all. We'll go and play golf.' The Geneva golf course was a nice easy one and I enjoyed playing on it, but not in these circumstances; the thought of disobeying such important instructions from Ottawa would make my slice even worse than usual. So I suggested that we try to get Mr Bennett on the transatlantic telephone and have our instructions changed. There had never been a telephone call before from our Geneva office to the government in Ottawa, and we had never before conducted business this way with a prime minister, especially one on an election tour. But Mr Ferguson was not one to worry about unconventional procedures, and so we put a call through from Geneva for the Prime Minister of Canada. He was discovered in his private car on the night train from Ottawa to Toronto where he was to have a final election rally that night. Mr Bennett was ushered from his car at breakfast-time to the stationmaster's office at Lindsay where the train had stopped and where a telephone call from Geneva awaited him.

I listened in on that conversation, at Mr Ferguson's request, from another phone in his hotel suite, and with some impatience as it was getting on to the hour when the Assembly would meet. Mr Ferguson explained the position and, with a great sigh of relief and satisfaction, which no doubt was audible across the ocean in Lindsay, I heard Mr Bennett, who seemed to be in a good humour, perhaps after a good breakfast, tell Mr Ferguson to use his own judgment with regard to the vote on the declaration of aggression. There were then a few jovial political exchanges between the Prime Minister and his High Commissioner.

'How is the campaign going, R.B.?'

'Fine, Fergy, we have them licked.' Optimism could go no further, for this was only a day or two before Mr Bennett received the worst defeat ever received by a party leader in a federal general election – that is, until 1958!

Much relieved, we went off to the Palais des Nations and were just in time to join all the members of the League of Nations, except Italy, Austria, and Hungary, in declaring that the fascist government of Italy had violated the Covenant of the League of Nations by committing aggression against Ethiopia. It was a narrow escape from making Canada look ridiculous on an issue of far-reaching importance.

Immediately after the vote, a Co-ordination Committee of the whole membership met 'to consider and facilitate the measures contemplated under Article xvi of the Covenant.' This, in effect, meant that it was to decide what sanctions should be applied to Italy, now a declared aggressor. The first instructions received from Ottawa regarding this committee were again negative. We were not to sit on any sanctions committee, even a committee of the whole. These were changed, however, on an appeal from Geneva and the Canadian delegate was authorized to serve. But Dr Skelton was anxious to put a brake on any possible initiative from the delegation. He would have had no difficulty on this score had Mr King been Prime Minister, but Mr Bennett's position was, simply, that we should discharge our obligations under the Covenant, and Mr Bennett carried on as Prime Minister until 23 October, when Mr King again took charge. So Canada became a member not only of the full committee, but also of the smaller Committee of Eighteen set up to do the effective work of organising and directing sanctions.

At the beginning, the two League committees acted speedily, smoothly, and almost unanimously. There were difficulties in Ottawa, however, after the change of government. Dr Skelton found that his views about sanctions and League policy in the Ethiopian crisis were much closer to those of Mr King than they had been to those of Mr Bennett. He had never shared my own satisfaction over developments in Geneva. At the beginning, in fact, he had opposed the decision that Canada should vote for the resolution declaring that Italy was an aggressor in violation of the Covenant, at least without an explanatory statement that this did not commit Canada to participate in sanctions. He felt that Mr Bennett's decision that we should sit on the full sanctions committee did not cover membership on the Committee of Eighteen. Indeed, after the change of government, he sent a message to Dr Riddell criticizing him for acting too hastily in joining the smaller committee. Dr Riddell, a mild man, took exception to this criticism, and rightly so. He pointed out that throughout the crisis he had kept the department fully and swiftly informed of developments but had great difficulty in getting any instructions from Ottawa in time to be of help in the decisions that had to be taken at Geneva; one of which had been the question of membership on the Committee of Eighteen.

If, at the beginning, the League was able to act effectively, this was because the members, and particularly the powerful ones, wished it to do so; while the strongest non-member, the United States, was co-operative. To the Soviet Union, action was being taken against a fascist state. To the United Kingdom, strong popular support for peace action through the League, recently shown in British opinion polls, was being satisfied. As for France, she was so torn between her declared policy of organizing collective security and her desire to keep Italy as a friend against Nazi Germany that she was at first unable to do anything except go along with the prevailing sentiment in the Assembly.

At the initial meeting of the Eighteen on 11 October, Mr Ferguson, in his final appearance as a Canadian delegate, had made a strong, positive statement which was well received: 'Let the committee,' he said, 'show the world that the League is no longer to be scoffed at but that it means business and that, when a breach of the Covenant takes place, it proposes to deal with the aggressor in the proper way.' He urged his colleagues not to get lost in legal arguments and to take immediate action, that very night. It was a long time since a League committee had heard such forthright talk from a chief delegate of Canada, and it helped to ensure that the initial resolutions on sanctions were passed without dissent.

Trouble was brewing, however, in Geneva as well as in Ottawa. The reversal of roles by some delegations at the League was too startling to be completely convincing. At the back of my own mind was the fear that later, if sanctions were not working, or if they were working too well, the tide might turn against League action; and Ethiopia, encouraged to fight on, would be abandoned. This is precisely what happened.

By 19 October, the full Co-ordination Committee had adopted five proposals for sanctions and had referred them to member governments for action. One of these was for an embargo on the export to Italy of certain key products, but with the noteworthy omission of the following strategic commodities: copper, zinc, lead, iron, steel, coal, and petroleum products. These omissions disturbed the Canadian delegate, Dr Riddell who, after 25 October, took Mr Ferguson's place. The list seemed both incomplete and weighted against Canadian exports, especially nickel. Dr Riddell felt that these omissions should be repaired, to make sanctions more effective and better balanced. He did not press for the necessary additions, however, at the meeting on the 19th because the new government in Canada had not yet had time to take over.

It was not until 29 October that Dr Riddell received information on the policy of the new government in a partial text of a press release issued that day in Ottawa announcing acceptance of these first five proposals for sanctions, but adding that no commitment for military sanctions be recognized unless and until it had been approved by Parliament. (This warning was not surprising as Mr Lapointe, a key figure in the new government, had asserted during the election campaign that 'Abyssinia was not worth the life of a single Canadian.') To Dr Riddell, this statement of policy came 'as a heartening surprise.' He was especially impressed by the words which assured the Canadian people that 'the Canadian government would take the necessary steps to secure the *effective* application of the economic sanctions against Italy proposed by the co-ordination committee.'

Dr Riddell, no doubt, felt after receiving this message that, even though he had received no direct instructions on the point, he could now press, as a member of the Committee of Eighteen, for additions to the list of embargoed exports to Italy which would make economic sanctions more effective and at the same time fairer to Canada. He thought he was right in taking this stand. He was. He also thought that in doing so, he was expressing the views of his government. He was not.

At a meeting of the Eighteen on 31 October the faint hearts of certain European intriguers began to make reservations or exceptions, or to give watered down interpretations of the sanctions which they had already undertaken to make effective. Dr Riddell, like Mr Ferguson before him, warned against any weakening. He went further. On 2 November he moved the addition of 'petroleum and its derivatives, iron and steel products' to the list of prohibited exports. This addition, he said, 'would put real teeth in sanctions.' It also put some Ottawa teeth into him – some weeks later.

Dr Riddell did not act hastily or without prior reference to Ottawa. He had previously sent two 'urgent' telegrams to Ottawa reporting the attitude of the other members of the Committee of Eighteen on his proposed amendments and which, as he pointed out, he had already advocated at earlier meetings. He had received no reply by 2 November. Therefore, after consulting with his British and French colleagues, who indicated support for his proposals, and relying on the positive statement on economic sanctions already made in Ottawa by the new Canadian government, Dr Riddell made his move. As a cautious official, however, he made clear in the text of his draft resolution that implementation would depend on a broad, international acceptance (he had the United States particularly in mind) of its terms. Further, he wrote to the chairman of the committee pointing out that he had made the proposal on his own authority and not on the instructions of his government. He believed that he had fully protected his position in relation to Ottawa, if indeed he needed protection. He was mistaken.

Dr Riddell's proposal was quickly endorsed by the Eighteen and referred to the full committee, where in turn it got quick and unanimous approval. The reaction in Rome was immediate and violent: 'Oil sanctions mean war.' It was a reaction likely to impress Mr King, Mr Lapointe, Dr Skelton, and those who shared their views, especially as the resolution was now designated everywhere as 'the Canadian proposal.' Some opposition in Canada developed. Other Canadians felt differently: 'Back the League and support oil sanctions.' A vigorous controversy ensued and the government became alarmed. Mr King at the time was in Georgia on a holiday and Ernest Lapointe was acting prime minister.

It was not, however, until 2 December, a full month later, that the government repudiated the initiative of its representative in Geneva for the extension of sanctions, while pointing out, however, that this was not to be interpreted as a repudiation of the principle of economic sanctions. The distinction did not impress opinion in Canada or abroad. This disavowal of its representative by the Canadian government played an important part in destroying any remaining hope that strong sanctions, collectively and effectively applied, would force Italy to halt its military aggression against Ethiopia.

The Canadian government was by no means alone in its timid attitude towards sanctions, an attitude potentially fatal, of course, to their success. To do just enough to satisfy advocates of collective action under the Covenant of the League, but not enough to risk an extension of the war or an Italian scuttle into the Nazi camp, had become the position of many League members, in spite of all their brave words at Geneva about standing firm for the Covenant, words often designed merely for home consumption. In brief, oil sanctions were too risky. This operation was to be acupuncture but not surgery.

The French government, in particular, and in spite of its formal stand in the committees during October and November, was determined that sanctions should not go so far as to run any real risk of a final break between Paris and Rome. London in its turn was willing to join Paris in a search for a 'peaceful' solution in spite of League resolutions on sanctions, even if this meant betraying Ethiopia. Dismayed by the prospect of a Berlin-Rome axis, the British and French governments worked out a settlement which, they thought, would be acceptable to Italy and enforceable on Ethiopia.

It was known as the Hoare-Laval agreement. That the British Foreign Secretary, who a few weeks before had so bravely pledged his country to steady and collective resistance to aggression, should sign this agreement was hardly more shocking than that his government, with its declared policy of backing the League, should confirm that signature. Laval's part, of course, was predictable. In England there was indignant popular reaction against the proposals. Sir Samuel Hoare defended his reversal by arguing that the alternative was the complete conquest of Ethiopia by Italy, or a general war, with Hitler supporting Mussolini. An aroused British public opinion was not impressed by this defence. The government had to abandon the proposals; Hoare resigned as Foreign Secretary to be succeeded by Anthony Eden.

In the middle of December after his repudiation by Ottawa, Dr

Riddell left Geneva for a meeting in Chile of the governing body of
the International Labour Office. He was chairman for that year, and
would normally have attended the meeting, but in the critical circumstances that existed he might have been expected to remain in Geneva.
He was certainly not encouraged to do so by Ottawa. His departure
was inevitably linked with the disavowal by the government of his
initiative on oil sanctions and a weakening generally of the position
regarding sanctions. I was appointed to take Dr Riddell's place on the
Co-ordination Committee and the Committee of Eighteen.

This was my first major diplomatic assignment. I was to represent
Canada on a League committee dealing with a very important matter, a
committee which had by now become an arena of international power
politics and in which a proposal by my predecessor had aroused strong
controversy in Ottawa and throughout Canada. While I was gratified
by this new responsibility, I was not enamoured at leaving my new
post in London, even temporarily, for a committee which had already
been sabotaged by the Hoare-Laval proposals and where I would have
little or nothing to do, or say. As I took my place at the committee
table, it soon became clear that all I had to do was be careful, and take
no initiative, to 'see no evil, hear no evil' and above all, 'speak no evil.'
This latter was particularly appropriate for me since I was suffering
from a severe case of laryngitis. Thus I had an easy time on the Committee of Eighteen where my presence caused no stir, not even with my
neighbours at the table: Laval, alert but with half-closed eyes and
nervously chain-smoking; Eden, brilliantly displaying the charm and
diplomatic skill of a chosen man moving upwards. During that December week when I was in Geneva, the committee, in fact, never got to
sanctions. They were too busy deciding how to bury the Hoare-Laval
proposals and with dropping, rather than applying, sanctions.

Ethiopia was left to its fate, and the aggressor, with modern arms
and uncontested air power, occupied Addis Ababa on 7 May. Admit-
tedly, there was no point in maintaining sanctions in futility and
hypocrisy. But it was sad to see timidity and narrowness of vision
triumph.

On 30 June 1936, a brave, lonely figure of impressive dignity and
unconquerable spirit spoke to the Assembly of the nations in Geneva
called to consider what should be done in the light of changed circumstances in Ethiopia.' At that meeting Haile Selassie warned the world:
'It is my duty to inform the governments assembled in Geneva, responsible as they are for the lives of millions of men, women and children,
of the deadly peril which threatens them, by describing to them the

fate which has been suffered by Abyssinia. Placed by the aggressor face to face with the accomplished fact, are states going to set up the terrible precedent of bowing before force?'

That is exactly what they did. The last act, however, was not to be played out at Geneva, but in Milan nearly nine years later, with a dead dictator hanging from a lamp post, his compatriots reviling his body and mocking his memory, while the Lion of Judah sat once more on his Peacock Throne in Addis Ababa.

Mackenzie King drew different and, as I think, less realistic conclusions than did Haile Selassie from the collapse of League action. Speaking earlier to the Canadian House of Commons on 11 February 1936, he said: 'I am not at all sure that when the whole story comes to be told, that but for the action of the government of Canada in this particular matter [of sanctions] at that particular time, the whole of Europe might have been aflame today.' My own view is that the failure in 1935 of the members of the League of Nations, including Canada, to stand up to a single aggressor, had much to do with the world war in 1939.

What went wrong? First, narrow national policies and interests were preferred to the untried experiment of collective security through international action. Second, some members of the League, again including Canada, were determined to prevent the world organization, especially when the United States was not a member, from becoming a 'war office' for the maintenance and protection of a European security policy based on the Treaty of Versailles. Those who held that view felt that economic sanctions which might lead to military sanctions must be rejected. For collective security to have real meaning for peace, all members must be prepared and willing to join in precisely the kind of action, economic or military, which is necessary to prevent or defeat aggression. Otherwise, an aggressor has nothing to fear from the international community but pin-pricks.

I end this chapter with a curious Canadian footnote. Mr Massey, by then our High Commissioner in London, recommended early in 1936 that a bust by Epstein of Haile Selassie which he had admired, and which was available, should be purchased for the National Gallery of Canada. The recommendation was rejected in Ottawa as the purchase might cause political controversy.

CANADA HOUSE IN LONDON

While these tragic events were unfolding in Geneva, there had been a change in my own position. One day in the summer of 1935, Dr Skelton told me that the Prime Minister, Mr Bennett, had approved my posting to Canada House in London under Mr Ferguson, and that I should plan for an early move overseas. A few weeks later Mr King became Prime Minister and confirmed this move.

There was some difficulty about my salary. No regulations had yet been worked out to cover a civil servant of my rank at Canada House. Dr Skelton suggested a salary which I felt was too low for what I was expected to do, especially as at that time there were no allowances of any kind for the extra expenses of foreign service. My Chief expressed pained surprise at my mercenary approach to this problem but agreed to increase the amount from $6800 to $7800. At the same time he warned me that Mr Bennett, Minister for External Affairs as well as Prime Minister, would not likely approve the higher figure. But he did; in fact, he increased it to a round $8000. Even that figure turned out to be inadequate for my duties as a representative of Canada in London; but, thanks to my wife, we managed.

Characteristically, though my transfer to London had been contemplated for some months, when I did finally move it was on a few hours' notice. The suddenness of my departure was due to a last-minute decision that I must first attend the Special Assembly of the League in Geneva which was about to open. Could I be ready for departure in a day or two? I could, but this meant that there was little or no time to say goodbye to my friends. I had worked in the department for nearly seven years; I left so suddenly that some of my colleagues did not know I had gone. More important, it also meant that I must, once again, leave my wife to settle our affairs, to pack our belongings and look after all the moving arrangements for the family. She might have been pardoned for suspecting that I had persuaded the department to do it this way.

It was not until October that I left Geneva for London where my family soon joined me and we began the business of settling in a great city in another country. It was not easy. Our means were limited, and our requirements were considerably greater than at home. It was not possible to find, as in Ottawa, a satisfactory house with a reasonably low rent, a daily to help with the housework, and a good public school nearby for the children. Life was more complicated at a diplomatic post in England.

After some false starts, however, and a few depressing weeks, we found a suitable, if temporary, house in Hampstead, with two private day schools nearby, one for boys and one for girls. We became established and comfortable, and were a happy family. We loved London and the British Isles. We came to know the fascination of the great city and the quiet beauty of the countryside; to appreciate the courteous manners of the people, and value their ancient and cherished traditions. I have always since considered London the only great city in the world fit to live in. I dislike all huge cities, but London is more like a community of towns, and much the better for that.

Life was most agreeable once we had become adapted to its differences from our Canadian ways. This adaptation was easier for me than for my wife, not only because she had to look after the management of a household, but because I had already lived in England for some years. As for the children, their adaptation naturally was quick and complete. Soon they looked, talked, dressed, and acted like English school children. In fact, a few years later when our son was at boarding school living a spartan, uncomfortable, and disciplined existence, composed about equally of games and study, he became rather embarrassed by his father's transatlantic accent and attitudes. On those occasions when proud parents are invited to appear, he carefully, if politely, kept me segregated from a too close contact with other parents, since he might be joshed later by his schoolmates for having a mid-western American as a 'pater.'

I worked hard and dutifully at Canada House, but found time as well for games and recreation; tennis, squash-rackets, and some golf. It was also a joy to go with my son to Saturday soccer matches, and even watch cricket, whose mysteries he appreciated better than I did. Then there were country weekends at the stately, but chilly, homes of England when we learned new rituals of rural living: early morning tea, walks in the rain, dressing for dinner, and so on. Equally if not even more enjoyable, were journeys of exploration in our Chevrolet when, sometimes with the children, sometimes with friends, sometimes alone, we roamed the island from Land's End to John o' Groats.

Most of these expeditions were great fun and without mishap. On one, I let my country down. We had been invited to visit a friend's country house in Scotland, and were delighted to accept, especially as it was on the way to Stirkoke Castle, near John o' Groats, where we were going to spend a week. Alas, I knew little or nothing at that time about the requirements of what was to be, I found, a grouse-shooting occasion. I had no gun, no skill at shooting, and no knowledge of the customs of the moors; I had not even the proper costume. My hosts no doubt felt some disappointment that I was quite unable to add anything to the day's bag. That would not have been serious, however, as they were very kind people, especially to Canadians. But even their friendliness must have been severely tested when, my first morning on the moors, as a carefully placed spectator, I saw a grouse winging past me and, with great speed and dexterity, but to the amazed disbelief of the guns nearby, I threw a stone at the rocketing bird. It was a fit subject for a Bateman cartoon and a guarantee of no further visit, at least for the shooting. Other summer holidays we spent with the rain in Harlech, on the Norfolk coast, or with sun and gaiety on the beaches of Brittany.

During the years when I was stationed in London, with the exception of those few weeks with Mr Ferguson, my chief was Mr Vincent Massey. He and Mrs Massey (they were so closely knit that it is almost impossible to talk of them separately) were very kind to the Pearsons in London. We spent many pleasant off-duty times with them. Mr Massey was not a man of gregarious social tendencies. No extrovert, he was by nature formal and reserved; but at home, relaxed with his family and his friends, he could be the life of the party. No one could be so clever or so amusing in the unusual charades we played; and no one possessed a keener sense of the ridiculous on such occasions. He was, I used to think, quite as good an actor as his brother, Raymond. An official or diplomatic occasion, of course, was quite a different stage.

I found the High Commissioner an understanding and considerate chief, a skilled professional in diplomacy, and one whose cultivation of mind and broad knowledge commanded respect. He was exceedingly conscious of his position as the representative of his country, and careful to surround it with dignity and, when necessary, with formality. In this he could hardly have been more unlike his predecessor, the earthy, very human Howard Ferguson. Mr Massey was more at home at the Foreign Office, the National Gallery, or Brooks Club than at a meeting of the Canadian Chamber of Commerce, or at a dinner of the Canadian Club. He did indeed discharge his duty gracefully and well on all occasions, but was not very comfortable in casual exchanges, with tourists at Canada House, for example, or with Canadian sports teams visiting England.

There was, I should think, no high commissioner who ever had more and closer contacts than Mr Massey in aristocratic or artistic circles. He and Mrs Massey were personal friends of the Royal Family, and Mr Massey seemed to know every duke by his first name. Many of the most exalted of the establishment, in fact, appeared to have been at Balliol with him. He was a firm believer in the crown as the great instrument for maintaining Commonwealth unity and for giving dignity and stability to British institutions. But he was also a nationalist who regarded the monarch as King of Canada, not of Britain alone, and believed that this constitutional fact should be recognized by Whitehall in their attitude toward the High Commissioner's relations with the Palace, and in other less august affairs. This gave rise, as we shall see, to occasional misunderstandings.

Mr and Mrs Massey were long-standing friends of Mr Mackenzie King. Mrs Massey was the only person I knew who called him 'Rex,' just as President Roosevelt was the only one who referred to him as 'Mackenzie.' During my stay in London this personal relationship seemed to lose its warmth, although there was never any outward sign of this when the Prime Minister came to London. There were reasons for this change. Mr King's determination to prevent Canada from becoming involved in British imperial or in European politics and his almost morbid suspicion of Downing Street led to a limitation on the High Commissioner's official contacts with the government at Westminster. His attendance at meetings might commit the government in Ottawa. If he sought information too earnestly from the Prime Minister or the Foreign Secretary, for example, this might imply an interest in British affairs which Mr King was anxious to avoid lest it lead to a misunderstanding of the Canadian policy of no advance commitments. The High Commissioner thought that the Prime Minister was over-sensitive in these matters, while the Prime Minister considered that the High Commissioner was rather too close to the makers of British policy – even, it might be, too colonially-minded and too easily impressed by the majesty of imperial splendour.

Mr King also, and of this I am quite sure, considered that the Masseys were almost too highly placed on the ladder of social-official life in London and that they lived in a manner too far removed from the sober simplicity of Laurier House, and perhaps in a style too exalted for a Canadian official in London. The fierce light that beats upon a throne should serve to illuminate only prime ministers. There should be no aura of aristocracy, and certainly no palatial structure in London to house a Canadian public servant, even a high commissioner. For this reason the government refused some years later to accept as a residence for the Canadian High Commissioner the gift of an eminently suitable house in Kensington Palace Road. This, it was no doubt believed, might give the occupant illusions of grandeur, a frailty to which Mr King probably, if mistakenly, believed Mr Massey was already dangerously exposed. I noted with interest, and regret, the declining personal relations between my Minister in Ottawa and my High Commissioner.

As for myself, I learned much in London apart from how to become a better foreign service officer. I could soon balance a tea-cup, a cocktail shaker, or a champagne glass as though I had never been brought up in a Methodist parsonage. I like to think that I was even a suitable partner for my beautiful wife at the high official and splendid social occasions which we now had to attend. I became accustomed to the costume of my trade: black homburg, short black coat, striped trousers, and furled umbrella. Anyone watching me enter my club, The Travellers, might have thought I was the patterned product of Eton, Oxford, and the Foreign Office, unless he heard me speak. For, as I have already suggested, I still talked Canadian. I had enough sense not to follow the unseemly example of some adult Canadians whom I watched as they tried to switch to English.

Canada House itself was a good place for work; there in the centre of London at Trafalgar Square, with Nelson and the pigeons to keep an eye on us. My colleagues were good friends and fine people. We had our frustrations and difficulties among ourselves but much more with Ottawa which often seemed to ignore and misunderstand our problems or even to forget our existence; but we had a good office and the morale was high.

Beyond Canada House, my contemporaries in the Foreign and Dominion Offices became far more than official contacts and, through our easy social relationships, made my work easier and more productive. I also had some old Oxford friends, as well as Canadians, living and working in London with whom we had many a happy time. I followed my invariable and, for me, rewarding habit of getting to know as many press correspondents as I could, whether Canadian, British, or American.

These were good years and exciting years for the Pearson family until, like so much else, they came to an unhappy close in 1939.

ॐ

Such, in brief, was the setting. What, then, of my work? When I reported for duty in October of 1935, no one seemed to know exactly what I was to do. This was, no doubt, partly because there was a new government in Ottawa and a new High Commissioner in London. My appointment, moreover, to London as a Counsellor, the rank I now achieved, was new. I was succeeding no one. I was the first of my kind, with detailed duties undetermined.

I had concluded from my talk in Ottawa with Dr Skelton that I was to be called 'political secretary' and my main responsibility would be liaison duties with Whitehall, particularly with the Foreign and Dominions Offices. Because of these duties, I was to have no administrative responsibilities at Canada House. These would be discharged by the official secretary, Georges Vanier, who was next in rank to the High Commissioner. Mr Massey was, I knew, anxious to organize Canada House more as a diplomatic mission than as a government department abroad and my appointment would, it was thought, fit neatly into that concept. There was, of course, also a large Trade and Commerce division at Canada House under an able and experienced head, Frederic Hudd, as there were officers of other departments of the Canadian government. But there was little integration or co-ordination of duties. This was to come later, and I was privileged to have something to do with bringing it about. Meanwhile, these branches had their own form of 'Dominion status.' Georges Vanier did not wish to be restricted to administrative and related matters and to be left out of the more interesting political work of liaison and reporting, which was to increase and to become more important during the years from 1935 to 1940. I could certainly understand and sympathise with his feelings. Our relations were most friendly, and, as reasonable people, we worked out an arrangement satisfactory to the High Commissioner and to ourselves for dividing responsibilities. Perhaps the most important element of this arrangement to avoid difficulties over division of duties was not substance but form, as so often is the case in these matters. To preclude

misunderstanding I was not to be called 'political secretary,' and settled
for no title at all.

Whatever my title, or lack of title, my work took me to Whitehall
nearly every day, often to The Travellers for lunch with a British civil
servant, or to an official dinner in the evening. I soon acquired some
skill in finding out what of importance was going on, and what the
British were about. Very often, I was more successful in doing this at
the right kind of dinner party or on a weekend visit than by visiting
Whitehall, where my contacts were largely in the Foreign and Dominions Offices. The Dominions Office, in its people, its attitudes, and
atmosphere, was similar to other civil service departments. But the
Foreign Office was the Holy of Holies, occupied by an aristocratic, well-
endowed élite who formed part of the British diplomatic service, and
who saw to it that the imperial interest was protected and enlarged in
accord with policies worked out in their high-ceilinged, frescoed, Victorian offices, to be accepted, they usually assumed, by their political
masters in Cabinet and Parliament.

Although the Foreign Office was changing and becoming more rec-
ognizable as a part of contemporary democratic society, its officers were
still formed very largely in the old privileged mould. That I used to
hear about a 'very bright and promising chap in the office who is the
son of an engine driver, you know,' or that two Australians were among
the most highly regarded senior officers, confirmed rather than removed the impression of caste. It is only fair to add, however, that
the members of the Foreign Office, caste or no caste, were extremely
intelligent, knowledgeable, and efficient, even if at times the procedures
they had to follow were drawn from the nineteenth century. The
younger officers, whom I knew better, were not only able and highly
qualified, they were in tune with the new world and its changes; they
were moving with the times without losing their professional pride in a
long-established institution.

Older or younger, senior or junior, they were invariably kind and
helpful to me. I got on terms with some of them which enabled me to
know almost as much about what was going on as they knew themselves. They were my friends and they trusted me; hence they would
let me see, without hesitation, many telegrams and despatches that
came to their desks, excluding, no doubt, any which might contain
references to the policies or lack of policies of the Canadian government. As a result, I was able to help my High Commissioner to keep
informed on developments in foreign policy, and he was thus, I hope,
better posted to inform Ottawa. The results of our reports to the de-

partment, however, were not always what we had hoped, either in ac-
knowledgment of their significance or in recognizing that we were able
to get the information without prejudicing in any way our insistent
Canadian policy of no entanglements. We often felt, this is a common
complaint of diplomatic officers abroad, that our despatches were
ignored and that we might as well have mailed a batch of local press
clippings. The further away from home the more sensitive you became
about neglect.

I knew that I had to be cautious in London about my methods of
work. Shortly after I joined Canada House, on 6 November 1935 (the
new Liberal government had just taken over), Dr Skelton instructed
me by letter not to seek any greater access to British information than
was given to the second man in the High Commissioner's office in
Ottawa. He did not want me to take any responsibility for reporting
anything to my High Commissioner, let alone to Ottawa, that the
British might want us to know merely for their own purposes. Indeed,
I felt that he was rather worried in general about my close contacts with
British governmental offices. My independent sturdy Canadian attitude
could be weakened, presumably, and I might be lured into the Whitehall net.

One of our main preoccupations at Canada House, in fact, was
over Ottawa's increasing worry about becoming too involved in
British policy. Canada's newly-won independence within the Commonwealth must be protected against the wiles of Downing Street and
Whitehall. The concept of 'our Empire' and 'our dominions' died hard
in Britain. Canadian officials there were supposed to stand on guard
against any move to revive this concept in any form likely to cause
controversy or division in Canada. Dr Skelton and, even more, the
Prime Minister were, as I have already pointed out, very suspicious on
this score. Our High Commissioner was also watchful lest any reflection on our status as a nation might among other things reflect on his
own position as its representative. At other times he was more sympathetic to the idea of a consolidated Commonwealth influenced possibly
by his close association with the imperial élite and the Royal Family,
but more, I think, by his growing anxiety that Canada was becoming
too Americanized.

ᵒᵀ

Apart from the events leading up to the outbreak of war, the most
dramatic episode affecting Canada House during this period from
1935–40 centred on the monarchy: death, succession, abdication, res-

toration. The impact of these events on popular opinion in the Commonwealth, still deeply concerned with the monarchy and its traditions, was striking. In addition to its effect on the public mind, it led to constitutional and political problems in Canada and in the other dominions. Here was a novel and perhaps final development in the relation of the Crown to British democratic societies and institutions. The Crown became 'hot news.' For more than a century the power of the monarch had, of course, been symbolic rather than substantive. But its authority and prestige were still great, based on tradition, on the qualities of the sovereigns and of the royal families, and on the conservative patriotism of the British peoples. On this patriotism, the abdication crisis of King Edward viii imposed some strain.

On the evening of 21 January 1936 I read in black letters on a newspaper hoarding: 'The King's life is drawing peacefully to its close.' He had served his people with sincerity and devotion, and the outpouring of grief when he died was deep and genuine. A new king succeeded. It has been said that his first act, shortly after his father's death at Sandringham, was to put back the clocks, which had been set forward a half-hour by George v in the interest of punctuality. The change was symbolic of a new dispensation in a new age.

When King George's body was brought to London, to historic Westminster Hall, I wrote in my diary: 'The procession was simple and without pomp; just the King on a gun carriage, followed by his sons on foot. King Edward looked young and lonely, with the loneliness, already, of those who live on the highest places.' It was not long before it became clear that he was determined to seek happiness and avoid loneliness in his own way. He soon displayed a will of his own, an awareness of new conditions, and proceeded to change the pattern of monarchy as well as to make his bid for a personal life which crossed convention and tradition. In doing so, the first steps were taken which led to the abdication. With the developments that followed, Canada House had some connection, although the channel for policy communications in a matter of such unprecedented delicacy as an abdication was often from Prime Minister to Prime Minister direct.

The abdication was of direct and great importance to the dominions, constitutionally and politically. The Canadian government was consulted, or at least the Prime Minister was, in all its stages. The King was the King of Canada and, unless we wished to keep Edward viii on his own terms, or to become a republic, the formalities of abdication had to be agreed with London and the accession of the new king timed to synchronize exactly in both capitals so that there would be no interregnum. Certainly Mr King did not wish to make Canada a republic. But he also did not wish to keep Edward as King of Canada, with Mrs Simpson as Queen. He had made it clear, as had the other dominions, that abdication was the only possible course. He saw eye-to-eye with Prime Minister Baldwin, both personally and constitutionally, on what had to be done.

He also must have realized that, while a divided crown was for Canada a constitutional necessity if we were to be an independent part of the Empire and Commonwealth, this division could produce its own complications when action had not only to be taken, but to be taken simultaneously by six governments, and in situations with which only one government, that of the United Kingdom, was in immediate, direct contact and for which it had primary responsibility.

When the moment arrived for the abdication to take effect legally by formal action in the House of Lords in London, it was essential that similar action at the same moment take place in Ottawa and other overseas capitals. Otherwise there would be a constitutional vacuum. We worked out an elaborate system of communications, a 'count-down' which in its precision would have been adequate to launch a moon-rocket. I was to be stationed at Westminster Hall and a telephone line was kept open to Canada House. I could tell the High Commissioner the very second the formal change had been made. He could then talk immediately to Ottawa on a line kept open, so that the necessary action could be taken there without the slightest delay. It was beautifully accomplished in all capitals except Dublin. The slip-up there did not take a form, as one might have expected, which would have eliminated the monarchy from the Irish Free State, if only for a short but symbolic time. The mistake in Dublin led to the very unexpected result of giving that state for some hours *two* British Kings. In the timing, one had ascended before the other abdicated.

The accession of George VI once again led to changes. An effort was made to restore important traditional elements to the atmosphere and character of the palace and the court. The new king was admirably qualified to make this effort successful, with his strong sense of duty, his irreproachable character, his dignity and decency, and his domestic happiness. The royal yacht was in calm waters again, and with a steady hand at the wheel.

The determination to 'repatriate' the monarchy into the solid and respectable comfort of English nineteenth-century traditions and mores occasionally expressed itself in exaggerated and even rather ridiculous forms. I recall a rather smug item in the Sunday papers shortly after

King George's accession that His Majesty had decided to ride only in English-built motor cars, thus reversing the precedent of Edward VIII who had had the effrontery to purchase and use a car made by General Motors in Canada; a country of which, incidentally, he was also the King. I felt it my duty, as a loyal Canadian, to protest 'personally and informally' to the King's Private Secretary that while action of this kind might strengthen His Majesty's place in the hearts of his English subjects, it would not make him more popular in Oshawa or with Buick dealers across our country. He told me to calm down as the notice had nothing to do with 'Buck House' though perhaps something to do with 'Buick House.' It must have been an unauthorized advertising stunt by the motor manufacturers. In any event, he added, King Edward's car had not been really Canadian, merely made in Canada by an American company; to which I gave the crushing reply that it was as much Canadian as their boasted cotton goods were English.

Then came the coronation. This had new constitutional aspects, as well as a minor personal involvement for me. There were moments, indeed, when I felt I was back in the days 'when knighthood was in flower' though I did not always comport myself, I fear, to that manner born. A coronation in London is the ultimate in joyous pageantry, a colourful throw-back to the days of medieval pomp and of later imperial grandeur. It is the efflorescence of the British talent for ceremonial; the easier and more impressive because it is based on deep historical roots and evokes genuine, not manufactured, emotion.

In North America we tend to suspect formal ceremonials as something, like good manners, personal service, and the recognition of status or rank, undemocratic and a shade demeaning. Perhaps that is why we focus so much of our ceremonial on the parading of garishly costumed teams of portly and cheerful middle-aged citizens from Tent 446 of the Knights of the Arabian Desert, or on marching bands and mini-skirted baton-twirlers at half-time. I must confess, however, that, while I appreciate good ceremonial as an onlooker, I am singularly uneasy when I have to take part in it. In later years my official positions often made this necessary. But whether inspecting a guard of honour or marching down a red carpet, I always felt uncomfortable and, on some occasions, a bit ridiculous; though I improved – I hope – with age and experience.

When the coronation date was fixed for 1 May 1937 and the complicated and detailed preparations began, the High Commissioner thought, as he so often did in such situations, that the Commonwealth significance of the occasion should be emphasized. One way to do this was to have the High Commissioner carry the Standard of Canada up the aisle of Westminster Abbey in the coronation procession, alongside the great Standard of England, borne by the Earl of Derby. The other dominions, of course, would also have their standard bearers. Indeed, the South African High Commissioner claimed the right to carry two standards because the British had three: one each for England, Scotland, and Northern Ireland. Why then only one for South Africa? This knotty problem was left to the Duke of Norfolk, the Earl Marshal, to settle. He was the unchallenged autocrat over all ceremonial rules and procedures, and resolved this issue by decreeing that a single banner for each dominion was acceptable.

Of a lower order of significance, but more important to me personally, was the decision that I, with three other Canadians, should be ushers inside Westminster Abbey for the coronation service itself; or rather, because it would never do to use such a plebeian expression as usher, we should be 'Gold Sticks in Waiting.' This was considered to be, apart from its Commonwealth significance, a privilege of sorts, which enabled the fortunate appointee to have a look at the ceremony from inside the Abbey, to wear knee-breeches and a sword, and be awarded as a souvenir and proof of his close association with the throne a wand painted in gold and red and embellished with a crown. It also gave me the pleasure of being in the Abbey on the great day from 4:30 AM to 5:00 PM, and the expense of renting a court uniform from that most British of all marketing institutions, Moss Brothers in Covent Garden.

In addition to adjusting myself to this new distinction, a great deal of my time at Canada House was devoted to helping with arrangements for looking after Canadian visitors to the coronation and dealing with other complicated and novel questions that arose, such as that referred to in the following telegraphic exchange with Ottawa:

From External to Canada House:
Commissioner RCMP states impossible to arrange earlier shipping date for horses [for Mountie contingent]. Extraordinary noise of street parades are part of regular training but horses are at present undergoing strenuous training in unusual noises. Commissioner does not expect any difficulty will be experienced with horses.

But the High Commissioner was still anxious and replied:

Am informed by high authority that the most experienced, even the most blasé, horse although habituated to usual and unusual noises will sometimes collapse with terror at sight of bearskin busbies as worn by the guards. Would suggest that this aspect of problem be brought to attention of appropriate authorities.

It was, but Ottawa remained unmoved. They curtly replied that Canadian Mountie horses needed no special training for London sights and sounds. And, of course, they didn't.

In the days immediately prior to the coronation, Canada House became a madhouse; and the thousands of Canadian visitors with their various demands made some of us suitable occupants for one. Unexpected crises always turn up on these occasions. With us, one arose out of the timber that went into the stand we built around Canada House to accommodate four or five hundred of the more favoured Canadian visitors. It was nicely decorated by bunting in a colour scheme of dirty green and drab russet with an occasional nondescript silver maple leaf pasted on it. If not a thing of beauty, the Canadian stand gave a perfect view to those whom we had decided (it was a most difficult choice from among the thousands of applicants) should be sold tickets at a reasonable price solely to cover the cost of construction. Naturally, being good nationalists, we told the contractors that Canadian timber alone should be used in building this stand. It was half completed when an angry Canadian timber commissioner rushed into my office, speechless with indignation, gasping that he had found, on inspection, that Swedish, even Russian, timber was being used. This was a real crisis. If a headline appeared in Canadian newspapers 'Soviet timber used in Canada's coronation stand,' it might mean the end of the Commonwealth or, at the least, the end of one Commonwealth government. It would certainly mean the end of our jobs. We jumped into action, told the contractor to pull down what had been erected, to remove the offending foreign planks, and build it again in national purity and strength. The honour of Canada was saved. Communist contamination was avoided. Canada House breathed easily again and the coronation could go on.

When I could get away from Canadian visitors – to say nothing of the Commonwealth Conference of Prime Ministers which was taking place – I attended rehearsals for the 'gold sticks' so that we would do our duty with efficiency on the great day. These were a waste of time. Any normally intelligent cinema usherette could have performed our duties without any rehearsal whatever and have considered it a day off, as each of us had to take charge of only a few seats. Nevertheless, we had more than one training session, including a final dress parade. We were a distinguished group of a hundred or so; young and vigorous, old and decrepit, ambitious young diplomats, sons of peers, retired admirals, and generals. At our briefings, the Garter King at Arms told us how to behave and how to handle any emergency in our sections. We were impressed by the warning that the success of the day and, therefore, the future of the Empire and Commonwealth, lay largely in our hands.

The rehearsals were very funny. We merely stood around, doing nothing in particular except watch our section commanders salute group commanders who would then rush off and salute the Chief Gold Staff Officer who saluted back, muttered a few syllables, whereupon the group leaders rushed back to the section leaders, saluted, and these in turn after returning the salute smartly would return to us and tell us that there would be a few remarks by our commander-in-chief after which the rehearsal would be over.

The last rehearsal, however, the day before The Day, was deadly serious. We clustered in the cloisters of the Abbey around our commanding officer who gave us final operation orders with a few solemn words of inspiration: 'England expects that tomorrow every man will do his duty.' We should be especially careful in dealing with 'special cases' of which there were thirty-eight. They required particular attention, and could be recognized by a large red cross which would be on the white ticket of admission. He picked out a few examples. The first was Lady A who was completely paralysed and would arrive in a wheelchair accompanied by a doctor and nurse. She would have to be very carefully ushered into her seat and continuously watched thereafter in case she died. 'This,' the Chief Gold Stick said, 'was a comparatively simple case.' 'Miss A [the small daughter of a prominent statesman] is too young to have a seat. When she arrives at Door 10 [my door], she will be conducted by the staff officer on duty there to the alcove in the Mary Queen of Scots Chapel where she will be turned over to ten little choir boys.' A third case, even more exciting, concerned the young Countess of X whose baby was due any moment. An usher's eyes must never leave her as it was feared that the excitement might bring on the baby. 'There must be no birth in the Abbey during the coronation' – thundered our commander.

I had thought that there would be one major advantage in being an 'usher.' I would get a perfect view of the historic ceremony. I was soon disillusioned. My post of duty was out of sight of the actual coronation, behind a pillar in an outer aisle. I decided that I would have done far better in the crowds lining the streets. On the great day, only half awake, but in accordance with orders, and in all my sartorial glory, I arrived at 4:30 AM at the Abbey, though the first guest didn't come for two or three hours. With nothing to do after my section was filled, I realized that I was going to stand there for hours with no remote possibility of seeing the coronation itself, unless I did something about it. The same idea had occurred to a South African friend in charge of the section next to mine. We put our heads together and decided to run the risk of court martial or deportation by deserting our posts, and scout for a spot to see something. We found a door in a tower, opened it, discovered spiralling steps, climbed them as far as we could and found an opening big enough to look out, and down. There we were, right over the Abbey's main transept with a wonderful view of the altar and the whole colourful scene. And there we saw the crowning of the King and Queen; while our charges looked after themselves with no trouble at all.

I should describe my costume. When I descended on Moss Brothers all I could tell them was that I wanted to rent a formal uniform for a 'Gold Stick in Waiting' at the coronation functions. The clerk was suitably impressed but wanted to know my Service and my rank. I drew myself up proudly and replied 'Counsellor, Canadian Diplomatic Service.' He looked baffled. He had never heard of this branch of His Majesty's Service and had no idea what its uniform was. Neither did I. However, Moss Brothers have never been defeated in all their centuries of existence by any rental request, so the clerk bowed, excused himself, and disappeared. He returned after a longish interval with an armful of garments, including a cocked hat and a sword (if that is a garment). I tried them on and felt, as I hope I looked, magnificent: knee breeches, silk stockings, buckled shoes, and a black cut-away coat with gold buttons right up to my neck.

When I arrived at the Abbey on the morning, long before dawn, in this impressive attire, I joined some of my Foreign Office friends. One of them, Gladwyn Jebb, took a look at me and said in a very rude and sarcastic way, 'My God, Mike, what are you supposed to be?' Stung by his insolence, I replied haughtily, 'A counsellor in the Canadian Diplomatic Service, sir.' At this, there was a general laugh. Jebb decided to inform me that, while parts of my costume might conceivably be correct, I was wearing a coat which had enough gold braid on it for an ambassador and my cocked hat was certainly that of an admiral. This made me feel even more impressive. He must have been wrong because I wore this costume at two or three coronation functions where feudal formality in dress was *de rigueur* and nobody seemed to mind, not even His Majesty.

I had one amusing misadventure on my first tour of duty as a Gold Stick on duty at Buckingham Palace at the first coronation ball. A select few were chosen for this prestigious assignment, to help the permanent officers of the Court ensure proper decorum at the Royal parties. My background, of course, in a Canadian parsonage made me a natural choice. Even more important, one of my best friends in London was Admiral Bromley (retired) who was the ceremonial and receptions officer at the Dominions Office. As such, he was on very friendly terms with everyone at the palace. So no doubt it was he who got me on the 'list.' He told me, in great glee, that my special duty at the first and grandest ball was to look after the Sultan of Zanzibar. I was suitably impressed.

'Brom' invited me to his home for a few drinks with some of his friends and my new colleagues on duty for the evening before we went to work. I arrived resplendent in my new costume and was greeted by a formidable butler who looked more stately and aristocratic than anyone I was to see later at the palace. In taking my hat and coat, he suggested I would be more comfortable during this informal part of the evening, without my sword. I agreed, though I hated to be parted from this status symbol even for an hour. How to dispose of it? You see, the sword belt was around my shoulders, across my body, down to my hip. But it was naturally underneath my black, gold-braided coat which buttoned right up to my collar. Did I have to unbutton all this before removing my sword? I assumed so and had just reached the last buttons, and was about to display my undershirt (for I needed no shirt under that coat), when the butler, who had been struck dumb, found words to express his amazement.

'All you have to do, sir, is unbutton the frog which holds the sword to the belt. Very simple, sir.'

I told him I was a Canadian primitive, unversed in these matters, and he actually grinned. He helped me get my coat buttoned up again. It was an uncertain introduction to my court life.

The ball itself was not as much fun as the preliminary party or as that which we had later after the ball was over. But it was, for me, unique. The Sultan whom I looked after was undemanding. He was a teetotaller and a non-dancer. So all I had to do was sit beside him as he watched the company dance, or talked to other distinguished guests. My own conversation with him was limited to answering one question,

'Where do you live?' My answer 'Canada' was greeted with some surprise and only one comment: 'Canada, cold.' That ended our oral communication. In due course, he was taken away to supper and I was left to my own devices.

So ended, for me, the coronation. My other duties at Canada House kept increasing and were a more serious tax on my intelligence and my industry.

7

THE DRIFT TO WAR

In January 1937 the High Commissioner told me that the Prime Minister had requested my services as secretary and general handyman to the Canadian delegation for the Imperial Conference to be held at the time of the coronation in May; I could also help in speech-writing. I was flattered by the request but not enamoured of the prospect, since I had already more than enough to do. I already knew, moreover, what it meant to assist Mr King in preparing speeches and statements. He was a most demanding taskmaster and discouraging in his insistence on reducing lively, colourful sentences to the flattest level of pedestrian prose.

In the sequel, however, my main function at this conference was housekeeping; trying to get my political masters settled contentedly into the accommodation made available for them in a new block of flats, Arlington House, behind the Ritz Hotel. This was no simple duty. It meant contending with impracticable suggestions from the department far away in Ottawa and with niceties of seniority so that each minister would agree that he had been suitably quartered; that no deputy minister would be given a smaller bathroom than an assistant deputy. On these and similar problems the efficiency and morale of delegations to international conferences often depend.

There were, of course, some complaints. One was that the Canadians had not been put up at one of the posh hotels, with all the services required or, if not required, available. For this I had a quick and easy reply. Ottawa did not let us know until the last moment who and how many were coming and by that time all the rooms in first-class hotels had been reserved by coronation visitors and other delegations to the conference. If our visitors at Arlington House lacked some of the amenities of a luxury hotel, Ottawa alone was to blame.

The conference itself proceeded without incident, overshadowed by the coronation. Mr King succeeded in listening to and talking about reports of dangerous European developments without committing himself or the Canadian government to anything, or making any concessions to the idea of a common foreign or defence policy, in spite of the visibly gathering clouds on the horizon.

Those clouds, I must confess, did not at that time seem particularly ominous to me. I was disheartened by the collapse of the League and its betrayal of collective security, and the farce of sanctions against Fascist Italy. I was depressed by the tacit assurance given to Hitler by this failure that he had nothing to fear from Geneva or from the world community as he made his own plans for aggression. The League of Nations had done nothing except to bring the Nazis, the Fascists, and the Japanese militarists together in a totalitarian axis outside the League. Disillusioned by the double-dealing and double-talking of the British and French, as they deserted collective security, I saw no reason why Canada should become involved in Anglo-French manœuvres to protect themselves against Nazi Germany. I was not yet fully aware of the menacing implications of Nazi policies. They were, I knew, aimed at destroying the foundations of the postwar Versailles settlement, but no one surely would go to war to shore this up.

Hitler openly admitted, even boasted, that Germany was rearming in spite of the provisions of the Treaty of Versailles. Yet, while the United Kingdom joined with France in protest against this rearmament, she had begun her own talks in May 1935 with Berlin which, in effect, sanctioned it, at least for the German navy. In spite of the three-power declaration of solidarity against the Nazis made at the Stresa Conference in April 1936, the UK accepted a month later as permanent and definite a 100–35 naval ratio with the Nazis which Sir John Simon, then Foreign Secretary, had summarily rejected when Hitler tried it on him during his visit to Berlin shortly before. It was not surprising that the French and Italian governments protested.

Sir Robert Craigie, a senior officer in the Foreign Office who pushed strongly for this naval agreement with the Germans, told me in October of 1935 in connection with these naval discussions that the Nazis (especially Ribbentrop) were 'pleasant and satisfactory fellows to deal with and that one felt that they were honest and straightforward negotiators.' The French and Italians considered the British action in making a naval agreement with these 'satisfactory fellows' was another betrayal by 'perfidious Albion.' As I wrote at the time:

Anyone not blind to the realities of the European situation must have realized ... that the intense resentment in France and Italy [over the naval agreement] would inevitably destroy the carefully built-up fabric of the Franco-Italian-British co-operation. Nor will the German government be slow to take advantage of this destruction. For the Nazis it is the long-sought-for opportunity to bring about an Anglo-German political rapprochement. It is well known that Herr Hitler's attitude towards England is based on the policy of Bismarck rather than that of Holstein, and that at all costs he is determined, as his great predecessor was, to make his arrangements with England secure before launching on any forward policy on the continent.

From the British point of view this policy may have two results:
1 public opinion may refuse to be tied to Nazi policy, and in an effort to placate it and win back France and Italy, Great Britain may rebuff the Germans; or
2 Britain may reorient her continental policy in favour of general co-operation with Germany. This, however, would be disastrous for all concerned ... It is frankly and avowedly the old balance of power without any of the 'collective' camouflage which has been so skilfully used in postwar diplomacy to conceal the grim reality of the pre-war power policy of alliances.

It would indeed be an ugly result if the United Kingdom, to ensure that Germany should not build another fleet to be sunk at Scapa Flow, found itself keeping step with Prussian militarism, more menacing now in a brown shirt than it ever had been in the trappings of Hohenzollern imperialism.

Certainly, the British government, in going ahead with this agreement, seemed to be moving away from the Franco-Italian front towards a new association with Germany. No information about even the possibility of Anglo-German naval discussions, the implications of which were obvious and important, had been given to the dominion prime ministers at the talks that took place during the jubilee celebrations shortly before. Indeed, during those talks the whole emphasis had been on the necessity of maintaining a strong European front against the Nazis. I was in London with Mr Bennett at the time and, when my friends in the Foreign Office took this line with me, I wrote back to Ottawa:

This united front against Germany will be difficult to maintain. The French and Italians will utilize it, and British participation in it, for their own purposes, and it will not be long before Great Britain will make some new move to conciliate Germany, the inevitable result of which would be to break the 'united front.'

I was assured throughout 1935, however, that though realizing the difficulties and possible dangers, British policy had now taken its stand alongside France and Italy, and henceforth would pursue a straight course; that while the door would be kept open for Germany, no further efforts would be made to lure Germany through that door by new concessions to her unreasonable demands. The naval agreement with Germany showed how straight was this predicted British course.

ᴕ

There now followed another Nazi violation of the Treaty of Versailles, the reoccupation of the Rhineland in March 1936. There were those who counselled firm action with France against this Nazi move; that German troops should be ordered out of the Rhineland under threat of war. I was one of the great majority in Britain and Canada who condemned such a threat as war-mongering. I agreed with the London *Times* as it thundered against a strong anti-Nazi policy and emphasized the danger of precipitate action against a Germany which, however deplorable its regime, was trying merely to free itself from some of the worst shackles of an unjust treaty.

There was, however, no danger of any strong action against the Nazis over the Rhineland issue. The popular and insistent feeling in Great Britain was that, while the Nazis were to be condemned, peace must be preserved at all costs. This meant that the French were to be pressured into showing 'statesmanlike moderation' while Hitler, in his turn, must be urged to make a real contribution to a general European settlement, something which the Führer was always ready to promise.

I recall how at this time, in pursuit of the policy which became known later as 'appeasement,' Barrington-Ward, an editor of the *Times* and an old Balliol friend of Mr Massey, came over to Canada House to persuade the High Commissioner to suggest to Mr King that he send a message to Mr Baldwin warning him that Canada would not support any strong or rash action against the Nazis over the occupation of the Rhineland. I was present at this talk. The idea appealed to Mr Massey, as indeed it did to me, and the High Commissioner in fact sent a telegram to Mr King along these lines on 13 March. In it he proposed that he should be authorized to state to British ministers a Canadian view which would encourage moderate opinion in the British Cabinet; or, even better, Mr King might do this himself in answer to a question in the Canadian House of Commons.

Mr King's reply was that, if anything should be done, it should be from Prime Minister to Prime Minister through written communications and not orally through the High Commissioner. Mr King, however, as might have been expected, though he strongly opposed any strong British and French reaction to the occupation of the Rhineland,

decided that Canada should keep out of this business. He had no intention of intervening in the affairs of Downing Street or of the Quai
d'Orsay, even if he agreed with the views of Barrington-Ward and
Massey on this particular issue. To give advice was to take responsibility and this was not an issue which should engage any Canadian
responsibility.

While the feeling was strong that Britain must now avoid extreme
policies, suspicion and dislike of Hitler increased. The Führer made
sure of this. The feeling was also growing that the country must now
rely on its strong, right arm for security. The anti-League and nation-
alistic viewpoint, given vigorous journalistic expression in the Beaverbrook and Rothermere press, rejoiced at 'the end of Geneva' and the
return to a national policy based on national power. It supported Mr
Chamberlain's effort, when he succeeded Mr Baldwin, to come to an
understanding with Fascist Italy in creating a London-Paris-Rome axis
to keep the Nazis in check.

My own views began to change before the next Nazi move, the occupation of Austria in 1938. This new treaty violation showed that Hitler
was determined to do more than recover what had been lost at Versailles and that, in doing so, he had the support of most of the German
people, together with the fanatical loyalty of a large section of them.
No longer was it possible for me to believe that Nazism was a temporary aberration in German politics, that the good sense of the German people would soon take care of the Führer, and that the greater
danger to peace was French over-reaction to Hitler's moves, with the
United Kingdom supporting such reaction. This feeling was replaced
by the fear of aggressive war brought about by the policy of a German
regime which now must be considered as evil and savage and an immediate menace to freedom and to peace. This regime could not be
allowed to triumph in Europe, for its triumph would be a threat to free
men everywhere. Indeed, the formation of the Berlin-Rome-Tokyo axis
emphasized the extension of this danger to the whole world.

There then followed Nazi pressure against Czechoslovakia which,
for the first time, brought war dangerously close. By now I had come to
the conclusion that war was inevitable unless Hitler abandoned his
objectives and his methods of achieving them, or unless Britain and
France, in their turn, came to terms with him, which would have meant
the triumph of Nazism in Europe and beyond. I saw no likelihood of
the first possibility but I now feared the second. With all my hatred of
war, and my suspicion of European manœuvres which might lead to
war, I had become convinced that nothing could be worse than the

domination of Europe by Hitler and the triumph of all he stood for. Nothing, I thought, could be more awful than the western world at the feet of that evil and cunning man. Therefore the only hope, however weak it might be, to avoid war without surrender was to arm; to unite the forces of freedom; to stand firm but without provocation against Hitler's threats and his aggressive moves.

In May 1938, it seemed possible that this strong policy would be followed. The mobilization of Czechoslovakia in that month against a suspected Nazi invasion and the British government's support of the Czechs was a diplomatic setback for the Nazis. It infuriated Hitler and encouraged those opposed to him. The democracies seemed now to be stronger and more confident. There were also optimists who thought that Hitler's appetite had been satisfied with the Rhineland, Austria, and rearmament. I remained unconvinced. On 25 March I had written to Dr Skelton:

Even if you accept the view that the boa constrictor, as Churchill picturesquely put it, will now uncoil and rest while the process of digestion goes on, events in Austria show that this process is pretty fast in our mechanical age. Furthermore, I simply cannot feel that this particular boa constrictor's appetite is going to be satisfied by the most recent sheep.

The official British position is now to refuse to say in advance that it will prevent or will not prevent any more victims from being eaten. The 'free hand' combined with the 'strong arm' is reaffirmed. I do not see how any British government could go much further at this juncture, but I do not feel that such a policy, in itself, helps the situation much.

What this government is banking on is:

1 That Germany will not provoke war or stumble into a position which will make war inevitable;

2 That she will not be able to dominate the whole of the Danubian basin;

3 That if a new war situation develops, Great Britain will have time to decide on her attitude, and work on public opinion; and, if war comes, to mobilize her strength while allies held the continental ring.

I am not satisfied that any of these things will happen.

As to the first, how can anyone really feel any confidence in the present directors of German policy, animated by ideals that mix as well with peace as gasoline and fire?

As to the second, the Danubian Basin, you will have noticed that within a week of the 'rape' or 'liberation' of Austria, it was announced that Göring was shortly to visit Hungary, Greece, Jugoslavia, and Turkey. I was at a small dinner the other night at which the Czechoslovak minister, Jan Masaryk, was present. He was emphatic that the Danubian states would like to resist German pressure and to live their own national lives. But he was equally emphatic that in default of an 'activist' policy by the democracies [France and Great Britain] which would encourage smaller countries to stand up to the Nazis, they wouldn't have a chance, would yield to the inevitable, and accept German domination.

As to the third – time; in 1914 Great Britain was given many months to arm, while France and Russia held the ring. In the next war, she would be lucky to get minutes.

As my views changed about the character of the Nazi menace and I became convinced of the likelihood, even the inevitability of war, I naturally became more concerned about the foreign policy of my country in its relation to this threat. That policy had been based on no prior commitments, no co-operation with London in defence arrangements which might lead to such commitments, or which might cause controversy and disunity in Canada. After 1938, however, the government in Ottawa itself became more alarmed over developments and went so far as to authorize a modest increase in defence expenditures for purely national purposes. But conciliation of Germany by the other European powers and a new European settlement still remained, in the view of the Canadian government, the objective to be pursued.

While very few in Ottawa thought we could escape involvement in a major war if it came, any more than we could in 1914, there were some, Dr Skelton and Loring Christie among them, who believed that such involvement should and could be limited to minimum participation. We should avoid the bloodbaths of the Great War and the political controversies which had so dangerously divided Canada in 1917. This was a view that might have appealed to me as late as 1936 but, by 1939, it seemed both wrong and unrealistic.

A cautious foreign policy for Canada reflected the feelings of the majority of the Canadian people, I believe, at least until the Nazi aggression against Czechoslovakia. The slaughter of 1914–18 was still a sad and living memory. I had been one of those who hoped that next time we could avoid any such senseless killing. Hitler had seemed far away from Ottawa, and distance obscured part of Nazi ugliness and evil. The savage shouts of the Brown Shirts and the maniac screams of the Führer could not be heard across the prairies as they could over the radio in London almost every night.

If Canada's slow and cautious reaction to the Nazi menace was understandable, it was more surprising that public opinion in Great Britain remained for so long calm and almost unconcerned. The most violent foes of the Nazi and Fascist ideology were on the left, but many of them opposed a tougher national foreign policy and stronger measures for defence. Many Tories, on the other extreme, while disdaining and distrusting Corporal Hitler, felt that he was not in fact so dangerous or bad as Commissar Stalin and that the decent Germans would, in due course, put a brake on the Führer and his wilder ideas. Those who tried to warn the nation of impending tragedy were dismissed as alarmists. Those who called for a crash programme of rearmament were war-mongers. All that was required, it was widely held, was a modest increase in British defence expenditures which would not put too great a strain on the economy, or challenge those pacifist and internationalist tendencies which the election of November 1935 showed to be still strong.

This was not enough for a minority now demanding much sterner action to meet the Nazi threat. At the head of this group was Winston Churchill. His prestige, however, after his stand during the abdication crisis and his aggressive, bellicose speeches on the need for more arms, was at a low point. Not many listened to him yet. He was still considered an irresponsible failure and an unreliable character.

I recall in March 1937 a dinner in a private room at Claridge's of one of those small but influential London clubs which meet occasionally to drink, eat, talk, alter the policies of the nation, and decide who is to do the altering. This particular club (the Thirty Club, as I remember, no doubt because it had fifty members) had as its guest that evening, Winston Churchill. During the dinner and afterwards Churchill talked with eloquence and passion about the 'gathering storm' and the need to stand up to the 'loathsome Nazis' and their Führer. I remember also, however, that he paid a reluctant tribute to Hitler as the 'little Corporal who had lifted the flag of Germany out of the mire of defeat and destruction when all the Hohenzollerns had fled, and planted it on the ramparts of a resurrected nation.' He was passionate about the need to push on vigorously with rearmament, to arrange for full military co-operation with the French, and to establish working arrangements with Russia. At that time he had almost no following in the House of Commons; when he pleaded with the members, as he so often did, to wake up to the perils ahead, more often than not they walked out. That night, however, he had a captive and enthralled audience, however small. For the first time, I was exposed to the force of his personality, to the magic of his words, and to the conviction of his argument.

At one stage he wished to illustrate a point of military strategy relevant to the war which he insisted was imminent. For this purpose he was able to mobilize and to manœuvre the considerable semi-circle of glasses in front of his own place, with extra rolls to reinforce his strategic exposition. After dinner, he continued to expound on the international situation and to predict the future with depressing but convincing certainty. I remember something else. Only two hours or so after our large meal with all its alcoholic supplements, Mr Churchill suddenly stopped talking. 'If I'm going to continue, someone has to get me a double scotch and a cold roast beef sandwich.' He waited until they arrived and went on.

I was impressed by his arguments that night. I was amazed by his vigour, his zest, and his capacity both as a trencherman and as a man. He was by now no youngster. He had been a member of a British Cabinet before the current prime minister, Stanley Baldwin, and his predecessor, Ramsay Macdonald, had even been elected to the House of Commons. One had now left public life and the other was about to leave, both wearied and exhausted men. Churchill's talk that night increased my anxiety for the future. My conviction also grew that business as usual was no way to face that future. Yet such an attitude persisted. There was no great sense of urgency in British policies, and none in Canadian, when the tragedy of Czechoslovakia became the prelude, not to peace in our time, but to a second world war from which my country, I was now certain, could not escape.

☞

The story has often been told. Hitler, contemptuous of France and Britain and all democracies; scornful of the League of Nations which had been mocked and defied by Mussolini; intoxicated with easy, successive diplomatic triumphs; fanatical with mad ambitions and an evil conviction of his own great destiny, decided to first dismember, then destroy, Czechoslovakia. Chamberlain and Daladier, men who reflected the weaknesses and divisions in their democracies, tried to appease the dictator and buy time at the expense of Czechoslovakia. It did not work.

The situation steadily deteriorated, and four-power discussions – the Czechs were left out – did little to improve it. One late afternoon, 27 September 1938 when things looked very bad, as I left to go home to Fairacres in Roehampton where we were now living, I noticed that the *Evening Standard* hoarding outside Canada House said in bold red type: 'Keep calm and dig.' It would be easier to dig than to keep calm. We had sent for our son at boarding school as we had decided that he and his sister should sail for Canada and safety on the first boat. That night Neville Chamberlain broadcast to the nation in such gloomy terms that the Pearson family was weeping as they were packing.

The next day, this man of peace, so obviously a civilian with his

black Homburg and his umbrella, got into an aeroplane for his flight
to Munich to secure, he hoped, 'Peace in our time' from a dictator's
promise that the Sudetenland transfer would be his 'last territorial
demand on Europe.' The Prime Minister returned, beaming, confident,
to be greeted by a people delirious with a joy born of escape from a
tragedy which had seemed so close. Joy and relief soon turned to regret
and shame. With security restored, as we thought, we could be bold
again and criticize not only the Nazis, but appeasement and the
appeasers.

I summed up my own feelings and made my own prediction and
assessment of British policy in a letter to Dr Skelton at the time:

The country has cheered Mr Chamberlain to the echo, the country has
thrilled to his German visit as a sporting and courageous step. And it certainly was. It's a great picture; that of a 69-year-old Premier, taking his
first trip in a plane, starting out to face Hitler, Ribbentrop, and the strutting
ranks of Nazidom, dressed as if for his morning stroll in St James Park,
complete with black hat and rolled umbrella.

Personally, I don't think there is going to be a European war over this
Czech business. The Nazis are going to get 95 per cent of their demands
without difficulty; or, if they insist on 100 per cent, with difficulty. I still
think France, and hence, Britain, will not fight them. The French are losing
their nerve and the British are relieved. If the Nazis do something incon-
ceivably stupid, and it's difficult at times to conceive of anything too stupid
for them, the thing might start; a quick brutal rush with their army might do
it. But I think what is more likely to happen is: trouble in Sudetenland, civil
war, German intervention, without any threats to France, but accompanied
by pacific statements from Hitler to the effect that he is not attacking Czechoslovakia – not at all, he is merely helping his tortured fellow-countrymen
defend themselves, he has no intention of crossing into the Czech districts,
and has nothing but the friendliest feelings for France and Great Britain who,
he feels sure, will respect his desire to help his kinsmen. He will also offer
them peace for fifty years and suggest an immediate conference to discuss
outstanding problems, or something like that. While London or Paris are
thinking it over the Czechs will have lost their Sudetenland. But at any rate,
we who have the misfortune to live by Trafalgar Square won't be dodging
bombs – for a bit.

And so it happened. The country came to the brink of war, and
retreated by the settlement of Munich. Yet opinion, after the first
shock of relief, again began to harden against Hitler. We wrote to
Ottawa from Canada House on 11 October:

The immediate reaction during the weekend of October 1st was, of course,
inexpressible relief that peace had been preserved. There was as little disposition to criticize Mr Chamberlain in the press as there was inclination in
the crowds outside Downing Street to refrain from cheering him. He was the

Peacemaker, as yet without any of the more difficult consequences that so often attend that role.

During the early part of last week, however, a more critical attitude became apparent. There were those who, recovering from the shock of imminent peril, began to question the method of their salvation and even to doubt whether it was salvation at all.

The question is still being asked and is never likely to receive a final and agreed answer.

Our own conclusions at Canada House, drawn from these events, were put in writing for Ottawa:

The crisis has shown, and the lesson has sunk in here, that Europe is at the mercy of any dictator with sufficient power behind him to enforce whatever demands he may care to make. The crisis has *not* shown that in the case of Germany there is any assurance that those demands will now cease, or will in the future be reasonable ones.

Here, there will be a policy of continued appeasement but with rearmament. The present government may be counted on to try to work with Germany, but, if that proves impossible, and, if and when rearmament is completed, there will not be the same hesitation to oppose her demands as has been shown during past weeks.

The one theme on which there is very nearly complete unanimity on all sides is the necessity of a great national effort to achieve adequate defence. The government have before them the lessons of the recent crisis. These should now equip them to do what is required. The country is demanding action with increasing insistence, action which involves definite, positive, and stimulating leadership in a vitally important task.

That task was to prepare the country to defend itself. Military weakness had been the most convincing argument to justify appeasement.

Whatever one may think of Munich, it remains true that time was gained and Britain *did* get stronger during that year of grace. Indeed, it could be argued that this saved her from defeat two years later. But public opinion worried that there was still not enough drive in rearmament. There were many now who felt that the government which had plucked peace out of the Munich crisis was not likely to be possessed with the necessary determination and energy to rearm against the next crisis which was inevitable. The ranks of the Churchillians were growing.

I was doubtful myself that all necessary steps to organize for defence were being taken and with enough vigour. I expressed this feeling in the following message to Ottawa:

The curse of this country is its determined and proud belief that it can always 'muddle through.' But in using that phrase it has always emphasized the last word. The only reason it has been able to get through, in spite of 'muddling,' is because it has usually found some ally or other to hold the ring while it pondered over the lesson of the most recent 'muddle.' But that day is gone forever. If war had broken out on October 1st, London would have been a front line in two hours. There would have been no leisurely gathering together of forces, while the French fought across the channel. All this is so obvious, and the implications of it so revolutionary, that you would think even the most easy-going politician, or hide-bound civil servant would sense it. They did during the first weeks of October, but they are getting over that crisis, at least they are in certain official and industrial circles; 'business as usual' and all that. At the moment the issue is in the balance: whether this traditional attitude of complacency, or the new spirit of action for defence, will prevail. That latter spirit, which would accept some form of compulsory national service, is now strong in the country, but it won't survive without governmental encouragement and leadership.

My own agony of mind over developments came out in a letter I wrote Dr Skelton at this time, from which I quote:

My first emotional reaction to the events of the last two months is to become an out-and-out Canadian isolationist. Yet when I begin to reason it out, it isn't as simple as that. I just can't find the answer to a lot of questions. For one thing, critical though I may feel of British policy leading up to the crisis, I can't sincerely quarrel with the decision taken last September not to fight. That being so, I have no right, I suppose, to assume that the present government is not as aware of past mistakes and present dangers as I am, and will not take effective steps to right the situation. In the second place, would our complete isolation from European events (if such a thing were possible) save us from the effect of a British defeat; and, even if it did, could we stand by and watch the triumph of Nazism, with all it stands for, over a Britain which, with all her defects, is about the last abode of decency and liberty on this side of the water?

If I am tempted to become cynical and isolationist, I think of Hitler screeching into the microphone, Jewish women and children in ditches on the Polish border, Göring, the genial ape-man, and Goebbels, the evil imp, and then, whatever the British side may represent, the other does indeed stand for savagery and barbarism. True, as Mr Massey often tells me, there are seventy-five million decent Germans, who love peace and, apparently, revere Chamberlain! They may eventually, with the help of friendliness and restraint on our part, cast out their own evil spirits. That's a hope, I admit. But though I am on the side of the angels, in Germany the opposite spirits are hard at work. And I have a feeling they're going to do a lot of mischief before they are exorcised.

I think that this is the general feeling in this country. Certainly it is among men of my own generation in all walks of life whom I have talked to lately. There hasn't been one of them who has not sneered at the idea that Munich meant peace with honour; or who has felt that Germany and England can now be good friends; or who has not sworn that, if this country does not soon put herself in a position to stand up to the next German challenge, the present government will pay the penalty. Events are going to move swiftly in the domestic and international spheres during the next few months.

They did, indeed, and I became more and more alarmed. It is true that Hitler made a relatively mild speech at the beginning of February 1939. But on this I could only write to Dr Skelton:

The speech had, of course, its purple patches, both in delivery and in reception, but on the whole I suppose it can be judged as a pacific performance. That very fact is, it seems to me, a measure of our deterioration. Twenty-five years ago this pacific speech would have shaken half the foreign offices of the world and caused more than an international crisis. Now, because Herr Hitler does not threaten us at once with fire, pestilence, and destruction, we heave a sigh of relief and face, if not the future, at least the next week, unafraid.

On 15 March 1939 Nazi troops marched into Prague and Czechoslovakia was absorbed by the German Reich. As an independent state, she ceased to exist. Her army disappeared and her modern munitions industry was at the disposal of the victorious invader. The humiliation and defeat of this tough, brave, and stubborn people was complete and recognized as such by all, including Chamberlain. He now accepted the inevitable and, almost in despair, rashly gave to Poland, which had behaved badly in the crisis of September 1938, the precise unconditional guarantee of assistance against any violation of her territory that he had refused to discharge for Czechoslovakia only a short time before.

There was, in fact, only one hope: to bring the USSR into a firm alliance with the British and French to stop the Nazis; the kind of alliance that had been the subject of discussions at Geneva the previous September. This conceivably might have preserved the peace or, at least, ensured that any war begun by Hitler would result in his defeat. It is doubtful whether such a coalition was now possible. True, a move against Poland was an even more immediate threat to Moscow than the one against Czechoslovakia, and it would be easier to come to Poland's assistance if the Poles could be persuaded to accept such aid. But Moscow's suspicions and contempt for the British and French governments had been strengthened by recent events. There would have to be strong and unshakeable evidence from London and Paris that they were serious about an alliance and able and willing to carry out their commitments under it. For Moscow was concerned solely with its own immediate security and was quite cold-blooded about the best means of ensuring it. Indeed, in a letter of 12 May I referred to a rumour, which seemed incredible, but which I thought should not be ignored, that the Moscow leaders were thinking of getting that security by a Nazi-Soviet alliance. I wrote:

The fact that these reports – which came in from various quarters – caused so much perturbation in certain quarters is, I suppose, an indication of the success of the Nazi policy of keeping our nerves upset. But with Hitler and Stalin controlling our destinies it's not safe to ignore even the most startlingly improbable reports. The incredible of yesterday can become the normal of tomorrow without too much difficulty these days. Opinion is now evenly divided as to whether the reports in question were 'planted' by the Nazis or by the Bolsheviks.

In the event, the Chamberlain government *did* make overtures to Moscow for a united front, but they were not pushed vigorously or conducted at a high political level. Stalin was able to say later that the last-minute British and French moves for collective action were not serious, and therefore his own last-minute move for a Nazi-Soviet alliance was necessary for the security of the USSR. The unthinkable occurred and Ribbentrop's visit to Moscow removed the last obstacle to Hitler's aggression against Poland, and to World War II.

☞

In tracing, very briefly and inadequately, the developments leading up to the war, I have mentioned my own change of attitude; from one of fear lest British and French policies in reaction to those of Nazi Germany might bring about war, to one of growing conviction that Hitler, with all that he represented, was bent on leading his country into aggressive actions which would, and were meant to, make war inevitable – and which must be firmly resisted. In these circumstances I found it increasingly difficult to believe that any Canadian policy of cautious non-commitment could be justified.

In short, I now believed that war was coming; that Canada could not or should not stand aloof and, therefore, we should co-operate with Britain and France in the only policies that had any possible hope of preventing war – policies of firmness, based on armed strength sufficient to deter the Nazis. I doubted if even these policies would succeed, but I saw no hope of any kind in anything else.

By the summer of 1939, however, the Pearson family was back in Canada. Home leave was overdue as I had not been back since 1935. As we sailed on the *Duchess of York* on 30 June, I was filled with foreboding. I was also looking forward to a good, uninterrupted holiday. It was not to be.

8

WAR YEARS IN LONDON

We settled down in a cottage on the shores of Lac du Bonnet in Manitoba with the Norman Youngs and their children. It was to be a family reunion. After the wedding we had shared, Grace and Norman Young had gone to the Gold Coast where Norman was to teach in Achimota College. They later returned to Winnipeg and founded Ravenscourt School. We had not seen much of them and their four children, so we were all looking forward to our holiday together. It was great fun, swimming and fishing and trying to keep up with six energetic and boisterous youngsters. Then one day I paddled over to the post office for the mail and saw an ominous headline: 'Nazis Threaten Danzig and the Polish Corridor.' This was it. The worst was about to happen and I should be at my post in London rather than at Lac du Bonnet. My wife, as always, understood. So our two-family holiday came suddenly to an end. It was the first and the last; Norman Young died within two years leading his company of the Cameron Highlanders of Winnipeg in that forlorn fiasco of the Dieppe raid, where so much blood was uselessly shed and so much courage wasted; or so it seemed at the time.

I was on my way to Ottawa by the first train and, on arrival, went straight to see Dr Skelton. I told him of my fears, and of my feeling that I should leave at once for London as Canada House would be pandemonium on the outbreak of war and everybody would be needed. He thought I was being too pessimistic but said my return was up to me.

That afternoon the Prime Minister learned I was in Ottawa and invited me to dine with him at his summer home at Kingsmere. He greeted me with that gracious friendliness which made it pleasant to be his guest and before dinner took me for a stroll around the grounds. It was a warm and peaceful summer evening and it was hard to think of war. Mr King was the only person I had ever known, or heard of, whose hobby was constructing ruins on his estate with stones from historic buildings which he collected whenever he could. By this time he had a quite respectable ruin put together. It appealed, no doubt, to his feeling for tradition, for links with the past which did not interfere with his plans for change in the future. That evening his ruins seemed to me more likely to predict the future than reflect the past.

I told Mr King that I was convinced war was near and therefore I planned to return to London immediately. He thought that I was wrong, that this crisis too would be resolved. He had seen Hitler not so long before and did not think he would risk a general war. Therefore, although the sentiments which prompted me to return to my post did me credit and all that, he advised me to rejoin my family and finish my leave. However, echoing Dr Skelton, he added that if I wished to go back to Canada House, that was my affair. 'But I feel sure there will be no war.' Those were his last words to me as I left Kingsmere. He was one among millions who felt that way. Another world war was unthinkable!

The next day I gave Dr Skelton further cause for surprise. I told him that if I crossed by ship I would be too late; war would have begun. 'Could I fly across?' Now he was convinced that I was in a panic. The transatlantic service by Pan American Airways had begun that summer, but to use it was still considered rash. No Canadian official had done so. Anyway, I would not be likely to get a seat on a plane. I told him I already had one, on a flying boat leaving the next day, thanks to a friend whom I had phoned at Pan American headquarters in New York. Dr Skelton gave up. He would take no responsibility for my decision, but he was good enough to arrange for me to fly that afternoon by a government plane to Montreal. From there, I got a commercial plane for New York which I reached that evening.

All that night in my hotel room I listened to the radio with its excited reports of the swift movement of tragic events. I knew I was right in my decision to return.

Early next morning, I boarded a Boeing Clipper plane which deposited me on Southampton Sound the afternoon of the next day. I shared a cabin on this large, slow, flying boat with two men; one a German reserve officer and the other a Polish reserve officer, both going home to fight; and perhaps kill each other. They became very friendly during the flight.

Only once did I doubt my good sense in rushing back by air. We had had to come down at Shediac, New Brunswick, because of engine trouble. When we took off again we ran into a fierce North Atlantic storm. I was in an upper berth in the plane, and feeling very miserable for I was then as prone to air-sickness as to sea-sickness. I looked out of a small oval window into the black night and found that we were flying only a few hundred feet above the wild waves. I hoped the engine had been well and truly repaired and I said to myself, 'What the devil are you doing here?'

Lionel Massey met me at Southampton and drove me to Canada House where I sent a telegram to Lac du Bonnet to say I was back in London. It was their first news that I had left Canada. I reached London only a few days before the outbreak of war. I was glad to be on the job for there was much to do. I was by this time second-in-command at Canada House, having succeeded Georges Vanier who had been made minister to France in January.

Life was active, exciting, purposeful, and, in those first days, confused and difficult. Canadian tourists were thronging our offices. They wanted to know if there was going to be war and, if so, how could they get passage home on the next boat. We were able to put many of them on the *Athenia*, which was torpedoed within the week with heavy loss of life. There were also resident Canadians who wished to move their children back home. There were messages from Canada to trace Canadians on the Continent. There were meetings with United Kingdom officials about arrangements for the evacuation of Canada House as soon as war began; for setting up our offices in the country, since the bombing, it was assumed, would make work in London impossible. These, and other activities, took up all my time during those last hours before the war actually began. My own domestic arrangements were simple. I went back to our flat and invited some married Canadian friends, who were looking for a home, to live with me until we saw what was going to happen.

It happened on 3 September. Inexorably and inevitably the moment arrived. 'German attacks upon Poland have been continued and intensified,' said Mr Chamberlain to a hushed House of Commons. 'I have accordingly the honour to inform you that unless not later than 11 am, British summer time, today, satisfactory assurances ... have been given by the German Government ... a state of war will exist between the two countries as from that hour.' No such assurances were received and war began. To those of us who remembered 5 August 1914 and the awful years that followed, this all seemed incredible. Before we had forgotten the dead of one war, our sons were to be killed in another. How could man be so mad?

At that moment, 11:00 AM (the very hour of the armistice on 11 November 1918), I was in my office which overlooked Trafalgar Square. It was a peaceful Sunday scene; fountains playing, children feeding the pigeons, Nelson high up on his pedestal looking serenely into the distance. Could this really be the renewal of the earlier horror of the war to end war? Then came the first air raid alarm. I had to admire the readiness, the efficiency of the Germans. We had been at war for only a few minutes and they were about to bomb London. Or so we were warned.

Canada House was fully staffed that Sunday morning to meet any emergency. According to instructions, as soon as the air raid sirens sounded we followed the High Commissioner down into the furnace room, which had been designated our temporary emergency shelter. Canada House itself was an old building, and we were led to believe, wrongly, that it would be unlikely to withstand the shock of a bomb within a hundred yards. So we took to the cellar which was probably the worst place to be when the building collapsed. But this was our designated shelter, so we crowded in. It became hot and very uncomfortable. Our orders, however, were to stay there until we got a message from Whitehall through a special telephone which had been installed in our shelter that it was 'all clear.' We obeyed orders. It got hotter and hotter. London might be in flames, but it couldn't be much worse than this shelter. Still the phone didn't ring; ours not to reason why, ours merely to swelter in the shelter. I begged the High Commissioner to let me go out and up, reconnoitre and report. He agreed. I reached the ground floor and looked out a window. Trafalgar Square was as sunny and peaceful as it had ever been with no sign of war or bombing. There had been a false alarm and the emergency telephone communication with our shelter had failed to tell us so.

Even more discouraging was our first experience with evacuation. I was supposed to be in charge of this operation at Canada House and was the only person, apart from the High Commissioner, who knew where we were to go if forced to leave London. The plan was a simple one. Immediately on the outbreak of war, an advance party was to move by bus to our new headquarters in the country, set up shop there, and prepare to receive the rest of us when we were forced to leave London. So secret was all this, though why I don't know, that even the official in charge of the advance party didn't know where he was to go. His orders were to report to a certain Bull Inn in a certain suburb where he would be given his final destination.

The advance party set out about noon. In about an hour I had a telephone call from their perplexed commander. They had reached the designated suburb, but there was no Bull Inn to be found. On inquiry, they discovered it had been knocked down or closed up some years before. So what was he to do now? Throwing secrecy to the winds, and with a fine disregard for orders or for the necessity of consulting White-hall, I told him, 'Go to the Ladies' College at Malvern for that is where Canada House is to function when London is being destroyed. But don't get any wrong ideas. The young ladies have already been evacu-ated.' A few weeks later the advance parties, having made the necessary preparations to receive the rest of us, who never came, returned sheep-ishly to London.

By then it had become clear that London was not yet to go up in flames. The Germans left it alone. The barrage balloons hung idly in the skies. Even the small British Expeditionary Force and the French army, of which it was a part, remained secure in the depths of the Maginot line or were patrolling a quiet front. This was not to be 1914. The German armies devoted themselves to the destruction of Poland, while Hitler divided the spoils with Stalin. Surely this was the time, when the main enemy forces were engaged on the Eastern front, to attack on the West. But, again, unlike 1914, there was no will to pro-voke a fighting war. It was 'All quiet on the Western Front' and a false sense of security prevailed.

It was certainly not quiet at Canada House, even though at the be-ginning we were not sure what part Canada was to play in the war. That decision would, of course, largely determine what Canada House would be doing. First, however, Canada had to declare war – this time, in contrast to 1914, as an independent member of a Commonwealth of Nations. There was time to make sure we were doing everything in proper form. The Canadian title-deeds to belligerence, authorizing us to kill and be killed legally and constitutionally, must be drawn up with scrupulous correctness.

For this war there could be no single declaration in London for all the King's dominions, other realms, and territories. His Majesty would declare war separately for Canada on the advice of his Canadian minis-ters, if and when the Canadian Parliament decided to authorize this advice. To this end Mr King summoned Parliament at once and the government's announced policy that Canada should go to war was ap-proved with virtual unanimity, as expected. Parliamentary and execu-tive action required a week before the formalities were completed. Dur-ing that week, technically we were neutral. This made evident our in-of certain badly needed war equipment from the United States could be continued for a week.

It is worth recording the formal steps that had to be taken by the Canadian government to declare war. At 10:15 PM on 9 September the Canadian Parliament approved the policy of the government to go to war against Germany. Shortly after midnight on that same day, an order-in-council was passed authorizing a submission to the King for the issue of a proclamation declaring war. Prior to this, on the afternoon of 9 September, a warning telegram had been sent to the High Commissioner in London to hold himself in readiness to make a most important submission to the King, possibly on the next day. A few hours later, the text of that submission was cabled, leaving the date to be inserted later. The High Commissioner was instructed to present this submission in writing to the King immediately upon receipt of a message authorizing the date to be inserted. Mr Massey was to communicate His Majesty's approval immediately to Ottawa for publication by proclamation in the *Canada Gazette*. The High Commissioner was also informed that a formal submission in writing signed by the Prime Minister would follow. Mr Massey carried out his instructions and, on the afternoon of Sunday, 10 September he cabled that he had been received by the King at Windsor and that His Majesty had approved the submission at 1:08 PM on that day.

This would seem to be speedy and efficient action by all responsible. This was not the view of our External Affairs masters, however, from whom we received, on 22 September, a querulous letter complaining we had been too casual and dilatory on that Sunday. In our innocence we thought, as did the palace, that we had broken all records for quick action; and we had. Indeed, during our week of technical neutrality we had tried to anticipate, expedite, and assist action in Ottawa by conferring in advance with the Foreign Office experts as to what exact form the Declaration of War should take. We had no experience in declaring war. I was told that the expert to see was Mr Dunbar, whom I knew personally, and he told me how the document should be drafted. I went back to my office and wrote out the proper words on a plain sheet of paper. Then I telephoned my friend, Tommy Lascelles, at the palace to ask whether I could show him the draft document for approval or amendment. He told me to come along, and in a few minutes I was in his office. He said that it looked all right to him but, since the King was in the office next door, he would 'pop in' and get royal confirmation. He returned in a few minutes to say that His Majesty had not only approved the text but had indicated this by signing it. This was satisfactory, but somewhat startling as it was only a draft for consideration. I was not sure what the King's signature did to it. When I told Mr Massey, he expressed great interest in the now royally authenticated draft. I had my own designs on it as a very special souvenir. But I knew that in this competition, I would lose to seniority. And so it turned out. I never saw the draft again, even after it was replaced later by the other more formal documents.

This replacement provided another interesting episode. The written, formal submission which was to follow the cabled one did not arrive for some weeks. This was indeed reprehensible delay because the earlier informal document, a cabled message, obviously could not have on it the Prime Minister's written signature. A legal purist could claim, indeed, that without such a written signature the submission had no legal effect and that Canada was not, technically, at war until the formal submission signed in his own handwriting by the Prime Minister was received and approved by His Majesty. Therefore, on 24 October Mr Massey had to telegraph Ottawa: 'Buckingham Palace enquiring when they may expect formal submission in writing.'

The High Commissioner followed this up with a letter to Dr Skelton a week or so later which explained that the preoccupation of the palace was owing, I quote,

to the fact that, according to Sir Alexander Hardinge, who wrote me on the subject as early as September 12th, the document which the King signed on the basis of cabled representations may well have no constitutional validity owing to the fact that it did not and could not bear the actual signature of the Minister.

This may be of course, as Sir Alexander put it himself, rather a 'quibble'. At the same time, it would undoubtedly provide material for constitutional pundits to prove that we are not yet legally at war at all!

These messages produced action in Ottawa. The formal submission was drawn up, signed by Mr King and post-dated 10 September 1939. It reached London by bag and was signed by the King on 27 November. I commented in my diary:

As the submission on which the Canadian Cabinet actually acted had been drafted here on cabled instructions, and, of course, couldn't be signed by a responsible Minister, there is some doubt whether it had any constitutional validity. And as Ottawa have been over two months getting the formal, written submission over here, who knows but that we haven't been at peace these nine weeks. The Prime Minister got over that difficulty by the simple expedient of dating his signed submission September 10th. The King will OK it now and some historian of the future will wonder how George VI and Mackenzie King could have been together on September 10th, 1939.

Having lost my own souvenir to the High Commissioner, I wondered who would secure for his own archives the interim cabled submission of 10 September. On 12 December the Prime Minister wrote Mr Massey asking for this document 'in order that it may be embodied in the permanent records of the Canadian Government.' Mr Massey's reply, supported by Buckingham Palace, was firm: 'May I say that His Majesty's Private Secretary pointed out at the time that this document had no constitutional validity owing to the fact that it did not and could not bear the signature of the Minister, and added that therefore it was desirable that it should not be embodied in the records of the Canadian Government.' So it remained in London, though whether in the possession of His Majesty or the Canadian High Commissioner, I never learned.

☞

It was one thing to declare war. It was something else to decide how Canada would implement that declaration. Would the pattern of 1914 be followed? There were those in Ottawa who felt that it should not, and that our involvement should be something less than total. One of them was Loring Christie, a man of great ability, deep sincerity, and considerable influence in the East Block. I knew his doubts about Canada's all-out participation in the war. Therefore the fact that soon after its outbreak he was appointed as Canadian minister to Washington made we wonder what the government's policy would be, now that we were a full-fledged belligerent.

I also knew Dr Skelton's views because he had discussed them with me on my last day in Ottawa. He felt, as Christie did, that we were bound to declare war if Great Britain did, even though he regretted the situation which made this step necessary. On 24 August, however, only a few days before the actual outbreak of war, he gave Mr King a memo emphasizing that the requirements of national and continental defence should be given priority over the dispatch of an expeditionary force and suggesting that if any military action were to be taken overseas it should be in the air. Dr Skelton argued that it was in the economic field that our aid could be most effective and 'most consistent with Canadian interests.' Mr King read this memorandum to Cabinet and noted that it met with general approval and that there was much disapproval of a possible expeditionary force.

The government, however, was soon to learn that public opinion throughout most of Canada would countenance no such half-way involvement; that Canadians would not accept a role to guard their bridges and their borders, to produce munitions and war supplies while British soldiers did the fighting against the Nazis. So it was not long before Canada House found itself the London headquarters of a nation participating in all aspects of the struggle.

After the first few weeks of excitement and confusion, of dealing with many war problems, life at Canada House settled down and became almost routine again, though a very busy routine with new conditions and circumstances to which we had to adjust ourselves, personally and officially.

I was living comfortably, though lonely for my family, in our flat at Roehampton. But it was rather far away from Trafalgar Square and when the fog and frost added to the discomfort of motoring through London in the black-out, I sublet the apartment and moved into a small flat off Piccadilly with Harry Crerar, now a brigadier, who had been posted to London at the end of October as senior officer, Canadian Military Headquarters Overseas. I lived with him for some weeks until Mrs Crerar arrived in London. As I said in my diary: 'I now have the rare and plutocratic privilege reserved for rich Londoners, prostitutes, and visitors, of being within walking distance of all the places one goes to – including the office.' This meant a lot in the conditions that existed even though we were becoming accustomed to them.

The British are great settlers down, and in London it soon seemed like business and pleasure as usual, although we blacked out with great thoroughness and a chink of light between curtains, or on your headlight, brought down the wrath of authority. Recruiting went on and khaki appeared once again on the streets. Yet there seemed to be neither the passion nor the parading of other patriotic wars. There was no blood-letting; no long daily casualty lists in *The Times* as was the case in 1914 and 1915. It all seemed unwarlike and unreal to anyone who remembered that earlier conflict. The theatres and night clubs were crowded, with women in evening dress and more men in dinner jackets than in uniform, though that began to change.

My own social life began to pick up with so many military and official friends arriving from Ottawa. In my diary for 21 September, I noted the important fact:

Today went to my first moving picture since the war – a newsreel at lunchtime and saw pictures of the war: German! No British pictures have yet been permitted. It taxed the ingenuity of the commentator to turn what really was very good German propaganda against its authors. He hardly succeeded. A notice was shown on the screen telling the patrons what to do and where to go if there was an air-raid. It closed with this gem, 'Above all, don't panic –

Remember YOU ARE BRITISH.' There was a burst of raucous laughter from the audience, which restored my faith in the British.

In all our minds, of course, was the question: how long will the war last; to which soon was added, when will it start?

After the quick and crushing defeat of Poland, and the division of the spoils with the Soviet Union, a move was made by Hitler, whether sincerely or not, to make peace. Mr Chamberlain told our High Commissioner, however, that Hitler's offer would be summarily rejected; that even if the terms themselves had been acceptable they would have to be backed by guarantees such as the disarmament of Germany, for he no longer believed anything that Hitler said or wrote. I commented in my diary, 26 September 1939:

Mr Chamberlain may have been a tardy convert to the view that Hitler can never be trusted but he has become 110 per cent converted. He is possessed now of only one idea – the Nazis must be destroyed. He is a determined, obstinate old man of limited vision and, I believe, with a limited tenure of office.

The draft of the British Prime Minister's speech in the House of Commons rejecting Hitler's offer had been submitted to Ottawa through Canada House for any comments they might care to make. Personally, I thought it was too negative. It was good on what we were fighting against but there was not enough about what we were fighting for. The High Commissioner and I, therefore, drafted some new paragraphs which were discussed with the other high commissioners. Ottawa and the other dominion governments also felt that the reply should be more constructive and include a reference to our war aims. But only a few minor changes were made to the text. The British government thought that this was not the time to put forward ideas for a peace settlement. They may have believed that Hitler would make further proposals after the rejection of his first one and that would be the time to put forward our own war aims. They were wrong.

Then came 25 December 1939, the first war Christmas for me since 1917 when I was also in London. This time, while I was not hurt and in hospital, I was even more homesick than I was twenty-two years earlier. My family were a long way off in Winnipeg. The children were at school there and my wife at home with her parents. I got regular and cheerful news from them but they were not with me. I decided to do something about this, at least so far as my wife was concerned. She had been anxious to return and the continued calm on the Western Front and in the air made this possible.

On Christmas Day I was permitted to put through a two minutes' overseas telephone call to the family, on condition that I would say nothing about the war. While the call was far too exciting to be wholly satisfactory, at least I was able to tell my wife to get a passage across the Atlantic as soon as she could, and to wish everybody a Merry Christmas. I dutifully hung up at what I thought was exactly two minutes when the operator rang back to tell me that I had twenty seconds left. She must have been a sentimental soul because she reconnected me with Winnipeg. It was hardly worth it, for, by the time the children had been collected again, I had time only to tell them that I had another twenty seconds. It was a kind Christmas thought, however, by that good telephone girl and I hope she ended the war as a superintendent of communications.

Canada House kept getting busier all the time as our war activities broadened. Messages to and from Ottawa by cable and mail were increasing by leaps and bounds. So were official visitors on war business. Mr Massey was, of course, the central figure in all our activities, with Mrs Massey always by his side in support. I was his chief of staff. As in all things, personal relationships became important as we tried to organize and administer so many new and unexpected duties. I have mentioned this problem in the all-important if long-distance relationship between the High Commissioner and the Prime Minister. It was also important in connection with Canadian ministerial and official visits, and with our relations with Canadian Military Headquarters in London.

The High Commissioner got on well with our Ottawa visitors and dispensed wartime hospitality generously to them, though his very real desire to make people welcome and assist them all he could was sometimes obscured by a certain formality and an official manner which was occasionally misinterpreted as coldness.

At that time the senior member of the Canadian colony in London was our ex-Prime Minister, the Rt. Honourable R.B. Bennett, who had decided to make his home in England after his electoral misfortunes in Canada. From the first Mr Massey did his best to establish friendly relations with Lord Bennett, as he became, but he was not successful. There was little or no contact between the two men. It seemed a good occasion to change this situation when war broke out, but Lord Bennett remained aloof from the representative of Canada who was also the Liberal friend of Mackenzie King. As a non-partisan civil servant, I was exempted from this cool treatment. He was kind to me and later during the bombing of London invited me more than once to visit him at his country home, Juniper Hall.

Early in February 1940 Lord Beaverbrook enquired of Mr Massey whether he would have any objection to the British government using Mr Bennett in a war advisory capacity. Mr Massey rightly replied that this had nothing to do with him, as Mr Bennett was a private citizen in the United Kingdom. At the same time, he pointed out that it would be unwise for the government in London to use Mr Bennett for contacts with the Canadian authorities which would normally go through the Canadian High Commissioner. The next day, a Cabinet minister, Sir Samuel Hoare, telephoned Mr Massey and said he wished to see the High Commissioner about a proposal that had been made in regard to the British government using a distinguished Canadian in an advisory capacity. It was obvious whom he had in mind though, according to Mr Massey, he brought the matter up 'very gingerly.' Mr Massey's reaction was equally cautious. The idea seemed to be that Mr Bennett should have access to certain cabinet papers on domestic, economic, and trade matters and give the British government the benefit of his advice thereon. Our High Commissioner told Sir Samuel Hoare that his attitude towards such an idea was very much the same as Sir Samuel's would be, he was sure, if the Canadian government proposed to use Mr Lloyd George as their adviser on certain trade and economic questions because he had honoured them by choosing Ottawa as a residence for his declining years. We heard nothing more about the idea which seemed to have been dropped; and, perhaps fortunately, did not get to Mr King's notice.

A happier contact for Canada House was made by a visit of the King and Queen on 17 October. By this time we had established a good working organization for our new wartime duties and our morale was high – as it remained throughout the war. We were ready for a royal inspection. My diary gave a light-hearted account of the visit.

The King and Queen paid us a visit on Wednesday to see how the machinery works at Canada House. The High Commissioner had told the staff the night before that it was to be a 'working' inspection, without ceremony, and that we weren't to make any special preparations. Everyone was to be at his job, in the normal way. One of our older English clerks took these instructions literally, and was so determined to carry them out, even at the risk of appearing to be discourteous to his sovereign, that when Their Majesties entered his sanctum, he refused to take any notice of them and kept on pushing his pen industriously and, he hoped, impressively. He had to be practically roared at before he would stand up to be introduced to the King and the Queen. However, he made magnificent amends by a bow which brought his forehead within a few inches of the floor, after which he hastened back to work again, to show how concerned he was about winning the war.

Most of our work naturally revolved around the civilian side of Canada's war effort. New and complicated questions arose relating to the legal and constitutional position of our forces serving abroad. There were also many economic, financial, and supply problems. There was thus a steady stream of ministerial and official visitors from Ottawa. It was our privilege at Canada House to do what we could to help them in their discussions and negotiations with their opposite numbers in London.

The first to come was The Honourable T.A. Crerar, then Minister of Mines and Resources, accompanied by officials and senior officers from several government departments, including Defence. This mission was concerned particularly with economic and financial matters, including the use of Canada as a source of war supplies: food, raw materials, and manufactures. There was a major argument within and between the two governments over wheat purchases, as always a matter of the greatest importance to Canada. Mr Crerar asked for a year's contract for UK bulk purchase at 93 cents a bushel. Too high by 20 cents, said the British. Mr Crerar replied that he only hoped he could get the Canadian wheat grower to accept the 93-cent figure. The British spokesman, Sir John Simon, of whom it was once unkindly written 'His smile was like the silver handle on a coffin,' replied 'Crerar, you know if you got 93 cents you would rush back to the prairies on the first boat and boast to your farmer constituents how, once again, you had put it over the British.' How little the Chancellor of the British Exchequer knew about the Canadian wheat farmer! If the British thought the price was too high, the Minister was told by Ottawa that it was too low. Indeed, there were some ministers who opposed any contract at all, leaving prices to be determined by the open market. So the Honourable 'T.A.' had to withdraw the offer at once. He had been left very far out on a limb and was in danger of being sawed off. I wrote:

The British may think we are bluffing and withdrew our offer only to avoid its rejection. But we are certainly not. On Thursday, the UK made a counter offer for three months' purchases at 85½ cents. Ottawa would, of course, have nothing to do with this and have told us not to enter into any contract of any kind. So now it's to be a fight between a monopoly seller in Canada and a monopoly buyer here. Bad business, this, in war time. Both sides are to blame. Our offer of 93 cents was a fair one and should have been accepted both here and in Ottawa. The fact that it has been attacked from both sides is the best evidence of its fairness.

In trying to resolve this difficulty over wheat, Mr King fell back on his usual practice of sending messages direct to the British Prime Minister, some of them dealing with details that even his private secretary should not have had to worry about. These messages no doubt were referred at once by Mr Chamberlain's private secretary to the British officials who were at the time discussing the problem with us in London. This, of course, made the position of the Canadian negotiators more difficult because it often meant that the British learned from Ottawa of a Canadian position before the Canadian representatives in London knew about it. As I plaintively recorded at the time, 'sometimes we don't know until they tell us here in Whitehall.'

The difficulty, though not in this case because a senior Canadian minister was in London, often arose out of the reluctance of the Prime Minister to deal with the British government through his High Commissioner. This was due not only to Mr King's constitutional and personal preference for communicating directly with the British Prime Minister but also to the feeling which was growing in Mr King's mind that Mr Massey was too close to the political and social élite in the United Kingdom to be a completely safe and sound Canadian intermediary. Any suspicions that Mr King may have had on this score were unfounded and unfair, but they existed. They added to our problems at Canada House and I believe made the position of the High Commissioner less comfortable at a time when life in London already had enough discomforts and even dangers.

There was, however, no cause for complaint on our part over the number of messages that the Prime Minister sent to Canada House on non-policy matters. Many of these seemed of no great significance but, because they came from the Prime Minister, had naturally to be given priority consideration. On this point, my diary for 2 October has this far too irreverent entry:

Is our PM breaking up? He sent a super-sealed double-enclosed letter to the HC marked 'Secret-Urgent-Most Immediate.' We thought it had information on Canada's war plans, or wheat policy, or something equally important but it turned out to be the copy of a telegram of thanks sent by Prince Felix of Luxembourg to the PM of Canada on his departure from the dominion. We can't get letters or cables from Ottawa on important matters but *can* get that kind of bumph!

I once received a very tactful personal message from Tommy Lascelles at the palace enquiring whether we could not gently put some kind of a check on Mr King's 'cable verbosity' in messages to Buckingham Palace. He said that the King had recently received (this was in April 1940) an eleven-page telegram from Mr King, in most secret cipher. This meant hours of work to decode it by hand, to say nothing of the risk of prejudicing the cipher by using it for such a long message. After all this work they found there was nothing in the message that could not have been sent in a single page of ordinary code. I told my

THE PEARSON GENERATIONS

top – with Mother, Father, Grandfather, and brothers, 1911
bottom – my children, Patricia and Geoffrey, 1934

WORLD WAR I

– in Alexandria, 1915

– learning to fly, 1917

CHICAGO DAYS

snapshot from a fishing camp in Wisconsin, 1920

Opposite page

OXFORD

top – scoring at Murren, Switzerland, 1921
bottom – St John's College 'Sophists,' 1924

TORONTO TRIUMPHS

– the happy honeymooners, 1925

– as coach with my senior intercollegiate champions, 1928

THE YOUNG DIPLOMAT

top – with O.D. Skelton on board the *Berengaria*, 1933
bottom – at Canada House, London, 1938

INTERNATIONAL JOURNEYMAN

top – meeting the press, San Francisco Conference, 1945
bottom – chairing the FAO Conference, Quebec, 1945

WITH THE GLAMOROUS AND THE GREAT

– Hollywood Dinner, 1945

– with Sir Winston, Ottawa, 1951

ALGOMA EAST

campaigning with Senator Tom Farquhar, 1948

friends at the palace that we had had similar difficulty, but that my diplomacy was not, I feared, equal to the task of drafting a message from Canada House telling a Prime Minister not to be so verbose, without offending him. I did, however, try to compose a tactful telegram suggesting that prime ministerial messages which did not require a high war-security classification should be sent in ordinary code. The High Commissioner, however, who had to see and sign all messages, decided that this one might better be filed than dispatched. No doubt he was right.

ॐ

To return to the Crerar supply mission. Another matter being discussed was the use of Canada as a base for industrial war production. We thought that this could be important for the British war effort and, incidentally, for the financing of our own. In these early days of the war, however, the British were slow, though no slower than Canadians, to recognize their supply needs. They did not think the war would last very long, if it ever began in earnest, and they thought that they could rely on their own resources to meet their war needs apart, of course, from food and raw materials. It was difficult to convince them of the importance of Canada's industrial war potential.

I recall one meeting at that time when we tried to persuade British officials that Canada's war industries could be of great importance to them, pointing out that American planes could be built in our country for the RAF as well as for our own Air Force. The British chairman was not impressed. He did not think that they would ever reach the point where they would need American aircraft which, in any event, were not much good. There was an insularity about it all which was irritating and which was soon to be shaken by events.

At this time we also had difficulty with the British government in the application to Canadians of their necessarily strict exchange regulations. The Treasury exempted Americans from exchange control if they had been resident less than seven years. No such exemption was given Canadians. We made a strong protest over this, but were blandly told by an officer of the Bank of England that the Americans were given favourable treatment because it was necessary to gain their friendship as neutrals. I was angry enough about this to write, intemperately, 'as we are *already* in their war, they don't have to give a damn about us.' When I reported this position to the High Commissioner he sent a vigorous complaint to Mr Eden, who was then Dominions' Secretary, about this intolerably unjust discrimination. The result was a letter from the Treasury a few days later to the effect that they would exempt Canadians resident in England if Canada House certified that their connection with Canada was closer than it was with the United Kingdom. To decide as to such certification was an unenviable responsibility. It was a perfect set-up for making enemies, especially as no criteria for 'closer connection' had been laid down.

One of the early applications for a certificate of 'closer connection with Canada' was from Lord Beaverbrook who had, of course, many investments in the country where he was born and with which he retained close contact. His banker telephoned me on 23 January 1940 to say that Lord Beaverbrook was somewhat surprised at our cool reception of his request for exemption, in view of the more positive attitude we had taken to an earlier informal approach which had been made on his behalf. I was mystified by this and asked His Lordship's intermediary, whom I knew well, what he meant. He referred to an earlier letter to Canada House giving information about the Canadian position of a 'Mr x' and asking whether this would qualify him for a certificate. We had interpreted 'Mr x' as referring to Mr Bennett. So I told my banker friend that the cases of Mr Bennett and Lord Beaverbrook were not at all the same, whereupon he replied that Mr Bennett did not come into the picture, as 'Mr x' was Lord Beaverbrook, whom he wished to keep anonymous while merely asking for an opinion. I found this surprising in view of the fact that he had described 'Mr x' to me over the telephone as a great Canadian public figure who had made all his money in Canada, and so forth. I naturally assumed it was Mr Bennett and still think it might have been. I then expressed my regret over this mix-up but thought in view of the details now given in Lord Beaverbrook's application it might be difficult for us to recommend him for a Certificate of Exemption as a Canadian. I noted in my diary: 'I am afraid the "little man," as his banker refers to him, is not going to be very friendly towards Canada House.'

Then Mr Bennett intervened to see if he could assist his friend by raising the matter with me at lunch one day in March. It was a very good lunch. Mr Bennett was very cordial and he gave me a learned talk about the law of domicile as it applied to Lord Beaverbrook's position regarding exchange control. I said in my diary on 19 March:

I felt like asking him why he wasn't applying for exemption on his own behalf, as his claims were much stronger. I found that out without asking. He stated that he had challenged last autumn the right of the Treasury to apply the regulations to him, as the Statute on which the regulations were based had no constitutional validity in its application to Canadians, because it

contravened the Statute of Westminster. R.B. said that he got a personal
letter back from Sir John Simon who said that the regulations would not, of
course, apply to him. I have been wondering for some months now when he
was going to ask us to give him a Certificate of Exemption, when it appears
that all the time he has had a letter from the Chancellor himself saying that
the Statute did not apply in his case. R.B. went on to say that, having made
good his legal claim to exemption, he then proceeded to Canada last December, sold about three-quarters of a million dollars' worth of Canadian securi-
ties and changed the proceeds into pounds for the benefit of the Treasury
here. This was a generous move on his part because it meant a substantial
loss in income to him.

There were other problems which arose out of contacts with Canadian Military Headquarters in the United Kingdom. In working out
arrangements covering the constitutional position of Canadian forces
overseas, Canada House had, in fact, the major responsibility. In World
War I, these problems had been dealt with by a member of the Cabinet,
the Minister of Overseas Military Forces, who was located in London
and who had a certain jurisdiction over Military Headquarters there.
Neither the Prime Minister nor Minister of Defence wanted any such
arrangement this time, one which had not worked very successfully
in the earlier war. So our Military Headquarters in London, although
working closely with Canada House, was responsible only to the
Minister of Defence in Ottawa, with the High Commissioner remaining the senior Canadian civilian representative in the United Kingdom.

Military discussions and negotiations with the United Kingdom were
greatly facilitated by the close personal relations established and maintained by Canadian Military Headquarters with the British Defence
Services. This was the easier because of friendships formed between
the senior officers of both countries, through service together in World
War I or attendance at the Imperial Staff and Defence Colleges. It was
not made easier, however, by the feeling sometimes encountered on the
highest political and military levels that Canadian formations overseas
were really an integral part of the British imperial forces and, as such,
subject to the direction and control of London. This was not at all the
position of the Canadian government who were determined to keep
control of their own overseas forces and maintain their separate Canadian identity. Insistence on this produced many problems which required for their solution goodwill and understanding on both sides;
both of which, fortunately, usually could be found.

We were also concerned with establishing the constitutional responsibility of the Canadian government for the disposition in action of its
forces overseas, subject, of course, to operational exigencies. For this

purpose we had many long discussions with the British authorities on
the application to our troops of the 'Visiting Forces Act.' These talks
were of educational value to many Whitehall officials who learned to
appreciate the difference between a Canadian division in 1939 and a
colonial contingent in 1914. In short, our government was rightly and
deeply concerned with bringing the position of its forces overseas into
line with our position as a fully self-governing state. This gave us much
work and some worry at Canada House; and also the opportunity to
convince our British friends that the nationalist position we adopted
would strengthen, not weaken, the common war effort.

The understanding of our position became easier as Canadian participation in the war grew in size and importance. In the early months,
however, it was difficult to remove the impression that we were once
more supplying men and formations for 'imperial' forces under British
management, or to convince our British friends that we had a legitimate
national interest in the general conduct of the war and in the direction
of its higher strategy, and that, at the very least, we had the right of a
partner to know what was happening or not happening, and why. This
seemed reasonable enough but was not always easy to secure. During
the visit of Mr Crerar in October 1939, for instance, the War Office
arranged for the Minister to visit the front in France. But he was
allowed to take only *one* person with him, General Crerar. The War
Office applied the same restriction to ministerial delegations from other
dominions who were then in London.

I thought this was a mistake and explained why in my diary for
Thursday, 9 November 1939:

The Honourable 'T.A.' and Brigadier Harry Crerar left for France this evening
to see the 'war.' You would have thought that the government here would
have been anxious to send all the dominion representatives, who were attending meetings in London, to France. The propaganda value of this would have
been great – as these men were all key people in their own countries. But the
War Office restricted the number to a minister and one other from each
dominion: even though the week before they had sent over a whole batch of
'back-bench' British MPs. This unimaginative ruling meant picking one from
the delegation, and Harry, as a soldier, seemed to be the obvious choice. One
result is that, Breadner, our second senior air officer, will go back to Canada
without having seen the Air Force in the field. This was very stupid.

It took time, patience, and firmness to change the colonial mentality
which lingered in certain quarters in Whitehall.

Our next ministerial visitor to London, in December 1939, was
Colonel J.L. Ralston, then Minister of Finance. The main purpose of

this visit was to make arrangements for the Commonwealth Air Training Programme then under active, and even at times acrimonious, discussion between the two governments. In the late thirties, the British government had proposed a Commonwealth Air Training Programme to operate in Canada. The Canadian government would have nothing to do with any such scheme which might prejudice its basic policy of 'no-commitments.' This attitude may have been understandable in a Canadian political peacetime context though its expression was, I think, overly negative and suspicious. Now, however, we were at war together and earlier political obstacles to co-operation presumably no longer existed.

Hence, shortly after the war began the UK government made another proposal for a Commonwealth Air Training Centre in Canada. I remember seeing a copy of a telegram from the Dominions Office to Ottawa on the subject. I noted:

The plan would virtually make Canada the centre of all empire air training during the war, with 20,000 pilots to be sent overseas to fifty-two training camps in the next twelve months. A stupendous programme which will stagger them in Ottawa. I wonder how they will react to it? To carry out such a plan will require vigour, imagination, drive and, above all, 100 per cent enthusiasm for the war. I don't yet see that combination of qualities in Ottawa. The High Commissioner, who has been consulted unofficially on the drafting of the message, is more optimistic than I am. We sent a long supplementary telegram today, asking for immediate information on points of detail concerning Canada's air training resources. The implications of this proposal are tremendous.

Most of the negotiating of the Air Training Agreement, difficult and contentious as it was, took place in Ottawa. We were involved in London in various ways, however, especially in the early stages when Colonel Ralston was in London. I attended most of the discussions that took place during that visit. It was clear from the beginning that the main difficulties would be over finance and control.

While Canada was willing to bear the major share of the financial burden, it was felt that the original British proposals were beyond our capacity and they were modified accordingly. Treasury considerations loomed much larger at the beginning of 1940, on both sides, than they did later, when men were fighting and dying and victory or defeat was in the balance. The Canadian government rightly insisted that the programme, carried out in Canada and largely financed by us, should be managed by Canadians. Colonel Ralston also insisted that the Canadian identity and control of Canadian aircrew who went through the training programme should be maintained. They were to be kept in RCAF formations to the maximum possible extent and not lost as individuals in the RAF. Indeed, we took the same attitude later in regard to army personnel. In this war our men were not to be Canadian units in a British army controlled exclusively by the British War Office and British Headquarters.

These discussions of finance and jurisdiction naturally went at times beyond the Air Training proposals. A note in my diary during December gives some indication of the general problem:

We have been trying to work out today a basis for talks with the War Office on how the Canadian government is going to pay for the maintenance of its troops over here. As a free and independent participant in this war – the boast of all our politicians' speeches on the subject – we can't allow the United Kingdom to pay any of our expenses. But how are we to pay our share of the cost of such things as barrack rentals, food for Canadian detachments with British units, etc.? It's even more complicated in the Air Force. We want all the Canadian pilots trained in Canada to form RCAF squadrons. But we haven't ground crews for them; nor could we finance their maintenance in the field. The British suggest we maintain as many RCAF squadrons overseas as our contribution to the Air Training Programme would cover; 350 million dollars. This should be about fifteen squadrons. The other Canadian air crews should join the RAF and, as a concession to our national feeling, they should be allowed to wear a maple leaf on their caps, or 'Canada' on their shoulders, or some such ennobling national device. These discussions are very exhausting.

It was inevitable that there should have been a great deal of time and energy spent on the reconciliation of control and cost, of nationalism and economics. Even in such a close war relationship as existed between Canada and the United Kingdom, these things were bound at times to come into conflict, especially in a period of war without fighting. Treasury considerations were also influenced on our side by a suspicion, not entirely groundless, that London was concerned with protecting its own hard-pressed financial and economic position, even at our expense, because we were such a rich and fortunate dollar country.

The haggling that occasionally went on over financial matters in those early days was more fitting for a market-place than for two countries fighting and working together in a war for survival. The trouble, as I have indicated, was that we did not know yet that it was a question of survival. After the initial shocks and fears disappeared, the war was not felt in Ottawa to be a life-and-death struggle requiring a total effort regardless of cost. The British could not seem to appreciate that Canadians did not yet feel they were in the war in the same way, psychologically and materially, as they felt themselves to be in the United Kingdom. Here, the people were in the front line, even if at the beginning there was no fighting going on. We were across the ocean, thousands of miles away from that front line with no feeling of danger, living securely, though we hated to admit it, under the protection of the United States. If the British had understood this better, they would not have occasionally made unrealistic and irritating comparisons of their war effort with ours.

In these financial and constitutional discussions, Canada could not have had a better spokesman than Colonel Ralston. He was a staunch and true Canadian, but he also appreciated that a narrow nationalism must not be allowed to interfere with winning the war. His fault was in driving himself too hard and becoming immersed in detail that he should have left to subordinates. He was overly conscientious and industrious, worked every day, all day, and never seemed to relax. He was more considerate of those who worked with him than he was of himself; he was as kind, generous, and unselfish a man as one could ever hope to meet.

On this visit, pressure and work took its toll and he became the victim of a very painful case of lumbago. He tried to carry on but it was impossible, so we persuaded him to go to the Canadian Military Hospital at Cliveden. I visited him there on Christmas day, 1939. He was lying flat on his back, as one does with bad lumbago, and reading a book. With his strong Baptist religious views, I would not have been surprised if it had been the Bible. I was amused to note, however, that it was a shocker called *No Orchids for Miss Blandish*. He looked fine. Having read the book myself, I'm sure that for the moment it took his mind off the lumbago.

ॐ

Before I returned to Ottawa, we at Canada House were privileged to be of assistance to other ministerial visits. C.D. Howe made the most spectacular appearance, after the harrowing experience of being on a ship that was torpedoed and sunk. I met him on arrival. Indeed, I was asked to do a broadcast of that arrival for the BBC as 'Michael Macdonald,' the pseudonym I used for my wireless reports to Canada during the Battle of Britain and the bombing. 'C.D.,' as those who knew him would expect, was completely undisturbed by his dangerous adventure and, immediately on his arrival in London, was ready to go to work on war supply and industrial problems.

I should also mention Norman Rogers, an old and dear friend who was now Minister of Defence and for whom even higher responsibilities were predicted. We spent one glorious late April day, in his crowded and busy visit, at Oxford trying to recapture the magic of those peaceful days when we were together as undergraduates. It was, alas, only a few weeks later that he was killed in an aeroplane crash. Rogers and his party had come to London armed with facts and figures to combat the feeling I have mentioned that Canada was not pulling its weight in the war. His effort in this regard illustrated a handicap that we sometimes gave ourselves in trying to combat this impression. While the Minister of Defence was making one case in London, the Committee on Public Information were making the opposite one in Ottawa by issuing a press release on Canada's war economy which began:

Canada enters the seventh month of the war well equipped to stand the economic strain. In the coming fiscal year, it is expected that the war will cost Canada around $500,000,000. Heavy as this burden will be, it amounts to only about 12 per cent of Canada's national income, estimated at $4,100,000,000. Compare the figures for Great Britain and Germany. Britain's war expenditure now calls for about 29 per cent of the estimated national income. German war expenditure is around 40 per cent of the estimated national income.

Once, during meetings with the British Minister of Supply when we were contending that orders placed in Canada were inadequate and should be increased, the same Committee on Public Information in Ottawa issued another release which called attention in most optimistic language to the large orders that had been placed in Canada by the United Kingdom Ministry of Supply. It was difficult for Canadians in London to try to melt the stony hearts of the Treasury so that the loganberry growers of British Columbia would still be able to sell their products in England, while our 'Ministry of Information' in Ottawa boasted about the 445 millions of their decreasing dollar supply which the United Kingdom had spent or would spend in Canada during the first year of the war on the purchase of war materials and other supplies.

Ministers came and went, conferences began and ended, but it was Mr King, in Ottawa, who determined the broad lines of policy. His attitude to the way the British were running the war seemed to me to be somewhat ambivalent. On 31 December 1941 (according to his diary) he told Churchill: 'They [the Canadian Conservative Party] had tried to pin the badge of isolationism on me. He [Churchill] could not find in Canada a man who had been stronger for British connection than myself, and for Empire unity.' Churchill's eyebrows must have lifted at this declaration of Empire unity because, even with Canada now fully in the war 'at Britain's side,' Mr King retained much of the old suspicion of Downing Street; though his public speeches gave no such impression. Our Prime Minister could, for instance, give vent to the most extravagant public praise of Winston Churchill when he succeeded Chamberlain. He could refer emotionally, when a public occasion or speech required it, to the unity of the Empire. Yet he would anguish over, and try to counter suspected Churchillian plans for centralizing control of policy of that Empire. He was suspicious of the tendency to treat Canada's military contribution as something turned over to Britain for direction and use. He was irritated by the exclusion of Canada from any real influence on the conduct of the war. At the same time, when there were proposals for imperial war councils in London, with full Canadian representation, or meetings of prime ministers to consult about war problems and plans, Mr King was cautious and often negative in his reaction.

The first invitation to such a meeting came from Mr Chamberlain in April 1940, a time when he must have had other and more pressing things on his mind. Of this I wrote on 24 April: 'I wonder whether Mr King will approve of this? It will be a crumb thrown to us for lack of active participation in the week-to-week direction of the war. I noticed that, at the Allied War Council meeting yesterday in Paris, Norway and Poland were both represented, but not Canada.' Mr King's reply on 8 May was negative, but subtle and verbose. I noted in my diary:

I had a feeling that Mr King wouldn't welcome this invitation very much, but I was wondering how he would get out of it. I found out this morning, because he sent a long personal telegram to Norman Rogers as follows: 'Am cabling Chamberlain direct tomorrow, Wednesday, regarding his recent request. If at all possible I wish you could see him personally to explain how all-important it is for me not to be obliged to leave Canada for any conference for at least some time to come. I would like you to tell him how strongly I feel it to be in interest of Allied Powers for me to be at seat of government here to deal with situations, both domestic and foreign, as they arise. Believe I can be infinitely more helpful by using my influence with colleagues in council at Ottawa to have right course taken and desired decision reached, with world situation changing and continuing to change, than I could possibly be to British government by being in London. In coping with unforeseen situations which may arise, you might explain the need there is certain to be to keep the Canadian war effort at maximum and Canada itself united. I also can think of nothing more important than to keep relations between the UK and the USA as cordial as possible. I firmly believe my presence at Ottawa might serve a more useful purpose to British government in helping to meet some critical situation in Canada or such as may be between USA and UK than would be possible for me to render in any other way. I also feel very strongly that such travelling and speaking as I may be able to undertake, once Parliament session over, should be done in different parts of

Canada and that my influence with Canadian people would be greatly prejudiced if, instead, I were obliged to be absent from Canada for any length of
time and, particularly, to be speaking or broadcasting from Britain. You
understand what the problem is. Please stress also the fact that I am Secretary
of State for External Affairs and President of Council as well as Prime
Minister and that especially in dealing with matters vis-à-vis the USA and
Japan, and questions, for example, such as those concerning Greenland,
Jamaica, which have come up in the past few days, my presence here is all but
imperative. Please explain to Mr Chamberlain delay in reply to his message
due to my absence from Canada, at the time of its receipt, and also desire for
full conference with colleagues before sending reply. I think I may say entire
Cabinet are of my point of view.

Norman Rogers was not very happy at this request to see Mr Chamberlain because it was his last day in London and he had many things
to do. More important, Mr Chamberlain was fighting for his life in the
House of Commons and would not be as interested in Mr King's message as he might otherwise have been. However, the Canadian Minister
was able to see the British Prime Minister without delay. With other
more pressing things on his mind Mr Chamberlain did not seem to care
very much whether Mr King came to the proposed July meeting or not.
Mr King had also sent a personal reply directly to Mr Chamberlain
emphasizing the value of his 'personal presence ... among his own
people' at this critical time. He assured Mr Chamberlain that 'the
present means of consultation with yourself and other members of the
Commonwealth appear to have been most satisfactory.'

Mr Churchill, early in 1941, renewed the invitation to a Prime
Ministers' Conference for the summer of that year. He certainly had
no plan or desire for any collective management of the war, Commonwealth or Allied, or for any machinery that would interfere with his
own direction of its policy and strategy, later to be shared with President Roosevelt. He appreciated the political value of Commonwealth
meetings, however, which could confirm and support his leadership.
Nevertheless, there is no reason to believe that he was disappointed
when Mr King again discouraged such a meeting, pointing out how
difficult it was for him to be absent from his wartime duties in Canada,
how well the existing machinery of consultation was working, and that
it could not be improved upon. If this caused us to lift our eyebrows in
London, a message from the Prime Minister eulogizing Canada House
as part of that machinery brought pleasure as well as surprise. This
'mention in despatches' assured us that our devotion and industry at
Canada House in 'difficult and often dangerous circumstances' was
'beyond praise.'

ॐ9ॐ

CANADIAN WAR PROBLEMS

It was natural that, during the deceptive months of the 'phoney' war, our work at Canada House was concentrated more on plans and preparations for the war than with problems arising out of its conduct. The fighting in Poland had soon ended and war on the western front had not yet begun. There was in consequence little to discuss or to report except plans or rumours of plans, or British preparations to meet the onslaught on the ground in France and in the air over Britain.

Questions of strategy and of policy were dealt with on a high political level, often from Prime Minister to Prime Minister, on those occasions when the Canadian government was taken into the confidence of the British. I can recall only one meeting in London which I attended in the early months of war, apart from those relating to the ministerial visits I have already referred to. This particular meeting concerned the defence of the Pacific. I noted in my diary on 20 November:

Most interesting part of this busy day was a meeting at the Cabinet Office at 4:30 to discuss defence of the Pacific. It was called at the insistence of the Australians who were uneasy at what they considered a lack of definite assurances from London to move capital ships at once to Singapore if Japan should ever declare war. [This was in 1939!]

Lord Chatfield [Minister of Defence] was in the chair, but the dominating personality at the meeting was Winston Churchill [First Lord of the Admiralty] who was looking as cherubically juvenile as ever; and puffing hard at the inevitable cigar. He radiates the impression of mischievous but invincible youth and energy.

Churchill gave a long and interesting talk on naval strategy; arguing that you don't protect a position merely by being there [this was aimed at the Australians]; that the government would be mad to promise that a certain number of ships would be at a certain spot at a certain time. But, while they must have a free hand in naval strategy, nevertheless, next to the protection of the homeland against the main enemy, they put the protection of Australia and New Zealand, and hence Singapore, even before the protection of their interests in the Mediterranean.

While the High Commissioner for New Zealand was quite happy about this, Dick Casey from Australia House was only partly satisfied.

Winston Churchill then ended the meeting on a very doubtful note; to the effect that when we win this war, we mustn't make the mistake of 1919. He didn't mean the avoidance of a harsh Versailles but of a mild one. We must really 'fix' Germany this time; not fall again for any disarmament nonsense; keep two British fleets in being, one for Europe and one for Asia, and never forget that during our lifetime and our children's lifetime our only security would be the British navy and the French army. What nonsense!

There were many meetings, of course, between service representatives of both countries dealing with purely military matters, at which Canada House was not represented. To gather and to forward to Ottawa military information and intelligence was the primary responsibility of Canadian Military Headquarters, now well organized and directed by General Crerar. With this Headquarters Canada House had the best of relations, both official and personal, and we kept each other fully informed on matters of joint concern. At times, Canada House was able to supplement information available to Military Headquarters, and to help our military command in various ways through the contacts and discussions which the High Commissioner and I had with British political and official authorities.

In those early days of the war, there was a complacency and an optimism in London which seems strange in the light of later events. It was often reflected in information we received. Canadian Air Force officers in London, for example, were not impressed by reports they received on the strength and effectiveness of the RAF. The High Commissioner, for his part, was disturbed by their pessimistic reports. So he arranged to have a talk with the Chief of the British Air Staff who reassured him on both the comparative strength and efficiency of the British and German air forces. My own faith in this optimistic assessment was somewhat shaken by the Air Marshal's remark to Mr Massey that there was not a single American aeroplane that was any good, hence they could not expect any effective help from the United States, even if Congress were to change the Neutrality Act. I had heard this opinion earlier from a senior British civilian official, but I was no more impressed when it came from the Chief of the Royal Air Force.

This attitude was all too prevalent in those deceptive early days. It was no doubt a fair reflection of the public mood. The work of recruiting, preparing, and training was going on, but without any great sense of urgency. There was much fatuous optimism about the strangling effect of the economic blockade of Germany and a pathetic confidence both in the genius of the French military leaders and in the invincibility of the French armies. As for the British navy, with Churchill again its First Lord, even the sinking of the *Royal Oak* and the *Courageous* did no more than cause a mild uneasiness.

Thus it was a quiet and calm conflict, at first. On 13 December the *Daily Express* printed the French war communiqués of the preceding two days: 10 December – nothing to report; 11 December – less activity than previously. I remember the complaint of a friend in the Foreign Office toward the end of October that it was going to be increasingly difficult to carry on a war without the excitement of fighting; that what was needed was a few thousand French military casualties and a German air raid on London. He was soon to have his wish.

Our minds at Canada House were distracted for a time from these larger issues by the arrival of the first Canadian troops. I went with the High Commissioner to Greenock to meet the First Division on 18 December. It was a stirring sight when the first ship of the convoy appeared out of the mist, with soldiers cheering from every vantage point. The sons of those who had crossed the Atlantic twenty-five years ago to win the war to end war had returned, but this sad confirmation of that earlier failure was lost in the welcoming celebrations.

Canada House had organized the press arrangements for this historic arrival. The news was to be kept absolutely secret for forty-eight hours, the time required to disembark and to get the soldiers to their camps. Any possible risk of air bombing at the port or en route would thus be avoided. But the press, naturally, had to be at Greenock to report the arrival. This would be very big news in Canada. We took all the journalists, Canadian, British, and American, to Glasgow by special train. They would thus get their stories on the spot but, we hoped, would hold them for release until the agreed hour. We were rather worried that some American might telephone the story at once to Dublin where it could be relayed to New York. Ottawa had asked us to ensure absolutely that no report would appear in the United States before its publication in Canada. There was no problem. We had only to trust the press. This we did, and all went as planned. But we forgot Winston Churchill who gave the entire story in a broadcast on the very day of the arrival. Mr King was disturbed by this breach of security and good manners.

The first battalion to land was from Toronto. The first Canadian soldier to leave the ship and step on British soil was the Battalion Sergeant Major. The press photographers, naturally, concentrated on him, and their pictures got national coverage the next day. This was unfortunate, for with the Sergeant Major was the regimental mascot, an Aberdeen terrier called Corky. Although the readers of British newspapers may have been pleased with the picture of the Canadian Sergeant Major, a zealous official in the Board of Agriculture must have noticed that Corky, too, had landed, thereby violating a sacred and inflexible British regulation that every dog entering the country must spend six months in quarantine. This regulation was a sensible one, to keep rabies out of the country.

Within a few days of the arrival of Canada's First Division at their camp, Aldershot, a civil servant called on the adjutant of the regiment and asked for Corky so that he could be duly quarantined. His request was indignantly rejected. Corky was their mascot and must stay with the regiment. The official wheels then started to turn. In due course His Majesty's government in the United Kingdom asked the High Commissioner of His Majesty's government in Canada to secure a dog, newly arrived from Canada now with the Canadian First Division in Aldershot, for a stay of six months in a canine internment camp at Basingstoke, Hants. I was selected to carry out these instructions and for that purpose got in touch with the battalion commander.

My mission succeeded, temporarily, and Corky went to his new home. The effect on regimental morale was bad. The Regiment vowed it would not go to France without its mascot, though it would be happy to march against the pound at Basingstoke or even the Board of Agriculture in London. This was discouraged. Instead, the proverbial enterprise and ingenuity of the Canadian soldier came into play and a plot was hatched. It was told to me later and while I cannot vouch for every dramatic detail, it is too good a story not to be true. A local Aberdeen was secured who might have been Corky's twin. Two of the best-looking, sex-appealing young soldiers were detached from other duties concerned with the winning of the war and dispatched to Basingstoke on indefinite leave. The pound there, it had been ascertained, was staffed by young and comely lasses of the Women's Land Army. The two Canadian soldiers were told to scrape up an acquaintance with two of the girls. That was easy, for our men were young and handsome. They were to ripen that acquaintance into the kind of friendship which would make it safe to tell one or both about a plan to substitute Corky II for Corky I. They were to secure the co-operation of their land girl friends for this exchange, at any price of promise or performance.

All went smoothly and according to plan. It may have been the most perfectly conducted operation of the war. So it was not long before Corky I was back with the regiment where, at the end of the quarantine period, he was joined by Corky II. I never learned what happened to the two land girls. I like to think that they later may have been among the thousands of young ladies who were brought back to Canada, after the fighting finished, as war brides. They certainly deserved some reward.

The arrival of the First Division, prematurely announced by Mr Churchill, certainly got maximum publicity, with the *Evening Standard* reporting in big, red headlines General McNaughton's declaration on arrival: 'We defend liberty.' That arrival was soon made evident in other ways. A day or so after reaching Aldershot a bus load of high-spirited Canadian soldiers on the town for the evening were creating more of a disturbance in London, so a phone call from the local authority told us, than the Nazis had yet been able to manage. The military police were unable to handle these sons of their fathers of World War I, who believed more in their desire and their ability to fight the enemy than in the need for British army discipline and good order on leave. This attitude, not always understood by the civilian authorities, gave us a new kind of diplomatic work, since Canada House had the unenviable duty of acting as liaison between the British civil and the Canadian military authorities in matters of this kind.

This included putting blunt Canadian military language into acceptable officialese designed to make a favourable impression at Whitehall when we wanted something done. It also meant interpreting austere Whitehall language into plainer terms more familiar to our own military authorities. I had been in the diplomatic service long enough to claim some skill in what I used to call quintuplet diplomatic communications, those requiring at least five copies. Indeed, I once agreed with a desk-bound soldier friend of mine at Canadian Military Headquarters that if we lost the war it would not be due to the German army but to the exhaustion of the supply of allied carbon paper.

These duties of interpretative communication went something like this. On my desk one morning I might find a letter from the War Office in more or less the following terms: 'I am directed by the members of the Army Council to ask the High Commissioner for Canada to invite the Canadian government to give favourable consideration to a proposal to charge Canadian patients in British military hospitals an extra penny for oatmeal at breakfast.' I would move into immediate action, throw red tape to the winds, grab my telephone, and call the senior officer at military headquarters. 'General, the UK authorities want the charges on oatmeal for Canadian soldiers' breakfasts increased by a penny. They need dollars. Will you agree?' He would say, 'Hell, no!' and slam down the telephone. Whereupon I would dictate a letter to the War Office somewhat as follows:

Sir:

I am directed by the High Commissioner for Canada to request you to inform the members of His Majesty's Army Council that the Canadian government has given long and earnest consideration to the subject of charging Canadian soldiers an extra penny for oatmeal at breakfast. My government regrets, however, that in view of all the circumstances, and having regard to existing financial commitments, it is not able, at the moment, to accept your proposal, but will re-examine it in due course.

☞

With Canadian forces safely installed at Aldershot, our next welcoming assignment was the arrival of the first Royal Canadian Air Force squadron at Liverpool. The routine was similar and the results equally satisfactory. But such ceremonies of war were not to alter normal regulations. The only reaction to my report to Ottawa on this arrival, of great historical interest as a first for the Canadian air force, was a note from the accounting office of the department that my expense account for the trip to Liverpool had included 2/6 for a gin and tonic at dinner. This was disallowed.

The Canadian forces were now well established, and I had frequent occasions to visit Army Headquarters. Now and then I also accompanied the High Commissioner to military ceremonials. The first of these, as I recall, was an inspection of the division, shortly after their arrival, by the Secretary of State for War, the colourful and controversial Right Honourable Leslie Hore-Belisha.

This visit somewhat disturbed the High Commissioner, who had hoped to have the honour of the first inspection for himself. Not anxious to play second fiddle in this particular Canadian programme, he decided not to accompany the British minister. This, in turn, annoyed General McNaughton who insisted that someone from Canada House must come with the Cabinet Minister and as the High Commissioner was not able to come, I must. Mr Massey, however, thought that it would not be right for the first civilian representative from Canada House to appear in Aldershot to be anyone but the High Commissioner. This is the kind of crisis that loses wars, elections, and friendships. It is also often remembered long after more important matters are forgotten. Once again a compromise saved the day and some faces. Mr

Massey would not escort Mr Hore-Belisha to Aldershot, but would meet him there. This he did, sharing the honours equally with the Secretary of State for War, on the platform, in the press, and in that wonderful world of public relations. The Minister alone, however, addressed the troops, with only partial success. His declaration that the Canadians were 'unbeatable' would be well received in Canada. Less happy was his observation that they were 'a lot better than those in 1914,' a remark fortunately dropped from the press release, or the outraged veterans of the First Canadian Division of the earlier war would have had the scalp of Hore-Belisha, whose greatest virtue was not tact.

The King's inspection, a few weeks later, went off smoothly, although the arrangements were much more complex. This visit was a great success and the Canadian civilians present had every reason to be proud of the appearance and bearing of the soldiers.

Although Harry Crerar was the Canadian officer I saw most often, both on and off duty, I was also happy to renew my friendly association with General McNaughton whom I had known and liked in Ottawa. Our relationship overseas was a very pleasant one and, as he told me more than once, helpful to him. To be perfectly frank, when he had occasion to take anything up with Canada House, General McNaughton preferred to talk to me than to Mr Massey. The reason was purely personal. He had known me for years. Mr Massey, however, was more official and reserved and the General did not, at that time, know him well. Their temperaments were at opposite poles and neither felt at that early stage very comfortable or relaxed with the other. 'Andy's' occasional explosions to me about diplomatic niceties and official red tape were often embarrassing in their bluntness.

General McNaughton soon made a favourable impact on the British public, as he already had on his Canadian troops. He looked, acted, and talked like a leader; he was forceful, forthright, and imaginative; unstuffy and even unkempt; very different from a normal British general out of Sandhurst, the Staff College, and the privileged classes. He was impatient of folly and undazzled by brass; at times frank to the point of indiscretion, and intolerant of opposition stemming from timidity or conventional thinking. His judgments on occasion may have been inspired more by zeal and emotion than by careful, painstaking analysis, but he made them quickly and decisively. He had my respect and admiration, but I wondered how he would fit into the top British military establishment or adjust himself to the complex civil-military relationship which so preoccupied us. Shortly after his arrival, I wrote in my diary: 'He'll be stepping on lots of toes before long in his restless zeal, his driving imagination, and his insistence on efficiency rather than "spit and polish." '

I remember the cold and foggy Christmas eve of 1939 when I accompanied the two generals, McNaughton and Crerar, to Euston Station to meet their wives who were arriving from Canada. The train was late and 'Andy' and I paced the platform while he told me of his hopes and fears about the war. He was vehement in his criticism of its military and political direction, whether in London or Ottawa. He damned all those cautious people who put financial considerations before full mobilization of everybody and everything needed for victory. He took a dim view of all politicians, but an even harsher one of the War Office, half of whose high command he thought to be 'nit-wits.' When not talking to me, he was borrowing cigarettes from porters, or swapping war stories with them. They must have wondered what kind of general was this, until they found he was Canadian.

A few weeks later when I spent a night with the McNaughtons at Aldershot, the General proposed that I put on the uniform and become a general staff officer. It would be my job to look after political and constitutional relations with the civil authorities, to help him write his despatches, and be generally useful. I was tempted to begin a second military career, not as a private but as a red-tabbed colonel. But apart from my doubts that I could fit comfortably into this niche, I knew that neither the High Commissioner nor the department would even consider my release to what they would undoubtedly regard as a less demanding and less responsible wartime job. No brass for me, no scarlet, neither crowns nor stars. I kept my short black coat.

The General, I recorded of this visit, was complaining once again of the slow methods of the British military authorities; also about the difficulty in convincing them that Canadians had different ideas about how to do things. For instance, he said, when the Canadian Division was the duty division of the area they received an order for 250 soldiers to be detailed for special fatigue duty. He enquired what this was and found out it was looking after officers' gardens, cleaning up their lawns, and doing general domestic work. This is apparently an old Aldershot custom, but McNaughton said that he wouldn't allow one Canadian to be used for such a purpose.

General McNaughton was a good Canadian as well as a good soldier. He was as anxious as any nationalist politician to maintain the Canadian identity of his army, and to ensure that its control would remain Canadian. But he always and rightly made the reservation of military necessity. He did not much enjoy, however, the long conferences we

had to have regarding the constitutional, financial, and economic implications of these political principles. He once complained to me:
'How can I fight the war if I have to worry about the Statute of Westminster?' Once, wearied by talk on economic and constitutional matters, he proceeded to extend our conversation to the war in general and
to the world situation. He astounded me by expressing the view that
the British government must purchase arms in Canada to build up a
large armament industry there, to be used, if not in this war, then in
the next. He hazarded a discouraging prediction that this was merely
the first of a series of wars to which we must look ahead for thirty or
forty years. Although sharing his opinion on the need for a long view,
a forty-year perspective seemed somewhat excessive. We should not, I
thought, condemn the British if they restricted their vision to the next
twelve months or so. My own was fixed on the one year ahead.

⌇

1939 ended in an atmosphere of unreality. We were at war but a war
with no battles. With the first few weeks of 1940, however, the deceit-
ful calm was disturbed. Those impatient and bellicose souls eager for
the fighting to begin so that it could end soon in victory were to see at
least one part of their wish come true before the year was half spent.

The winter war of the Soviets against Finland was the first sign of
change. A storm of emotion was aroused to help the Finns, all the
stronger because the over-powering aggressor was a communist state.
Plans for assistance were accordingly concocted with the French. Their
futility, as well as allied weakness, were soon exposed when it was
found that one of the three divisions to be sent to Finland would have to
come from the western front. The transfer, moreover, would depend on
Norwegian and Swedish consent to the passage of these 'volunteers'
across neutral territory.

Canadian troops, accustomed to cold, snow, and northern terrain,
were considered perfect material for this adventure. On 7 February,
when we first got the news at Canada House of these plans, I wrote:
'The intervention will be on the approved Spanish-Italian model, with
very little attempt to disguise it. It will be prepared by emphasizing the
gravity of the news from Finland. What the Germans will do about it
remains to be seen. If they consider it endangers their iron ore supplies
from Sweden, they might go to any lengths.' But there was no need to.
The expedition was abandoned and Finland left to its fate. Scandinavia,
however, remained the focus of interest for a blow against the Nazis.
This blow could be delivered by cutting off supplies of Swedish iron

ore to Germany. When the idea was first considered by the British War Cabinet, I noted, on 11 January:

The great issue at the moment in the conduct of the war is whether to stop German ships proceeding with Swedish iron ore through Norwegian territorial waters. The excuse would be the use of those waters by German subs; the reason, it would cut Germany off during the winter from her supplies of iron ore. The dominion high commissioners have been telling Eden the proposal is a most unwise one; that whatever advantage would accrue from stopping the iron ore would be more than neutralized by the Nazi invasion of Sweden and Norway which would likely follow; to say nothing of the ill-will, and possibly resistance to the allied action that would be aroused in Norway and Sweden ... Eden has told the War Cabinet the views of the high commissioners. Chamberlain has decided to squash the proposal, though whether dominion views had anything to do with this or not, I don't know.

At the beginning of March the matter was brought up again, presumably by Churchill who continued to advocate action to prevent German use of Norwegian territorial waters as, in his words, 'a covered way' for war material. Once more Eden discussed the subject with the High Commissioners. They all remained sceptical, especially as aid to Finland was still under consideration which, if attempted, would require the tacit co-operation of Norway and Sweden. Their negative attitude was confirmed by all the dominion governments, except the Canadian. Mr King refused to take any view, even a personal one. Indeed, he was irritated that his government had been asked to express one. With an election campaign in full swing, and ministers scattered across the country in the search for votes, the government was in no position to give this important question the full consideration it required. Mr King was saved from embarrassment, however, when the British government again dropped the matter; but not for long.

At the beginning of April it was decided to close Norwegian territorial waters to German shipping. This would not only cut off German supplies of iron ore but might have the further result, still considered to be desirable, of opening up the war, presumably as the only way of winning it. This time the dominion governments were *not* consulted. My own reaction to this omission was mixed. I was indignant that, for all our boasted independence, we were not even told in advance about a decision which, as I put it, 'may conceivably result in Canadian troops fighting in Scandinavia within the next few months.' Yet I could hardly blame the British government, which already had so much evidence of Mr King's reluctance to give any opinion or become enmeshed in any way in these Scandinavian questions.

In any event the war was opened up and in a way which must have brought no satisfaction to those responsible. German reaction was swift, ruthless, and decisive. It was also unprecedented in the use of new techniques of war and for the violation of neutrality. This should have been a salutary warning of what was to follow. Denmark was overrun in a matter of hours, with no hope of help from outside. Norway was able to mount a sturdy resistance, but it was bound to fail without help from others. The British government decided to mount a combined operation of sea, air, and land forces against the Germans in Norway. It had already made preparations for such intervention if action to close Norwegian territorial waters resulted in German counteraction by invasion.

My diary for 8 April read:

Harry Crerar was telling me that he had a talk with Dick Dewing [Director of Plans at the War Office] who said that they still have troops on board ship ready to go to Scandinavia if they should be invited. The only chance for such an invitation is that the measures which the Allies are now going to take in Norwegian territorial waters result in drastic counteraction by the Nazis which would in turn force the Scandinavians to ask for help. I doubt that they would ever get such help in time, even if it should be invited.

There is only one British division in this country now sufficiently equipped for immediate action overseas. The Canadian division is next in line for active service and it is far from being ready. If three divisions were sent to Scandinavia, two of these would have to go from France. If the country knew this there would be an explosion; at least there *should* be.

Canada soon became directly involved in these developments, in both Norway and Greenland. The Canadian government proposed that it should assume responsibility for protecting Greenland, especially the cryolite mines in Ivigtut which were of vital importance for the Canadian production of aluminum. We were anxious to get there before the Nazis, or the Americans. The United Kingdom government welcomed the Canadian suggestion to 'occupy' Greenland, as they put it. They then proceeded to advise our government gratuitously on the desirability of telling the Americans in advance of the action proposed. The advice was contained in a memorandum to Canada House certain to make the worst possible impression in Ottawa. I persuaded Mr Massey to let me paraphrase it before sending it on in order to remove some of its more irritating language. I learned later that the original, which we kept at Canada House, was written by a senior official recently transferred from the Colonial to the Dominions Office. It was in a form to which he had no doubt become accustomed in communicating with North Borneo or British Guiana. The Greenland plan, however, was satisfactorily carried out and Canada looked after Ivigtut and the cryolite mines throughout the war.

The Norwegian situation was more important and more complicated.

From the beginning it was understood in London that a Canadian contingent might be included in any force sent to Norway. Nevertheless, on looking out of my office window across Cockspur Street at noon on 16 April, I was startled to see on the hoarding for the early edition of the *Evening Standard* the big red letters 'Canadians in Norway.' Within a few minutes I had a call from the Canadian Press wanting to know about this sensational story on which they had been scooped and about which they could get no information of any kind from Canadian Military Headquarters.

I knew that no formal decision had yet been taken in Ottawa to include Canadian troops in any expeditionary force to Norway and that there could not possibly be any Canadians there. So I said the story was 'poppycock' but that to make doubly sure I would check and call back. I immediately got in touch with General Crerar who had just returned from the War Office. To my amazement, he told me that under no circumstances was I to deny this report, for two reasons. Firstly, the War Office was anxious to deceive the enemy and make it appear that there were more forces in Norway than was the case. This may have seemed clever, but did not take into account a probable immediate denial from Ottawa. And second, though no Canadians were in Norway, they might be shortly, as a formal request for their deployment was to be made at a meeting with Generals McNaughton and Crerar set for later on that same day.

In World War I, a similar request for Canadian troops would have been, I suppose, almost automatically acceded to, but times had changed. There were several questions at issue, not all of them military. For that reason, I asked Crerar if McNaughton was going to deal with a formal request for the use of Canadian troops without referring it first to the Canadian government. He felt sure that General McNaughton would act on his own, because of the military urgency and because he felt he had full authority as commander to designate troops under his command to serve in combination with British forces at any time, if the military situation warranted. I noted in my diary:

If the whole thing turns out badly and they cannot drive the Germans out of Norway, then I would not wish to be in McNaughton's shoes if he agrees to the use of Canadians in this way without prior authorization from Ottawa.

General McNaughton had no such worries and agreed to the inclusion of a Canadian contingent in an operation against Trondheim which, it was hoped, would restore a rapidly deteriorating position in Norway.

On the evening of 17 April General Crerar showed me a telegram that was being sent to Ottawa to the effect that a Canadian detachment would be leaving for Norway on the next day for the first Canadian military operation of the war, and a daring one at that. I persuaded him to send this message through our office to ensure that the Prime Minister would see it at once, as important non-military considerations were also involved. The reaction was immediate. McNaughton's acceptance was confirmed, but the government was disturbed. Even if McNaughton himself had authority to make the decision, and this was a matter of opinion, the government insisted that it should have been informed immediately the idea was first suggested by the War Office.

This plaintive telegram was not well received by the General who exploded to me that evening about interference from those 'trying to run the war while 3000 miles away.' I helped him draft a conciliatory reply, however, which pointed out the difficulty of sending information to Ottawa in advance when events were moving so rapidly; and that a telegram on the 17th about a request made on the evening of the 16th surely was prompt action. Furthermore, to wait for the government's approval might well have held up an emergency operation which had to be planned and mounted in haste.

While the General's impatience was understandable, he would have been wise to have sent an immediate telegram to Ottawa once the possibility of a request for a Canadian contingent was first mentioned to him. He may have judged that, if he had done so, his power to make quick decisions later would have been fatally weakened. The government was not satisfied with the General's explanation, but no recrimination or protests resulted, since the military situation in Norway led to the cancellation of the operation against Trondheim. The Canadian contingent, frustrated and disappointed, returned to its Aldershot base from the port of embarkation.

The proper chain of command, however, and the precise authority of a Canadian commander confronted with such circumstances remained to be clarified. The problem at issue was how Canadian forces could be detached to serve in combination with British forces, under a British commander, whilst recognizing both the ultimate authority of the Canadian government and the immediate requirements of a military emergency. Ottawa doubted whether a Canadian commander overseas had authority to take action except when the military situation made this imperative in the course of operations actually in progress. His authority could not embrace a decision to send part of a Canadian division out of the country to initiate military action. This delicate matter, the reconciliation of civil and military authority, was made no easier to resolve when the forces were overseas but not yet in action, and when the government and the Commanding General had definite but not always similar views on the subject. The Norwegian episode was, in a sense, a dress rehearsal for the future. Partly because of this experience, the problem of authority was clarified, if not completely resolved, before the war began in earnest.

I wrote at the time in my diary, 30 April:

I have been hard at work most of the day on two memoranda. One was on the legal and constitutional position arising out of the application of the Overseas Visiting Forces Act. The Norwegian project has shown us our difficulties in this regard and I am making certain suggestions which should, I think, remove them. The other memorandum was on the question of wartime communication and consultation. I am suggesting that something should be done to get us out of our present situation where we have as much influence on the conduct of the war and not much more information about it than, say, Burma. Certainly, we have much less influence than we had in the last war. I am not sanguine about any results being achieved in this regard, as I know there are people in Ottawa who would prefer to be left in ignorance and without influence rather than agree to the setting up of some imperial machinery which might, in their suspicious minds, start a centralizing development which would continue after the war. So far as I am concerned, I dislike having our forces being considered as 'unpaid Hessians.'

I admit that I put our nationalist grievances too strongly and rather peevishly in this memorandum, but it was preferable, I think, to err on that side than on the other, if legitimate Canadian interests were to be protected. This became even more important – and difficult – when the western alliance came to include the United States.

The fact is that in an alliance of nations at war there is no way to prevent the big leaders, the big partners, from making the big political and strategic decisions. Canada was as much concerned to win the war as any other member of the alliance, and its own war effort and sacrifices were substantial. Nevertheless we were bound, at times, to subordinate political considerations of national interest to military factors. Yet if a government is to be politically acceptable to its people, it has to see that national interests are protected, even in wartime, and that an appropriate national control over its own fighting forces is maintained. This means maintaining their unity and separate identity under national command, except when a military emergency or prior agreement dictates otherwise. The government also must insist on full consultation and information on all matters of concern to it, except, again, when this is impossible for valid military reasons.

I shall have more to say about these matters when I write about my work in Washington. I believe that the Canadian government in World War II was successful, on the whole, in reconciling its international responsibility to the common cause with its national responsibility to its own people. This success may have been made somewhat easier by Mr King's realization, as the war continued, that insistence on participation in top-level decisions of high strategy and direction would mean that a greater war effort and more expenditure by Canada might be expected to follow. As Dr Skelton once put it: 'If you wish to call the tune, you have to pay the piper.' There were occasions, of course, when the swift movement of events, political or military, made exchange of information, let alone consultation, impossible. The offer that was to be made in June 1940 of political unity with France made by Churchill as a last desperate effort to keep France in the war was one such occasion. The dominions who were directly and deeply concerned with the effect on them of the acceptance of this offer did not even know about it. But this was inevitable in the circumstances. Far less easy to understand and to accept was the kind of decision made by the British government to retaliate for the shackling of prisoners taken by the Nazis at Dieppe without any consultation with the government of Canada, though nearly all the prisoners were Canadians. But I anticipate.

The Norwegian disaster should have been a warning, as well as a shock, politically and militarily. As for the former, it showed that neutrality and rigidly correct international behaviour gave no immunity from Nazi attack. On the military side, it proved that the Nazis had learned much from World War I and were not going to rely for success on obsolete concepts of tactics and strategy. These, however, still greatly influenced thinking in the British and French war establishments, and the complacency, which should have been shaken by the events of April, persisted.

There was an amusing footnote to Canada's association with this Norwegian misadventure. When the War Office thanked General McNaughton for his willingness to send a Canadian detachment to Norway, the letter did not give even the correct designation of the Canadian infantry regiments detailed, which were cited as 'the Princess Pats Connaught Light Infantry and The Edmonton.'

Humour was not always so easily found amid complacency and punctilio. Earlier in March I had experienced more depressing evidence of the pedantic approach. A Canadian military party had been invited to go to the western front on a 'Cook's tour.' The High Commissioner agreed with the suggestion that I should join the party as a civilian observer from Canada House. I was delighted at the prospect of an exciting break from the heavy work of the office. The War Office decided, however, that a civilian should not be allowed to travel across the Channel on the leave boat with the military party and that I would have to make my own arrangements to reach Calais by the ordinary commercial Channel steamer. I could then join the party at Arras. I decided that this wasn't good enough and that, unless I could be included from the beginning as a member of the group, I would not go. I had no intention of going through all the red tape of securing a ticket, an exit permit, French francs, spending five or six hours travelling from London to Calais and another two or three motoring through the blackout to Arras, reaching there in the deep night to join our soldiers. I phoned our Military Headquarters to say that they could leave me out.

On the return of the Canadian party to London I was interested to see the official report of the visit. They had been most hospitably treated, skilfully briefed, and shown what was likely to create the best impression. Their report reflected the optimism of their hosts on the strength of the western front and tended to support the official British and French view: 'If only the Germans would attack!'

I got, however, a very different private and personal report from a friend who was on the mission, Colonel Burns, as he then was, who was later to have such a distinguished career in national and international service. I had learned to respect the independence and wisdom of 'Tommy' Burns' military judgment so I was impressed, and depressed, when he told me that he was profoundly disturbed at what he had seen. The French seemed permanently and comfortably installed in their Maginot Line which they considered, with some reason, to be impregnable. It could be outflanked, however, as indeed it would soon be when the Germans attacked to the north of it, where the French relied for defence, on the terrain, on second-class troops, and on Dutch and Belgian neutrality. Burns told me that this reliance would soon be exposed as foolish and fatal. He even pointed out on the map precisely where the attack would take place and he was right. As for the British, they had not done nearly so much as they should have during the winter to prepare for an attack, but they had certainly established themselves comfortably. Burns thought that, once the Germans moved, they would break through the northern front with ease and the Maginot Line would be left untouched, to be outflanked and fall later without resistance.

It was a sombre but, as it turned out, an accurate picture – but not one for public showing.

❦

The Norway venture, however, had important political consequences, even if its military warnings were largely ignored. The defeat was a serious blow to Mr Chamberlain and strengthened the conviction that he was not strong and decisive enough to be a wartime prime minister. The demand grew that he should be replaced, and that with him should go all the Men of Munich.

At the club, our favourite subject of political discussion centred on how much longer Chamberlain could hang on and who would take his place. I noted one such talk in my diary for 1 May, when Chamberlain's position was very shaky:

We speculated on who would take the place of Chamberlain and came up against the usual blank wall ... Hume Wrong suggested that it might be necessary to call out old Lloyd George and make him head of the government, for a time at least. The fact that this suggestion was not received with the amazed incredulity which it would have aroused three months ago is, perhaps, the best indication of not only the weakness of the present Prime Minister but also the lack of agreement on any successor.

I had discussed the same subject with the High Commissioner a few days earlier. He admired and respected Neville Chamberlain but now agreed that he would not do as the leader of a nation in arms. He then asked the inevitable question, 'But who is there to take his place?' 'Winston Churchill' was my answer. His total rejection of this rash suggestion was emphasized by the incredulous tone in which he repeated 'Winston Churchill!'

After Norway, however, the words 'Chamberlain must go' were more and more often followed by 'Winston must take over.' Churchill, of course, was already active and influential in the government as First Lord of the Admiralty. He seemed happy and content in his old post and his sense of loyalty rejected any temptation to manœuvre as Lloyd George did in World War I to replace the Prime Minister.

He was giving the service to his chief which he was soon to demand of others. Furthermore, while the eyes of the nation were more and more turned toward him, there was still questioning as well as invitation in the glance. The naval war had not been without mishaps which recalled Churchill's misadventures in World War I; misadventures, as I have always believed, which might have been triumphs had his plans been adequately supported. Indeed they showed at that time strategic imagination the absence of which in other leaders led to the horrors of the years of trench warfare with advances by yards and daily body-counts by thousands. Yet Churchill still suffered from these earlier mishaps and from his chequered and unsteady political record in the twenties and thirties.

Although the succession remained uncertain, Chamberlain's own position became untenable after the sitting of the House of Commons on 7 May. I watched that debate from the gallery. It was one of the most dramatic ever held in a chamber where great drama was common. I reported it as follows:

I took the afternoon off to go to the House of Commons to listen to the beginning of the debate which may conceivably decide the fate of the government. I don't think I have ever seen the House quite so crowded. We were sitting on top of each other in the gallery, while the members were all over the floor below. I sat there for six hours. Chamberlain was Chamberlain – sure of himself, unperturbed by recent developments, calm and, in his own way, vigorous. He got a bad reception, however, from the House. There was a moving speech from Sir Roger Keyes, who is almost inarticulate but was very convincing by his sheer sincerity. Amery was extremely good, I thought; one of the best speeches I have listened to in the House of Commons. His peroration was something to remember when he quoted Cromwell's remarks on the dismissal of the Long Parliament: 'In the name of God, go!' He pointed an accusing finger at the Treasury Bench as he almost hissed out this last sentence. The effect was somewhat reduced, however, as there was only one minister on that bench at the time, Sir Kingsley Wood, and he didn't seem very interested, no doubt because he was already about to go. I left about 9 o'clock and at that time it was doubtful whether the government would be seriously affected by the debate. Tomorrow will tell.

It did not, for on that day the Germans attacked in the west, and the centre of interest and concern shifted for the time being to France. On 10 May I wrote:

While the difficulty in Paris is to prevent a Premier from resigning, the difficulty in London is to get one to resign. Dick Law, who has had a great deal to do with the development of opinion in the House of Commons against Chamberlain, dropped in to see me this afternoon and told me that the political situation was still confused owing to the development of the military situation, which may give the government a few days more life. Chamberlain, however, has agreed to resign and the Labour people are deciding tonight whether they will come in to the National government under another leader, presumably Churchill. Dick said he was talking to Churchill this morning, who was complaining that for twenty years it had been said of him that, though he had courage, audacity, and energy, he had no judgment; and now it was being said of him, in connection with Norway, that while he showed judgment, he showed no courage, audacity, nor vigour. Dick also said that Churchill told him that he didn't wish to be Prime Minister. I suppose all men say that at times like this.

The announcement of the all-out German assault – blitzkrieg, as we learned to call it – which was in the form and place predicted by Colonel Burns, was at first greeted with greater relief than alarm. A generation which remembered the falling waves of attackers over those same fields in World War I might be pardoned for thinking that the allied armies would mow down the enemy and end the war before it could bog down into years of trench crouching and crawling. I noted the circumstances in which I heard the first news of the German attack:

Well, the war has at last really begun. I nearly always listen to the 8 o'clock news from the radio in the flat above, while reclining peacefully in bed. This morning, however, I couldn't hear it, the reason being that the Germans were on the move in Belgium and Holland, were over France and possibly over England, and therefore the BBC had weakened its wavelength. I am writing this at noon and everything is still indistinct. Mr Massey came back from an early meeting at Downing Street and says that there is almost a feeling of relief there that the thing has begun. Harry Crerar was in and he says that the War Office feels the same. The British Expeditionary Force is moving into Belgium this afternoon, and I do not think the Germans will have the walk-over there that they enjoyed in 1914. At the same time, it looks as if they have created complete confusion in Holland. The report has just come in that they have invaded Switzerland. Harry was with me when it arrived. This is not yet confirmed, but he echoed my thoughts when he said it would be a rather good thing if it were true. From a purely selfish point of view, the more Neutrals we get in this war now, the better.

A long telegram in from Rome reports an interview between Ciano and the Ambassador in which the former was very reassuring. It seems that Italy will now sit back and see how the Blitzkrieg gets along. If the Germans make headway they will stab us in the back at once. If not, they will remain neutral and ask later for their reward for being good boys!

There was, of course, violent indignation that once again 'brave little Belgium' was not to be saved from the violation of a scrupulous neutrality and that this time brave little neutral Netherlands was to join her in the sacrifice. Looking back now, it is hard to understand why anyone should have believed that neutrality could have protected these countries from Hitler. Yet this neutrality had been so meticulously observed, even after the experience of Denmark and Norway, that both governments refused to discuss plans for possible defence co-operation with Paris and London up to the very eve of invasion.

The first feeling of optimism soon gave way to surprise, then alarm, then shock, as the German blitz tactics developed with such quick and dramatic success. We waited, with hope gradually turning to dismay, for the counter-attack from the invincible French army under its great leader, General Gamelin. It never came, as the enemy raced on and familiar names began to appear in the communiqués, bringing back memories: Arras, Amiens, the Somme, Boulogne, Calais – and finally Dunkirk. It was hardly possible to believe that the French army had been routed, that the British had been cut off from them and were retreating to the Channel; that a new front could not be established; that Paris had fallen; that the aged and weak Marshal Petain had formed a government to sue for a peace of capitulation. My own diary expressed, for me, the emotion and shock of those terrible days:

The whole thing still seems unbelievable; that the much-vaunted French army would fold up; that the lauded Gamelin was no good and some of his army commanders worse; that Germans could wander at will in parts of France which they couldn't reach in four years in the first war; that they could take towns without difficulty on which British communications depended; that they can now look across the Channel from Boulogne; well, it just doesn't seem possible. What about the doctrine of the impregnable defence? The trouble is, of course, our people were thinking in terms of conventional war; and the Germans in terms of revolutionary rashness based on air, tanks, and disintegration by treachery.

And again a few days later, 9 June:

This has certainly been black week with a vengeance – beginning on Monday when we listened to the 9 o'clock news telling of German advances; Italy's entry; Norman Rogers' death ... and ending with the tramp of Nazi troops up the Champs Elysees, the swastika flying over Versailles, and a German guard over the tomb of the French unknown soldier. The whole thing has been a nightmare. Sometime in the distant future it may be called the week that changed the world. But in the midst of it I have had too much to do to worry about history.
    If the French cease organized resistance what happens next? Can we get their government, and above all, their air force and navy to carry on, possibly from North Africa? If so, we can give the Germans a warm time even yet; especially if the Americans come across with supplies and equipment as they are beginning to do. But if France makes the best peace she can – folds right up – what then? Will the USA come to our help, alone? If not, what do we do then? Follow Churchill to the last beach, the last hill, the last town, the last colony? People here are in the mood for resistance to the end. But they haven't been attacked yet.
    Meanwhile they are looking pathetically across the Atlantic; but not to Canada! At times I think they are rather overdoing this 'appeal to America' business. Having messed around with their own defence for nine months of war and for years before that, they are now making a great clamour for salvation by US help. The only thing that justifies such a clamour is 100–110 per cent effort on their own part. And at last that effort is being made. But is it too late?

During those dreadful June days it was difficult to keep up with events; for some it was impossible. I recall lunching one day shortly before the collapse of France with a friend at The Travellers and expressing some gloomy views. I was chided for being too pessimistic and was told to remember that the British always won the last battle. I finally exploded at this attitude which seemed to me to be not calmness in the face of crisis so much as a silly smugness in the face of catastrophe. 'One day,' I replied, 'you people will lose a battle and only then realize it was the last one.' My friend's reply ended all further discussion of the matter: 'But, my dear chap, if it was the last one, we wouldn't lose it.' I was better able to appreciate this attitude in the testing and terrible times ahead than at that particular moment.

However stiff the upper lip, the British did in fact realize that they had lost more than a battle, that they had lost a campaign, and were in danger of losing a war. They were aroused. They now knew that a tremendous struggle for survival was ahead. They also knew they had a leader for that struggle. Churchill was in charge, John Bull incarnate. He seemed to glory in the awful responsibility that now was his. His powerful personality, his inspired words, began to rally the British people to the task ahead; to give them that pride and defiance in defeat which, to adapt a quotation from another time of crisis, was to save themselves by their efforts and the world by their example. From Churchill: 'We are now alone' became not a cry of despair but a shout of defiance. His new government gave new hope, largely because it had a new leader. Churchill himself made the difference. Looking ahead further than was necessary or perhaps advisable at this critical time, I noted:

My impression of Churchill's government is that it is going to be a good war government but I shudder to think of the PM himself, Lord Lloyd, and Duff Cooper at the peace conference. However, the main thing now is to win the war and this government is certainly a step in the right direction so far as that is concerned.

It was at this grave moment that another name, de Gaulle, began to appear. It belonged to a man who was to do for France, in reviving and rallying its spirit, what Churchill did for England. One bright ray of hope in the gloom was the rescue of so much of the British army from capture in France. The British Expeditionary Force had been split from the French and had fought its way to the Channel where it was surrounded and seemed doomed. Then came the miracle of Dunkirk. What a time it was to be in Britain, with the people of that beleaguered, but now aroused and undaunted island!

I have one personal memory of Dunkirk. Charles Ritchie, my colleague and friend at Canada House, and I shamelessly exploited our contacts where they mattered, to wangle the various passes and permissions required to get to Dover at the height of the evacuation. An unbelievably calm Channel in the perfect summer weather, the great work of the navy and RAF, and the organization of the most heterogeneous collection of craft and volunteer sailors ever assembled was resulting in the steady removal of ever more soldiers from the beaches in France to the homeland.

It was at the very height of this amazing operation that Charles and I set off in my Chevrolet for Dover on a lovely Sunday morning in early June. We reached the harbour, in spite of the removal of all road signs and other identification marks, done presumably in the hope that the German invaders would get lost on the way to London. Cleverer than Nazis were expected to be, we found Dover harbour, though we were stopped by military police more than once, who examined our credentials with special care when they heard my transatlantic accent. Ritchie, fortunately, spoke good Oxford English!

At Dover we reported, as instructed, to the office of the chief naval officer. There had been stories in the newspapers that volunteers were needed to man the 'little boats' and so we thought that perhaps two sturdy inexperienced landlubbers might be required at that particular moment for a rescue trip across the Channel. The officer to whom we made known our heroic intention was singularly unimpressed. It seems that we were redundant and only our official papers prevented us being turned around and sent back to London at once. As it was, we were told to go down to the quay if we wished to see what was going on and keep out of the way.

A lot was going on, and it was intensely interesting to watch. Every kind of craft from small boats to naval destroyers and excursion steamers would come in crowded with troops, dock and transfer the remarkably cheerful Tommies to the trains alongside. Two sights remain vivid in my memory. A large Thames garbage scow unloaded a hundred or so German officer prisoners, mostly airmen. It was the only invasion of Britain during the war and it was comforting. There must be some hope if the British could evacuate not only their own men, but German officers as well.

The other sight was a British destroyer pulling in a French one which had been cut almost in half. An hour or so later we saw this wounded destroyer again. It had been secured against the dock. French sailors were lounging on the deck and four of them were huddled with smiling fascination over some postcards which I had to believe were 'feelthy.' This also was comforting; to realize that though the French had been defeated, their morale remained firm and on unshakeable foundations.

In the summer evening, we left Dover and the Channel to find our way back to London. As we drove through the streets of the old town, the people were going to evensong, and children were still playing in the streets. The town, away from the docks, seemed just as it was in happier times; quiet, with a Sunday drowsiness, quite unflustered by the fact that a few miles across the water the enemy were looking at their chalk cliffs, the guns were firing, and the bombs dropping as the drama of Dunkirk was played out and a disaster barely averted.

We returned to London strangely consoled and with some feeling of security.

The Commonwealth now stood alone to face a Nazi Germany, triumphantly bestriding Europe; seemingly invincible on land, dangerous under the sea, and powerful in the air. True, the spirit of France was kept alive by de Gaulle, but French military power, on which we had relied so much, had gone. The United States was sympathetic and its economic and financial assistance was important, but this would not win the war. Indeed, while one could continue to insist 'We will not lose,' it was difficult to put much conviction behind the words, 'We are bound to win.' Yet at this critical time, in these depressing circumstances, and in spite of the dismaying state of Britain's defences, Churchill had the courage and the nerve to move troops, including armoured formations, to North Africa where they were to scatter the Italian army while the navy routed Mussolini's ships on his 'mare nostrum.' With this kind of faith to inspire them, the people could still hope. They never gave up, whatever the odds against them. It was, indeed, their 'finest hour.'

Nor did the British lose their sense of humour. In the darkest days of June 1940 there was a sharp controversy on whether or not movies and all other forms of entertainment should be closed. Britain was in mortal peril and invasion seemed certain and imminent. But the *Daily Express* reflected public opinion accurately when it came out strongly against this timorous proposal with the deathless words: 'We shall all fight the better for an occasional glimpse of Ginger Rogers' legs.'

It seemed as if they would soon have the opportunity to fight, for surely the German momentum of victory would soon take the Nazis across the Channel. The first invasion since 1066 was in the offing. The danger and dimension of this threat were something new in British history.

ᏩᎦ

For the Pearsons, there was a hard decision to make. My wife, on her return to London, apart from looking after our home, had been active in war work. She was happy in that work and comforted by the knowledge that the children were safe and well cared for in Winnipeg. But the disaster in France and the apparent imminence of an invasion of England created a new situation. She and her two friends, Joyce Wrong and Verse Crerar, had no doubts about the future as it concerned them. They would stay and join every other man, woman, and child in this beleaguered island, in obeying the Churchillian command to stand firm and resist the invader. To this end, and to their husbands' mixed feelings of dismay and amusement, they were learning to use a revolver; and to be ferocious Amazons when the parachutists dropped from the skies and the tanks rumbled up the streets. The husbands, however, believed strongly that the wives should join their families in Canada, and so decided. It was one thing for us to decide; it was something else to have them accept our decision! My wife and I argued long and hard over this. At last she reluctantly accepted my view that her first duty was to be with the children, even if all her instincts and wishes demanded that she stay with her husband.

It was hard to say goodbye again, at this time and in this crisis, and to see my wife leave with Joyce Wrong; Verse Crerar had gone on ahead. Mrs Pearson got back to Canada safely, but, to the amazement of Mr Wrong and the chagrin of Mrs Pearson, Mrs Wrong turned up at Roehampton the very next day. At the last minute she had changed her mind, disobeyed instructions, had her luggage taken off the ship, and took the first train back to London. Even though her children were older than ours and family circumstances were different, my wife felt that she had been badly let down. She naturally resented her companion's return to London to share with a husband the drama and peril of the days ahead, while she sailed away. So, for the next year, I lived with the Wrongs while my wife settled down resignedly with the children in a small house in Ottawa to await my return; a return that at the time seemed remote.

OTTAWA INTERLUDE

At first, it looked as if I would not be long in our London home. The immediate future seemed grim. England on the ground seemed quite defenceless. But not, thank God, in the air or on the sea. Indeed, with the Expeditionary Force having lost so many men and virtually all its equipment in France, and with the home forces neither fully trained nor equipped, almost the only troops in a state of readiness to meet an invasion were Canadian; and they were few. A brigade of the First Division had moved in June across the Channel in a last desperate effort to help keep the fight going in France but had returned almost at once, fortunately with its equipment intact. The division then took up a position along the Channel, as part of a very thin line of defence against a land invasion by a victorious and powerful army.

Home Guards drilled on every village green or city square, with rheumatic and bemedalled old generals in the ranks and retired sergeant majors barking at them. It was a gallant and impressive expression of the nation in arms. The Royal Air Force, including some Canadians, saved us from having to discover whether it would have had any effect whatever against the kind of armoured invasion that had overrun France. The Battle of Britain, fought by legendary young heroes, backed by a totally united people, under the inspiration of Churchill's words, was about to begin.

At Canada House we were again busy with Canadians anxious to get home, and young Britishers bound for new homes in Canada. There were also many Canadian refugees from the continent. One evening,

Mr Massey invited a few of us to supper at the Dorchester, where he was now living, to welcome Pauline Vanier back from France. She had had an arduous and perilous journey by sea from Bordeaux, the final stage of many tragic days. (Georges was still in France.) She was exhausted, at the end of physical and nervous reserves, and distraught at the tragic collapse of the France which she so deeply loved. But this was also the France which, as many Britishers saw it, had failed to fight, and after ignominious surrender, had made peace with the Nazis. There was a slight echo that evening of these feelings. Then over the radio we heard the true voice of France in General de Gaulle's cool but ringing defiance from London of all those across the Channel, French or Germans, who would betray and destroy his country. It was a memorable moment.

The summer and early autumn days went by, warm and sunny. The country never looked more beautiful, or London more worth defending than during those critical weeks. We did not fully grasp it at the time, but it *was* being defended, and an invasion prevented by the Royal Air Force which was mocking Göring's boast that his Luftwaffe would quickly drive it out of the skies.

It was eerie to sit in the garden at home and watch the Spitfires and Hurricanes streaking over from an air station not far away to intercept 'bandits' over Kent, or even to watch dogfights directly overhead. It was more disturbing to be around when bombs began to fall, although until the night bombing some weeks later, marking the victorious end of the Battle of Britain, there was little danger and not much damage to Londoners, except in the East End dock area. The Germans concentrated on air fields, air factories, and radar stations. They were dangerously near to a decisive success in putting them out of action. How near, of course, the British people did not then know. I did, because I had access to daily reports which showed what was happening.

The people of London seemed characteristically unexcited and carried on as normally as possible while their future was being decided. A typical display of British sang-froid was the BBC treatment of the 9 o'clock news on the crucial day of the Battle of Britain, the day when the issue was virtually determined by the huge German losses suffered. The announcer began, in calm, precise Oxford English: 'This is the news read by Horace So and so. The weather promises to be uncertain tomorrow with the prospect of rain as a depression moves slowly eastwards from Iceland. Today the RAF shot down 189 enemy planes in an impressive victory.' There was no sign of emotion or even special interest. It was a contrast to turn the dial to a German station and listen – there was, of course, no restriction on doing so – to the ravings of 'Lord Haw-Haw' out of Berlin.

I described my own feelings and activities during this great air battle in a letter home:

This has been quite a week but, anyway, the invasion hasn't come off, even if the bombs have. We rather thought the Nazis might try it last weekend but, if they had intended to, the combination of a break in the weather and the battering of the invasion bases by the RAF must have stopped them. If no invasion does take place, the feeling will be a mixture of relief and disappointment. The reason for the relief will be obvious; at the same time, an invasion defeated and thrown back into the sea would be a great tonic.

You will be amused at how we spent the hours on Sunday during which the 'greatest air battle of all time' was taking place. Roger Makins [a friend in the Foreign Office] had come out for some golf with Hume, Joyce, and me. As the alert went we were sitting down to a late lunch at Roehampton Club. Then about 3.00 we teed off. Just as I was about to drive, my caddy, a picturesque old chap, advised me to keep well over to the right: 'slice more than usual, Sir, because there is a time bomb buried over on the left of the fairway, by that red flag.' So I gave my slice free rein – and kept over to the right so successfully that I almost hit a gent in front of the polo house. Personally, I don't think it was a bomb at all; merely an unexploded AA shell. But erring on the side of caution is, no doubt, wise in these circumstances .

Our match progressed without incident for a few holes when suddenly we discovered an additional bunker in the form of a bomb crater on the fifth fairway and then another and deeper one right in front of the eleventh tee. As if golf isn't a difficult enough game without these extra war hazards, including the noise of bombs and anti-aircraft fire. We had a lot of fun. Every time I heard any signs of aerial activity I would put on my tin helmet which I had strapped to my bag, not so much as protection against falling shrapnel as to improve my score by forcing me to keep my head down.

Some time later after the bombing had become heavier, the Department, with its constant regard for the Canadian taxpayer, decided to save money at our expense. The pretext was that the dislocation and difficulties of war must have cut down official entertaining; therefore the allowances we now had for that purpose should also be cut. It seemed to me a singularly ill chosen time for this decision, and I expressed my feelings as delicately as I could in a letter to Norman Robertson in the department:

Dear Norman,
Just a few words on last week's sequence of exciting events.
Monday, August 12th
British official figures show cost of living up 33%.
Tuesday – breakfast
No eggs (3/ – dozen).
Tuesday – 11 am

Notice from landlord that rent is due (no reduction).
Tuesday – lunch
Three Canadian soldiers to lunch (no reduction).
Wednesday
Letter from my wife to effect that it is expensive to maintain household in Canada (including keeping 3 children not our own).
Thursday
Air raid shelter for 1½ hours during day.
Friday
Suburban station next to mine hit by bomb in evening – streets nearby machine-gunned.
Saturday
Cable from External: 'Your allowances are cut by 10%.'
Sunday
Cable from External [after a heavy night bombing]: 'You are all much in our minds.'
PS Please get us out of your minds at once. We don't want another cut.

The bombing of the West End and the suburbs was comparatively light in the early weeks, compared with the damage done to the East End with its docks, its industries, and its crowded slums. It seemed unfair that it was the poor in those districts who suffered most. I remember vividly a tour of that part of London, made with the High Commissioner and British officials on Sunday, 22 September. There had been heavy bombing on Saturday and we wished to see how much damage had been done and how the people were bearing up. I made notes of that sad inspection:

One spot will remain in my memory. A small lane – Alice Street – had been destroyed, though the front walls of most of its 20 houses or so remained standing. On the wall of a centre house of the block was a small shrine – a memorial to the 'Men of Alice Street who fell in the Great War.' It was a simple home-made memorial, a wooden plaque with the names of nine men. Above these was a glassed-over triangle for flowers, and underneath the motto: 'Give us peace in our time, oh Lord.' Alice Street was a ruin, every house had been hit, every pane of glass and doorway shattered, but that little shrine was untouched. Its pathetic expression of a hope now vanished was intact, the glass not even cracked.

Our return journey was by the south side of the river, where the damage, though bad enough, was not as great as on the north bank. We crossed the Thames again by the Tower Bridge, noticed that a bomb had fallen into the Tower moat, and that a number of buildings in the City proper had been hit. Going further west, the Sunday crowds were still feeding the pigeons in Trafalgar Square, and at Marble Arch soap-box democracy was in full swing a few yards from the bomb crater where many had been killed the other night.

When the stepped-up and indiscriminate night bombing of London and other cities began in October it meant, although we did not know it at the time, that Hitler had replaced his project of invasion with the hope of destroying by terror from the air Britain's resolve to continue the war. All it did, of course, was to strengthen that resolve. The British people do not give in to terror. Their qualities of calmness, stoicism, order, and discipline, and their confidence in winning through in the end (so irritating over that luncheon at the Travellers' Club), stood them in good stead now.

Life became more difficult and dangerous. Yet the spirit of the people was never better, their morale never higher than in those weeks of night bombing. There was no sign of panic. Instead, there grew up a sense of solidarity, a community of suffering and sacrifice, and cheerful co-operation. There was the attitude you find in the face of a common danger, and which unhappily dissipates when the danger is past and you return to the competitive, acquisitive society where men are unequal and insecure.

I tried to convey this feeling of determined solidarity in one of those Michael Macdonald BBC broadcasts which I was sending to Canada by short-wave. A brief sample on 21 November is typical:

This has been a mixed week in London, so far as the subject which interests us most is concerned. I mean air raids. We've had our rough and noisy nights – and others calmer and quieter. There was one when the sirens didn't go off at all. Believe me, that's news. Our fortune, bad or good, in regard to night bombing, seems to have a good deal to do with the weather. We're lucky it's getting pretty bad now that winter is on us.

A year ago, when I left my office in the black-out (which begins at all too early an hour in winter) – I'd look at the sky, and if by some chance it was clear and moonlit I'd thank my lucky stars and decide it mightn't be a bad idea to dine in town and go to a movie or show. Now, a clear sky, stars, and, what is worse, a moon, cause mutterings of disappointment and apprehension. But if it's wet and murky, or even better, if a London fog has descended on the city, you heave a sigh of relief as you pick your way home because that means, probably, a quiet, or at least a quieter, night.

And if the night starts off quiet, then it's always a burning question with many whether to stick to the bedroom on the top floor or, playing safe, to descend to the coal cellar – now reinforced and made into a nice, comfortable shelter. I'm a bed addict myself. I'm afraid of getting a shelter complex, of becoming a tube-dweller where the real danger is not bombs, nor germs, but as one person put it last week, 'of going native and not coming up again till after the war when you will emerge with a large family and speaking another language.'

I wish I were Walter Winchell and could end this broadcast with some exciting flash; you know, 'five bombs have just landed by the microphone'; flash – that explosion was a Messerschmitt which has just crashed outside the door.'

I'm afraid I've nothing like that today, so I think I'll just wander out and get a bite at my favourite Soho restaurant – that is if it's still standing!

Under these conditions, life changed in many ways. Barriers were broken down. Britons began to speak to perfect strangers, even in the West End; the Cockneys of the East End were always chummy enough. At 'Fairacres' we finally got to know people in neighbouring apartments. If glass was breaking and walls were falling down during these weeks, so were many peacetime restraints and inhibitions.

The situation brought out the best in most people, though occasionally, for some, the worst. At our office, after successive nights of bombing, with disrupted transportation systems, it was difficult to get to work. Yet every person on the staff would turn up at the office at the regular time each morning, however bad the bombing or awful the weather. The effect on individuals was, of course, uneven and unpredictable. Some of those whom you would have expected to be the strongest and steadiest began to show signs of strain while others, normally timid and dependent, seemed to revel in the heavy going and the danger.

In the office there was a typist, a spinster in her fifties, who had always seemed nervous and insecure. Once the bombing began, she became a new person, perky, cheerful, and energetic; always ready to work late even if that meant trying to get home after the bombing began. We had also a Canadian girl in indifferent health, who was bombed out of her flat twice but on both occasions turned up at Canada House for work next morning on time and ready for the day. Then there was our 'Nelly,' maid of all work at 'Fairacres.' If Hitler had ever met Nelly, he would have had to realize that he could never bring these islanders to their knees, if only because it would never occur to them to adopt such a posture. Nelly, who had not, I admit, the brightest mind in London, lived out. One morning she came to work as excited as she ever could be. Two cottages near hers had been blown up in the evening: 'Do you know, sir, the rescue party, seven or eight hours later, found a canary still in its cage, chirpy and very much alive!' I asked her about the people, her neighbours, were they saved? 'I don't rightly know about them, sir, only the canary!'

We all, of course, had our bomb stories and the bomb bore became a garrulous new species. Aware of this danger, I venture to add, nevertheless, one more story.

Our most exciting time at 'Fairacres' was during one night about the middle of October. Some fire-bombs landed on the roof and on the garage and the porter's lodge. Things began to light up. This was the first good opportunity for those querulous old air-raid wardens, ex-admirals, professors emeriti and retired executives, to spring into action. For thirteen months now they had been badgering the tenants about infinitesimal 'chinks of light.' Indeed they had become so conditioned to thinking that chinks would lose the war that they seemed, or rather one of them did, unable to cope with a real fire. On this night I noticed flames behind a window in the Porter's Lodge. I noticed also that this warden who had always been rather pompous and authoritative, was standing fatuously below the window shouting, in a reaction by now no doubt automatic, 'Turn out those lights.' When I told him it was not a 'chink' but a fire, he agreed to do something about it. Meanwhile I had noticed two fire bombs burning on the flat roof of the main building. (Fairacres was a sprawling semicircle of apartments with only three stories.) I was about to go up the stairway with another tenant, armed with a stirrup pump, when the head porter halted us. He was a magnificent specimen, a retired Guards Sergeant Major, obviously in charge of this entire emergency. Ignoring our intention to save the main building and win a George Cross, he asked us, very politely, what we were up to. We paused to tell him that we were going up to the roof where a fire was beginning. 'Tenants, sir, are not permitted on the roof.' 'But there's a fire there.' 'I'm afraid it's the rule, sir. I'll deal with the fire.' And he did.

The horror, the brutality, the callousness of war were made cruelly evident by the bombing of London, Coventry, Amsterdam, Belgrade, Hamburg, Dresden, Kiev. Fighting men know that they have been selected, or have volunteered to kill or be killed. That has been war over the ages. But this time, and now for all time, there was no sanctuary for women and children, for the old and the helpless. This element of barbarism was enough to strengthen any man's resolve to do what he could to banish the horror and enormity of war, if he came through this one.

☞

Meanwhile, work went on at Canada House. Meetings were held and problems resolved; men and messages were sent to, and came back from, Ottawa. Some of the return traffic spurred us into new and urgent activity. One or two tested our sense of humour, something important to preserve those days. One of these messages came from the Prime Minister himself on the day following the bombing of Westminster Hall. It reached Canada House about ten at night marked 'Secret and Most Immediate.' Our instructions were that a telegram with those markings, if not sent to the High Commissioner personally, was to be dealt with by me at once. At this hour I was home, so our coding clerk phoned me from his eyrie at the top of Canada House. I could hear Spire's chuckle, 'This is a funny one, Mr Pearson, and I'm sorry to disturb you with it but orders are orders and it is marked "Most Immediate." ' I told him to read it. The telegram was from Mr King asking if it would be possible to get a stone or two from the ruins of Westminster Hall, reported as bombed the previous night. He wanted the stones for his own ruins at Kingsmere. This urgent and unusual war message having been delivered, I went back to chinese chequers with Mrs Wrong. But the request was not to be taken lightly. It came from a Prime Minister who had seized an opportunity to add to his own cherished, if symbolic, ruins some stones from the structure of the most honoured and revered of parliaments. Yet the Office of Works was now overwhelmed with repairs and reconstruction vital to the very life of London, and might take a jaundiced view of a suggestion to find, pack, and ship some shattered stones to gratify a Prime Minister across the Atlantic. I would not have been surprised if the request had been greeted with an immediate and indignant refusal. It was not, and this historic and heavy freight was shipped safely through the submarines to add a new distinction to Mr King's ruins at Kingsmere.

As always, new and unprecedented conditions brought about adaptations soon to become routine. London itself, after some uncertain first weeks, became amazingly well organized for the emergencies it had to face. The Air Raid Precautions organizations and the fire-fighting services functioned with a calm and courageous efficiency beyond praise. However heavy the enemy action, however great the destruction, transportation, communications, and essential services were maintained except for short periods after very heavy bombing. The taps ran, the lights shone, the water pipes were repaired, the unexploded bombs were defused, the holes were filled, the milk and even the newspapers were delivered every morning. The soldiers on leave had all the enjoyment and entertainment they sought, even if there was not the same feverish gaiety or the 'eat, drink, and be merry for tomorrow we die' attitude of those on leave from France in the first Great War.

The Canadian troops, increasing steadily in number, were becoming uneasy and impatient for action. They had come overseas to fight but they had known only the boredom of training and the restlessness of being so far away from home. There were difficulties with civilians, with girls, with the authorities over many things, though not more than was to be expected. This was especially true after the fall of France and the return of a brigade of the First Division following a tantalizing momentary taste of active service and a cancelled embarkation for the others. No wonder the morale of the troops was low. They were 'fed up.'

Our work at Canada House included the handling of complaints about the misdemeanours of the sometimes licentious soldiery. Some of these complaints came direct, some through the British authorities. Some were genuine and warranted redress. Some were grossly exaggerated to the point of blackmail. I remember one in this latter category. A father came to Canada House to protest the behaviour of two Canadian soldiers at Oxford. They had taken his virginal young daughter for a boat ride on the Cherwell. It was June; the river, with a punt and a pretty girl, could be enticing to active but lonely overseas soldiers. This, however, was no ordinary accusation. The two had navigated the punt under Magdalen Bridge where, it was alleged, they had stripped and raped the daughter. I agreed that this was lamentable and should be punished if the culprits could be identified and brought to justice. But the father went too far. He claimed that the soldiers had then pushed the punt ashore and fled with those items of his daughter's clothing which were marketable, telling her that they were going to sell them to a second-hand dealer. That charge I put in the blackmail category and indignantly rejected. No Canadian soldier, however wicked, would attempt to make a profit out of such a situation.

An experience of a different kind occurred when one day I received a call from a secretary at 10 Downing Street. It was during the tense period of imminent invasion when Nazi spies were thought to be everywhere, having been planted as respectable residents years before, or parachuted down the previous night. My Downing Street friend told me that a Canadian soldier had turned up with, as he claimed, important security information which he wished to give at once and personally to Mr Churchill. He was asked why he hadn't passed it on to his own military superiors who would be able to deal with it quickly. His reply showed the independence and healthy irreverence for the brass which characterized Canadian civilian soldiers. 'This,' he said firmly, 'is a very important matter, vital to the winning of the war and not to be entrusted to the military.' Naturally, they were impressed at Downing Street but persuaded the soldier to pass his information to the highest Canadian civilian authority in the land, the High Commissioner. I was warned that he was on his way to Canada House. Unhappily, he never turned up. I wish I had met him.

In the early part of 1941 the detailed negotiations between the United Kingdom and the United States took place, which concluded the Bases for Destroyers' Agreement. Our office took part in these negotiations because of Canada's responsibilities for the defence of Newfound-land, where the Americans proposed to locate some of the bases for which they were negotiating.

When, however, the UK and US governments first began to consider an agreement, there was no recognition of any Canadian interest which would justify Canadian participation in the talks. Newfoundland was merely lumped with the other British colonies affected, Bermuda and the West Indies. In spite of strong but too long delayed representations, we were unable to secure separate discussions on Newfoundland, to which Canada would be a third party. The Americans objected to Canadian participation in any form though they finally agreed that we should attend as observers when matters concerning Newfoundland were being considered.

The conference was not an easy one since urgent defence considerations had to be reconciled with those of longer-range political interest. How do you compare the need for fifty destroyers to meet a war emergency with a 99-year lease of your territory to a foreign government? The urgency, however, was great and after much bargaining an agreement was finally reached which did recognize Canada's interest in and responsibility for the defence of Newfoundland.

My diary gives the Canadian point of view. On 26 February I made this entry:

This conference is not going very well, as the Americans are taking advantage of British necessities and exploiting the situation, so it seems, in order to prepare the way for ultimate acceptance of their sovereignty over the territories in question. Our interest, of course, is restricted to Newfoundland. If the United States makes good its claim to certain rights and powers which it is proposing to exercise over Newfoundland, we would find ourselves in a rather difficult position. Unfortunately we are only observers at the Conference and cannot take a very active part. So far all that I have done [I was the Canadian observer] is to keep the High Commissioner and Ottawa informed of what has been going on and of the difficulties and changes in the situation. In return I have not had a single word from the department; if they are not worried, I don't know why we should be!

Ottawa, however, later did become worried by the US demand for rights and powers in Newfoundland, and returned to a suggestion made previously for a separate conference and agreement covering this off-shore island. We tried again to win UK support for our position but got nowhere. We had left our protest too late because the discussions were now coming, so the British hoped, to a reasonably satisfactory conclusion. But we persisted. My diary for 11 March reads:

This day was mostly taken up with trying to persuade the British government that there must be a separate agreement for the Newfoundland bases acceptable to and signed by Canada. We didn't get very far. The High Commissioner and I left the Colonial Office after a very unsatisfactory interview and went straight to the United States Embassy. The High Commissioner put the Canadian case very convincingly and clearly, but the most we could get out of Winant was that Canadian interests in Newfoundland should be recognized by notes to be exchanged at the time of the signing of the general agreement, between the governments of the United Kingdom, United States, and Canada; these notes to recognize Canada's special position in Newfoundland and (this in response to a suggestion from us) that if there were any conflict between the defence arrangements in the agreement and those of the Canada-US Joint Defence Board, insofar as Newfoundland was concerned, the latter should prevail. The Americans thought that this could be done and that by it we should accomplish the same purpose as if we had a separate agreement over Newfoundland.

The next day, 12 March, not having yet received any reaction from Ottawa regarding the proposal for an 'exchange of notes' to cover Newfoundland, we drafted such a document ourselves in order to have something ready in case it was needed. It was. The Canadian government, though most reluctant to abandon the idea of a separate agreement for Newfoundland, accepted the procedure of an exchange of notes, and agreed generally with our text.

The next step was to get UK and Newfoundland members of the conference to agree with the Canadian draft. On this I noted, 19 March:

Struggled with the Dominions' Office, Service Departments, and the Newfoundland delegation over our draft Agreement on Newfoundland. At times I almost felt that they were more suspicious of Canada in this matter than they were of the United States. Finally I got a bit impatient and put the question to the Newfoundland delegates bluntly as follows: 'After all, it is a very simple matter, whether you prefer to be raped by the United States or married to Canada.' Emerson replied that they would prefer the latter if they didn't feel that after the war was over they would be divorced! There is something in what he says. However, it is all settled now and we are simply waiting word that the Americans have also agreed to our draft.

My last diary reference on 27 March to this conference reads:

We signed the Bases Agreement and the Protocol this afternoon ... While we were waiting for the champagne to be brought in, to celebrate the occasion, Churchill paced up and down the Cabinet Room like a caged lion, puffing away at his cigar, occasionally stopping and bursting forth with an expletive of some kind or other. He is certainly showing no signs of mental or physical fatigue. When we finally got our glasses filled, the PM gave a toast, as follows: 'The King and the President of the United States.' Then, 'to the heroes of Belgrade' [a pro-Nazi government had just been overthrown there]. 'Long live liberty. To hell with tyranny. Blast it – off the record.' This sally was greeted with great applause. The PM then added, 'I said "off the record" not that I was ashamed of the sentiment but merely because the expression thereof might be considered a little vehement.'

As for the Agreement itself, I noted in my diary: 'No matter how much we may applaud it now, or toast it in champagne, it is a victory for the United States and means the beginning of the end of British rule in the West Indies.' Without Canada's intervention, it might also have made more difficult Newfoundland's entry into Confederation a few years later.

ॐ

On 28 January 1941, a cold wintry day in Ottawa, Dr Skelton, driving back to work after luncheon, slumped over the wheel of his car and died. He had worked himself to death and was as much a casualty of the war he so deeply hated, and had hoped Canada could avoid, as any soldier killed in action. He was the firm foundation of our department, at home and abroad. He was more. He was at the centre of all its decisions and of many of those of the government. He appeared to be irreplaceable. Of course, he was not – no man ever is – but his death left a gaping void. It had also an important effect on my own fortunes, for it brought me back to Ottawa.

I confess that I hoped to return as Dr Skelton's successor. I was the only officer of senior rank in the service who had served for any considerable time both in the department and abroad. My record seemed to have been satisfactory. It is true that Hume Wrong was senior to me in the service. He was also superior in intellect, though not, I believe, in ability to get along with people. But he had had no service in the department at home. There were also three senior French Canadians: Laurent Beaudry, Jean Désy, and Pierre Dupuy. I leave out Georges Vanier, as it was assumed he would go back to Paris as head of mission as soon as France was liberated. Laurent Beaudry was, I understood, not in line for the deputy's post, as he was reported to have no desire to take on that heavy responsibility. The other two, Jean Désy and Pierre Dupuy, had made it clear that they wished to remain in diplomatic posts abroad. Indeed, Dupuy, who was making quite a reputation for himself by his skilful and daring work as Churchill's liaison officer with Vichy, subsequently went to great lengths to avoid transfer to Ottawa, a place, presumably, which he much disliked.

These men were all fluently bilingual. I was not. I did not realize then as much as I did later what a grievous handicap this was to anyone who wished to make a career in the federal public service. It certainly did not prevent me from reaching the highest positions, as it would now, and rightly, but I came to feel self-conscious and defensive about my inability to be fluent in Canada's two official languages. I learned some French in Ontario schools, but this was woefully inadequate. French was not required in the modern history course at the University of Toronto. Nor was I pressed to remedy this deficiency during the years I worked in the department at Ottawa from 1928 to 1935. I did take lessons spasmodically and this, with the little I had learned earlier at school, enabled me to take a stumbling part in a French conversation; to understand it fairly readily, and to read it somewhat better. But this was inadequate for an officer of the federal service, especially in the foreign and diplomatic branch. My deficiency was my own fault, but it was regrettable that I was not told on entering the service that, if I hoped to advance in my career, I must become fluent in French within, say, three years. Conditions have now changed, and for the better. I am glad to have had something to do with making this change effective.

It may be that Dr Skelton was reluctant to insist that young English-speaking candidates for the department have, or secure, at least a working knowledge of French because neither he nor his first assistant deputy, nor, indeed, his minister, had any proficiency in the language. Moreover, the business of the department, as of every other department, was conducted almost exclusively in English.

Whatever the reasons, I was in 1941 a linguistically uneducated Canadian foreign service officer in London, hoping none the less to be chosen by the Prime Minister to be head of the department. Presumably my deficiency in French was not considered decisive because the man whom Mr King chose was no better qualified than I was in this regard.

Norman Robertson had joined the department as a third secretary shortly after I joined as a first. He had served in Ottawa with increasing distinction in positions of increasing responsibility. He had worked very closely with Mr King and Dr Skelton, particularly since the outbreak of war. His chiefs had come to rely on him greatly. He was close to them both and they were in a position to appreciate his work and his worth. It was, therefore, no surprise in Ottawa when he was made deputy minister. My diary for 27 February included the following paragraph:

This afternoon I receivd a letter from Norman Robertson, very friendly and apologetic, as he seems to think that if I had been on the spot I would have undoubtedly taken over Dr Skelton's work. He is worried because he had suggested six months ago to Dr Skelton that he, Norman, should come to London and I go to Ottawa for a time, but the suggestion was not proceeded with. He asked me how I felt about accepting one of the new South American legations. It seems I could go to the Argentine or Brazil as minister if I wanted to, but I don't want to. As Norman himself stated 'there is no shadow of doubt in my mind, or anybody else's, that your London job is bigger and more important than either legation.'

While I was disappointed at not becoming deputy minister, my disappointment was lessened by the fact that the Robertsons and Pearsons were the closest of friends. I was one of Norman's greatest admirers. I knew him to be as modest and kindly as he was erudite and wise.

One of his first acts was to ask me to return to Ottawa as his chief assistant. He had two things in mind. First, he thought that I was entitled to return home after long service in London, recently in the trying circumstances of war; I could rejoin my family and he knew that this meant much to me. Secondly, he may have felt that I had done well in London as second-in-command, looking after administrative and personnel matters in a large organization under difficult conditions; thus I could take this burden off his shoulders in Ottawa, a burden which, I knew, he did not like and in consequence bore with only partial success.

The first reason appealed to me. The family pull was strong. The second was much less convincing. I had no great desire to be in charge of departmental administration and no great aptitude for that kind of work. I would have preferred to stay at Canada House and in London, to both of which I was now deeply attached, than to take on work in Ottawa with little appeal to me. Robertson's letter, however, was soon followed by a message to the High Commissioner from the Prime Minister instructing him to send me back to Ottawa for a new posting. When the Foreign Office learned that I was going to fly back to New York, they asked me whether, as a 'King's Messenger' for one trip, I would carry a top secret brown envelope to be delivered at a certain room on a certain floor of a building in New York, the headquarters of British Security Co-ordination. I agreed.

I shall always remember this journey. I was flying from the war to peaceful, unharmed Canada; from battered and beleaguered London in the hour of her agony and honour to the safe, far-away city on the Ottawa River. I had left London the day after the heaviest and most damaging air raid of the war. When I drove to the airport fires were still burning fiercely and some buildings which had been hit were only a few yards from Canada House. That old structure, however, continued to escape serious damage. I was happy at the thought that I was getting away from all this, but saddened by the feeling that somehow I was deserting.

The contrast between that last night in London and my first exposure to a city not at war was staggering. As we flew over Lisbon, there were lights, actually lights! As we landed, we saw German and Italian planes. We went through, not military, but civilian inspection. On the way to the hotel, the shops, gaily decorated, displayed fruit and flowers and candies. Very strange! I had been met by a secretary of the British Embassy. While driving me to the Palace Hotel at Estoril, he warned me that it was the centre of Nazi and Fascist espionage. This made me very conscious of my brown envelope. I became more anxious after an experience on entering the hotel. The first person I saw looked familiar. With a start I recognized him as a German whom I had known in Geneva during the disarmament conferences, when he was a secretary in the German delegation. He had gone to Harvard, and had the accent and manners of a young, aristocratic Bostonian. He was a very friendly fellow. I was impulsively about to say 'hello,' and he seemed to share the same impulse, when suddenly I realized, as he may have too, who we were and where and when. We turned away, and it was just as well because my British escort, who knew his way around Lisbon, pointed him out to me later as one of the principals in the German intelligence services in Spain and Portugal.

My career as courier was off to a shaky start, but there were no further incidents. No Mata Hari dropped her handkerchief before me in the dining-room or at the casino. Nobody tried to snatch my brown envelope from under my pillow that night. I guarded it carefully during our stops at the Azores and Bermuda. On landing in New York I took a taxi at once to my destination and rode an elevator to the appointed floor of British Security Co-ordination. As I got out of the elevator I expected to be stopped and asked to produce my credentials; or, if not there, certainly outside the particular room where I was to hand over my envelope. Nobody bothered me. There was indeed a New York policeman in a chair outside the door of the office I was seeking. But he was dozing and ignored my entrance over his outstretched legs. Within the office a receptionist glanced at my credentials, signed for my envelope, thanked me, and said good-bye. This all seemed very casual for a secret service, a first impression of carelessness which I later found to be deceptive.

If not yet home, I was now on the North American continent. Next day I was in Ottawa, joyfully reunited with my family. How those children had grown! My loving wife concealed her emotions as is her wont; the deeper they were, the more concealment was required. She told me I needed a hair-cut.

I really *was* home!

☙

The department, of which I now became second-in-command, had greatly changed since I left in 1935. It was much larger, and more important in the Ottawa scheme of things. Its work at this time was, of course, largely concerned with the war. Norman Robertson was one of Mr King's closest advisers from the civil service on all matters related to the war, which by now meant almost everything. On most of the interdepartmental committees would be found an External Affairs representative, usually Norman or myself; with our Deputy very often the chairman. Through this interdepartmental mechanism most of the business of government on the official level was conducted. The committee members were nearly always from the same group of senior civil servants who had become personal friends as well as official colleagues. Indeed, they did a great deal of their work, and their thinking, in informal sessions over food or drink or both. The Chateau Laurier cafeteria and, in the summer, the Five Lakes Fishing Club became almost as important centres for discussion and decision as the conference rooms in the East Block. This was a closely knit group, and no government could have been more fortunate in the high quality of their service and in their devoted and untiring dedication. Nearly all of them were good friends of mine, and I fitted into the milieu easily and happily. I also enjoyed my association with the outside academics and dollar-a-year men brought in to help for the duration. Fortunately some of these 'temporaries' remained as permanent officials after the war and did their part in strengthening the high and well-deserved reputation of the Canadian Civil Service. The atmosphere was stimulating, the contacts agreeable, the activity engrossing. I was very content with my life and work, though I missed the frontline feeling of London and my former comrades there.

With other young activists in the East Block, however, I often became impatient with the Prime Minister's apparent lack of clear-cut purpose in directing Canada's war effort. He still seemed obsessed with ensuring that the British government would recognize our constitutional independence and our special internal problems. I have already written about these matters but I came more directly into contact with them now that I was again in the East Block in Ottawa.

Of course, I did not have now, any more than I had in London, the information and knowledge that the Prime Minister had. Nor was I aware, as he was, of all the domestic and international factors that had to be taken into consideration in long-range policy and planning. But I felt, as did many of my friends, that Canada's war effort was often obscured, even hindered, by a preoccupation with political and constitutional matters more appropriate for peacetime; that we were lost in the imperial scene dominated by Churchill. Indeed, we often longed for some proud and inspirational words from a Canadian Churchill. Mr King was wise, if often inscrutably so, and far-seeing; but he certainly was not Churchillian. Nor was Canada the tight little closely-knit island of Britain now under savage attack and fighting for survival. Yet surely, with the whole world in danger of Nazi domination, with freedom, as we knew it, in grave jeopardy, we did not have to be quite so defensive in Ottawa over the reaction in the country, and especially in Quebec, to every move that was made to strengthen and broaden our war effort. That is how it looked at that time, at least to some of us, as we tried to understand our Prime Minister's subtleties and apparent hesitations. This understanding was not made easier by his enigmatic and contradictory personality, with that combination of charming friendliness and self-centred calculation, of kindness and ruthlessness, of political vision and personal pettiness which so many who worked for him found disconcerting.

My immediate responsibility, however, was the effective working of the department, rather than the involuted policies of the Prime Minister. I was, after all, a civil servant, not a policy-maker, and I had much to learn about my new job after an absence of six years.

These years of foreign service had made me very conscious of the requirements and the difficulties of work in an office remote from headquarters. From personal experience I realized the necessity for the department to keep in closer touch with its officers abroad who cannot do their work effectively unless they are kept informed of what is going on at home. I was able to make some improvements in this regard. I was also given responsibility for much of the administrative and personnel work of the department, for which, as I have noted, Norman Robertson had little liking. While I have never thought of myself as a management expert, I was able to create a feeling of loyalty to an office or to an organization, to maintain good morale, and to get the best from those who worked with or for me. I have always considered this more important than technical organizational efficiency, or familiarity with form charts, flow sheets, and all the devices that now tend to substitute mechanics for man.

Much of my work was concerned with our wartime relations with London and, especially after Pearl Harbor, with Washington. My duties included problems of security and, in particular, the formation and development of a Canadian intelligence unit which worked closely with similar British and American agencies. Our unit was concerned with breaking enemy codes, not with the more glamorous work of snaring and shooting spies, but it did outstanding work in its own field.

The two most important developments in the war situation which occurred during what turned out to be my relatively short sojourn in Ottawa were, first, the entry of the USSR into the conflict on our side, and, later in the year, the attack by the Japanese which made the USA an ally. I doubt if ever before in history have two powers miscalculated so disastrously the consequences of a military attack, as Germany and Japan did at this time.

In Ottawa the sudden transformation of Russia into an ally caused some understandable bewilderment. I was a member of a board at that time, under the direction of the RCMP, which was responsible for domestic security. This meant, among other things, watching and, if necessary, interning suspects. These suspects included certain communist leaders who had followed the Moscow line even when it twisted to an alliance with Hitler. They therefore agitated against the 'imperialist' war and were interned in consequence. This, of course, all changed after 22 June 1941 when the USSR became 'our gallant ally' and whose sacrifices, in a very real sense, became our greatest hope of victory. The war suddenly became a people's war to the Canadian comrades and they grew zealous in its support. It seemed silly, therefore, to keep them locked up, let alone to continue adding to their number. But security authorities do not adapt easily to sudden changes. I recall arguing strongly in favour of new security policies, which recognized communism as a source of support, however temporary.

An equally important and dramatic change occurred on Sunday, 7 December when the Japanese attack on Pearl Harbor brought the USA into the war. I shall not soon forget that day. I was working in my office in the department when the first news flash appeared. I called home, to find that my wife had already heard. She had an amusing story of how someone else had heard, our old friend General Crerar, now chief of staff. He was out for an afternoon stroll in Rockcliffe and had dropped in to say hello. I was at the office and my wife was upstairs. But our daughter, Patsy, aged 13, welcomed him. She decided to entertain the General with casual conversation until her mother appeared. Her opening gambit had an immediate and startling effect. 'Wasn't that bad news, General Crerar, about the Japanese attack on Pearl Harbor, but at least it will bring the Americans in on our side.' The General leaped from his chair with an incoherent mutter of astonishment, fled precipitately and was seen no more that day by us or, I presume, by his family, as he no doubt arranged for summary court martials for his high-ranking Intelligence officers who had allowed a child to 'scoop' them.

A declaration of war by Canada soon followed. By now we had learned the technique. Earlier in June when the Germans invaded the Soviet Union they brought into the war Finland, Hungary, Roumania, and Bulgaria. In consequence action had to be taken to declare war on these new enemies. This meant, among other things, a number of orders-in-council. Mr King relates in his diary how he had been signing orders authorizing these declarations of war when the papers on Bulgaria appeared. He decided that he had declared enough war for one day and put Bulgaria aside for the time being. He never did get around to it again. This omission, however, was of such little practical importance in the prosecution of the war that it was never detected or rectified. Therefore in 1946 when the time came to join the others at the Paris Conference in making peace with Bulgaria we were in real trouble. How could we make peace when we had never declared war? We solved this problem simply. We merely took no part in the work of the Political and Territorial Commission of the conference dealing with Bulgaria. No one seems to have missed us.

By the time of the Japanese attack, we had acquired such technical efficiency in using our flexible constitutional machinery for declaring war that we found ourselves formally at war with Japan even before the United States – on the assumption, of course, that a cabled unsigned submission to the King is valid.

The entry of the United States as an ally greatly increased the importance of our mutual relations and multiplied our diplomatic and administrative contacts. New and more elaborate arrangements were required for the conduct of these relations and for the smooth working of our joint affairs. Fortunately, our official relationship had already become so close and cordial, with many personal friendships to facilitate it in both capitals, that essential new procedures could be made readily effective. We had to be careful here, however, as in London, to insist that we should be treated not as a subordinate to be ordered, but as an ally to be asked and consulted; an ally, moreover, that had been in the war from the beginning, as in World War I. If occasionally Washington acted as though Canada were another state of the union, we tried to be tolerant, realizing that our American friends, unlike the British, had not been educated to respect our national sovereign status – and our sensitivity. They too would learn this, under our firm but friendly teaching, or so we hoped.

The first wartime lesson of this kind was given to the American government through their minister in Ottawa, Mr Pierrepont Moffat, whom most of us in the East Block knew well and respected highly. The problem arose over our relations with Vichy France, and here we were at odds.

There was now a Free French mission in Ottawa which had the department's complete sympathy and support. For Vichy and all its works we had scant respect. The United States, however, with a projected invasion of North Africa in mind, were anxious to maintain a correct relationship with Vichy, and to avoid driving that government further into the German camp. For this purpose, de Gaulle and his Free French must be discouraged from taking any action against Vichy likely to disturb the delicate balance which Washington was trying to establish. This policy was all the more agreeable to the President and to the Secretary of State since they had already been alienated by de Gaulle's arrogant and difficult attitude.

It is probable, therefore, that Pierrepont Moffat viewed with some anxiety our close association with the Free French mission in Ottawa. There was no trouble, however, until Admiral Muselier descended on St Pierre and Miquelon and took over those islands for General de Gaulle. The Americans thought, wrongly, that this seizure had been made with the knowledge and approval of the Canadian government. Cordell Hull, a courtly but explosive southern gentleman, was particularly angry and tried to browbeat us into forcing the 'so-called Free French' (a phrase which made us as angry) from the islands and restoring them to Vichy. Mr Hull was informed through his minister in Ottawa that the Candian government would do no such thing. We were on such good terms with Mr Moffat that we could use the frank language which often marks Canadian-American confidential exchanges. We made it clear to him that we were no banana republic to be pushed around by Washington. Our position was accepted and the controversy was settled, but it was unpleasant while it lasted.

ℰ

For me it was a happy year. Our family was together, the children were progressing at school, we had old and congenial friends close by, and the work was absorbing. I played tennis in the summer, with frequent forays up the Gatineau and to the fishing club. I was also doing a certain amount of outside speaking about life in wartime London, at Canadian Clubs and war bond drives.

In the autumn of 1941 we took an important step in putting down roots in Ottawa. We bought a house. I might have known that to do this was tempting the fates that determine the destiny of foreign service officers and that we would shortly thereafter be moved. So it happened. I was told early in 1942 that I would be going to Washington as Minister-Counsellor in the Legation, as it then was. As for the house, we felt that we would now be spending some years abroad and we did not want to be bothered by owning property in Ottawa as absentee landlords. That turned out to be another mistake. A few years later I came back as Deputy Minister, but by this time we had sold our house for about one-third the price we would have received later, and we had no place to live. I was never very astute at managing my own affairs.

I was surprised and pleased when I was posted to Washington, now becoming the centre of the whole Allied war effort. The Canadian minister at this time was Mr Leighton McCarthy, an elderly gentleman who had been a prominent and successful lawyer-businessman in Toronto. He had been persuaded by Mr King to leave private life and go to Washington as Minister after the death of Loring Christie in April 1941. Mr King once remarked to me that he owed his leadership of the Liberal party to Mr McCarthy who had refused, so he said, to be a candidate at the Liberal convention of 7 August 1919 which chose Mr King as the successor to Sir Wilfrid Laurier. If Mr McCarthy had stood, Mr King added to my great surprise, he would have been successful. Perhaps a more important qualification for the post was Mr McCarthy's long personal friendship with President Roosevelt. It was helpful, of course, to have been trained in diplomacy and the conduct of foreign relations but, in the Washington of 1940, it was presumably considered to be even more important to have a direct line open at any time to the White House and to be able to call the President's private secretary by her nickname.

Mr McCarthy had as his second-in-command one of the best and most experienced career officers in our service, my old friend Hume Wrong, who had the further advantage of having already served in Washington. The combination of the able and shrewd Toronto lawyer and the professional diplomat did not, however, work out with entire success. There were problems of incompatibility. Mr Wrong, therefore, went back to the department in the spring of 1942 to take my place and, at Mr McCarthy's request, I went to Washington to take his. I remained there until 6 October 1946.

ON TO WASHINGTON

Our first problem in Washington, as in London, was to find a house. This was extremely difficult in overcrowded wartime Washington, with rents soaring far beyond my rental allowance. After many frustrating weeks of search, the Canadian government, in its wisdom, moved our military attaché, Major (Bud) Drury, into a more active field of warfare where he distinguished himself greatly. We inherited his comfortable old house in a nice quiet district, with some trees, a garden, mice in the cellar, and a good cook.

Perhaps I should continue here with the story of domestic life and arrangements in Washington. On my promotion later to be head of the Mission, we moved into the Embassy at 1746 Massachusetts Avenue, and were inclined to think our household worries were over. The house, however, was more magnificent than comfortable, especially as we occupied the second and third floors only, while on the others were offices of the Mission. It was a building worthy of the spacious days of imperial diplomacy, and, with my simple parsonage background, I was suitably awe-struck. So was my wife, but for different and more practical reasons of housekeeping. How I was going to live up to my surroundings was only a minor worry.

Though we had the large residence, we did not have the domestic staff to go with it. They had all, to our sorrow and chagrin, been discharged by our predecessors. This made our arrival somewhat forlorn for, with all the larders, the wine cellar, and the big kitchen, there seemed to be no food of any kind. We felt lonely and lost in the big, empty house. To overcome this unworthy first feeling, we decided to have a drink. We had brought with us two bottles, adequate for that stimulating purpose, but they had corks and we could find no cork-screw in all the facilities of that diplomatic establishment. But things soon improved once I applied all my ingenuity and strength to get the christening bottle opened.

A butler, of course, was required for this diplomatic splendour. My wife eventually found, so we thought, the perfect one. James had fine references from the most aristocratic of English employers. He was a veritable stage butler in his manner and his appearance. He also had a quiet efficiency and a courteous kindliness, without undue familiarity. I only hoped that I would be worthy of him. He was really a very good person and he certainly knew his job. Indeed, there never was a better Jeeves – or one more British. Once we had a member of the Royal family to dinner who asked James the name of the white wine (a Lieb-fraumilch) he was serving. Very conscious of the presence of Royalty and the impropriety of using German words in wartime, especially in such august company, James did a quick and literal translation: 'Milk of the Virgin, your Royal Highness.'

I found it difficult to live up to James. In my clothes cupboard, which was the size of a small room, there was a series of wooden shelves for my footwear. I felt humiliated, when showing the new butler our quar-ters for the first time, to see the strange look that crept over his face when he looked at those boot shelves and saw only a pair of brown shoes and an old pair of sneakers. I did, of course, also have a pair of evening shoes but they seemed to have disappeared. It was a shock-ingly inadequate display of ambassadorial footwear and I felt I had let James down. Would he stay? A few days later I was wondering whether we should keep him. I wrote in my diary: 'I don't mind him laying out my dinner clothes, etc., but if he continues to call me "Your Excellency," he goes!'

Soon he became indispensable. James, however, had one major weakness. He was an alcoholic, not in the sense that he was a steady and excessive drinker, but that he couldn't take even a sip without being trapped by what, in fact, was a disease. It took us some time to discover it, because when he joined us, he had become a teetotaller and was doing his best to remain one. Unfortunately, under the pressure of ambassadorial entertaining, he slipped and began to take just a drop of sherry before an official dinner or luncheon to soothe his nerves. This soon proved his undoing; and ours. He could not be counted on when needed most. Once when we were giving a luncheon, James took the fatal drop in his own room to steady his nerves. One drop led to a bottle, until James became unconscious. My wife missed him and began to investigate. She found him so far gone that he seemed lifeless. Alarmed, my wife phoned the military attaché to see if he knew of a Canadian Army doctor who could examine him. There being none, Colonel Gurney phoned the emergency hospital authorities. His message was misread by somebody at the telephone: 'the Canadian Ambassador's butler had collapsed,' was transmitted as 'the Canadian Ambassador had collapsed.' An emergency squad with pulmotors and other equipment from the fire department was rushed over. Disappointed, no doubt, because the Ambassador was in good health, they took James to the emergency hospital along with the keys to our wine cellar which were in his pocket. However, he was back a couple of hours later, as hospitals were too crowded to deal with minor things like intoxication. Meanwhile, we struggled through our luncheon without a butler's help and with the depressing feeling that the Governor General was arriving next day with no James to look after him. He swore that he had had his lesson and that it would never happen again. We certainly hoped so, but it did. James, in consequence, took his leave with our best wishes. We missed him, especially as I had begun to train him not to worry too much about my clothes or my bourgeois habits.

When one got used to it, diplomatic life was not without its pleasures. Indeed, for those who loved entertaining and being entertained, it could be positively exhilarating. My wife and I were not in that category, but we did our social duty, both as hosts and guests. We preferred both to give and to attend small parties, luncheons, and dinners. We gave our share of these for diplomatic colleagues, government officials, journalists, and others. These could be not only pleasant but extremely useful in making friends and in acquiring the kind of information often difficult to get in a State Department office. As time went on, we were fortunate to find that the people we found it most useful to invite professionally were also among those we most wanted to invite as friends.

Big receptions and cocktail parties we greatly disliked, finding them meaningless, exhausting, and expensive. We gave no more than protocol required. We had to go to many, of course, but we kept the time spent at each to the minimum required by politeness. In time we divided embassies in Washington, not by the country represented, but into those that had a separate entry and exit, which meant you could be in and out in one minute, the host on the receiving line quite unaware of your departure; and those which had only a single door, which meant you had to stay long enough to avoid a displeased look from your host over the shoulders of those still coming in.

There was one social occasion that I remember well since it marked our daughter's unofficial, almost accidental, debut into Washington society. It was the President's birthday dinner at the Mayflower Hotel on 30 January 1943. This from my diary:

It was a noisy, crowded affair, juvenile and boisterous, notwithstanding the presence of the dignified diplomatic and high official world who, however, were very definitely second string to the film stars who graced the occasion. It was their presence that made Patsy urge us to take her along, at least for the pre-dinner reception. She had on her first evening dress and was goggle-eyed with excitement as she shook hands with the Hollywood celebrities. In fact, she shook hands with them twice, as she insisted on going around the line a second time. James Cagney apparently spotted her second appearance and said: 'Haven't I seen you before, little girl?' He had, fifteen minutes before. Her special attraction was a teen-age movie actor named Roddy McDowell, by whom she had been badly smitten.

An important part of my life and my work was to get to know and to keep in touch with not only American officials but diplomatic colleagues. Some of this was tiresome and of no great value; our talks were merely an exercise in taking in each other's clean linen. Much of it, however, was rewarding as well as pleasant. It was natural that, among the diplomatic corps, we should keep specially close professionally and socially to the Commonwealth representatives, the senior of whom was considered, understandably, to be the British Ambassador. Canadian relations with the British Embassy, while I was in Washington, were always friendly. The Ambassador was Lord Halifax. I had had no great admiration for his policies as Foreign Secretary but as an Ambassador, and as a man of simplicity, sincerity, and quiet conviction, he won my respect and affection. He was always himself and refused to try to create, or allow to be created for him, an image to impress the Americans. They, in turn, gradually acquired a high regard for him. When I became Ambassador, we spent a good deal of time together and I benefitted from and greatly valued our association. Lady Halifax was the perfect wife for a British Ambassador, while the civilian and military members of the British Mission were highly competent and co-operative.

With all this diplomatic activity, social and official (the two were sometimes hard to separate), private life and personal pleasures were, in a sense, circumscribed. But the Pearsons managed to have their own fun with their own friends. The fact that official life enveloped one in

Washington made our family holidays in Canada all the more welcome. These, however, for me were few and short, so busy was I in Washington and at international conferences. Our family life was once again disrupted. Our son, Geoffrey, was getting a good education at Trinity College School at Port Hope, while Patsy, after a short initial period at a day school in Washington during which she acquired more teenage sophistication than education, was well and happy at Bishop Strachan School in Toronto.

To keep fit was a problem, with so much office work, travel, and the good, or at least the calorific life. But for exercise I did play some tennis and boisterous soft-ball on the week-ends with a group of Americans, most of them senior government officials. The baseball games, however, which really mattered – apart from those of the Washington Senators in the American League, which I loved to watch whenever I could – were those between the Canadian Embassy and the State Department, which took place from time to time. We had a reasonably good team, thanks to a few experts from the Canadian military mission. Our diplomatic worry was that we might prejudice our good relations with the State Department by beating them too easily. At the same time national pride would permit no defeat by the foreigner. So we worked out a unique and most ingenious method of handicapping. We placed a jug of martinis and a glass at each base and negotiated an agreement under which, whenever a player reached that base, he had to drink a martini. This ensured a record number of men stranded on third base and, if anyone did try to make home plate, he could easily be tagged. The scores were remarkably even. It is a tribute to the steadiness and good condition of the players on both sides that every game did not end 0–0.

My wife's problem was one of exhaustion, not exercise. Apart from the tiring and demanding work of running a diplomatic household, she had become a nurse's aide in a hospital in one of Washington's poorest districts. Together, however, we managed. If the life was new, the work was familiar, after my six years in London. It was also unceasing, demanding, and, at times, confusing.

As the United States more and more became the headquarters of allied war activity and of increasing importance to Canada's own war plans and policies, most of the departments and agencies of the Canadian government had to be represented in Washington. An inescapable interdependence developed between the Canadian war effort, in all its ramifications, and that of our powerful neighbour. Whenever a new US agency was set up, it seemed that a Canadian and his staff moved to Washington to liaise with it. Thus Canadian officials there grew in number, both in the Embassy and in separate civil and military offices. Canada was well served by these men and women. Whether permanent civil servants or temporary wartime volunteers, they added to the high reputation of our public service.

The Ambassador had general supervision of all Canadian official activity in Washington, even though much of it was carried on by officers responsible also to their own departments in Ottawa. This important function of supervision and co-ordination was done by the Embassy, through regular meetings of heads of all Canadian agencies and in less formal ways. The physical work of keeping in touch with mushrooming American war agencies was a problem in itself. They grew fast and their personnel changed often. The official to see today was some place else tomorrow.

Washington was alive with action in those days and a very exciting place in which to live and work. It became even more so for me when I was asked to undertake a number of international assignments which I shall be describing later. My work required frequent trips also to New York and Ottawa, usually by a long, uncomfortable, and exhausting rail journey with the train always late and over-crowded. Jets were not yet in operation to make travel quick and easy. Wartime travel by rail, and I did a lot of it, is one of my least agreeable memories of those days.

Until I became Head of the Mission at the beginning of 1945, my immediate responsibility, of course, was to Mr McCarthy. He and I worked very well together. He left largely to me the administration and organization of the Mission, as well as State Department contacts, meetings, and reporting, though I was careful to keep him informed of what I was doing and, of course, he had to approve all official messages sent to Ottawa. He looked after White House liaison and kept in personal touch both with Mr Roosevelt and Mr King. As Minister, and after January 1944, our first Ambassador, he had the responsibility for formal representational work, giving and going to official parties and receptions. This was something he didn't like much, and Mrs McCarthy liked less.

Nor did Mr McCarthy relish travelling about the country to make those 'educational' speeches about Canada which have become an important part of ambassadorial activity; most of this he managed to avoid. When he had to make a speech, it was my duty to prepare a draft. I became his 'ghost writer.' He seemed to welcome my help in this regard, although demurring at my objections to his use of old-fashioned nineteenth-century references to the great British Empire on which the sun never set. Mr McCarthy, in fact, combined a strong Liberal political faith with fervent, Toronto-Tory emotions about the mother country. It was instinctive with him to accept British leader-ship in an imperial family and the superiority of British policies and practices. On specific issues, however, he could take, when he saw fit, a very independent Canadian stand. He used to complain, good-naturedly, that when he had to make a speech he was only 'Charlie McCarthy' to my 'Edgar Bergen.' In fact, he was a strong character and nobody's dummy. But he was new to the practice of diplomacy and the conduct of international affairs and seemed glad to get what help he could from me in the techniques of this profession, especially in draft-ing speeches, messages, and despatches, and in attending meetings.

Once in Washington I was even a ghost writer for President Roose-velt, though he may never have known it. The President wished to send a message of congratulation to Mr King on the third anniversary of the British Commonwealth Air Training Plan, a project in which Canada now took a great and justifiable pride. I was surprised when a friend on the White House staff, ignoring all rules of diplomatic propriety and without telling the State Department anything, asked me whether I would be kind enough to do a draft of the message for the President. I did. So on 1 January 1943 the Prime Minister of Canada received a very impressive letter lauding Canada as the 'aerodrome of democracy' drafted by me but signed by the President of the United States! This must be some kind of unorthodox first.

Though ghost writing was never one of my favourite occupations, at this or any other time, it had one advantage for me in Washington. When, later, as Ambassador, I made speeches of my own, I could always quote from Mr McCarthy's earlier ones and with genuine approval, 'As my predecessor once put it so eloquently and wisely ...' Indeed, I was able to quote myself even before I became Head of the Mission for, as second in command, I often accepted invitations to speak, frequently in place of the Minister who, as I have said, had no liking for this kind of activity. My subject was usually Canada's war effort, something about which the Americans were woefully ignorant, as they were indeed about Canada generally.

I considered, in fact, the projection of Canada – propaganda, if you prefer – a very important part of my duties in Washington; as it should be for any Canadian representative in any foreign country. Bad or excessive propaganda, however, can backfire and do more harm than good. Moreover, it embraces far more than speeches or broadcasts. Press contacts are equally, or even more, important, as are the cultivation of good relations with Congressmen and officials of the government. All this is, or should be, a very important part of diplomatic duties.

In my public relations and propaganda activity in Washington, and also to secure all the information I could, I naturally made as many friends as possible among the press. The press corps in Washington included some of the most knowledgeable, intelligent and influential men in the country. I came to know many of them, some very well. I suppose no Ambassador spent more time at the National Press Club than I did. This was an agreeable and useful activity, for it was a good place to find out what was going on, who was going up, or who was going out. It was quite as valuable a source of information, and rumour, as my colleagues in the diplomatic corps, or even my friends in government departments.

While the Canadian government may have had reason to complain about the inadequacy of official consultation by the United States or British governments on questions of policy, it could not complain of lack of information from its diplomatic servants. In our reporting duties, as in other ways, we could invariably draw upon a generous fund of American goodwill and cordiality. Of this goodwill there was an abundance, but it was combined too often with a profound ignorance of Canada. This made us not infrequently the targets of critical shafts. 'Canadians were not sacrificing enough on the home front to win the war. There was no conscription in Canada. Canadians seemed to be better off than Americans. Canada's food rationing was less severe,' and so on. This kind of criticism of a country which had fought and suffered from the first day of two world wars was hard to take.

To counter it was another reason for my willingness to accept invitations to speak about my country, its war effort now, and its place in the future. If I was to do all I could to correct misconceptions about Canada, I could not restrict my contacts to the State Department and other government departments or follow only customary and formal diplomatic routines.

My extra-curricular activities in public relations caused, I believe, some misgivings among my friends in the State Department, some of whom thought that a diplomat should deal only with them, not directly with Congress or the press, and only prudently and blandly with the public. I fear that I was unconventional in these matters. If Americans were prone to treat a Canadian as one of themselves, why not get the benefits as well as the risks of this special relationship? I talked, therefore, about Canada to all sorts of people in all sorts of places, whenever I had the opportunity.

On one occasion, a Congressman, Mr Clare Hoffman of Detroit, got me into some difficulty over my public relations activities. I did not know him personally, and what I knew did not make me one of his admirers. In Congress he had said something derogatory about Canada's part in the war. His facts were wrong and his conclusions rubbish. I ventured to point this out in a stiff letter to Hoffman which I gave also to the press, leading to headlines 'Pearson raps Hoffman'; 'Representative Hoffman All Wet on Lease-Lend Affairs says Canada.' While pleased with the success of this corrective action, I was mildly concerned by my identification with 'Canada'! At the same time I was gently rapped over the knuckles by the State Department. Their expert on Canadian affairs, an old friend, suggested that I deal with Congressmen through official channels or, and this was more helpful, if I wished to write letters in defence of my country, I might ask an information officer to sign them. Diplomats should never by-pass the State Department, or forget the rules of their trade.

On the whole, however, Canada received a good press during my years in Washington. When we were criticized, it was usually the criticism made of a close friend, and more in sorrow than in anger. Our complaint was not of unfriendliness but of irritating ignorance and indifference.

My desire to take full advantage of every occasion to talk about my country and to do my small bit to reduce American ignorance of Canada meant for me a great deal of extra work, much travel and some unusual experiences. Americans, even more than Canadians, are addicted to service and other similar clubs which seem to enjoy having guest speakers. Hence I had plenty of invitations, even if many of them came to the Embassy simply for 'a Canadian speaker.' I could tell many stories of my adventures on the speaker's trail in furtherance of Canada–United States understanding. I was always given a warm, friendly welcome even if my remarks did not stir much excitement.

My information work in Washington was not confined to Canadian affairs. In 1943 and 1944, as I became more and more immersed in United Nations questions, I became active on the international publicity front. Some of this activity arose from my membership on the United Nations Information Board set up in Washington by the United States government in 1942, but transferred to New York in 1943. This board was designed to assist in maintaining good morale and ties of solidarity and co-operation among the members of the United Nations in their struggle for victory and peace. It met often, talked much, planned many good things, put much high-minded idealism into words, but did little to convince governments to take any collective action, or to set up collective machinery, which would foster the idea of the United Nations and help bring it to life in political terms. The governments were then too busy trying to win the war to worry about postwar international organization and solidarity. I once suggested to the board that we should celebrate the first anniversary of the publication of the United Nations Declaration by having President Roosevelt call a conference in Washington of representatives of all the United Nations who would reaffirm their unity in winning not only the war but the peace. We all thought this a fine idea but it got nowhere – as so many fine ideas do.

᳁

Information and public relations activity, while important, was not the most substantial part of the work of our Mission. Our major concerns were with wartime military, economic, and political problems. As the United States effort increased, continental co-operation became more and more important, especially in the mobilization of industrial and agricultural resources. This co-operation also extended to the area of strategy but, here, Canada was more often concerned with carrying out decisions already made by others than with participation in the making of those decisions. We were not consulted about plans and decisions at high levels unless our agreement was essential, and this was seldom. Often we were not even informed in advance about those plans nor our interest in them recognized except as part of a 'British Empire.' Indeed the Big Two saw nothing incongruous in deciding to meet, or to have their representatives meet in Canada without even telling the Canadian government about it beforehand.

We usually had to ferret out information on what was going on at the top, whether in civilian or military affairs. We became adept at this. We had very friendly relations with senior officers and high officials, both American and British, who usually were most co-operative and willing to tell us all they could. The fact that we were both 'British' *and* 'North American' was a valuable asset in our access to information, though not in certain other matters. We could play both sides of the street, if we did so carefully and without trickery.

This triangular relationship was, of course, changing. The American side of the triangle was becoming more important for us, as the United

States grew in world power and influence, and as the comparative strength of the United Kingdom declined. It was obvious that Canada's most difficult international problems, in contrast with the twenties and thirties would now, and in the future, arise out of relations with its neighbour. These would often be affected by our old and close association with the United Kingdom as a mother country in the Commonwealth of Nations, and, even more, by our own growing and sensitive nationalism.

These relations (USA-UK-Canada) had become my main preoccupation while I was in the department, even before going to Washington. I produced a memorandum in 1941 on the subject for the Under-Secretary, hoping he would then make it a departmental document for the Prime Minister. This he did after modifying some of my stronger expressions of concern. The first paragraph of this memorandum gives the viewpoint which I held throughout my stay in Washington:

In recent years Canadians have tended to take it for granted that the United States will continue to follow a friendly and co-operative policy toward Canada. Our general relations with the United States are all based on this assumption, which is, I think, a fundamentally correct one. There have been a number of warning developments in the last year or so, however, which suggest that we should not be too confident that the United States will always regard Canadian interests as a close second to their own and appreciably ahead of those of any third country.

After less than a year in Washington, I sent another memorandum to the department which included these paragraphs:

Suspended somewhat ambiguously in the mind of so many Americans, between the position of British colony and that of American dependency, we are going to have a difficult time in the months ahead in maintaining our own position; in standing on our own feet.

This difficulty in 'standing' should make us particularly careful in choosing our direction each time we start to move. If we don't exercise such care, our role of interpreter will result in bringing the US and UK together but in such a way that we may find ourselves uncomfortably squeezed between them.

During the war, however, our difficulty was more often to avoid being squeezed out, rather than squeezed between.

I soon learned that it was no easier in Washington than it had been in London to maintain Canada's position as a separate partner in the war. In some respects it was more difficult now that the United States was a belligerent, and *two* strong leaders of *two* great powers were managing matters on the allied side. Indeed, the Americans were more likely to ignore our national interests and feelings, through ignorance of our position and insensitivity to our pride, than the British were through imperial habit. Moreover, if London offended, traditional Empire sentiment in Canada could sweeten, and at times even disguise the pill for national consumption. If the British sometimes forgot the Statute of Westminster, the Americans hardly knew that it existed. If imperial sentiment caused the British at times to forget our status, American officials too often thought of Canada in colonial terms as part of the British Empire. As such, we should be content to be part of 'Empire' representation at meetings and on boards or committees. This was simpler for them as it helped to centralize control.

Paradoxically, on other occasions Washington found it more convenient to consider us as North Americans. This was natural and even easy. We both spoke English with the same accent, except for 30 per cent of our people who spoke French and whose separateness the Americans ignored, as English-speaking Canadians so often did. We played baseball, not cricket; and our boundary, so after-dinner speakers always insisted, was undefended and almost unnoticed. Therefore, as North Americans, so like 'Americans' in so many ways, we should be willing, even happy, to accept the war leadership of Washington. If we insisted on being 'British,' then we were fortunate to have a great man like Churchill and his Empire to speak for us and to look after our interests.

We knew, of course, that in time of war, concentration of authority was necessary for quick decisions. We realized further, especially after Pearl Harbor, that Canada was only one member of a coalition of United Nations against Hitler. But it was frustrating to be lumped with 'other Allies,' whose contribution in many cases to the war effort, by circumstance or by choice, was very recent and very small or even non-existent. It was annoying to be told that making a distinction between Canada and Santo Domingo was impossible. We were very conscious and proud of the fact that for many long months after the fall of France the nations of the Commonwealth had stood alone against Hitler, and that Canada was now the third strongest of the western Allies. Indeed our war effort was *relatively* greater in terms of fighting men and war production than that of the United States. Hence the argument of non-discrimination was as functionally unrealistic as at times it was politically insulting. While these misunderstandings created problems which we could not ignore, we tried not to be unreasonable in our assertion of Canadian rights and to remember that the first and over-riding objective was to win the war.

A specific example of our problem was to be found in the machinery set up in Washington for the direction and control of the total combined war effort in all its aspects. This was done through a series of joint or combined agencies of the United States and the United Kingdom. On the military side, the body at the top was the combined Chiefs of Staff on which only London and Washington were represented. The US government felt that on this committee, as on other related military bodies, Canada should be represented through its association with the British. For this reason the Americans did not wish to accept a Canadian military mission in Washington, using the same old and irritating argument that others would want missions too. They even opposed a Canadian military mission in London, insisting that the channel of communication between the Canadian Chiefs of Staff and the Supreme Commands there should be through the British Chiefs of Staff and not through any separate Canadian military organization in London.

Canadian insistence, it is true, resulted in a Joint Staff Mission in London, but it did not succeed in Washington. However, while there was no formal military mission, the United States government in time accepted a Canadian Joint Staff under an able and effective chairman, Major-General Maurice Pope. It was, in fact, if not in name, a mission. But it was only our persistence that secured this kind of military representation.

On the civilian side, we also had to struggle to have our position recognized in the way it deserved to be in the many agencies dealing with supply and munitions, having regard to Canada's importance in these areas. We had close association with these combined boards and participated in the work of most of their committees, but we secured full membership only on two, although all of them dealt with questions with which Canada was directly and importantly concerned. Our failure to secure representation on one of these boards which dealt with munitions assignment was in part our own fault. There arose a difference of opinion between Colonel Ralston and the Department of National Defence on the one hand, who were anxious for formal membership, and C.D. Howe and the Ministry of Munitions and Supply on the other, who saw no reason for it. Mr Howe had his own way of making his influence felt, in Washington, as in Ottawa. His procedure was personal and informal and his own strong position and prestige made it effective.

While the British did not press our claims for representation on these joint boards and while they naturally preferred 'dual control,' they were far more sympathetic to our desires and more understanding of our difficulties than the Americans. They were also helpful, as were some

Americans, in keeping us informed of what went on at the working levels.

The principle we wished to see adopted in solving these problems of representation and responsibility was what we called 'functionalism': membership on bodies and committees would include those, but only those, who had a very real and direct interest in the work and could make an important contribution to it. This principle of representation was never realized as we hoped, though lip service was paid to its fairness. Political considerations stood in the way. These favoured concentration of control in the hands of the two major Allies since this, among other things, would avoid problems of discrimination between other Allies.

It could be argued that we did not protest strongly enough on the highest political levels whenever we considered our national interests were being ignored. Mr King, for instance, could smoulder privately and order his officials to reflect his anger by taking a strong stand with their British or American opposite numbers. But in messages or talks between heads of governments he was usually smiling, friendly, and mild in his reactions.

The leaders of the British and American governments seemed to feel that all would be well if they played up to Mr King's egoism; by an invitation, for instance, to attend a conference such as the one that they had decided to hold at Quebec; or by posing with him for pictures, or on other occasions sending him fulsome letters. His reaction to this treatment was all they could desire in terms of friendly understanding. As long as it *seemed* to Canadians that he was one of a 'Big Three,' neglect to consult and inform him did not appear to matter quite so much; protests on matters of substance could be made on lower official levels.

It was discouraging, however, to an official who had been instructed to make a strong protest in London or Washington over some sin of omission or commission by the British or United States government to find that ministers, even the Prime Minister, when the matter reached higher political levels, accepted the situation with a mild complaint or none at all.

ॐ

As in London, there were also constitutional and jurisdictional problems to be solved, arising out of our war relationships with the United States. I thought that I had seen the last of these problems when I left London. Not at all. Our problems in Washington, however, were mostly in reverse: the position of *their* men and *their* activities on *our* soil. Ottawa became worried, and rightly so, about encroachment on our sovereignty by American activities. These kept growing in number and importance, especially in our northwest, where the Canadian presence was not very noticeable and where, more through carelessness than calculation, an increasing number of Americans were inclined to operate as though they were in their own country. I fully understood Ottawa's anxiety in this matter but warned that, if they were going to get tough, they should choose their ground carefully so that they would not be pushed from it later by the argument of military necessity which was certain to be advanced.

A specific problem in this connection arose regarding US criminal jurisdiction over its forces serving in Canada. On this issue our government decided to refuse to give the US military authorities full jurisdiction. I told the State Department about this decision informally on 22 January 1943 before I gave them a formal note, as instructed from Ottawa. I felt that, if we were forced to modify our stand later, as we were, this procedure would be less embarrassing for us. The US government was disturbed by our firm stand and began to bring pressure to bear on Ottawa to change it. The matter came to a head when the British Columbia authorities insisted on exercising jurisdiction over a black American soldier who had attacked a white woman. To forestall this, the US military ordered an immediate court martial. I was at a dinner party one night in February 1943 when I received four calls from Ottawa instructing me to get the US to drop the court martial proceedings immediately and permit the Canadian courts to try the soldier. I managed, at least, to get the court martial postponed until the bigger problem of jurisdiction was settled, where, as I expected, each government modified its stand.

The Americans were at first quite unreasonable in their demands, insisting that exclusive military jurisdiction should apply even to their individual soldiers on leave in Canada. In our most extravagant nationalist moments, we had never asked for this in respect of our own troops in England or anywhere else. The Americans eventually agreed, however, that these jurisdictional rights should not only be modified but made reciprocal. This reciprocity may have been a help politically, but I got no comfort from the thought that every Canadian soldier on leave in New York who, after a few drinks, got into trouble with some American who claimed that they alone were winning the war, and was duly apprehended, would be turned over to us for disposition and trial by the Canadian authorities. In return for reciprocity, the Canadian government backed down from its earlier position and gave the American authorities wide, though not total, rights of jurisdiction over their forces on our territory.

The lesson to be drawn from this and other similar incidents (I base my judgment on many years' experience as diplomat and politician) is never to go out on a limb, above all formally and officially, from which you are likely to have to crawl back or be cut down. There is a great deal to be said for 'velvet glove over the iron hand' diplomacy, but nothing for the 'iron glove over the velvet hand.'

While we had our difficulties and differences with the Americans, we were accustomed to discuss and settle them in the frank and outspoken manner which had now become customary between us. We pulled no punches in our official and confidential expression of viewpoints. It never occurred to me that I had to be more punctilious and polite in dealing with Americans in Washington than with Canadians in Ottawa. Naturally, a different attitude had to be adopted in public statements in accord with normal diplomatic propriety.

Our British colleagues in Washington used to envy our ability and our inclination to talk frankly and, when necessary, critically to Americans. They were usually more restrained in words and manner. Once, in March 1943, the Assistant Secretary of State for Economic Affairs, Will Clayton, gave a luncheon for a supply mission from London. When the head of this mission, the Right Honourable Oliver Lyttleton, was called on for the inevitable few words, a fixed ritual on all such occasions, he made a brief but polished and polite speech in which he said that Anglo-Americans had their difficulties and disagreements (his mission had certainly had theirs) but they were always able to work them out satisfactorily. When they left London for Washington in depression, they always returned with hope. I was then asked to say my piece and told my American friends that, when Canadians went from Ottawa to Washington, they left in hope and returned in confusion. When Lyttleton afterwards congratulated me on this pertinent and, to him, witty observation, I asked him why he had not made it himself, since I knew that it more accurately expressed his feelings and those of his colleagues than what he had said. His reply was illuminating: 'You Canadians can say anything over here and get away with it but we have to be more careful.'

In fact, we did not 'get away' with everything, and did not try to, but I think that our tactics, when pursued amicably and inoffensively, were more effective than polite public concealment and acid private criticism when no Americans were present. Sometimes I felt that there was too much of this kind of criticism among Commonwealth representatives in Washington. We used to meet regularly at the British Embassy, in the friendly family atmosphere which reflected our good, close personal relations and also the nature of our Commonwealth association at that time. At these meetings we learned much from pooling and exchanging views and gossip. We also told each other about our problems, whose source was nicely balanced between the stupidity and delays of our home offices and the confusions and difficulties of dealing with the government departments in Washington. The British were less critical about their London masters than the rest of us but concentrated on how many and grievous were the mistakes of the Americans as 'new boys.' John Maynard Keynes, after a visit to Washington, once put this point of view wittily, if unkindly and unfairly, when he characterized American officials as 'flying confusedly about like bees, in no ascertainable direction, bearing with them both the menace of sting and the promise of honey.'

Those family gatherings were very much off the record; at them frustrations and irritations could be soothed by complaining that most of them had been caused by American talk and American action or inaction. I thought that this therapeutic process was occasionally carried rather too far.

All this, of course, was merely part of the inevitable difficulties of an alliance trying to wage total war, embracing civilians and soldiers alike. These difficulties were aggravated by an easily understood British sense of greater knowledge and experience in the conduct of war, and also by the real and justifiable conviction that they had made sacrifices from 1939, not from 1942, of men and resources that were far greater than anything comparable in the United States. On the American side there was the feeling that the British were too slow and conventional, neither energetic enough nor willing to adopt modern ideas and methods.

Misunderstandings and misconceptions that had grown up for a hundred and fifty years were never far beneath the surface. Hence, it is a very real tribute to both sides that in the Washington of those days British and Americans got on so well together even if there were mutterings and tacit criticisms. This co-operation was made easier and more productive by very warm Anglo-American personal relationships that were often established. Canadians, of course, could look on this Anglo-American relationship with the detachment and understanding of a third party who knew well the good, and the not so good, qualities of both sides, even if we possessed our own share of each from our heritage and our environment.

I found this role of observation, with occasional intervention, a fascinating one. While discounting the interpretative role so often given to us, more often by ourselves than by others, I know that there were times in Washington when I could talk, I believe to some effect, to the Americans as a Britisher and to the British as a North American. In any event, I had many opportunities to do this which added to the interest of my work. It was my own preference during these years to discuss and argue and negotiate with the professionals, the career civil servants, rather than with the political appointees and the dollar-a-year men who flooded the capital. Some of these temporaries became good friends. They were efficient and helpful and did fine work for their country. Not all, however, found it easy to fit into governmental procedures or recognize official inter-relationships, and this could lead to confusion and misunderstanding. This danger was increased by the normal inclination of the business executive to make quick decisions which, it would be discovered later, he had no authority to make and which were not, therefore, implemented. Or decisions would be made in a way to cause trouble later through by-passing well-established procedures in trying to speed things up.

American procedures were also occasionally disconcerting to us because we were used to the parliamentary system of government where the chain of responsibility was recognized and firm. This was not true in Washington. The congressional system was not designed to work that way, especially in the forcing times of war. There could be no certainty that even those presidential directives which did not require congressional approval would be carried out. At the beginning of 1943, for example, the President sent a letter to Mr Churchill outlining the arrangements reached with Oliver Lyttleton during his mission to Washington covering the allocation of war supplies for Britain in 1943. This was a most important agreement to the British, as Churchill acknowledged in a reply to the President. I drafted a letter on the subject matter for Ottawa:

I can understand the satisfaction with which Mr Lyttleton's report and President Roosevelt's letter were received in London, as they 'contain assurances on the major points which can be regarded as adequate and satisfactory.' I feel, however, that I should report that in British circles in Washington the satisfaction at the assurances given is qualified by the feeling that the American agencies concerned with their implementation may be neither able nor willing to carry them out to the letter. In this connection, I should point out that the President's assurances have not yet even been conveyed to the various departments of the United States government concerned, who are, officially at least, quite unaware of them and who do not therefore feel that they are yet bound to implement them.

Possibly the anxiety of these British officials would not be so great if they did not know that, in the past, agencies of the United States government have been able, by interpretations and by other means, to alter the effect of political pronouncements on the highest level; and also because in this particular case the commitments in question are still personal from the President to the Prime Minister and have not yet even been seen by those officials of the United States government on whose whole-hearted co-operation in carrying them out their realization will largely depend.

Mr McCarthy decided not to sign this letter because he considered it a reflection on the President's personal honour to suggest that promises he had made would not be fully carried out. The fact remained that at times commitments to other governments made on one level in Washington were not or could not be fully implemented on another. This was not due to bad faith but to the lack of co-ordination of the activity and authority of so many unrelated decision-makers.

There could be no denying, however, the energy and enthusiasm of everybody, or almost everybody, with whom we had to deal in Washington; especially with the dollar-a-year men. This was quite a contrast to the business as usual atmosphere of London in the fall and winter of 1939–40. As one of my friends once remarked: 'Washington is a place of bewildering confusions, strong passions, contradictory policies, *but* energetic performances!'

Government offices, especially the temporary wartime offices, were crowded not only with dynamic executives determined to get things done, but also with public and press relations officers who were determined that these results should be publicized; that people should be stirred by stories of amazing triumphs in production as well as in military operations. Let me give an illustration. In 1943 the greatest danger of losing the war came from German submarines. Sinkings of allied shipping were increasing at a frightening rate. Hence shipbuilding became a vital war operation and the Americans threw themselves into it with energy, enthusiasm, and skill. One day in March of that year I had a visit at the embassy from some excitable public relations men who wished to dramatize the amazing shipbuilding results then being achieved by giving maximum publicity to the launching of five ships simultaneously from one shipyard. I was assured that they could make this launching the biggest event of 1943 if they could get the Canadian quintuplets to participate; five girls for five ships. I felt almost sad when this coup did not come off.

12

MADE EXCELLENT

In writing about my life and work in Washington, I have made little or no distinction between my successive positions. As for official work, there was not in fact much distinction to be made, although there was in responsibility and in representational duties. As Ambassador, I had a position of greater importance, of course, than I had as Minister-Counsellor or Minister, but I had already become a public figure of sorts largely because I was the Canadian representative at United Nations conferences meeting in the United States or on United Nations agencies centred there.

It was in the summer of 1944, after Mr McCarthy had decided to return to private life, that I first heard that I was being considered by Mr King as the next Ambassador. I was both elated and worried. The elation was natural. The worry was not so much whether I was qualified to take on this new responsibility but whether I could afford it financially. Mr McCarthy, I knew, had had to use his private resources to make ends meet. Our work was increasing and I expected to be a very active Ambassador. I would be doing more official entertaining than my predecessor, for one thing. I also had family obligations which he did not have. So my expenses were likely to be greater.

I therefore wrote to the Under-Secretary to the effect that, to do the job as Ambassador as I felt it should be done if I were offered the post, I would need more staff (there was no problem here as an increase was already in the offing) and larger allowances. I pointed out to him that my predecessor had had to use his private income while in charge of the mission but this was impossible for me because I had none. University teachers and civil servants rarely amass fortunes. When I was appointed, the salary remained unchanged, but the allowances were increased and we were able to carry on, not lavishly, but without financial worries, and without curtailing any necessary activities.

Mr McCarthy's report to the Prime Minister on my performance was presumably reasonably good or I would not have been chosen as his successor. More important, I must have satisfied the Prime Minister himself, though his diary indicates that he was at times uneasy over my tendency to press ahead with things and take unnecessary initiatives. I was not, obviously, Mr King's ideal of a prudent bureaucrat, but he made me Ambassador at the post where I had been serving. Promotions of this kind within the mission are unusual in a diplomatic service. Normally a subordinate is transferred to another post before bringing him back later as head of the earlier mission. This would be all the more likely in Washington, the most important mission in the Canadian foreign service. So I would not have been surprised if Mr King had appointed some prominent Canadian to replace Mr McCarthy, instead of promoting me.

My new position, of course, increased our social responsibilities. These are often derided as an expensive waste of the taxpayers' money, but they can in fact be very important in the discharge of diplomatic duty, if properly conducted. They can make friendships, and friendship is the foundation of official as well as of personal understanding. A diplomat who can not make friends, without exploiting that friendship in the wrong way, is never a master of the profession. This aspect of my life in Washington was indeed important, even though at times exhausting. A major social-diplomatic duty was to get to know and to keep in touch with one's diplomatic colleagues, and with officials of the State Department. This became a much more important responsibility for me when I became Ambassador in January 1945.

The mission had been elevated from legation to embassy in early 1944. Mr King was reluctant to agree to this change in status. He thought it might cost money and give the head and members of the mission those illusions of grandeur to which he suspected diplomatic representatives abroad were prone.

The arguments that convinced him to agree to the new designation were, first, that it would cost nothing and, second, that all countries were making this change so that the old distinction between embassy and legation based on national power and prestige was becoming meaningless. When every Latin American mission in Washington, even the one from the smallest country, and every United States mission in Latin America, was an embassy, it would be absurd if Canada were to remain in the theoretically junior grade. There was, indeed, no point in one country trying to maintain this moribund distinction. So the change was made.

The first duty of a new ambassador, after presenting his credentials, an ancient ritual, is to pay formal calls on the high officials of the country to which he is accredited, and on his diplomatic colleagues. This demands, in Washington and other great capitals, weeks of visiting. I thought that the diplomatic calls would be an unmitigated nuisance and an extravagant waste of time. I learned, however, that whilst these formal diplomatic courtesies were indeed demanding of my time, some of them were of real value, for both personal and official purposes. My only misadventure in these calls was when one ambassador, an aristocratic and indolent representative of the old diplomacy, complained that I had asked to be received at 10:30 in the morning, 'practically in the middle of the night.' Having made that point, however, he gave me a very interesting and frank analysis of the attitude of his government toward the Dumbarton Oaks draft of a United Nations Charter.

Of the calls on American dignitaries, I shall refer later to that on the Vice President. The only other call I need to mention was that on the Secretary of State, Edward Stettinius, whom I had already met. He gave me warm greetings and congratulations on my new dignity, then added to the uneasiness I have already expressed over these bland expressions of goodwill toward my country by assuring me that there were no outstanding or troublesome problems between Canada and the United States and 'that is all very comforting these days.' So I thought fit to mention a few problems, even on this ceremonial occasion. I made particular reference to the Dumbarton Oaks proposals for a United Nations organization. The Secretary seemed to think that we were worrying ourselves unnecessarily in matters of 'detail' about Dumbarton Oaks, and then proceeded to confirm my concern by adding: 'You people in Canada really have nothing to worry about in these things. You are in a sense part of us and you are also part of the British Empire. You are really very fortunate because you have such good and strong friends.'

Senator Austen of Vermont, whom later I got to know so well at the United Nations, made the same point to me shortly afterwards. Indeed, he underlined our good fortune in having as neighbour and friend a country whose 'foreign policy always had and always would be based exclusively on altruism, which was why the rest of the world had so much confidence in it.' The Senator, a fine, Christian gentleman, was both serious and sincere in this observation; as indeed he was a few years later during the bitter Jewish-Arab disputes at the UN over the partition of Palestine, when he observed that 'we could settle this Palestine conflict quickly enough if only the two sides, Jews and Arabs, would behave like good Christians.' There were times when I thought that the approach of Mr Stettinius to international affairs was almost as naïve.

❧

Another ambassadorial responsibility was to receive and entertain official visitors, most of them from Ottawa. All roads led to Washington in those days and those from Canada to its embassy. I shall mention only two of my Canadian visitors, both of the highest rank.

The first was the Governor General, the Earl of Athlone, and his delightful wife, Princess Alice, who surely had found the secret of perpetual youth and charm. Their natural simplicity and kindliness made them easy and welcome guests. My experience of people has been that the more exalted they are in the social or official hierarchy, the less snobbish or difficult they are with others. I admit there are some exceptions.

The Governor General paid his state visit to Washington in March 1945. He was given the full, red-carpet, head-of-state treatment, interesting in itself since he was not, of course, a head of state but the viceroy of that head, the King. Perhaps the few Americans who were aware of such a fine distinction might have been more impressed by this evidence of our separate national status had the Governor General been a Canadian and not a member of the Royal Family.

The viceregal visitors on arrival at the station were met by the President and Mrs Roosevelt. We had been given our ceremonial drill orders, but when the time came no one seemed to know exactly what to do. The arrival therefore was more informal than planned, and the better for that. This was my first experience of a VIP cavalcade, with motorcycle escorts roaring in front, in the rear, and alongside. I was to have many of these splendid dashes in later years and the experience has always given me a thrill; a sense of power as we roared through red lights, of fear that we might have a spectacular accident, and of embarrassment at this assertion of exclusive privilege over pedestrians and other motorists. My own experience has been that this escort routine was most excitingly done, as was to be expected, in Chicago; with the greatest flourish in newly independent ex-colonial countries; and most efficiently in Montreal. But the city where I most enjoyed this attention was Paris since the sturdily recalcitrant Parisians, true inheritors of the 'rights of man,' often refused to give way, or to be pushed aside, by any provocative demonstration of authority. Any attempt at coercion was countered by a ribald volley of insults, a decided slowing down of the pace, and, for me, a new faith in the cranky independence of the aroused citizen.

On this particular occasion, in Washington, our procession swiftly reached the White House where the Marine Band welcomed us with three national anthems. The President had insisted, as this was a matter of high Canadian policy, that I should make the decision between 'Oh Canada' and 'God Save the King.' I played safe and asked the band to touch all the musical bases.

The first event on the viceregal visitors' programme was the White House correspondents' annual dinner. Here the Governor General was the President's guest. Notwithstanding, he received scant attention. There were too many local celebrities present. I doubt whether the Earl of Athlone had ever before attended such a function and I doubt even more whether he would have wished to do so again. He did not seem impressed by the earthy humour of Jimmy Durante, Danny Kaye, and Fanny Brice, all of whom reduced the President and the Canadian ambassador to helpless laughter, but left the Governor General only vaguely bewildered. It was not precisely the kind of humour that would have commanded roaring applause at Buckingham Palace or Rideau Hall.

If the first night was not a smashing success, the rest of the visit went off very well. My diary gives my impressions:

This was one of the most exhausting days I have ever spent, full of Royalty, ceremony, striped pants and all that.

I began by going to the White House and accompanying the viceregal procession to Mount Vernon, Arlington, etc. I found myself seated in the first car with the Governor General and the Princess Alice. I rode flap-seat, a most undignified position in which to place an Ambassador and one which I believe caused Mr Massey acute humiliation during the visit of the Willingdons to Washington years ago. I was uncomfortable, but not humiliated. I was also exhausted trying to answer the numerous questions of the Governor General. He wanted to know about every place we were passing. He is a born tourist, and a very nice, amiable man. The viceregal party were most enthusiastic about the beauties of Washington.

That second evening we went to the state dinner at the White House. My diary noted:

It was not nearly so dignified or so impressive a function as I had expected. The Cabinet Ministers and their wives were the only guests beside the vice-regal party, ourselves, and the Speaker of the House of Representatives. There was very little pomp and ceremony and no particular effort made to see that the people had a chance to talk with the guests or with the President and Mrs Roosevelt.

The President proposed the health of the King in a few words, not particularly apt. The Governor General replied with a toast to the President, and the poor man had a hard time getting any words out. He played safe by talking about the beauties of the cherry blossoms. For a minute I thought he was going to call them 'Japanese' cherry blossoms, but he stopped just in time and substituted 'Oriental.' I had warned him about this!

The next day the acting Secretary of State gave a luncheon at Blair House, a lovely old place used as a government guest house where, as I know from experience, you are most hospitably entertained.

After this very pleasant affair our guests left by train for Ottawa. The President and Mrs Roosevelt accompanied them to the station, which was gracious of them. Indeed, they went out of their way to make this visit a compliment not only to the Athlones, but to Canada. The President had a better understanding of the position and importance of Canada than most Americans in official places.

I went with the Athlones as far as New York and did my best to get the Governor General to tell me about his private discussions with his host at the White House. But I got nowhere. Either there had been no discussions or the Governor General was not going to talk about them. He did mention, however, which was not news, that the President spoke very critically about France 'Which can never,' he said, 'become a Great Power again'; and about one Frenchman in particular, General de Gaulle.

This was a short, if successful, visit, and my excuse for giving so much space to it is that it was the first state visit with which the Pearsons were concerned as principals. But not the last. There were many to follow over the years and in all of them I did my best to have a minimum of formality and a maximum of friendliness and easy atmosphere.

It was not long before the Governor General had to return to Washington for the President's funeral. On this sad occasion, he was alone and stayed at the embassy. He endeared himself more than ever to the Pearsons by saying that before he left he would like to meet the domestic staff individually and thank them for their kindness to him. Our appreciation of this courtesy was heightened by the fact that Pearl, our cook, had threatened to leave and go back to Jamaica. I told His

Royal Highness about this menace to our domestic and diplomatic welfare and suggested that it would be very helpful if he could direct a few well-chosen words from the Royal Family to this very British subject, indicating that her loyalty to the crown and her duty to help ensure a British victory in the war required her to remain at the Canadian Embassy. Lord Athlone got the point, said just the right things, and Pearl remained for a few more months until the lure of Jamaica, or someone in Jamaica, proved too strong to resist.

I was able to repay in part the Governor General's kindness a year or so later. The Athlones were back in London where postwar life had its problems, even for Royalty. Princess Alice had great difficulty in finding the white stiff linen collars her husband required; and in getting those that he still had, laundered. She had heard from an American admiral about the paper collars used by US naval officers, which were indistinguishable from the linen variety but disposable and costing only a cent or two. Could I secure some? I could and I did; some dozens of them. It was pleasant to think that I had solved a collar problem for a member of the Royal Family.

☞

The other visitor I should mention was Mackenzie King. He came several times to Washington during the war but was our guest at the embassy only once. We were more worried about that visit than any other. He was reputed to be difficult to please as a guest. More important, he was the Prime Minister and Secretary of State for External Affairs of Canada.

The visit got off to a bad start. We showed our guest to his quarters. On the mantelpiece in his sitting room was a bowl of flowers. They were beautiful and colourful, but they were artificial. Fresh, natural flowers, though not so perfect, were in the bedroom. The very first thing Mr King did on entering that sitting room was to go straight to the mantelpiece and smell the artificial flowers, another confirmation of his psychic qualities. But everything else went off satisfactorily. Mr King was in his most kindly and benevolent mood, when no one could be more charming.

In his other visits to Washington Mr King stayed at the White House or in his private car at the station. He particularly enjoyed being in the capital with Mr Churchill. One night in May 1943, a few hours after the arrival of the British Prime Minister, I had a call from Norman Robertson in Ottawa that a telegram was on the way inviting Mr Churchill to Ottawa. Could I deliver it to him immediately and personally at the White House? It was evident that I was also delicately to convey to Mr Churchill the impression that, if time made it impossible for him to come to Ottawa, Mr King was prepared to accept an invitation to Washington. I got the point at once since I knew how Mr King liked to convert these Big Two meetings into Big Three or even to 'Big Two and One-Half' ones. Who could blame him?

I knew the technique and sent the telegram at once to Churchill's secretary, Leslie Rowan, asking him by telephone to show it to the great man immediately, mentioning that a very early reply would be appreciated as Mr King would undoubtedly be questioned in the House of Commons that afternoon on whether he had been invited to Washington or whether Mr Churchill would come to Ottawa on this short visit to the United States. If the Ottawa visit was not possible, I was confident that Mr King could arrange his affairs to come to Washington. Rowan understood and sent me a telegram before lunch for transmission to our Prime Minister. It was to the effect that Mr Churchill deeply regretted he could not get to Ottawa this time, but that he and the President would be delighted if Mr King could come to Washington. Mission accomplished.

The people at the State Department, however, were annoyed that the invitation came from Mr Churchill, the guest, and not from Mr Roosevelt, the host. So another telegram was sent from the White House in which the President expressed his delight 'that you can accept *my* invitation.' Mr King's cup of pleasure was now running over. He had a most satisfactory few days in Washington, during which he called at the chancery, talked to the staff, and was most amiable to all.

On this visit, Mr Churchill invited our Prime Minister, Colonel Ralston, and our three Chiefs of Staff (who were with Mr King) along with the Commonwealth Ambassadors to a meeting in the cabinet room of the White House. I thought at the time that this was an unusual place for a Commonwealth gathering. Normally they were held in the British Embassy but, on this occasion, Mr Churchill was staying at the White House, so we all went there. The British Prime Minister had, of course, a strong sense of history which prompted him to observe that on the last occasion when so many Britishers had met at the White House during a war they burnt it down.

Mr King's next visit to Washington was in March 1945, on the invitation of the President. There was at first some uncertainty whether he was to stay at the White House or the embassy and I was asked to clear this up discreetly. This I did by getting a written note from the President to telegraph to Ottawa: 'Dear Mackenzie: I am looking forward very much to seeing you at the White House on Friday afternoon.'

During this visit Mr King had useful discussions with Mr Roosevelt on some pressing matters: the Dumbarton Oaks draft of a UN charter; Canada's part, if any, in postwar armistice arrangements; the war in the Pacific; the repatriation of troops after the end of the European war. On this last point Mr King received an assurance, very important for Canada, that priority would be given to North American servicemen with the longest service overseas.

The Prime Minister, pleased with these talks, asked Norman Robertson and me to do a 'colourful' statement which he could hand out at a press conference before departure. This we attempted in co-operation with two officials on the American side and soon found that our colours began to clash. For instance, we wanted to put in some words to the effect that Canada and other middle powers would be asked to play a part in the organization of the peace which would match their contributions to the winning of the war. The Americans, with an eye on Latin America, did not think much of this one. Nor did we think much of their attempt to slip in a few phrases advocating the removal of 'all trade discriminations' which would certainly be interpreted as applying to imperial preferences. We found suitable compromises on these points, as one can with press communiqués, by resorting to ambiguous or meaningless phrases as the price of agreement.

The Prime Minister was delighted with the communiqué, with the press conference, and with President Roosevelt's laudatory references to him. The communiqué was, in fact, a modest enough document and we were amused when one Canadian Press correspondent christened it 'the White House Declaration for Political Co-operation and Freer Trade.' A more cynical appraisal was that it was the first shot in the forthcoming Canadian election battle.

If Mr King's visits to Washington helped me to become better acquainted with him, which is not the same as knowing him better, my frequent visits to Ottawa for discussions had the same result. On one of these visits, in the spring of 1943, I accompanied Anthony Eden who was to report to the Canadian government on talks he had had with the President and the Secretary of State. Mr Eden, who was a most attractive person and, as the heir-apparent to Churchill, a powerful one, made a very favourable impression in Ottawa. He was extremely frank in his views about British relations with the United States, present difficulties, and prospects for the future.

I recall the dinner that Mr King gave for him at the Country Club on this visit. Our Prime Minister, while as always the gracious host, was at his post-prandial, oratorical worst (his Country Club speeches were as variable as the climate) in taking thirty-five minutes to propose the health of his guest. I was unkind enough to record in my diary:

The PM wandered all over the map of Europe, and the life of Eden, with a lot of stories about the League of Nations and how he had once, on Eden's advice, almost returned to London from Geneva via Berlin so that he could see Hitler. His welcome to Eden was excessive – and rather too obsequious, I thought, for the head of a government which is determined to play a strong and independent part in the United Nations. He is, however, a very kind and genial host and positively exudes an appealing warmth and friendliness. You would think of him on these occasions as merely a kind, simple, old man and you could hardly be more mistaken.

As Ambassador, I was privileged to meet and talk with the powerful men of the allied world, all of whom appeared in Washington at one time or another while I was there, and most of whom were entertained at the Canadian Embassy. Naturally we sent reports to Ottawa about these visits and what we had learned from the visitors, in the hope, not always vain, that in Ottawa they would be read and might be useful.

Winston Churchill's visits, naturally, over-shadowed all others. He dominated the Washington stage by his very presence, and he played on congressional, official, and public opinion with sure and masterly skill. I met him during his visits and I remember them all – not surprisingly, since any encounter with Churchill is not forgotten. At this point, I am disposed to add to the ever-growing collection of Churchilliana, although this will take me beyond my days in Washington.

It was customary at the end of a Churchill visit to Washington for the British Ambassador to call a meeting of the Commonwealth heads of mission, together with the senior British military and civilian representatives in Washington. On these occasions, Mr Churchill would greet us and, if he felt so disposed, tell us in his own inimitable way what had gone on, adding a few brief but usually pungent comments on those he had met and his talks with them. In return, the others would report on their work to the British Prime Minister in the hope that this might be of some interest to him. Sometimes it was, if the report was brief enough and to the point.

Though I would be the first to admit that he was awe-inspiring, I was struck by the very deferential manner of these high-ranking Britishers in the presence of this great man. At one meeting in September 1943, Sir Ronald Campbell (who was presiding in the absence of Lord Hali-

fax) was going around the table inviting the civil and military representatives to make their reports. He came to the huge figure of the head of
the UK Supply Mission, Field Marshal Sir Henry Maitland Wilson,
known affectionately, for everybody liked him, as 'Jumbo.'

The Field Marshal said that things were going well enough in his
department but that they were having some difficulty in securing
enough trucks, especially for troop transport purposes. Churchill cut
him short. 'Trucks, Jumbo! You mean lorries, I presume.' Jumbo reacted like a startled schoolboy after an unexpected rebuke by the head-
master, while Churchill muttered something about the danger of
Americanizing the glorious language of Shakespeare. He also began to
give us a little lecture on war and troop movements. 'In my day,' the
Prime Minister said, forgetting that he had been a cavalryman, 'men
marched to war. Now,' he snorted, 'they are taken by ships or planes
to the area of conflict, transferred to charabancs that take them to the
battlefield, where some official opens the door, touches his cap, and
announces "Gentlemen, the battlefield." ' It was very graphic and the
result on his audience was, as usual, all that Mr Churchill could desire;
even though Field Marshal Dill remarked that neither the German
army in France in 1940 nor the British Eighth Army in North Africa in
two very successful campaigns did much marching. When it came to
David Bowes-Lyon's turn to report on political warfare, Churchill gave
him also a short lecture: 'Concentrate your propaganda on two main
targets, my boy: Prussian militarism and Nazi tyranny, without defin-
ing too closely what they mean, so we won't be committed to anything
definite when the Nazis are beaten.'

I had my own exchange with Mr Churchill at this meeting. It arose
in connection with a British proposal, then under consideration by
governments, for a Commonwealth discussion of postwar civil aviation
arrangements in the hope that some 'all-red' routes could be worked
out.

Ottawa did not like this imperial approach. They felt, and we had
been encouraging the feeling, that these talks might be misunderstood
in Washington as ganging-up against the Americans, and our own
continental air interests might therefore be prejudiced. When it came
my turn to speak at this meeting I ventured to point out that as the
Prime Minister had been in Ottawa so recently, he would undoubtedly
be aware of the preoccupation of the Canadian government with questions of postwar civil aviation. Had he anything to tell us about this
matter? He faced me squarely, frowned, waved his cigar, and told me
that he did indeed know of our worries but that there was going to be

an early Commonwealth discussion of civil aviation questions before
we talked with other countries, whether Canadians wished to attend or
not, or whether other powers (he really meant the United States) liked
it or not. He had already mentioned the matter to the President who
quite understood the situation. In view of my interest, however, he
would bring it up again with Mr Roosevelt the next day. But in working out their policies for an air transport fleet adequate to their needs
and consistent with their resources, he felt sure that the Commonwealth could present a united front. Anyway, he said, with a final
admonitory wagging of his cigar in my direction, they were going to
try, with or without Canada. He sincerely hoped the former. I could
have told him from what I knew of Mr King's attitude on the subject
that, so far as Canada was concerned, his plans were going to fail. But I
refrained. I had already said enough to ruffle the calm of the meeting
and to startle my colleagues by drawing thunderbolts from Jove.

At this meeting, finally, Churchill gave us his views on Anglo-
American relations. I quote from my report to Ottawa:

Mr Churchill then went on to talk in a very sincere way – he obviously feels
strongly about this – of British-American co-operation, now and after the
war. He said this was working out satisfactorily, and should be allowed to
take its course without too much planning. A start had been made in the
statements of himself and the President that the Combined Chiefs of Staff
would remain in existence. He felt that the habits of friendly co-operation
developed in the Combined Staff and among Anglo-American Staffs in the
Mediterranean were a happy augury for the future. The Prime Minister was
on the whole very optimistic about Anglo-American relations, more optimistic
than some of the British officials who spoke afterwards. Incidentally, he
added that one of the advantages of this co-operation would be the presentation of a united Anglo-American front in discussions with the Russians. He
warned British officials in Washington that they should cultivate the friendliest relations with Republicans as well as Democrats; they should not lay
themselves open to the charge of consorting only with the government. As
for him, he added that President Roosevelt was his 'war comrade and no one
could take his place'; but that was a purely personal view.

Two years or so later, Mr Churchill was in Washington again, now
as Leader of the Opposition. The British people, after thanking him for
saving them in war, had told him that they thought Mr Attlee would do
a better job in helping them to recover from it. I was on the *Queen Mary*
when that election took place, en route to United Nations meetings in
London and Geneva. Lord Halifax was also on board. We were having
coffee after dinner when a message was given him that Churchill's
government had been defeated. If I was surprised, he was flabber-

gasted, and at first refused to believe it, claiming that there must have been some mistake in transmission. There was no mistake.

On this postwar visit to Washington, Mr Churchill was on his way to Missouri. At the request of President Truman, he had accepted an invitation to give an address at Fulton College in that state. This college was not Harvard or Yale or Princeton, but any college where Churchill spoke was, on that day, pre-eminent. Churchill had worked long and hard over his speech. He intended it to be important. Having respect for Mr King's knowledge of the United States and his judgment of the reaction of American public opinion to speeches made and ideas put forward by outsiders, he called the Canadian Prime Minister from the British Embassy where he was the guest of Lord Halifax. He wondered whether Mr King could visit him in Washington to discuss his proposed speech or, if this were impossible, could he, Mr Churchill, send the text to Ottawa for comment and advice. The last thing Mr King wished to do was to take any responsibility, however indirect, for anything Mr Churchill might say at this time. The war was over. The Canadian Prime Minister could revert to his earlier mistrust of London and speeches on the 'Empire' by British Prime Ministers or ex-Prime Ministers. Mr King hedged. He suggested that as there was so little time and as parliamentary duties would keep him busy in Ottawa, his 'dear friend' might like to consult the Canadian Ambassador in Washington who knew his views on these matters and had his confidence. This idea probably had little or no appeal to Mr Churchill, but he was apparently polite about it. I was informed of this exchange by Ottawa and told to stand by in readiness for a message. It soon came from Lord Halifax with an invitation to call at the Embassy the next morning, Sunday, at 11 AM, to discuss with Mr Churchill his forthcoming speech. I turned up at the appointed hour, was told by Lord Halifax that his guest was somewhat grumpy, and ushered into a bedroom. There he was in bed without the top half, at least, of his pajamas, propped up by a couple of pillows, behind a portable breakfast tray-table, with a big cigar in his mouth and a glass on the tray that evidently did not contain water. On the tray, also, was his manuscript which he had been reading.

Lord Halifax left me to his guest. 'Your Prime Minister tells me,' he said, 'that you are an authority on US opinion and could advise me on this speech.' I modestly disclaimed either honour but would be privileged to help him in any way I could. He then suggested he might read it to me. This would have been a memorable experience for me, I know, but of course I would have heard him out without daring to interrupt the performance, which may have been what he had in mind. Hence I suggested that he let me take the script into a nearby room where I could read it with the care it deserved. If I had any views about it that could conceivably be of any interest to him, I would come back and give them. Somewhat to my surprise, he agreed to this suggestion. After reading a page or two, it was clear that this was indeed going to be an important speech. It certainly needed no comment from me on its main theme, Anglo-American co-operation as the 'Iron Curtain' descended. I was, however, able to correct a factual error at the beginning, concerning the position of Missouri in the American Civil War. I also doubted the wisdom of that part of his peroration where he gave the recent world conflict a name for history: 'The Unnecessary War.' The reasoning behind this designation was valid enough; that the war could have been prevented by the right policy and action in the twenties and thirties. But the term could easily be interpreted, especially in the Middle West where the christening was to take place, as a justification of United States isolation and avoidance of foreign entanglements for the future. Mr Churchill was courteous enough to agree with my two small suggestions and to thank me for them. This was my contribution to the famous Iron Curtain speech; a tiny footnote to contemporary history. The orator thanked me again when I sat beside him at a luncheon in Washington on his return from Missouri. He also told me then how much he appreciated Mr King's telephone call after I had left. This, incidentally, I had not heard about.

My suggestions for a small change in the Fulton draft reminded me of a revision to the draft of another historic Churchill speech, the one to Congress on that visit of 1943. There was one sentence in that speech dealing with the saturation bombing of Germany, which went: 'If [the German people] do not like it, they can disperse.' Mr Churchill's own version of this sentence, which his staff only with great difficulty persuaded him to alter, was: 'If they do not like it, they can take to the hills and watch the home fires burning.'

If I may anticipate further, my next encounter with Sir Winston was some years later on 9 December 1951. He was Prime Minister again and I was now Canada's Secretary of State for External Affairs. I was invited to Sunday luncheon at Chequers during a visit to London. I arrived in good time at this beautiful old country house, of great historic interest and, as the home of the British Prime Minister, of even greater contemporary importance. I was taken by Lady Churchill into the Great Hall, where the Prime Minister, clad in his own special boiler suit, zippered and baggy, was lost in a large chair, dozing before an enormous, blazing fireplace. He showed no signs of pleasure at being awakened to greet his guest. Indeed, Lady Churchill had to remind him that I was not only an invited guest but the Secretary of State for External Affairs of Canada. Just then the pre-lunch drinks arrived and things looked up; our host came to life. He got even livelier as the lunch went on, with its accompanying wines. Over coffee and brandy, Sir Winston continued to get brighter and brighter as I got droopier and droopier.

He gave me a lecture on European policy. It was the pre-de Gaulle era when France was pleading for a European army and European unity. The PM was emphatic that Britain would not and should not join or support it in the form proposed. Forgetting the lessons of this century, he insisted that the British would fight with, but not in, European forces. The proper way to bring armies and peoples together, he asserted, was to maintain their national identities, to bring them together as a 'bunch of separate sticks' bound together by common interest in their own salvation. He did not believe in the 'wood pulp' theory of unity. So, while Britain would help France if she were attacked, she would not merge herself in Europe. British association with the European unity movement would be close but not organic. Alas for June 1940 and the European Common Market of the 1970s! I noted at the time, 'Mr Churchill seemed somewhat of a romantic reactionary in discussing this subject.'

He then changed the subject and vowed that he was a great friend of Canada, and of Mackenzie King and his successor, Mr St Laurent. He painted a glowing picture of Canada's future, even predicting that the centre of power would one day shift to the northern half of the American continent. But he warned us to maintain and strengthen our British connection and the old traditions which would help us to stabilize our progress. In this connection, he was very disappointed by a recent move in Canadian policy. I wondered what it could be and was both relieved and surprised to discover that it was merely an order of the Minister of National Defence that the official anthem of the Royal Canadian Navy was to be 'Vive la Canadienne' and not 'Rule Britannia.' I attached no particular significance to this gesture, whether national or sexual, to Canadian unity. But Sir Winston was quite distressed by the demotion of 'Rule Britannia,' whose verses he then recited. Inspired by his own eloquence, he next gave me some other patriotic verses he had learned at school. Indeed he was now prepared to spend all the time that was necessary to educate me in the grand traditions of the Royal Family and the imperial navy. But by this time I was as sleepy as he had been when I arrived, so I pleaded an appointment in

London. As he saw me off, his last words were, 'Now, please, beg of your Prime Minister on my behalf to restore "Rule Britannia." ' I promised to do my best.

That promise, I hate to admit, I completely forgot until the day of Sir Winston's arrival for his farewell visit to Ottawa on 29 June 1954. As I saw him, I was suddenly reminded of 'Rule Britannia.' I knew that the two Prime Ministers were to meet that afternoon and that there was to be an official dinner that night at which I was to be present. I was certain that Mr St Laurent would be reminded about 'Rule Britannia' and 'Vive la Canadienne.' I hastened to warn him by telephone of the inevitable encounter. Then I had an idea. The dinner that night was to be a very formal affair with a Services band in attendance to do the musical honours. I got in touch with my friend, Brooke Claxton, the Minister of Defence, to see whether he could arrange that the military band give Sir Winston a special musical greeting as he took his place at the head table. Why not 'Rule Britannia'? Claxton agreed that, though unusual, this would be appropriate. It would be a simple matter to insert this musical flourish into the programme, and no rehearsal would be required.

That evening as I sat at a table immediately below the centre of the head table, I awaited with keen anticipation the procession of honoured guests. As Sir Winston stopped opposite me, the band, to the surprise of everyone but amid great applause, struck up 'Rule Britannia.' Our famous guest was delighted. It may have been my imagination but I will swear he winked at me as I stood applauding below him. He may have assumed that 'Rule Britannia' had been restored to its rightful place in Canadian naval hymnology. I learned later that the matter had not even been mentioned in the talks with Mr St Laurent.

On that happy note, I end my small contribution to the Churchill legend and return to work in Washington.

✵

As Mr Churchill towered over all other visitors to Washington from abroad, the President was equally unrivalled in power and personality at home. Only General Marshall even approached his standing and his prestige.

As Canadian Ambassador, I was close enough to the White House to witness the decline and death of a great man. It was sad to see this deterioration of President Roosevelt after the autumn of 1944. It became all too obvious in the early part of 1945. Friends back from Yalta told me that the President was really in no condition there to deal with Stalin; he was losing his grip, and the ability to manœuvre and to manage, which in good health he had possessed so abundantly. Yet this was a conference that could decide the fate of the postwar world. 'The prospects ahead are grim' was my summing up to Ottawa on FDR's return.

Mr King, who had been with the President in March on his return from Yalta, although in his diary he confirmed the gloomy reports of the President's condition, told me at the embassy that he found Mr Roosevelt in very good form and that he was reassured, especially after all the alarming reports he had been hearing. I was far from being reassured. My mind kept going back to that day in January 1945 not long before he left for Yalta, when I presented my Letters of Credence to the President on succeeding Mr McCarthy as Ambassador.

On these occasions there is a formal exchange of official messages, after which the two principals usually withdrew for a chat, short or long, friendly or perfunctory, depending on the relations between the two countries, or the two gentlemen. On this occasion, the President was as amiable and talkative as if I had been a staunch Democratic supporter in Congress. But his words, though they came easily, and his thoughts, though they were far-ranging, were not impressive. I recall some observations he made about the French fact in Canada which it was impossible to take seriously, but which made it also impossible not to be anxious about the state of his health. I had, of course, every reason to be alarmed, as events were soon to show.

On 23 March the President gave the state dinner at the White House, already mentioned, in honour of the Governor General and the Countess of Athlone. I was shocked by his condition; his hands shaking, his voice halting. My wife and I wondered how long he could go on; and whether the harrowing experience of President Wilson's last months was to be repeated. We were soon to find out.

In the late afternoon of Thursday, 12 April, I was having a talk at the embassy with my friend, Scotty Reston of the *New York Times*. I used to see a good deal of him, both privately and professionally, a distinction not always easy to observe in the world of journalism. I learned much from Mr Reston and repaid him by occasionally correcting his facts or improving his conclusions from them! We were in the midst of an argument over the proposed voting procedure in the draft UN Charter which had emerged from Dumbarton Oaks, when we were interrupted by a telephone call that the President had died from a cerebral haemorrhage. I wrote in my diary that night, under the spell of strong emotion:

It was like a physical blow ... we could not believe it at first. I phoned Ottawa. Norman Robertson had not heard and almost dropped the receiver ... It is hard to realize what has happened. The President was so much the centre of this age, and now President Truman, a Missouri politician, is thrown into the most powerful place in the world at almost the most critical time in the world's history. He may rise to the occasion, but what a chance to take! There seems to be a feeling that there will be quick changes in the Cabinet. Probably Stettinius will go. Everybody was wondering about San Francisco, but not for long, as Truman said that the Conference would go on. All evening long, tributes came over the air. All the doubts and criticisms and suspicions of deterioration are rolling away and the President is being placed in the position which undoubtedly he will retain as one of the great men of all time. What would we have done without him in the period 1939–1942? Without him, indeed, the Allied Armies would not tonight be closing in on Berlin. At least he lived to see the victory in war. If he had lived another year, would he have seen victory in peace? Certain telegrams I read today about Russian activities in Poland, Rumania and Bulgaria make it very difficult to answer this question in the affirmative.

I was asked to take part that night in broadcast tributes. The words which I put together in great haste expressed my feelings in a more formal way:

Franklin D. Roosevelt was more than a great President of a great land. He was a leader of free men in every land in their fight against oppression and aggression and evil. He was a leader of the United Nations and as such he belonged to us all. So tonight we share with you the grief and tragedy of his loss. With you we take pride in the majesty of his achievements; we stand humble before the inspiration of his vision. My country is Canada. We Canadians knew the President well and he knew us. He was, in fact, close to us, in a sense that no other President ever was ... He spent his summers on our shores. He fished our northern streams. His fireside talks were heard in our homes; his ringing declarations uplifted our hearts. He understood our problems and our possibilities. It was at his Hyde Park home that he and our Prime Minister worked out an enduring scheme for solidarity in war and peace between two friendly neighbours. It was at Quebec that he and that other great leader of embattled democracy, Winston Churchill, worked out those plans of victory which are now on the threshold of fulfilment. Above all, we Canadians, conscious now of the sure approach of total triumph, remember what the great President meant to us when we were passing through the valley of the shadow of defeat. He held ever before us the hope of final victory and he backed his hope with help. At this time, above all times, we do not forget.

Now the President has joined the gallant company of those who fought and won and fell. We, from all the United Nations, can pay the best tribute to his memory and offer the highest homage to his greatness by carrying forward the fight from the point where he fell; the unslackening fight to win the war, the determined fight to win a peace worthy of him and all those other valiant souls who have died for it.

I attended the funeral service in the White House. I felt that it was not worthy of the man whom the country and the world had lost. I cannot help but compare it with the funeral of his great companion-in-arms in St Paul's many years later. That was a tribute, embodied in a ceremony which brought pride by its impressive dignity and solemnity, tears by the sincerity of the emotion it represented so perfectly. The afternoon of April 1945 in the White House, Washington, was far from being so moving. The service was in the East Room. It was unimpressive. The clergymen droned; the singing, with a piano accompaniment, seemed unfitting. There were too many people, and there was too much noise. We were crowded into a hot room; some standing at the back, some leaning against the wall. There was little dignity. People shuffled about, shook hands, talked, stood around. The guards from the four armed services, around the coffin, were singularly unsoldierly in their bearing. It was no fitting farewell to such a great man.

Now Mr Truman was President. The ex-haberdasher and Missouri politician who had become Vice-President by political manœuvring and President by a tragic death was now the possessor of great, possibly even decisive, power in determining the future of the world at a vitally important moment in its history.

I had not met Mr Truman until he became Vice-President. My first meetings were not encouraging. As a new Ambassador, in accord with custom, I made an appointment to call on the Vice-President on 2 March 1945. Mr Truman was busy when I arrived so I was invited by an assistant in the outer office (he later had some trouble with the law over influence peddling) to take a chair and make myself at home. This I did, and waited for some time with growing impatience not entirely removed by friendly chat about baseball and Democratic politics; or even by the generous offer of a 'peanut chew.' It was fortunate that I was not the Ambassador from Upper Ruritania, or I would have felt that my country had been insulted.

Eventually, I was taken into Mr Truman's office and presented in an off-hand manner. We had a pleasant talk about nothing in particular, interrupted by the unannounced entrance of a Senator. There were more introductions and some cheerful political banter. As I left, both gentlemen assured me emphatically that our countries were and always would be great friends and, that if only all countries were as neighbourly and reasonable in their relationships as we were the world would have nothing to worry about. This, from the Vice-President and an influential Senator, was nice to hear. It also illustrated once again the need to impress on our American friends that there *are* serious Canadian-American problems; that they will increase in number and importance; and that they will not be made easier by the tendency to treat Canada as, in effect, another state of the Union, north of an unguarded border, but without congressional representation.

My next exposure to the Vice-President was even more informal, but rather less agreeable. It was at a big party given by the Press Club in his honour. As is normal on these occasions, it was a ribald and boisterous evening. Toward the end the Vice-President was called on for a few words. He made what he no doubt thought was the kind of speech expected for such an occasion, a 'stag party' bit with jokes that were more vulgar than funny. He then played his theme song, the 'Missouri Waltz,' while a lovely young actress, also part of the programme, was hoisted on to the edge of the grand piano where she exposed a stretch of leg, daring in 1945, though today it would be considered old-fashioned modesty. The cameras flashed, the company cheered. I was not amused or impressed. I thought: 'Can this man rise to the awesome responsibilities likely to fall on him soon?' I was not long in finding out.

A few hours after being sworn in as President, Mr Truman received the heads of diplomatic missions. He entered the room, where we had been assembled, to receive our respectful good wishes. He was a different person, dignified, serious, formal in dress and manner. His short talk was exactly right. This was a President of the United States of America.

I saw Mr Truman on several occasions during the rest of my stay in Washington and, as time went on, acquired for him a deep respect and admiration. He was decisive, without being rash, courageous without being foolhardy, progressive without being visionary. He chose good men to be with him and he knew how to get the best from them. The United States, and the world, was fortunate in this succession.

ॐ

There were so many happenings during my years in Washington in which I became involved, that I have not space to deal with them even if they are worth recounting. In one way or another they all seemed to be connected with the war.

There is one incident I should mention, however, even though it was not important in the context of the world conflict, and normally our Washington Mission would not have been officially concerned with it. I refer to the landing of allied forces in Sicily in July 1943.

By this time, the morale of the Canadian forces in England was suffering from their long period of camp life and training without action. This deterioration began to modify the insistence in Ottawa that the Canadian forces overseas remain as a single unit under Canadian command, except to meet a grave military emergency. Such a policy, right in principle, had to be re-examined when British military action increased in North Africa, and when plans were being made for the landing in Sicily. Were Canadians to leave the fighting to others, because political reasons compelled them to remain together as an army? Resentment against this attitude grew, especially among the troops, not many of whom, I suspect, volunteered for overseas service to confirm Canada's independent political status. Mr King soon sensed this feeling (no man was quicker to sense a feeling than he was), and was prepared to modify the decision not to break up the army. In fact, he took the initiative in pressing for Canadian participation in the landing in Sicily. Earlier suggestions to send a Canadian division to the Eighth Army in North Africa had never been seriously considered but the return to Europe was something else. The government felt that Canadians should take part in it.

During the visit, therefore, of Mr Eden to Ottawa at the end of March 1943, both Mr King and Colonel Ralston brought up the possibility of including Canadian troops in any invasion of Sicily. Indeed, Mr King stated that it was the fixed policy of the Canadian government and the Canadian High Command that Canadian soldiers should be employed wherever and whenever they were needed. He added that he wished to remove any idea in the minds of the British government that the Canadian army could not be broken up. I heard the Prime Minister say this with some surprise, because, however realistic militarily, it meant a complete reversal of policy. In any event, when the first Allied soldiers returned to the continent of Europe, not as raiders but as invaders, Canadians were with them.

In planning for this invasion of Sicily, which became imminent after the expulsion of the Germans and Italians from North Africa, General Eisenhower's Headquarters in Algiers drafted three documents to be issued in his name, at the appropriate moment: (*a*) an initial communiqué announcing the landing; (*b*) a message to the French people; (*c*) a message to the Italian people. These documents were sent to London, Washington, and Ottawa. Their texts used the words 'Anglo-American Forces' and 'Forces of the United States and Great Britain,' and this was resented and objected to by the Canadian government. Since a Canadian division was an important part of the landing forces, and this was the first stage in the liberation of Europe, the angry feelings aroused in Ottawa by the use of the words 'Anglo-American' can be understood. Our reaction was swift and decisive. References to 'Anglo-American' forces must be changed to 'British-American-Canadian' forces. Efforts to do this, however, through London and through General Eisenhower's Headquarters in Algiers, were unsuccessful.

On the evening of 8 July, therefore (the invasion was to begin in about 24 hours), I was asked (the Minister was on leave) to do what I could in Washington to get the desired changes made. From this point, my diary tells the story:

I immediately telephoned Robertson and told him that there was no use in my going to the State Department, who would disclaim any responsibility and possibly even any knowledge of the matters in question. There was only one thing to do, and that was to see the President himself. The only way I could do that in a hurry was to get Mr King to telephone Harry Hopkins or, even better, the President himself and tell him that he wanted me to go to the White House at once and discuss a matter of urgent national importance with Mr Roosevelt. Norman agreed to take the matter up with the PM. Within fifteen minutes (who said Mr King cannot work quickly?) I had a call from Hopkins to say the President would be glad to receive me at 9.40.

The telegram I sent to Ottawa gives the result of the visit:

I saw the President and Harry Hopkins at 9.40 tonight on the matters mentioned in your telegrams. I found them both most friendly and sympathetic to the position which I took, namely, that any mention of 'armed forces' in official statements announcing 'HUSKY' operation without inclusion of the word 'Canadian' alongside 'Anglo-American forces' would be objectionable and would not be understood by the Canadian people; also that references to the 'Canadian government' should be made when the UK and US governments were mentioned. The President at first thought the presence of French troops might complicate matters, but later agreed that as they were so few in number they might be disregarded in this particular connection. He also wondered whether the phrase 'British Empire-American forces' might not be satisfactory. However, he ended by accepting the view that a specific mention of Canada was preferable and said he would take steps to see that this was done and that the Canadian position generally was safeguarded in any proclamations or official announcements to be made on the launching of this operation.

I was pleased with my success, hurried back to the Legation, and sent my telegram to Ottawa. It was, I thought, a good evening's work.

There still seemed to be doubt in London and Algiers, however, whether the changes could or should be made. I was sure the President would follow through, but was there time?

I left the Legation just before midnight and started for home. As I was driving up Connecticut Avenue, listening to dance music on the car radio, I was startled to hear a voice break in: 'We interrupt this program to make an announcement. "British, American, (pause) and

Canadian troops" have commenced landing operations in Sicily.' I heaved a sigh of relief and satisfaction.

As I opened the door at Ashley Terrace, the phone was ringing. It was Norman Robertson from Ottawa to say that the Prime Minister and everybody else were very happy. On 12 July I received a telegram from Mr King. 'I would not wish the occasion to pass without expressing my warm appreciation of your efforts of the past few days with regard to the announcements dealing with the participation of Canadian Forces in the Combined Allied Offensive against Sicily. I am sure that it was with deep pride that the Canadian People heard that our Forces together with Forces from Britain and the United States are engaged in this great action.'

The results in the United States were also satisfactory. I wrote to Robertson on 12 July:

The fact that 'Canada' was mentioned in the first official communique seems to me to have made absolutely all the difference in so far as the impression made on public opinion in this country is concerned. Since midnight Friday, 'Canada' has appeared almost automatically alongside 'United Kingdom' and 'United States' in press and radio references (except, incidentally, in radio comments from North Africa where I notice the phrase 'British and American' seems to be used).

There have been moments since last Thursday when concentration on the necessity for adequate and separate recognition of Canada's part in the operation has tended to obscure in my mind the operation itself. Our own particular tree seemed so important! But I've been looking at the forest again lately and it certainly is encouraging. We shall have the Axis out of Sicily before long.

I hope in the enthusiasm of our initial publicity success we are not tempted to try to prove to the world that Canadians are solely responsible for this achievement.

13

PREPARING FOR PEACE

In completing the account of my years in Washington, I wish to mention four other matters with which I was associated. They were international in character and of far greater and more continuing importance than the problem of how to refer to the landing of troops in Sicily. Dealing with them will require skipping forward and back again in time but this will, I hope, result in a clearer picture. These developments were all centred in Washington since that capital had become the headquarters of allied war policy and planning. I will try to show how I became closely concerned with them, for this had far-reaching consequences on my career.

I have already mentioned my deep interest in the United Nations aspect of my work in Washington. From the day the United Nations Declaration was signed I hoped that the concept embodied in it could be translated into reality by multi-national planning and policy. To this end, I felt that the allied meetings and conferences that were beginning to take place should be held not only in the name of the United Nations, but should also be organized and conducted by them. I suggested to the State Department early in 1943 that an international committee of officials should be set up, representing several countries, which could do the preparatory and organizational work for United Nations conferences, and supply the secretariat for them. Dean Acheson, with whom I discussed the matter, thought it was a good idea, but I feared that nothing would be done about it and I was right. The Americans had decided to look after these meetings themselves.

Looking back, I can see that this was almost inevitable in the circumstances of that time. The Big Two felt that, as they were directing the war successfully, they should also take responsibility for the development of the United Nations, with the co-operation, if they could get it, of the 'Third,' Stalin.

There were many fine and intelligent Americans who believed that there should be a far broader basis than this for co-operation and I was fortunate in having many friends among them. They were deeply, almost emotionally, international in their views of the future world. They were men of the highest ideals, for their own country and for the international community; but few of them were political decision-makers. Among these few, to my surprise, was that superficially aloof and unemotional person, Sumner Welles, who once talked to me with burning conviction of the absolute necessity for a postwar collective security system based on an international police force to enforce international law.

This international idealism which flourished in certain circles in Washington at that time was too imprecise and unorganized to stand up against the practical realities of war and politics, national and international. Differences of this kind between 'Yogis and Commissars' are common to all political societies but this is particularly evident in the United States, where public opinion is vigorous, broadly based, and assertive, but where idealism and politics often become confused. I remember one of my British friends telling me a story about meeting Eisenhower in North Africa after the Casablanca Conference. The General was complaining that he was criticized by American and British liberals for having no ideals because he approved of deals with men like Admiral Darlan. Ike claimed that this was most unfair and assured his British companion, 'I am idealistic as hell.' While many Americans were 'idealistic as heaven,' they found it difficult to ensure that these ideals should be reflected later in the plans and policies being worked out by the Big Three.

☞

The first of the international events which I wish to describe arose from the President's decision to begin organizing postwar international co-operation in the field of food and agriculture. Mr Roosevelt had adopted with enthusiasm Vice-President Wallace's welfare approach to world peace and human progress, with priority to be given to the elimination of hunger and malnutrition. It was hoped that a 'hot meal every day for every Hottentot' would bring happiness and contentment to the world. The fact that a conference on these relatively non-controversial matters might keep the United Nations busy and allow Roosevelt, Churchill, and Stalin to run the war may have been a contributory reason for calling it.

It was in March 1943 that we first heard of the President's plans for this initial UN conference. He announced them, rather vaguely, at a White House press conference, explaining that no date had been fixed for the meeting because the replies to the invitations had not all come in. There was a good reason for this: none at that time had been sent out. Indeed, the State Department knew nothing about the President's plans. This uncertainty was cleared up and the invitations did go out. But nobody seemed to know what the conference would actually deal with, or how it would operate. We knew only that it was to be organized and run by the United States, who would choose the chairman and the secretariat and draw up the agenda. The White House also decided to hold the Conference in Hot Springs, Virginia, where it would be easier to keep the press away than in Washington. The first United Nations conference was to be in secret.

There were to be five Canadian delegates and I was one of them. The head of the British delegation was my old friend, Dick Law, now Parliamentary Under-Secretary in the Foreign Office. Prior to Hot Springs, we had a meeting of Commonwealth delegates in Washington. I attended for Canada, as the other delegates had not yet left Ottawa. Naturally, I was asked to outline Canadian policy at the conference. If we had one, I had not been told anything about it. After long experience with such situations, however, this caused me no embarrassment. It was like old times. There was a unanimous feeling at the meeting that the conference was not likely to accomplish much. This also did not depress me. It is always better to be pessimistic before a conference than in despair afterwards.

On Monday, 17 May 1943 the delegates left Washington for the first formal conference of the United Nations to be held among the beautiful green hills and healing springs of West Virginia. I naturally referred to this historic event in my diary:

We left in our special train for Hot Springs today, five hundred assorted United Nations nationals, including Russians, Ethiopians, Icelanders, Liberians, and others. We are a motley crew, and I do not envy those responsible for organizing us into a conference in such a way that at the end of two weeks or so we will be able to produce a report that means anything. It took us most of the day to get to Hot Springs, the last fifteen miles very much uphill. Once or twice I thought we were going off the rails. I hope that going 'uphill' and 'off the rails' is not symbolic; or the fact that it took four engines to haul us the last part of the journey. At any rate, we got to Hot Springs without mishap; a lovely spot, high up in wooded hills. A very luxurious hotel. I wonder what the Russians, who have just flown here from their hard-pressed and devastated country, or the Ethiopians from Addis Ababa, think of this haven of peace and luxury, so very remote from blood, sweat, and tears ...

The arrangements for our accommodation are all very satisfactory, but they have done one very silly thing. They have a military guard around the hotel day and night, and you cannot get in or out without showing your pass. They say this is to protect us from the press, but it gives one, more or less, the same feeling that the Japanese, German, and Italian diplomats must have had when they were interned in this hotel after Pearl Harbor. None of us have been shot yet trying to escape!

The opening session on 18 May was the most original of any international conference I have ever attended, and I have attended many. The chairman, a good Democrat from Texas, tried to blend dignity with bonhomie; to combine the Congress of Vienna with a Rotary meeting. We opened with a silent prayer and ended by singing, not 'Hail to the United Nations,' but the 'Star Spangled Banner.' None of us was quite sure what we were to pray about and none of the foreigners knew the words of the American national anthem. In between, we were given a message of greeting from the President, a speech by the chairman, who neglected not a single cliché, and an inaudible reply from a Chinese delegate on behalf of the forty-two foreign delegations.

At the end of this inaugural meeting, the chairman introduced another new idea into international gatherings. He called the roll of all the countries present and asked each chief delegate to stand up for recognition, as his country was announced. The applause would indicate his country's or his own popularity.

Food and agriculture were important subjects to Canada and, since the steering committee of the conference would be making the important decisions, we were anxious to gain membership on it. This was not my first or my last experience with the tricky and fascinating business of international lobbying. We were successful on this occasion and as a consequence were able to play an active part in the work of the conference, much of which, as is always the case, was done behind the scenes and even in constructing scenes behind which to do it.

The conference accomplished more than the pessimists predicted; indeed, it made a good start. It was only a start, however. A continuing interim commission was set up to carry on the work and to draw up detailed plans for a permanent international body.

In a personal initiative, I proposed to some British, American, and other friends that the conference should issue a short, non-technical, but inspirational declaration on the determination of the United Nations to deal with the problems of hunger and malnutrition once the war was over; something that would be valuable not only now in the political warfare that was being waged against the Nazis and their allies, but might help also to convince opinion in all countries that, this time, international co-operation and action would not fail after victory was won. I was punished for such initiative by being invited to draft the declaration; it was published two weeks later in Washington but the world paid little notice.

The closing days of the conference saw a certain testiness develop between the British and American delegations, the two which, with ours and one or two others, did most of the work. My last diary reference to the Hot Springs Conference on 30 May mentions this:

The Americans are getting the feeling that the British are playing too big a part in these closing days and taking charge of too many things. One of them said to me that the Americans called the conference, but the British have captured it. In contrast, the British feel that they are really doing the hard work, that the American contribution, in the final stages, is not a very effective one. There is something in this. The particular points of uneasiness are the General Resolution, which the Americans are criticizing and which criticism the British resent, as they claim the Americans have not contributed any really worthwhile ideas; and the efforts of the Americans to slip into the report of a committee several pages of social and economic theory as an introduction to the specific resolutions. The British do not like this at all.

The Russians entertained us tonight at a vodka party. This certainly was a test of our sobriety and also of our powers of collaboration with the Soviet, as it is hard to be friendly with your host when you cannot talk to him. We all sat around, glass after glass of vodka was drunk, to the accompaniment of much smiling and a few broken exchanges of words. I tossed off five toasts in rapid succession and then staggered back to the main lobby to listen to a woman playing the violin. That sobered me up.

On our return to Washington, the Interim Commission began its work. It consisted largely of United Nations diplomats in the capital, and I was the Canadian representative. It continued to work throughout the summer of 43 and with it my hopes of a holiday with the family in cool Canada disappeared. I had been approached by Paul Appleby, the Under-Secretary for Agriculture and a most dedicated American internationalist, to see whether I would take the chairmanship. I did not much like the idea, since I had more than enough to do at the legation, but passed the invitation on to Ottawa, through my Minister, thinking that he and the government would tell me to regret my inability to accept. They did not do this. So I was elected chairman and spent a great deal of time during the months ahead presiding over the commission or, more often, over its small executive committee. This committee did most of the work, as the representatives of forty-two states would get nowhere slowly in the task of drawing up a constitution and regulations for a United Nations organization on food and agriculture.

This working group laboured steadily and effectively on the project for many weeks and we gathered together some highly qualified experts to give us advice and assistance. The result was that, when an international conference met in Quebec from 16 October to 1 November 1945 to consider the draft constitution for a United Nations food and agricultural organization, the preparatory work had been well and honestly done. Presiding over that work was the most important responsibility which I had yet undertaken. I learned much from it and made many friends from the four corners of the globe.

One result of my chairmanship of the commission was that I was asked to preside over the Quebec Conference. A further result was pressure from many quarters at Quebec to become the first Director-General of the first United Nations agency, the Food and Agriculture Organization, which had been brought into being by our work. I was not willing to let my name go forward, however, though I was assured that I would get more than enough support for election. I did not want to leave the Canadian foreign service for a post which, however important, was not one for which I was really suited, since it dealt with matters in which I had little experience. I felt the more strongly about this because Sir John Boyd-Orr was one of the British delegates in Quebec and no one could possibly be better qualified for the post of Director than he. He had devoted his whole life to precisely those questions of food and agriculture with which the new organization would have to deal, and had become a world authority in the field. He was elected and served in a manner which abundantly justified his choice. I went back to Washington very happy over the success of the work which had begun in Hot Springs two years before. By now I had become an old hand at UN meetings.

The Quebec Conference stimulated our hopes for progress in international action; at least in technical and non-political fields. But we also discovered that there were few subjects, however technical, that did not have political implications, and that these usually created obstacles to understanding and co-operation. This was particularly true in dealing with the USSR and its friends. The Quebec Conference gave me a discouraging experience of Soviet suspicions and negative reactions to what seemed entirely non-controversial, technical proposals, as well as of Soviet diplomatic tactics in general.

A Soviet delegation had attended the Hot Springs Conference. They had worked in the Interim Commission and had managed to get a number of changes made in its report and in the proposed constitution. Some of their suggestions were good ones. Some, we thought, were not but were accepted as part of the process of bargaining to secure unanimous agreement. Then, when the final document setting up FAO was accepted in Quebec, the USSR decided to have nothing to do with the organization, and flatly rejected a constitution which had been drafted with its participation and included some of its own proposals. This Soviet tactic was disturbing. We were to experience it often in the years ahead.

They were not always to blame, of course. Very often western delegates did not show enough patience with, or understanding of, Soviet doubts and suspicions. But, after making all allowances, Soviet methods were disconcerting and were going to make it very difficult to build up an effective postwar structure for international co-operation, even in areas where this co-operation was of obvious practical benefit to all countries.

ℭ

A second United Nations initiative in Washington with which I became associated concerned the relief and rehabilitation of liberated territories. As early as June 1942, at a time when nothing had yet been liberated or indeed looked like being liberated, the Canadian government agreed, in principle, to a draft proposal made by the United States government for the creation of an international relief and rehabilitation organization. From that day the United Nations Relief and Rehabilitation Administration, or UNRRA as it became known, brought much work and many headaches to the Canadian Mission in Washington and to me in particular.

We became deeply involved in the arrangements and negotiations that followed, not only because of a strong Canadian interest in this work but also because, as a rich and physically undamaged country, with ample supplies, we would be expected to play a part commensurate with our relative affluence and good fortune. But while we were expected to play such a part, only the Big Four, USA, UK, USSR, and China, were to be on the Central Policy Committee of an UNRRA Council, which would largely control the organization and decide how it was to operate.

The Canadian government reacted vigorously, and rightly so, to this exclusion. In a note to the United States government we argued strongly for appropriate Canadian participation in UNRRA policy-making as well as in the working of other postwar international institutions. The position we took was as follows:

There had to be a proper relationship between the place of Canada in the Council of UNRRA and the anticipated importance of Canada as a supplier of relief.

The Canadian people could not be expected to accept the sacrifices which relief and rehabilitation contributions would entail if they were not satisfied that their government was properly recognized in making decisions on UNRRA policy.

Representation on the policy committee of international economic organizations should be determined on a functional basis on every occasion when this was practicable.

No workable international system could be based on the concentration of influence and authority in bodies composed of a few great powers to the exclusion of all others. The largest powers did not always make the greatest contribution to the work of these bodies, or have the greatest stake in their success.

In presenting and supporting this note, I told Dean Acheson at the State Department that they should take it seriously. I warned him that if we were refused membership on the Policy Committee of UNRRA, we might not be able to sign any relief convention.

The State Department, however, was more concerned about political difficulties that our stand was creating with the Soviet Union than they were about the merits of the Canadian position. The Russians would not agree to add Canada, or any other state, to the Policy Committee. This might mean that the Polish government, which was not then communist, would insist on membership. The Americans also, and this was becoming an old and tiresome excuse, thought that Brazil and perhaps another Latin American state would have to be included if Canada were.

We remained adamant. So did the Russians and Americans. The latter preferred a row with Canada to one with the USSR or Latin America. The British were sympathetic but could do little to help. Mr Churchill, for instance, seemed to take this whole business of relief rather casually. Once when the subject came up for discussion at a meeting of Commonwealth Heads of Missions in Washington, he dismissed it with the remark that when the time came he was sure they 'could make up a hamper' for the rescued people of Europe but, he added, the goods

would have to come from countries that had made fewer material sacrifices than the British. That was true enough, and was a major reason
why Canada, bound to be a major contributor, should have a part in
policy-making.

Our friends in Washington were finally convinced that we were not
bluffing. So they agreed to consider a compromise, which I had already
proposed to them informally and personally, by which Canada would
become chairman of the proposed Suppliers Committee, with a clause
in the UNRRA agreement under which the chairman of that committee
would be invited to sit in at the meetings of the Central Policy Committee whenever supply questions were under consideration. In effect,
that would mean practically every meeting. This, at first, was not good
enough for Ottawa. I tried to make it more palatable to our government
by getting the words 'will be invited to sit in' changed to 'will become
a member of,' but the best I could secure from the Americans was 'will
be invited to participate in.' The whole dispute was becoming ridiculous
and the Big Four were showing themselves to be rather petty. However,
I sent the change of wording to Ottawa.

The Prime Minister was not made more conciliatory when he learned
at this particular moment (1 February 1943) that the United States
government had decided to publish a note to the British government
proposing a conference between British and American representatives
to alleviate the plight of war refugees, which would be held *in Ottawa*.
Not only was the Canadian government not invited to attend; we were
not even informed that it was to be held in our capital. I noted: 'Jack
Hickerson has phoned me, grovelling with apologies, that it was all
done hurriedly and that he knew nothing about it. I asked him if they
had already requisitioned the Chateau for their conference. I phoned
Ottawa about the matter, and they were furious. The whole thing is a
stupid mix-up.'

On 4 March we sent another message to the State Department from
our government, with the information that their compromise, even with
the verbal improvement, was not satisfactory. My instructions from
Ottawa contained a paragraph from a letter written by the Deputy
Minister of Finance reflecting the prevailing view there. It read:

We are still trying to run a democracy [in Canada] and there is some historical
evidence to support the thesis that democracies cannot be taxed without representation. We have tried to lead our people in a full-out effort for the war,
and we had hoped that we could continue to lead them in such a way as to
get their support behind the provision of relief and maintenance for battle-
scarred Europe in the postwar years. We will not be able to secure their

support for such a programme if it, as well as the economic affairs of the world generally, are to be run as a monopoly by the four Great Powers.

Mr Acheson was irritated. I felt, myself, that *we* were now too negative about the compromise offered which would certainly have given us the substance of what we rightly insisted on. The British also felt that we were being too stubborn. Ottawa, however, remained unmoved. Indeed, they thought we had not pressed the Canadian case strongly enough in Washington. This angered my Minister who threatened to go to Ottawa and protest to the Prime Minister. On this I noted:

I hope he doesn't, because Mr McCarthy thinks favourably of an idea that the British and Americans were playing with, by which a Canadian on the Policy Committee would represent the 'British Empire.' I told my friends at the British Embassy that this was a non-starter but was a shade disconcerted when the Minister took a different position at a Commonwealth meeting with Eden [who was then in Washington]. I knew, of course, that Mr King would summarily reject it.

However, Mr McCarthy went off to Ottawa to see the Prime Minister, where Mr King gave him a lecture on the structure of the Commonwealth.

Another complication was that the Russians began to think that our efforts to become a member of UNRRA's Policy Committee confirmed their suspicion that the 'Anglo-Saxons' wished to dominate postwar relief activities for political purposes. Far from the Supplies Committee being an unimportant subsidiary body, as they feared in Ottawa, Moscow thought it would be the most important one and demanded the right to sit on it. This strengthened my feeling that we should accept the US compromise proposal.

To further this, at the end of March, I went to Ottawa myself. I found that the most violent opposition to the 'compromise' regarding UNRRA came from our Deputy Minister of Finance, Clifford Clark, a very real power in Ottawa in those days. He was emphatic we should have nothing to do with any relief convention which did not put Canada in an equal position in every way with the Big Four. He had little or no appreciation of the obstacles in the way of achieving this. Mr King was more realistic when I had a private talk with him and said he was impressed by my arguments that we should not turn down lightly the 'compromise,' adding that he had not previously understood what it really meant. I had some difficulty in appreciating this as I knew it had been explained carefully enough to him by his staff who, though they previously favoured rejecting the 'compromise,' were now coming around to my view.

Mr Eden, who was then in Ottawa, argued at a meeting of the War Committee of our Cabinet that the 'compromise' recognized Canada's special position in a very satisfactory way. Neither the Prime Minister, nor any minister, disagreed. Mr King contented himself with saying they would reconsider the matter in the light of this 'new' proposal. He wondered, however, how other countries would react to Canada becoming the chairman of the Supplies Committee and also whether we had a Canadian who was capable of handling the job. I was present at the meeting and knew, after hearing Mr King say this, that he had decided to accept the compromise. I was happy about the result but felt I had been left out on a limb by my political masters. I had told Mr Eden and his officials that they were going to hear some really strong, tough complaints from the Canadian ministers about the way Canada had been treated. The Cabinet's reluctance to make any complaint at all made me look rather foolish, and their own strong telegrams to the mission in Washington more or less meaningless.

In any event, what had been a long drawn-out and at times a somewhat heated conflict was settled when on 8 April 1943 we received a telegram from Ottawa saying that the Government of Canada accepted the proposal. The difficulty was resolved. It should never have been allowed to develop. The Americans should have been more understanding of the Canadian position from the beginning. We had a strong case. We were going to be a very important member of UNRRA and contribute more to its resources than any other country except the United States and the United Kingdom. Why the Americans did not recognize this at once and at least try to get the USSR to recognize it was due, presumably, to their confidence that, notwithstanding our strong views, when the decision had to be made we would be 'good boys' and help them in their difficulties with Moscow and with Latin America.

However, when a compromise *was* worked out in Washington which *did* recognize the Canadian position in a reasonably satisfactory way, Ottawa, especially some of the senior officials there, were too negative and stubborn in their reaction to it. After the matter was settled, I noted: 'I hope we play our cards right and put a good man on the Supplies Committee.' I cannot very well comment on that as I was the man chosen and became its chairman. I also said: 'We have a chance to play a big part in this organization.' Both of the directors-general of the organization, Governor Lehman and Fiorello La Guardia, have testified to the importance and effectiveness of that part.

The chairman of the Supplies Committee was, in fact, a full member of the Policy Committee of Big Powers in everything but name. The first Council meeting was at Atlantic City in November 1943. I recall it well because it was there that the organization laid down the principles and procedures to govern the work that was to be done. I recall it also for a less serious reason. We had been working amicably and usefully with the Soviet representatives on relief matters, even though they often introduced political considerations into humanitarian discussions and also kept insisting on the claims of their own devastated and liberated areas to first priority in aid. These claims certainly needed no reinforcement, but they were not helped by Soviet demands for exclusive control over the distribution of all relief supplies in their territory, or in territory controlled by them. They were also too suspicious about the possible political activities of UNRRA missions. In spite of differences and even disputes, I was on very good terms with the Soviet representatives, especially with one of their leaders, Sergeev, whom I got to know and like.

At Atlantic City they lavished hospitality on other delegates in traditional generous Russian style, with special emphasis, of course, on vodka and caviar. I was their guest at dinner on the last night of the meeting. It was an occasion which required stamina and stability beyond the call of duty. It was a great feast with many toasts drunk to honour irreproachable people and things. As I returned to my room, I was thinking of two things: of peace, which we must have toasted a half a dozen times that night and, secondly, of the instructions given us to have our luggage in the corridor outside our rooms by two AM, to be collected and taken in advance to the special train which was to take us all back to Washington, leaving at eight AM. So before going to sleep, and dreaming of peace, I finished my packing and put my bags outside the door. On rising, not too brightly at seven, I discovered that I had packed so thoroughly that I had nothing left to wear but pajamas! It was a desperate situation, but my baggage was retrieved and the train was delayed no more than five minutes. This proved to be a lesson to me, but of what, I am not sure!

The Atlantic City meeting was the responsibility of our Director General, Mr Herbert Lehman, who had been appointed to that post by President Roosevelt. I have not met an American of finer quality. For reasons which remain obscure to me, Mr Lehman, who had been Governor of New York and a US Senator from that state, later retired from UNRRA and was succeeded by the former mayor of New York, the fabulous Fiorello La Guardia. While Mr Lehman had been quiet, gentlemanly, and conservative, Mr La Guardia was excitable, domineering, unpredictable, and explosive. He had an almost frantic energy, and in his determination to get things done did not care much about whose feelings were hurt in the process. It was impossible to ignore him, to stop him, or to reject him. He revelled in giving shock treatment which at times, no doubt, the organization needed.

He seemed to like Canada and Canadians. Once during a long drawn-out discussion which was becoming contentious and getting nowhere, he astonished me, and the committee even more, by telling me to make a proposal – any proposal – and that would end the matter because he would insist that it be accepted. This was perhaps not the best way to resolve a dispute, but, in this instance, it worked.

The third meeting of the Council was at Montreal and I was chosen to preside over it. We had a useful and constructive meeting as by this time the work of relief and rehabilitation was in full swing. I fear, however, that I remember it for a different if less important reason.

I opened the first session by warning the members that I did not want them to raise points of order, for two reasons: first, because their discussion wasted a lot of time and, second, because I knew little about rules of order and procedure. My wife, attending this opening session, heard with surprise and anxiety this admission on my part of ignorance and inability. I noticed that she disappeared but returned in twenty minutes or so. A messenger then handed to me, in the chair, a small parcel which turned out to be a neat little book, well-indexed, entitled *Parliamentary Procedure at a Glance.* I was so overcome by this wifely devotion and solicitude that I didn't hear one of the delegates who was raising a point of order!

The fourth meeting of the Council was in London in August 1945. The war was over. Occupied territories in Europe, Southeast Asia, and the Pacific had been liberated. There was much to do in relief and re-habilitation and this was being done. If there was inefficiency in the doing and some corruption, nevertheless, without UNRRA, there would have been infinitely more suffering and destitution after the war and a far slower rate of recovery and rehabilitation.

On this journey to Europe I motored through the devastation and destruction of the Rhineland, visited Canadian troops, and then went on to Berlin. I was almost as shattered as the city as I trudged through the ruins and gazed in and around the fatal 'bunker' in the garden of the Reichs Chancellery where Hitler killed himself. It all looked as though it had happened only yesterday. This, then, was the Thousand Year Reich. Would we read aright its lesson, or fail once more? I wrote to a friend that it was inconceivable that Germany would get back on her feet for years and years, although they were already working with great energy among the ruins. I should have known better. I was de-pressed and distressed and saw little light for the future, none at all, unless the promise of San Francisco could become a reality.

The next and, for me the final, meeting of the UNRRA Council took place at Geneva in the summer of 1946. It was strange to return to that peaceful and lovely city which, once again, had escaped the horrors and destruction of war. It was almost eerie to go back to the Hotel de la Paix after ten years to be calmly greeted by the porter, 'Nice to see you back, Mr Pearson,' as if I had been there last week; and to be asked at the desk whether I would like to have my old room. In a world of chaos and change, some things remained undisturbed; even the red plush curtains of my room and the rich black cherry conserve with croissants for breakfast. Perhaps, however, it was not the best atmosphere in which to discuss how to deal with the distress and devastation of Europe. I told La Guardia that we should have met in tents at Dachau or in the ruins of Warsaw.

It was a short and useful session. I remember, among other things, that it gave me an opportunity to become better acquainted with that doomed but delightful person, Jan Masaryk. By accident of alphabet, we sat beside each other at the Council. He had no illusions about what was happening in his country and about the price which he and other Czech democrats would have to pay for collaborating with Czech communists who had already their own plan for a takeover, with Soviet support and power behind them. Masaryk was a gay and highly civilized person. He was also an uninhibited conversationalist. His comments to me about the USSR, its satellites, and their representatives were restrained neither in content nor delivery. They were invariably witty, but dangerous for him if overheard by the wrong persons. This was likely to happen because some of those wrong persons were close by in his own delegation. I remember that once he leaned over to whisper to me that the Czech sitting behind him was the real 'boss' of his delegation because he was the senior representative in it of the Czech Communist party. Soon afterwards Masaryk met the fate that he knew was inevitable.

After the Geneva meeting I accompanied La Guardia on an inspection of UNRRA activities in Germany, Poland, and the USSR. To accompany Fiorello La Guardia was to ride a whirlwind – physically and emotionally. There never was a dull or even a calm moment. It was a tour which I shall never forget, not merely because La Guardia was the conducting officer but because of what we saw; the human and material wreckage of war, and the hopeful signs of rebirth and rebuilding.

The refugee centre we visited in Germany was crowded with the survivors and the victims of the Nazi concentration camps. The two cities we saw, Warsaw and Wroclaw (formerly Breslau), were more completely shattered even than Berlin, if that were possible. We went for a day into the country near Warsaw and watched the farmers cultivating recent battle-fields, often with dug-outs as their temporary homes. We talked to some. I shall never forget one old (at least she looked old) and stooped lady, who paused for a moment from her work and with moving sincerity and great dignity told us her tragic story, and also of her hope for a better future for those to come when war might be no more. She then quietly thanked us for visiting them and honouring their poverty and their work. It made one feel very humble.

We had a picnic luncheon that day with our Polish hosts at a ruined village at a bend of the Vistula River. It had to be outdoors because no house remained. I was seated beside a Polish political leader who told me that at this very spot the USSR had condemned Warsaw to death by making the decision to halt their relieving forces, thus permitting the Nazis to exterminate the heroic freedom fighters in the city, only a few miles away. My surprise at his statement was owing to the fact that he would make it, for he was a leading member of the Communist party.

After our meal, the villagers greeted us. Their children, thirty or forty of them, marched by in a pathetic little parade. It was also, for me at least, a frightening one. The boys and girls looked happy and excited. This was an event. They had been scrubbed and tidied. It was all very pleasant and normal. But they marched by in separate groups and each wore the coloured blouse or shirt of their parents' political party: green for the peasants' party, blue for the socialist, red for the communist. There was no white for peace and humanity. There were merely the symbols of that political and ideological division which had had so much to do with the ruin of their own village and all the other thousands of cities and towns and villages that once made up Europe. What did this mean for Poland's future? We soon learned that it meant one thing: only red shirts would be parading in the future.

We were about to leave Warsaw for Moscow when I received a telegram from Mr King in Paris asking me to see him there as soon as possible. So instead of flying east to the Soviet Union, I went the other way to Paris and, after a short visit there, on to Washington. But not for long. Another change was in the offing. Before writing about it, however, I must explain my association with the other two international questions with which I became concerned in Washington. The first was atomic energy and takes me forward to the autumn of 1945.

ॐ

On 3 October of that year Mr Truman told Congress that he proposed to initiate discussions with Great Britain and Canada and then with other nations 'in an effort to effect agreement on the conditions under which co-operation might replace rivalry in the field of atomic power.'

It was an important and encouraging move on the part of the American government since it faced up to the terrifying implications of the unprecedented power for destruction now horribly unleashed in the bombing of Hiroshima and Nagasaki. The United States had a monopoly of atomic power at that time, but this monopoly would not last long. Therefore this was the right moment for the American government to begin the effort to ensure that atomic energy should not be used again for destructive purposes. This could only be achieved by international agreement. The proposed Washington meeting was to be the first step in this process, including as it did the three governments which had worked together during the war to harness and apply atomic energy for military use. The results were now for all the world to know, and fear. We had seen the future and how it could work – for total destruction.

Mr Attlee and Mr King accepted Mr Truman's invitation. Their talks began on Saturday, 10 November. As Ambassador, I took part. Never before had there been meetings of such potential import, with the fate of man and his world as the agenda. The memory of these sessions remains vivid. At the first meeting at the White House, Mr Truman and the two prime ministers, accompanied by Mr Byrnes (Secretary of State), Admiral Leahy (Chief of Staff), Lord Halifax, and myself, discussed the nature of the problem and made arrangements for the subsequent talks.

The next day was Sunday, 11 November. Armistice Day could never be more relevant. It reminded us in a special way that peace may have little to do with victory, an armistice even less to do with peace. Nor could there have been a more appropriate ceremonial to emphasize this than the laying of wreaths and the two minutes' silence at 11 AM at the Tomb of the Unknown Soldier at Arlington Cemetery. I had not missed an Armistice Day silence since 1919, but never had the two minutes seemed so long, so pregnant with meaning, so evocative of memories, or so challenging to a renewed and more resolute search for a better world. We then motored to the Navy Yard, boarded the Yacht *Sequoia*, and began to move down the Potomac in damp and cool November weather. No record was kept of the talks but I made my own that evening.

The seven participants sat around a circular green baize covered table in the yacht's dining room. President Truman asked each of us in turn what should be done to ensure that atomic energy would never be used again for destructive purposes. When my turn came I might have been excused, in that company, and with my own Prime Minister having already spoken, for saying nothing. I could not resist the opportunity, however, to plead for a deep and broad international effort through the United Nations to control this new and final threat to human survival, an effort which must be made before other atomic powers appeared. I emphasized as strongly as I could what seemed to be so obvious, that we could prevent global catastrophe only by global agreement of an unprecedented character, and that this would undoubtedly require some delegation of sovereign rights to a supranational agency. After twenty-seven years I am still convinced this is the only solution, but I am more aware now of the almost insuperable obstacles in the way. The discussions continued. There was a good deal of thinking out loud, and no restraint or restriction in the exchange of views. But it was discursive talk, unfocused, unrelated to any specific plan of action, or any concrete proposal. There was, however, full agreement on the necessity for both national and international action and, less definitely, on the principles that should govern this action.

Monday was devoted to setting down the ideas and proposals put forward in the earlier discussions. The United Kingdom's delegation was the first to circulate the draft of a statement which might be issued by the three heads of government. I had previously prepared a 'memorandum on atomic warfare' which, with some changes by Robertson and Wrong, had been submitted to Mr King as a possible Canadian proposal. He approved it but decided not to table it. He would use it for possible amendments to the British draft, or to the American one shortly to be circulated.

The Canadian approach to the problem is given in this memorandum from which I quote:

Before any sound policy, national or international, can be laid down in respect of the development, manufacture, and use of atomic energy for warlike purposes, the following assumptions must be confirmed.
1 That the atomic bomb is not merely a new weapon in a long succession of weapons, since man first began to fight with clubs, but something revolutionary and unprecedented, a new departure in destruction and annihilative in effect.
2 That the atomic bomb dropped on Japan, if development is not controlled, is only the beginning, not the end, of the use of atomic energy for destruction; that even more devastating bombs are being or could be developed which will be to the present bomb as a machine gun is to a breech-loader.
3 That the secret of the atomic bomb cannot be kept and that within, say, five years a country like the USSR will know all about it.
4 That the manufacture of the atomic bomb is possible in any industrial state which knows the secret.

5 That projection by rockets with accuracy over great distances is now or will shortly be possible ...

It is assumed that the above statements are substantially true. If this assumption is correct, then no government has the right to give its people a feeling of security, which can only be false, by basing its policy on the opposite assumption, that a national or three-country monopoly of development and production is possible. Even if, for some years at least, such a monopoly *were* possible, its value to enforce peace would not be great because other countries would know perfectly well that Anglo-Saxon public opinion would not permit the aggressive or even preventive use of such a terrible weapon.

It follows, therefore, that any constructive solution of this problem of the war use of atomic energy, must be international – not national. There is, in fact, no national solution.

This does *not* mean that the three countries concerned should make a gift of their atomic knowledge to other countries without conditions. That would be folly. It means that they should exploit the temporary advantage they now possess in order to bring this weapon under international control, so that it can never be used by anyone. This can be attempted by trading the knowledge of invention and manufacture they alone possess at present, for renunciation by all nations of the right of production or use, except, possibly, on orders from the United Nations. This in its turn means international supervision and control of the development and use of atomic energy. If an honest offer of this kind, made by the United States, United Kingdom, and Canada, were refused by any other state, that refusal would certainly disclose which nations were to be trusted and which feared.

Our memorandum then went, in some detail, into the kind of international agreement which would implement these principles.

On Tuesday we began the discussion of a suitable statement to be issued by the three heads of government. Neither the British nor American draft was felt to be adequate for the purpose, and further consideration was postponed until the next day, Wednesday. A revised US draft was then submitted for consideration to which Mr King suggested certain amendments based on our own memorandum. These were designed to .nake the US draft more positive in character; to emphasize the importance of safeguards; and, characteristically, to take out all words that suggested that the agreement was between governments rather than between heads of governments only. Mr King's changes were accepted, as also was his suggestion that the draft be carefully examined to remove any impression that the three conferees were shelving the problem by sending it to a commission of the United Nations, as had been proposed in the US draft, and that they had no definite ideas themselves for a solution.

Things became more complicated when the United Kingdom also produced a redraft of their earlier proposal. It was an impressive statement (British drafts nearly always are), especially in its emphasis on the fact that prohibition alone was worse than useless since it gave merely a feeling of false security without doing anything to make that security effective.

At the close of the meeting on Wednesday afternoon, President Truman suggested that a committee of Dr Vannevar Bush, the US atomic scientist, Sir John Anderson, Lord Privy Seal in the UK, and I should produce a new document which would combine those parts of the US and UK drafts and the Canadian amendments, on which there had been general agreement, and which would also include any other ideas that had been put forward during the day and found acceptable.

This was a rather difficult assignment as we were to report back by ten that evening. But we began our work at once and when our chiefs met at the appointed hour we had a new document ready for them. They went over it, sentence by sentence, and with a few unimportant changes, had agreed on it by midnight.

It was signed the next morning at eleven and immediately afterwards was read to the White House correspondents who were summoned and came charging in to the President's office. Mr King left for Ottawa that afternoon with Mr Attlee. I left for my home and sleep.

The 'agreed declaration' was an impressive statement of the problem and made constructive proposals to find a solution to it, as follows:

In order to attain the most effective means of entirely eliminating the use of atomic energy for destructive purposes and promoting its widest use for industrial and humanitarian purposes, we are of the opinion that at the earliest practicable date a Commission should be set up under the United Nations Organization to prepare recommendations for submission to the Organization.

The Commission should be instructed to proceed with the utmost despatch and should be authorized to submit recommendations from time to time dealing with separate phases of its work.

In particular the Commission should make specific proposals:
a For extending between all nations the exchange of basic scientific information for peaceful ends.
b For control of atomic energy to the extent necessary to ensure its use only for peaceful purposes.
c For the elimination from national armaments of atomic weapons and of all other major weapons adaptable to mass destruction.
d For effective safeguards by way of inspection and other means to protect complying States against the hazards of violations and evasions.

The work of the Commission should proceed by separate stages, the successful completion of each one of which will develop the necessary confidence of the world before the next stage is undertaken. Specifically it is considered that the Commission might well devote its attention first to the wide exchange of scientists and scientific information, and as a second stage to the development of full knowledge concerning natural resources of raw materials.

Faced with the terrible realities of the application of science to destruction, every nation will realize more urgently than before the overwhelming need to maintain the rule of law among nations and to banish the scourge of war from the earth. This can only be brought about by giving wholehearted support to the United Nations Organization, and by consolidating and extending its authority, thus creating conditions of mutual trust in which all peoples will be free to devote themselves to the arts of peace. It is our firm resolve to work without reservation to achieve these ends.

These were fine words and noble sentiments. There was a solemn warning in them but there was to be little effective action to follow. Have they become merely the expression of another 'might-have-been' of history?

Today the answer seems to be 'yes' and it could mean humanity's greatest and final failure.

14

THE BIRTH OF THE
UNITED NATIONS

Of these international issues with which I was involved during my war years in Washington, the fourth and most important of all was the question of how to make a just and lasting peace and create a United Nations organization to maintain and strengthen it. If this was not done, then victory once again would be nothing but another brief interval between wars.

As early as 1942 some thought was being given in Washington and in London to the peace settlement. Public and private, official and unofficial discussions began to take place. I made a number of speeches myself on the subject, both in Canada and the United States. Certainly no subject was closer to my heart, and the more I thought about it the more convinced I became that the time to make plans and agree on policies was during the war itself.

I was certain that if we made no progress in drawing up the blueprints for a new world when the agony of war and the unity of purpose in a common struggle were drawing us together, we would find it far more difficult to do this later when nationalist prides and prejudices would become strong again and narrow concepts of national interest prevail. I also felt strongly that the planning should be broadly based. My Minister, after a visit with Mr Roosevelt at Warm Springs in April 1944, once startled me by telling me that the President had assured him that the next peace conference would be no long, drawn-out affair. He and Winston and Stalin would settle everything quickly. Just like that!

This seemed to me to be a dangerously narrow view of the organization of peace after victory.

It may have been understandable, even if often unacceptable, to concentrate all the authority of the United Nations in the Big Three powers while the life-and-death struggle was going on. It was intolerable to do this in plans for a peace settlement that would, hopefully, prevent another war. Did President Roosevelt's remark which I have just quoted mean that Canada and other similar countries would have to fight for the right to appropriate participation, as independent countries, in making and implementing these plans? Were the Big Three to have the exclusive privilege of redrawing the political map of the planet, and of assigning rights and responsibilities as they saw fit to other countries in any world organization? Some light was thrown on these questions in the discussions that went on in Washington.

On the Anglo-American official level, these discussions included interim measures to be taken immediately the fighting ended. At the Canadian mission we knew little about them. An incident in the summer of 1944 underlined the desirability of knowing more. In a visit to the State Department I saw a draft of the first pronouncement that would be made to the German people after their defeat. I was amazed to read a reference to that defeat having been brought about by the armies of the United States, the United Kingdom, and the USSR. As with the landing in Sicily, there was at first no reference to Canada or any other country. Of course, we managed to get this changed; but the obtuseness that brought about this wording in the first place made one worry about the kind of planning that was going on for longer-range postwar settlement.

To explain our Canadian worries, I must recount in some detail the developments leading up to the Dumbarton Oaks talks and the resulting draft of a United Nations Charter. For this I should go back to March 1943 when Anthony Eden told the Canadian cabinet that he had been delighted to find in Washington that British and American views on war aims and peace objectives were closer than might have been expected: Germany and Japan should be disarmed and kept weak. East Prussia might have to be given to Poland and any move for separate German states encouraged. Populations might have to be transferred to prevent minority problems. This all sounded to me more like the Versailles of 1918 than a peace settlement that would avoid its mistakes. But war feeling against Germany was deep and bitter; cool, rational thinking on these matters was difficult.

As for a postwar international organization, the British and Americans were contemplating, Eden said, a council of eight or ten members, consisting of the Big Three plus China, and others to be elected for specific terms by some agreed method. Mr King and Mr St Laurent were quick to make clear, even at this early date, that Canada would expect separate representation on all UN bodies and would not be willing to be included in any British Commonwealth representation. Whenever this matter came up in Washington, we told our American friends that this position would be maintained. It had also been made clear in London, or so we thought. A few months later, in September of 1943, the Canadian government was shown a Declaration on General Security drafted by President Roosevelt and to be made by the Big Three. To this document Mr King suggested changes to ensure greater recognition of the rights and responsibilities of others of the United Nations in the maintenance of peace and security.

This US proposal was considered by the Big Three in November 1943 at the Moscow Conference, and was embodied in a Declaration which included the following:

They [the three governments] recognize the necessity of establishing at the earliest practicable date a general international organization, based on the principle of the sovereign equality of all peace-loving States, and open to membership by all such States, large and small, for the maintenance of international peace and security.

For the purpose of maintaining international peace and security pending the re-establishment of law and order and the inauguration of a system of general security, they will consult with one another and as occasion requires with other members of the United Nations with a view to joint action on behalf of the Community of Nations.

This Declaration and a British Memorandum explaining it, entitled 'The Future of a World Organization,' was considered at a conference of Commonwealth Prime Ministers in London in 1944.

The steps leading up to this conference go back to 3 April 1943 when Mr Churchill proposed such a meeting 'in order to show to the whole world the strength and unity of what we should call in future,' he said, 'The British Commonwealth and Empire.' The Churchillian prose of his personal message was reduced to more sober terms in a telegram from the Secretary of State for Dominion Affairs on 15 April with the formal invitation to a conference in London to discuss both short-term and longer-range postwar political and economic arrangements. June or July was suggested for this meeting.

This invitation disturbed Mr King. He was afraid that at this conference the British government might begin the pressure, as they did at the end of World War I, for postwar centralization and unification of the Commonwealth, especially in matters of defence and foreign policy. He worried lest the United States, and other governments of the United Nations, might think that the Commonwealth countries as a unit were ganging up on them in respect of postwar arrangements. He was also afraid that Canada might be asked to take part in the policing of Europe, or even of Japan, after the fighting ended and before a peace treaty was signed, but without separate representation on any allied political machinery which was set up to exercise control.

While Mr King reluctantly accepted the invitation he hoped that the meeting could be postponed until 1944. He was therefore relieved when the Quebec Conference, and the difficulty of finding a date suitable for all the Prime Ministers, made it impossible to hold the conference before May 1944. In London, Mr King gave guarded approval in principle to the Moscow Declaration and the British memorandum, though more time, he added, would be needed for careful study. However, he took advantage of the opportunity to explain once again to his Commonwealth colleagues Canada's thinking in these matters. It was along familiar lines. It was important that power and responsibility should correspond in the international organization of peace and security. This meant, he realized, that on the smaller council of the proposed world organization the Big Powers should have a special position, with permanent membership. But it should not mean an exclusive one. Appropriate recognition should be given to the other members of the United Nations according to the 'functional' principle.

Canada was to push hard, from 1944 to 1946, for the recognition of this principle which meant not only an acceptance of the difference in power and responsibility between Canada and the United States but also of that between Canada and Luxembourg. Mr King was emphatic that in the organization of peace it was essential to secure the loyal co-operation and support of all states. This required that nothing should be done to make, or appear to make, three or four powers controllers of the world's destiny, with all the others, without distinction, grouped together as 'other members of the United Nations.' This was the line which we took also in all our discussions in Washington.

There was another point which Mr King made in London. It concerned British representation on the proposed Security Council, or the 'World Peace Council' as he called it on this occasion. Mr Churchill had suggested to the Conference that on this council 'the British Commonwealth and Empire' might take its place as one of the Great

Powers. This aroused all Mr King's old fears and suspicions, which we who worked for him knew so well. The Commonwealth, he said, so politely that his firmness might have escaped another audience, the Commonwealth could not be a single power when its policy could not be controlled by a single government.

On this occasion Mr King agreed that United Kingdom representation on the Security Council was indispensable. But he felt that as a Great Power she would be even stronger, 'because of "the alliance potential" which she was able to command when her policy was such that her interests were also those of her friends, the most faithful of whom, in two great wars, had been the other nations of the Commonwealth.' Mr Churchill, though no doubt somewhat bemused, perhaps even disappointed by Mr King's stand, was never one to believe in unconditional surrender for himself; so he tried another tack by suggesting that there would be obvious advantages if the United Kingdom were able to speak on the World Council for all the Dominions; but only, of course after the closest consultation with them. Mr King was even more polite in not accepting this proposition, which must have shown him how hard it was to teach Mr Churchill to accept the realities of association without integration in the Commonwealth. How often, Mr King must have thought, was it necessary for him to save the Commonwealth from the centralists who would destroy it in the name of unity? How long would he be unfairly criticized in Britain and Canada by those whose 'Commonwealth and Empire' he was trying to preserve by rejecting the misguided ideas of its centralizing supporters?

ॐ

The Moscow Conference of November 1943 had agreed that discussions should go forward at Washington on an official and organized basis. The following resolution had been adopted:

It was recognized as desirable that representatives of the United States of America, the United Kingdom, and the Soviet Union should conduct in a preliminary fashion an exchange of views on questions connected with the establishment of an international organization for the maintenance of international peace and security, the intention being that this work should be carried out in the first instance in Washington, and also in London and Moscow.

As a result the Dumbarton Oaks talks, which later were to include China, began on the official level in Washington on 21 August 1944.

Our duty at the Legation was to maintain close touch with these talks in order to make the Canadian position known on points of concern to us, in the hope that this would avoid, or at least reduce, public

differences and disputes later at the United Nations conference to follow Dumbarton Oaks.

For this purpose we had to find out what was going on. Though we
could not secure, and indeed did not expect, formal participation in the
talks, we hoped to maintain close, if informal, touch with them and to
be consulted by our British and American friends about them. We had
no problem with the British who, as a matter of policy, kept Canada
and the other dominions well informed about these preliminary negotiations. We occasionally felt, however, that the State Department was
more concerned with consulting their Latin American than their Canadian friends. The United States government had proposed, for instance,
a Pan American Conference for the autumn of 1944, to be held in
Mexico City to discuss Dumbarton Oaks, without inviting Canada.

When I heard of this, I told my friend Jack Hickerson, the Canadian
expert at the State Department, that one might have thought that consultation with Canada on this subject was more important to the United
States than with Bolivia or Guatemala. He refused to admit that we
had any complaint whatsoever. For one thing we were not members of
the Pan American Union and naturally could not be invited to a conference held under its auspices. He might have added that at that time,
in contrast with their later policy, it was the United States which was
keeping us from membership in the Union. What was more important,
Hickerson claimed that we were the only country apart from the Big
Powers that was being kept informed about the progress of the discussions at Dumbarton Oaks. The British had not only convened a
Commonwealth meeting on the talks in London, but they were also
briefing us continually in Washington, as were some American officials. So Hickerson wondered what we were grousing about. He
thought that if anyone had a right to complain it was the Latin Americans over the preferential treatment we were being given. Moreover, he
added, he and his colleagues were beginning to get annoyed at Canadians for passing to the British information and comments made to us
by our American contacts. I reminded him that we often reciprocated
by giving the Americans the British point of view when we were able
to obtain it. Moreover, the British welcomed Canadian ideas and gave
them serious consideration. I was not sure that the Americans did. Indeed, I sometimes suspected that they thought we were a nuisance,
especially when we disagreed with them. In any event, I told Hickerson, he must have known that in these activities we were merely dis-
charging our sacred and historic duty of trying to interpret one country
to the other, acting as a 'bridge' or 'link' or 'lynch-pin.' It was the kind
of free-swinging exchange which we were accustomed to have with our

American friends, and which I greatly preferred to diplomatic politeness and empty pleasantries.

Notwithstanding these verbal jousts, the fact remained that, while
not a participant, we managed not only to keep in close touch with the
Dumbarton Oaks talks, but also to make our views known informally
on points as they arose to both the British and American representatives in Washington; and also more formally in Ottawa to the two
governments. When the Dumbarton Oaks draft of the Charter, therefore, was officially sent to us on 10 October 1944 (the day it was made
public), Mr King could commend it to 'the careful and earnest study
of the people of Canada,' in the knowledge that a great deal of thought
had already been given to it by Canadian officials.

Two days later, 12 October, I wrote to Norman Robertson:

It has occurred to me that, in addition to consulting with the great powers
and with the nations of the Commonwealth, it might be useful if, before the
beginning of the United Nations conference, we discussed the problem informally with France and with the principal middle powers, such as Brazil
and the Netherlands, and perhaps Czechoslovakia, Norway, Belgium, and
Mexico.

The French will be happy that they are to secure in due course a permanent seat on the council, but it is likely that they will be far from satisfied
with other provisions of the draft Charter. Since they are the only great
power which has not participated in the drafting of the Charter, they may,
for prestige reasons, be tempted to propose numerous amendments. But
considerations more important than prestige will enter into their calculations.
They will, I think, want to see created a more powerful international organization than that envisaged in the Charter. They may push hard, for example,
for the proposal which has already received Soviet and Chinese support, that
there be established an international air police force. They may also propose
inclusion in the Charter of provisions which would, by themselves, give rise
to obligations on the part of member states to assist in imposing military
sanctions. It would only be with great reluctance, I think, that they would
concur in a Charter which, like the present draft, entirely shelves this problem, and leaves it to be met by subsequent security agreements, some of the
more important of which may never be concluded or, if concluded, ratified.

I realize, of course, that before discussions of any kind can begin, we have
to formulate, at least provisionally, our own views. In the consideration that
is no doubt being given to this matter in Ottawa, may I make one suggestion? Any proposals of ours for revision of the Charter will emphasize, I
take it, the necessity of narrowing the gap between the rights and obligations
of the great and the lesser powers. I suggest that we make clear also that a
solution of this problem is associated in our minds with changes for strengthening the Charter so as to make it a more effective instrument for the maintenance of peace and for peaceful change. My own view is that Canada's
national interest would be served by such changes, some of which, as I have
pointed out above, are likely to be put forward by the French. Certainly the

international interest would be served by them. But equally certainly it would be more difficult to support them if the 'great-powers' – 'other-powers' gap is not narrowed.

On the morning of 11 January 1945, Canada's views on the Dumbarton Oaks draft were officially requested when a member of the State Department handed to me a list of questions on which he hoped we would comment. Most of these questions had been the subject of earlier personal discussions between myself and the State Department. Now, however, an official position had to be taken. This was done in part when the government presented its views on the membership and powers of the Security Council to Washington, London, Moscow, and Chungking on 12 January 1945. On the vital question of enforcement action under the Charter, we wrote:

It is suggested that decisions of the Security Council under Chapter VIII B should be binding in the first instance only on states which are members of the Council. States not represented on the Council should be required to take positive action only when the decision has been endorsed by a two-thirds majority of the Assembly (when it would become binding on all members), or when the country or countries concerned have by special invitation participated on the same footing as elected members in the Council's proceedings, or when they have individually agreed with the Council to join in particular talks of enforcement. The adoption of these suggestions would make it far easier for states other than the great powers to enter into agreements making available to the organization substantial military forces, facilities, and assistance, and would thus increase the effective power at the disposal of the Council. Their adoption would also help to secure the requisite public support in countries not permanently represented on the Council.

On another section of the Dumbarton Oaks draft in which we had a particular interest, the role of the Economic and Social Council and UN specialized agencies, our position was as follows:

There is no doubt that the responsibilities of the Assembly and the Economic and Social Council need more careful definition and that they should be developed so as to provide satisfactory machinery for coordinating the activities of such diverse bodies as the ILO, the International Monetary Fund, the Organization of Food and Agriculture, the International Civil Aviation Organization, and a number of other functional agencies which are likely to be established.
    It is inevitable that Canada will be deeply interested in this aspect of the work of the World Organization and we should be prepared to make a positive and valuable contribution to the development of this side of the scheme. Our delegations at the various technical conferences of the last two years have won a high reputation and we shall be expected to live up to this.

We felt that, in general, Chapter IX of the draft dealing with 'Arrangements for International Economic and Social Cooperation' had received scant consideration in the Dumbarton Oaks draft and we indicated our desire to rectify this at San Francisco.

The first Dumbarton Oaks draft was reviewed later at the Yalta Conference by Roosevelt, Churchill, and Stalin. A few changes were made there. One of these, which the President announced on his return to Washington, greatly disturbed us. In the General Assembly of the proposed world organization the United States and USSR would each have *three* votes. The reaction in my diary was:

It is the most ridiculous thing for the President to have done ... Of course, the old argument of six British Empire votes was used. I thought that had been buried twenty-five years ago. But not so. I tried to get Norman Robertson to persuade the PM to issue a statement at once in Ottawa, laying this ghost. But to my surprise they do not seem nearly so disturbed in Ottawa about these developments as we are here. I had Jack Hickerson to lunch and told him what I thought of it all. He admitted it was as much a surprise to the State Department as to me and they had no idea what line they should take. The whole thing is a mess.

Even some of the Americans, notably Senator Vandenberg, opposed this proposal. Then the President, almost at once, announced that he had dropped the whole idea of three US votes, making his original announcement a few days before even more difficult to understand. It soon became clear that the Big Three had agreed at Yalta to stand firm on their draft. Any changes, not acceptable by all three, would be opposed. This set the scene, of course, for our major arguments at San Francisco.

I think it can be said that when the San Francisco Conference opened, the Canadian preparatory work had been thoroughly done and that the views of the government on a draft Charter for the United Nations had been clearly established and made fully known to those four governments that were to submit the draft to the conference.

I was myself most concerned over the proposals that dealt with the organization of security and with measures to prevent and defeat aggression. This would be, of course, the core of the Charter. On these matters I wrote Norman Robertson on 15 March 1945, before going to San Francisco:

We are hearing far too much these days that there is no use of the world organization even contemplating the imposition of sanctions against a Great Power. I can recognize that certain immediate political considerations in certain countries may make it necessary to take this line, but I see no reason why we should encourage it in Canada; especially as it is a completely defeatist line and represents a considerable retrogression from the League

Covenant. Notwithstanding, the State Department here goes merrily along trying to convince the people that the Dumbarton Charter is much better than the old League Covenant because it has teeth in it. What is the use of having teeth if you cannot use them? What the Dumbarton Oaks Charter needs in fact is a little dentistry.

On 20 April I found myself on a special train leaving Washington with delegates for the San Francisco Conference where a new world was to be born. I reported my journey in my diary as follows:

My start was inauspicious, as I found that my compartment had already been allocated to a member of the Australian delegation. However, we got that straightened out without too much trouble. I find myself in a compartment between Senator Connally and Dr Evatt. All the other people in the car are Australian.

Dr Evatt kept bobbing into my compartment to point out the iniquities of the Dumbarton Oaks Charter; to suggest that Australia should be given a better position in the proposed World Organization; to criticize the British and the Americans for their handling of these matters. He is an arrogant and aggressive fellow, but intelligent and well informed. His views seem to me to be pretty sound, but his expression of them a little too forceful to make him popular. He praised the Canadian position as put forward at the recent Commonwealth discussions in London and added that, on further study, he realized that he should have supported that position more strongly. He promised to do so at San Francisco. There are a flock of conference celebrities on the train but I have kept as much as possible to my own compartment and have read two good Canadian books: *Earth and High Heaven* and *Two Solitudes*. The latter is particularly good. I tried several times to go over the Dumbarton Oaks papers again but each time they gave me a headache! So I eventually gave up.

The journey itself was interesting, especially to me, as it was the first time I had crossed the continent. We had only one longish stopover, at Salt Lake City, where we were taken to the Mormon Tabernacle and exposed to an organ recital. We arrived at Oakland, California, on Tuesday at four o'clock, where a ferry took us across the bay to San Francisco; at least, it took all of us but Lord and Lady Halifax, who were sheltered from exposure to the masses by being whisked across in a private launch. San Francisco is an extremely impressive city in appearance, especially when approached by water. We were met at the docks by various welcoming committees, put in motor cars, and whisked at break-neck speed to our various hotels, with motorcycle cops rushing madly ahead, sirens screaming. To make it all more exciting, they took us up the wrong side of the road and against red lights. It was a rather fantastic and nerve-racking performance. We arrived at the St Francis Hotel pretty shaken. At this hotel I found everything in a state of complete chaos and confusion. Our delegation from Ottawa had arrived the day before, but the office accommodation promised was not available and nobody seemed to know what to do about anything. The organization of the conference seems to be pretty hopeless, as indeed has been the organization of any conference that I have attended in this country. Why they do not know how to do these things better, beats me. As soon as I reached my room (without my luggage, which had been lost at the station) I found a note to say that the delegation was having a meeting. I hurried to the conference room and found the PM and all the rest of them. The PM had just begun an exposé of the Canadian position. It was rather amusing to notice how careful he was to prevent the Opposition party delegates thinking that he was taking too much responsibility on himself. Graydon and Coldwell responded by being equally co-operative. For a few weeks at least, Canada will probably have a national government – at San Francisco!

The other Canadian delegates were Mr St Laurent, Mrs Cora Casselman and Senators King and Moraud. The alternate delegates and advisers, in addition to me, included Norman Robertson, Hume Wrong, Maurice Pope, and my fellow Canadian ambassadors, Wilgress, Désy, and Chipman.

The US delegation at the San Francisco Conference was the largest and the most influential. Mr Stettinius, as Secretary of State, was head of the host delegation and, in consequence, chairman of the conference. I noted at the opening session that he was 'eager, nervous, and a little bewildered by it all.' During those first days he was not an effective chairman, especially where it counted most, at meetings of the Steering Committee of which Canada had been chosen to be a member. But after the conference had been in progress for some time, and Stettinius had acquired more experience in the chair, I was able to note :'Stettinius is improving. However, he gets on the nerves of the old "conferenciers" with his manner, which is a combination of a Rotary President and a Bible class leader.'

Nevertheless, Stettinius did not acquire a strong personal standing at San Francisco. His strength was derived from his official position. Of the other US delegates I will mention only two – Senators Connally and Vandenberg. Senator Connally, from Texas, whom I had met occasionally in Washington, was a very important member of their delegation, as befitted his position as Chairman of the powerful Senate Foreign Relations Committee. We were not likely to forget that in 1919 that Committee, through another Chairman, Senator Lodge, had been largely instrumental in keeping the United States out of the League of Nations. Senator Connally was more impressive in his senatorial manner than in his knowledge of international affairs. A week or so earlier, however, when I called on him at his office, he had surprised me by being far more understanding of, and sympathetic to, the Soviet position than most of his colleagues in Congress.

I took advantage of this visit to give him a short lecture on Canada's independent position in the British Commonwealth which I reported to Robertson as follows:

Senator Connally's mention of the three Russian votes gave me an opportunity to remark that it was most unfortunate that, in the discussion of this matter, reference should be made so often to the six 'British Empire' votes. I added that, as he would appreciate, there was a great difference between the position of Canada and that of the Ukrainian Soviet Republic. If we, for instance, had wished to stay out of this war, we could have done so. Even if we wished to get out of it now, the United Kingdom government would not intervene. I hesitated to think, however, what would have happened to an official in the Ukrainian or White Russian Republics if he had argued against participation in the war in 1941 or for withdrawal from the war in 1945. Senator Connally said that, of course, he appreciated the position of the British dominions in this matter. I hope he does, as once or twice in the past there have been suggestions to the contrary.

Senator Vandenberg, the ranking Republican member of the Foreign Relations Committee was, of course, another important delegate. I got to know him very well and to value his international viewpoint and his willingness to express it. The prominence he achieved at San Francisco pleased him for he liked the limelight. He was not unique in this respect among the politicians at San Francisco. He was, in fact, a key figure on the American political scene in the postwar organization of peace. As a leading Republican, he was perhaps the most important single influence in Congress in ensuring that the repudiation of the President in 1919 would not be repeated in 1945.

I recall a long talk which I had with him before the San Francisco Conference opened. He was most encouraging in his assurance that this time the United States would not only take the lead in the international organization of peace, but would follow through in the discharge of its responsibilities to the world. He amazed me on this occasion by telling me that he had never been to an international conference in his life and was looking forward to San Francisco so that he could see 'how one of these things worked.' I noted: 'He is also a little worried about his position as a possible Republican presidential candidate in a Democratic delegation.'

The British had a strong all-party delegation headed by Anthony Eden whose reputation was then at its highest. One of his assistants was my friend, Dick Law, now Minister of State in the Foreign Office, with whom I kept in close touch and had some frank discussions on policies. I remember in particular an almost violent argument we had one night after the day's work was finished and a few members of our two delegations were having a drink together. There had been some controversial discussions in the Committee on Trusteeship and the British were upset at the anti-colonial feelings expressed. It looked to them as if this conference, under the leadership of the Americans, was doing what Winston Churchill said he would never do: 'preside over the liquidation of the British Empire.' I ventured to suggest that nothing now could prevent the early liquidation of all the old empires. Therefore the British had a great opportunity to direct this process with a minimum of disorder by turning over voluntarily all their colonies, except India, now on the verge of self-government, to the United Nations as trust territories. The British would then undoubtedly be asked by the UN to administer these territories until they were ready for independence. Hence they would have lost really nothing and would have saved themselves from future trouble and conflict. I added that, after their sacrifices and efforts in two world wars, the British obviously could not bear the imperial burden much longer, so they would do well to recognize this and withdraw gracefully and gradually under the auspices of the UN. When Dick Law heard these remarks and concluded that I was not trying to be funny, his British pride and imperial patriotism exploded with rage and he could hardly find words to tell me what he thought of such heretical views. He would, I think, have reacted differently fifteen years later.

The British experts and advisers, most of them from the Foreign Office, were able, well-informed, and experienced professionals. We worked with them closely. Even my onslaught, as Dick Law regarded it, on British colonial policy was an indication of our freedom to say to one another what we thought. It may have been easier for me since almost all the British officials were personal friends of long standing.

Among other Commonwealth delegates, General Smuts was very naturally regarded as a pré-eminent statesman, of great influence and prestige. He seemed, however, a somewhat remote figure, aloof from the strife, to be consulted as an oracular being. The Australian chief, the redoubtable Dr Evatt, was outstanding for other reasons: his drive, determination, and his incredible energy. He was in effect a one-man delegation, as he rushed from committee to committee urging the Australian viewpoints on all matters, clearly taking great pleasure in contending with the Great Powers and in trying to reduce their representatives to size. He became in effect a public defender, a belligerent champion of the smaller countries, anxious to prevent the United Nations from becoming a private preserve of the Big Powers. In this role, he proposed and pursued vigorously amendment after amendment to the

Dumbarton Oaks draft of the Charter. His refusal to withdraw or to accept compromise made him a hero to many of the delegations from smaller states. He was saved from the snares of his courage (or, if you like, from his pig-headedness and vanity) by other delegations, including our own, who undertook the unspectacular but essential task of finding compromises for a Charter which had to be signed by the Soviet Union and by Liberia alike. In doing so we were charged by Dr Evatt with weakness, but I think that deep down he knew that our policy of moderation and of reasonable compromise prevented the conference from being wrecked by some of his amendments if they had been carried against the opposition of the Big Four. It was impossible, nonetheless, to ignore the energy and dexterity of the Australian delegate. In a sense, his was the outstanding personality at the conference. He revelled in the excitement of his own initiatives, though often saved by others from their consequences.

The other chief delegate from the Antipodes was the Prime Minister of New Zealand, Peter Fraser, a shrewd Scot. He talked as much as Dr Evatt, but with less effect, though I think the Big Three often found his needling harder to take than Evatt's hammer blows.

The end of the war in Europe came when I was in San Francisco. Those who were trying to organize the peace, however, were hardly conscious that the fighting in Europe had ended, no doubt in part because we were facing the Pacific where the war was still raging bloodily. My diary for 3 May had this:

I don't know whether it is because we are too absorbed in conference activities, or whether we have become numbed by repetition to the impact of great events but, whatever it is, the fact remains that headlines such as 'Hitler Dead,' 'Mussolini Hanged by the Feet,' 'Berlin Captured,' 'Nazis Collapse Completely,' all leave me about as cold as the headline, 'Yanks Win Two Games.' All we have been struggling for in the last six years has come to pass, and we seem almost unaware of it. What a contrast to the atmosphere and attitude of November 1918.

On Monday evening, 8 May, I had returned to the hotel from a delegation party and had been asleep, it seemed, for only a few minutes when Ben Cochran of the British delegation phoned me (it was actually about 2:30 AM) to tell me that VE Day would be announced that morning at 9 AM and I might wish to tell our Prime Minister. I replied that if I woke the PM at that hour, another war would start and that, if he called me again at such an unearthly time, he also would be in serious trouble. Ben rang off muttering about the ingratitude of these

Canadians who were always complaining that they were never informed in advance about important developments. The next day I
noted:

The end of the war, but you would hardly know it around here. There was a
meeting of the Executive Committee this morning, and at eleven, Stettinius
called for a minute's silence. He followed this up by saying he would give the
photographers a minute and a half in which to take pictures. He is not a very
sensitive person. The Executive Committee was held up for half an hour
while Stettinius and some of the Foreign Ministers were trapped in an
elevator. They might have been held up for an hour without damage, because
we did not do anything anyway as everybody had to leave at noon to broadcast. I came back to the hotel and listened to a very moving program from
London. It was the first time I realized what VE Day really meant.

I will write no more here about the San Francisco Conference and the
United Nations Charter that emerged from it. No one who was in the
lovely and hospitable city of San Francisco at this conference will ever
forget those weeks. It was a busy and exciting time. Our delegation,
which soon became one of officials as the politicians left for the election
campaign at home, was, I believe, effective and hard-working and won
many tributes from other delegations for its contribution not only to
the big debates, but to the exhausting and important work that went on
in the committees. Much has been written elsewhere on the successful
work of our delegation, particularly with regard to Article 44 of the
Charter and to those articles dealing with the Economic and Social
Council.

As for me, I was forced to leave some time before the signing of the
Charter because of other commitments in Washington and elsewhere.

❦15❧

MINISTER OF THE CROWN

After San Francisco and the UNRRA mission overseas, which I have already described, I returned to the Embassy. The work continued to grow, both in volume and variety, and there was a corresponding increase in the staff to deal with new duties and responsibilities. I could write many pages about that work, but the following summary taken from our annual report for the department for the year 1945 will suffice:

A wide variety of subjects was dealt with by the Embassy during the year, including the following: diplomatic reporting on relations of the United States with other countries and on developments in the United States; economic and political warfare; information and public relations; income tax problems and United States Revenue legislation; surplus war property disposal; telecommunications; international civil aviation; selective service and manpower problems; fisheries; boundary waters; price control and rationing; relief and repatriation of Canadian prisoners-of-war and civilians; Red Cross matters; treatment and repatriation of enemy prisoners-of-war and aliens held in Canada; passport, immigration, visa, and nationality questions; military relief; refugees; customs matters; import and export problems; registration and protection of Canadian nationals; international educational matters; extradition and other legal matters.

There were other matters that do not appear in this list, two of which deserve special mention. One concerns the Washington repercussions of the Gouzenko spy affair, which I shall deal with in more detail in a later chapter on security. The other was the selection of the first Secretary General of the United Nations with which I became personally concerned.

During the first UN meetings at Church House in London, the 'Big Four' considered whom to recommend to the Assembly as the first Secretary General of the world organization. As each one had a veto over the choice, there had to be unanimity. The USSR felt that, as the UN was to be situated in the United States and as the first President of the Assembly (they had agreed on M. Spaak of Belgium) was to be from the West, the secretary generalship should go to their choice. For that purpose they put forward the communist Foreign Minister of Yugoslavia, M. Simic, more for bargaining purposes than with any hope of having him chosen. On the Western side – we were talking about 'sides' even then – the United States with British support nominated me. It had been agreed from the beginning that the Secretary General should not be a national of any of the countries with permanent seats on the Security Council. This eliminated such distinguished persons as General Eisenhower, Anthony Eden, and others who had been mentioned. The Soviets objected to me not, so they assured me at the time, on personal grounds but because they felt, for reasons I have mentioned, that the Secretary General should not be a North American, particularly one whose claims were being pushed by the Americans and British. This seemed to me to be a reasonable position. I certainly did not wish to become a subject of controversy between Washington and Moscow, so I told Mr Byrnes, now the US Secretary of State, to withdraw my name. He demurred and asked me to allow it to stand, assuring me that there was no danger of any bitterness with Moscow over the selection. I did so, and Moscow then vetoed me. M. Simic was similarly rejected, to nobody's surprise, as he had only Russian support. This left the way open for a compromise candidate – which is, no doubt, what the USSR had in mind from the beginning. The Americans and British may at first have thought that I would be acceptable to Moscow, but when it became clear this was not the situation, they could also use me for bargaining purposes, if necessary. That is international politics.

Eventually a compromise was agreed on in the person of the Foreign Minister of Norway, Trygve Lie. Indeed, he may have been the choice of the USSR from the beginning. If this were true, they must have later regretted the success of their tactics. Trygve Lie was a Socialist and he was favourably regarded in Moscow. But he was a strong man with no liking for communism, and soon showed that he would be an independent Secretary General. He aroused the bitter hostility of the USSR before long and they did their utmost to get him replaced, while he later did everything he possibly could to get me elected his successor.

I was not particularly disappointed about not being chosen Secretary

General. I would naturally have been gratified if I had been selected. It would have been a tribute to Canada and a great honour to myself. I felt too that it was a position I could fill and one which would have given me an unrivalled opportunity to work for the things in which I believed; peace, security, and international co-operation. But I was very happy with the work I was doing as a Canadian public servant. I had been given unusual opportunities in my various appointments to pursue my interest in international affairs. Otherwise I would never have become known to those who wished me to become Secretary General of the UN. These opportunities were likely to continue if I remained in the Canadian service. I was quite content.

My Minister, who was still the Prime Minister, seemed also content. Mr King recalls in his diary that when Stettinius at the San Francisco Conference mentioned my name to him as a possible Secretary General of the UN, he, Mr King, indicated that he would not stand in my way. Indeed (I was amused when I read this) he reassured the US Secretary of State that I was a scholar as well as a diplomat. However, Mr King doubted my wisdom in even considering the post, because of his own growing conviction that the UN would not really amount to much or be able to do anything effective to heal the dissensions and divisions that were already appearing in the postwar world, especially between communists and non-communists. As he confided at the time to his diary: 'I doubt if the UN would ever be other than a creaking house with nothing of a solid structure about it.'

On 11 January 1946, after a talk with Mr King at Laurier House on a visit to Ottawa, he noted in his diary:

I can see that what was most on Pearson's mind was his possible appointment as Secretary General of the United Nations Organization. I felt quite sure from the way he spoke that he intended to accept the appointment, if offered, though he said there were some things he would want to know first. I told him that of course we would not wish to stand in his way if he were inclined to accept the appointment. I told him, however, that if I were similarly situated I would prefer the freedom of the position of an Ambassador in a country in the position Canada was to that of an official of an international organization, as important as that was. I thought he would find a great difference in trying to serve many masters instead of one master.

If I was not to go to the United Nations, neither was I to stay in Washington. By the end of 1946 I was back in Ottawa as Deputy Minister. For a time, however, it looked as though the move would be to London, this time as High Commissioner. Mr King told me on 29 June when I was dining with him at Kingsmere that London might be my new post. This would have given me the greatest satisfaction, but I knew that there had been an understanding that Norman Robertson should succeed Vincent Massey as High Commissioner, as a recognition of the tremendous burden Robertson had carried so ably and unselfishly during the long years of war as Mr King's principal adviser. It seemed to me that I should let Robertson know about Mr King's new idea, and find out whether this was agreeable to him. He was surprised and disappointed. I urged him to see Mr King and to remind the Prime Minister of the earlier commitment. He did this, and in consequence there was a triple shift in the autumn after Mr Massey's retirement; Robertson to London, Hume Wrong to succeed me in Washington, and I to return to Ottawa as Deputy Minister. I had told the Prime Minister earlier, during our talk at Kingsmere, that I would of course be glad to serve in London, Ottawa, or at any other post, if I were to be moved from Washington. However, while willing to go back to the Department, I would have preferred to remain at the Embassy. A period of less than two years as Ambassador was not in fact long enough to take the measure of this job and to work at it with full effectiveness.

The government had accepted my recommendation to use the Massachusetts Avenue building solely as a Chancery for office purposes as our staff was increasing steadily, and to buy a separate residence for the Ambassador. We were told to find a suitable house, adequate for our purposes, but neither too grand nor too expensive. After weeks of searching, my wife found the right place, and began to arrange for its decoration and its furnishing. Everything was in readiness for the Ambassador and his wife in the new and very attractive residence. We did our packing, however, not for Rock Creek Drive, but for Augusta Street in Ottawa.

My years in Washington had marked an important stage in the development of my career and views. As for my career, at the age of forty-eight I had reached the summit of the Canadian diplomatic service. I do not think it immodest to observe that I had done this without outside influence and without financial resources, apart from my salary. I had done it by hard work and long hours, by making it evident that I was available for whatever was to be done; by welcoming every opportunity for new and more responsible duties; and by accumulating all the experience possible in all the varied aspects of my profession. After eight years in the Department in Ottawa, five-and-a-half in London, and four-and-a-half in Washington, I had the background and the training to fill the senior post as Under-Secretary of State for External Affairs.

The only upward step that I could now take was to delete the 'Under.' But this would require me to abandon the professional for the political which then I had no thought of doing.

It would have been strange if my ideas and, I hope, my judgment had not matured as my career moved ahead. My opportunities for development in the field of international affairs had been exceptional; in my departmental work, in international conferences and intergovernmental consultations, and in contact with many men of power and position whom I had been fortunate to hear, to observe, and, frequently, to get to know.

In describing my work in Ottawa and in London before the war, I have said much about the paramount need for nations to ensure peace and security by international collective action, the only acceptable way it can be done, and of Canada's obligations and opportunities to play a positive and constructive role in this process. Everything I learned during the war confirmed and strengthened my view as a Canadian that our foreign policy must not be timid or fearful of commitments but activist in accepting international responsibilities. To me, nationalism and internationalism were two sides of the same coin. International co-operation for peace is the most important aspect of national policy. I have never wavered in this belief even though I have learned from experience how agonizingly difficult it is to convert conviction into reality. I felt then, as I do now, that the growth of the United Nations into a truly effective world organization was our best, perhaps our last, hope of bringing about enduring and creative peace if mankind was to end a savage tradition that the strong do what they can and the weak suffer what they must. With all its weaknesses, which soon became clear but which, after all, were only those of its member states and the system of international anarchy in which they had to operate, the United Nations was at least a foundation for a new world on which we could build. Canada must play, then, her full part in strengthening that foundation and in helping to design and complete the structure. I knew that Mr St Laurent, for whom I was to work in Ottawa, believed this. I was never sure that Mr King did, notwithstanding the ringing speeches he made during and just after the war in favour of collective action for collective security.

I made my own views known on these matters whenever and wherever I could. On 1 February 1944, I summed them up in a long letter to the Department of External Affairs which included these sentences:

Certainly we now know that there is no safety in a League of Nations which does not make adequate provision both for peaceful change and for police action against the aggressor. We shall, I think, have to revise our attitude toward any future Article x or Article xvi of an international covenant. We have also, I think, learned something from our Commonwealth experience. We had little to do with British foreign policy leading up to the present war, but we were as deeply involved in the results of that policy as Great Britain herself. That being the case, surely we should seek to influence British policy in some way when it appears to be going in the wrong direction. I do not mean by this that we should adopt certain ideas now being thrown out by various British Commonwealth leaders which look to the British Commonwealth as a unit in international affairs. If we act as a unit, I do not see how we can also act separately and maintain the national and international position Canada has gained ... Acting in unison as separate states is one thing; acting as a unit is quite another.

Canada is achieving, I think, a very considerable position as a leader, if not *the* leader, among a group of states which are strong enough to be necessary to the Big Four but not important enough to be accepted as one of that quartet. The position of a 'little Big Power' or 'big Little Power' is a very difficult one. The big fellows have power and responsibility, but they also have control. The little fellows have no power and no responsibility, therefore are not interested in control. States in between sometimes, it seems, get the worst of both worlds. We are necessary but not necessary enough! I think this is being felt by countries like the Netherlands and Belgium as well as by ourselves. That is why these countries are not only looking toward the Big Powers, but are looking toward each other for support. There is, I think, an opportunity here for Canada, if we desire to take it, to become the leader of this group. This might be not only desirable in itself, but also would supply a useful corrective to those who think that we should exercise no influence except within the confines of the British Commonwealth.

These were the principles which I thought should guide Canadian foreign policy in the years immediately after the war. They were far removed from those which we followed in the thirties.

By 1946 when I returned to Ottawa, I would have altered this letter in one important respect; by emphasizing that the country whose policies would now concern us most would be not Great Britain but the United States. That country was now the super-power. Washington, not London, would determine, with Moscow, whether peace, progress, and even survival were possible. American policies, therefore, must be watched closely. From their consequences Canada could not escape, no more than we could from those of Downing Street from 1920 to 1939.

We Canadians had a special reason to be concerned. We were on the same continent as the United States. She was our neighbour. Our economic dependence on her was increasing and her pressures on us of many kinds were also increasing, friendly though they were. My experience in Washington convinced me that relations with our neighbour were bound to be far and away the most important part of Canada's foreign policy. Moreover, while we could count on goodwill and friendliness in this relationship, we could not assume that our rights and interests as a nation would always be respected, or even understood. It was clear to me, when I returned to Ottawa, that Canada's continental policies would be not only vitally important, but increasingly complicated and difficult; and that the importance, the complications, and the difficulties would increase with every year.

It promised to be an exciting and challenging period in the acceptance of new responsibilities by Canada in international affairs and in working out policies for their discharge. I looked forward to the part I could play in this work in my new position.

ơ

We missed Washington; the excitement of life there, its political and diplomatic activity; the friends we had made and the pleasures we enjoyed; the sense of being at the centre of great events and important developments, of knowing many of those who were directing them, and the feeling that you were playing at least a small part in their unfolding. Ottawa was home, however, in a sense that Washington, or any other American city, could never be. Life was more normal and, in that sense, more comfortable in the house we purchased in the Sandy Hill district of Ottawa than it could ever be in an embassy in another country. It was an old house, one of the first built in that district. My aunt once told me she used to play on its lawn when she lived there as a girl in the early eighties when my grandfather was the Methodist minister at a nearby church. This was all very nice and sentimental, but old houses are often inconvenient houses, as my wife learned. However, as always, she met and surmounted any domestic difficulties and this side of life soon reverted to the contentment and comfort, for me, that had characterized our earlier years in Ottawa.

We were still, however, too often without our children who now were away at college and home only on holidays. We seemed doomed to be separated from them in these years of their growing up, which were to lead all too soon to their own separate lives. We remained a closely knit family and the senior members of it were very proud of the progress and achievements of the children. Both of them were soon to receive their Arts degrees from the University of Toronto. Patsy then moved from the academic to the very practical, when she decided to become a nurse; due less, I suspect, to any desire to follow Florence Nightingale than to follow a young medical student whom she was to marry before long and in due course begin the duties of nursing five babies of her own.

Geoffrey made us proud by winning the same scholarship to Oxford that I had enjoyed many years before. In doing so he continued to show a healthy independence of paternal precedents. When he first went to the University of Toronto, I assumed that he would follow his parents into Victoria College. Not at all; he went to Trinity College. I expected also that he would become a member of my college fraternity of which I had such happy memories and where I made so many lasting friendships. But he saw no point in living in a fraternity house when he was comfortable in residence at college. So I might have known that I was rash in assuming that when he won a scholarship that enabled him to go to Oxford he would go to St John's College where I had had such a wonderful two years; he went to New College. I hoped he would continue his studies there in Modern History which had been my subject; he chose Politics, Philosophy, and Economics. I was also very far from the mark when I took for granted that he would take full advantage of the healthy, happy, robust male life in college. He married and lived a domestic existence in 'digs.' The wisdom and good judgment of this I was only able to appreciate fully later. However, after securing his Oxford BA, he did follow my example in passing the examinations for entry into the Canadian Foreign Service. I am sure he will not follow me in deserting it for politics.

Life, of course, was simpler on Augusta Street than in an embassy. It had to be. We received only one-fifth of the income that we had enjoyed in Washington, for our allowances were naturally cut off when we moved back to Ottawa. I should add that our expenses were also reduced, if not by the same proportion. I had no embassy to maintain, no ambassadorial social responsibilities to discharge, no need for a diplomatic limousine and chauffeur to drive me about. I could walk to work or drive my own car. While there was really no great financial sacrifice in this transition, you can too easily become accustomed to a certain standard of living made necessary by a diplomatic appointment abroad, and if you yield to the temptation to try to maintain that standard when you are transferred to Ottawa, and you haven't the private means to do so, you can get into difficulty. We had no problem here.

The change was made easier for me because not only was much of my work a continuation of what I had been doing, but many of those with whom I worked in External Affairs and in other government offices were old friends. It was easy to join the fellowship of Deputy Ministers and sit once again on interdepartmental committees which seemed to be even more numerous than in 1941.

I was fortunate also in knowing so many of the members of the Cabinet, some of whom – Brooke Claxton, Paul Martin, Doug Abbott –

were personal friends. My contacts with the Prime Minister had naturally increased as my own responsibilities as a civil servant increased, although I never felt that I really knew Mr King. Who did? He was still Secretary of State for External Affairs when I returned to Ottawa but was soon to transfer this portfolio to the Minister of Justice.

I had met Mr St Laurent on several occasions and had learned to respect him as a man and for his sense of public service in entering the Cabinet during the war when his personal wish was to remain in private life. I admired the important contribution he had made then to national unity, so essential to the successful Canadian war effort. But I did not know him well. That changed after he became my chief, as the first Secretary of State for External Affairs who was not also the Prime Minister.

I naturally saw much of my new Minister. I like to think that the official association soon developed into a deep and enduring friendship. It certainly did on my part. I have never known a finer gentleman, or one who had a greater sense of public duty. His service to his country was without any thought of self, without any meanness of spirit, or ever alloyed with personal or unworthy motives. While his Irish temperament could occasionally show in bursts of transitory anger, he was a man of the greatest courtesy and kindliness, considerate of others, patient, fair-minded, and understanding. One of my greatest privileges in public life was to have been so closely associated with him during these years.

As Deputy Minister, I had the major responsibility for putting the department on a peacetime basis. It had expanded tremendously from 1939 to 1946, but much of this expansion was temporary and due to the exigencies of war. Many of our wartime duties could now be wound up; our temporary officers could return to their usual work. Many of the wartime practices and much of the wartime organization had also to be altered. Earlier routines were re-established without, I hoped, new ruts being created. This work of reorganization and re-establishment occupied a great deal of my time and attention though I delegated as much of it as I possibly could, in line with my practice and preference, which I believe is the right one, to decentralize responsibility for planning and administration to the greatest possible extent.

It was, however, neither possible nor desirable to return completely to the prewar organization of the department. Some of the new duties undertaken during the war years continued in peacetime. Our responsibilities in the field of foreign relations had grown and, with postwar problems crowding in on us, were more likely to increase than decrease unless the government wished to go back to the cautious, no-commitment attitudes of the thirties. I knew that Mr St Laurent thought that this was both undesirable and impossible, and I agreed with him. Moreover, Canada's diplomatic relations had been greatly enlarged during the war and the immediate postwar period. There was no way of escaping this, even if we had wished to. Canada emerged from the war a strong and respected sovereign state. Practically every country in the world wished to establish diplomatic relations with her. The problem was how to keep inevitable expansion under control and within our resources of finance and trained personnel.

When the war broke out in 1939, we had seven missions abroad. By the end of 1945 we had twenty-two. This expansion of political, diplomatic, and administrative activity meant that I was taking over the department at a very exciting and challenging time. It made my position a very busy as well as a very enviable one for I liked change and activity and responsibility. In addition to my strictly departmental duties, I was active in the work of the United Nations and attended many of its sessions as a Canadian representative. During this period, and even more when I later became Minister, I often felt like a commuter between Ottawa and New York. I will write more in later chapters about these international activities.

The department was also concerned with the preliminary work in negotiating a European, and later a Pacific, peace settlement. It was necessary for the government not only to formulate its views but to ensure that they would be heard and considered in the negotiations. We had had little or nothing to do with the terms of surrender and the temporary arrangements for the control of Germany after the surrender. Indeed, there was no desire in Ottawa to become involved in many of these arrangements, territorial and political which, we hoped mistakenly, would only be temporary in character. Therefore their obvious faults, even their dangers, would disappear when the permanent peace treaty was made. However, we did insist that we should have an appropriate role in the negotiation of that treaty. We would accept nothing imposed on us from above by the Big Four who apparently wished to keep control of peace-making as well as of war-making. Their agency for this purpose was the Council of Foreign Ministers. In that Council of Four, they were having their own problems in reaching agreement, both on questions of substance and of procedure, and they did not welcome demands from others to participate and be consulted. The USSR, represented by the rigid and suspicious Molotov, 'Old Stone Face,' was particularly intransigent about admitting any participation from countries like Canada, particularly, of course, in connection with a German peace settlement. However, when a satisfactory arrangement was eventually agreed for a peace conference with Italy and the lesser axis powers, Canada was represented, made her views known, and signed the resulting treaties. Austria was a separate problem whose solution was left to the Four Powers. Here we could state our position only in a memorandum which expressed also our dissatisfaction with the procedure that we had had to accept.

It was with the German peace settlement, however, that we were primarily concerned. On this vital question we could get no access to the Council of Foreign Ministers, except through their deputies. To them we submitted, as requested, Canada's views of what should be included in a German peace treaty, while insisting that this procedure was no substitute for full participation in any formal peace conference, and the right to sign any treaty or treaties that might result from it. We emphasized that any peace treaty must be considered in relation to the problem of European economic recovery and, above all, to the prevention of another war. The mistakes of Versailles must not be repeated. If Germany was to be demilitarized, her ethnic frontiers should be respected and she should not be economically destroyed. Our views were sensible but they were of little import. The Council could not agree among themselves or accept Soviet policy to prevent the restoration of any but a pro-communist Germany. In this situation, they were not likely to pay much attention to the views of any other country. Thus the German peace treaty remained undrafted, the peace conference postponed indefinitely, and the Cold War took over.

On the economic front, our department had little or no responsibility for purely domestic matters. As Deputy Minister, however, I took part in meetings concerned with economic questions when international factors had to be considered, as was often the case. The government expected severe economic dislocations and difficulties in the re-entry of hundreds of thousands of ex-servicemen and women into the labour market. It was thought there might be high unemployment and economic recession. This, fortunately, did not happen. The change-over was made smoothly and successfully under plans that had been previously drawn up. War veterans were quickly absorbed into the labour force. They were also treated more fairly and generously, with far more efficient plans for their civil re-establishment and training, than we had been after World War I.

On the international economic front, Canada was concerned with the re-establishment on a stronger and better basis of the trading and financial relationships disrupted by war. There was also the need for assistance to countries which had been physically or economically damaged by the conflict. In this area questions of direct concern to Canada included financial and commercial relations with other countries; relief and rehabilitation programs; loans; the supply and financing of food and other commodities to countries still suffering from the war and its aftermath; foreign loans; exchange and balance of payments problems; shipping, aviation, and telecommunications questions; relations with existing international economic agencies, and the establishment of new ones.

There were many conferences and negotiations on these matters, both bilateral and multilateral. The latter were usually related to our membership in the UN, more particularly in the Economic and Social Council, to which we had been elected when it was first set up. Canada played an active part in ECOSOC, and in the conferences held under its auspices in Geneva and Havana to organize international trade in a way which, it was hoped, would avoid the conflicts and restrictions which helped to bring about the economic depression of the thirties. While it was impossible to agree on an International Trading Organization, partial success was achieved in the acceptance of the General Agreement on Tariffs and Trade (GATT) which soon began its important and productive work.

We had, of course, special and very important trading relations with the United Kingdom and the United States. These involved many and difficult discussions, in which our department played an active part. The re-establishment of sound and mutually profitable trading and commercial relations with the United Kingdom was made more difficult by its serious financial and exchange problems, due largely to Britain's tremendous war effort which had required the sacrifice of most of its dollar assets. Canada was not in the sterling area, and if the UK was to continue to import from us, in conditions where free convertibility of the pound was not possible, she had to receive financial help. This meant dollar loans, and price concessions on new and old food contracts. It was in our own interest, of course, to help put the UK in a position where she could buy our goods. But it was also important to be fair to our own producers, and especially our farm producers, in doing so. The reconciliation of these points of view was not easy and the discussions to that end were long, complicated, and difficult. At times this taxed the patience and goodwill of both governments.

These discussions also confirmed the view, which I had formed in earlier negotiations and conferences, that the British are as shrewd and tough bargainers, especially in trade and commercial matters, as are to be found anywhere, although their arguments are usually presented in a calm and dispassionate way, in the best Oxford accent, by very cultivated and intelligent persons. Off duty, they are friendly and hospitable, operating on the assumption, which is only rarely condescending, that we are all members of the same Commonwealth family and in that spirit everything will be worked out amicably and equitably. Even if their methods may seem at times a shade subtle, their word can be relied on and their engagements, once made, are kept.

The Americans are much more outspoken and aggressive in putting forward a case. Their attitude is more informal, their toughness more obvious, and their talk more emphatic. Their arguments are often easier to understand and to counter than those of their British counterparts. The political and commercial pressures on official negotiators are often more obvious. It is foolish, of course, to generalize, but I would normally prefer to face the Americans than the British in difficult intergovernmental economic bargaining.

In prewar years, there was a triangular relationship in trade between Canada, the United Kingdom, and the United States in which we could use the surplus sterling from the UK to meet our dollar deficits with the US. With inconvertible sterling, however, this could not happen, so our trade deficits with the US became a serious problem. Measures therefore to protect our dollar from this imbalance, which I will not discuss in any detail, became a major subject of negotiation and discussion with Washington. It is interesting to note, in the light of what has happened since the situation was reversed, that we did not act in Ottawa to protect our position without prior consultation with our neighbour. It would be comforting to think that this was due to a higher sense of international responsibility. But it is also true that we knew that action on our part, which could be considered arbitrary or unfair, would invite retaliation, and that in this kind of conflict we would be bound to suffer most. This did not mean then, as it should never mean, that we have to abandon a right and strong Canadian position. It does mean that before we decide to stand firm on that position, we should be certain that it is based on principles that we must maintain whatever the cost.

It was at this time that I became interested in examining the pros and cons of a reciprocal free trade arrangement with the United States. We were authorized by Mr King and Mr St Laurent to do this on a purely official and non-committal basis and to discuss it in Washington on the same basis. I have mentioned the fear that the transition from war to peace, the re-establishment of stable and prosperous international economic relations, would be very difficult and the risk of high unemployment very great. When an international situation of this kind seems to be developing, or could develop, Canada is bound to think first of her trading relations with her neighbour – her largest market and her largest source of imports. The examination that was made and the discussions held about a possible free trade arrangement went into the matter in greater depth and detail than is generally known. They showed that a strong economic case could be made from the Canadian point of view for continental free trade. I know that Mr St Laurent was impressed by the economic advantages for Canada and that he hoped any necessary arrangements could be made, for this was an essential factor, without prejudicing Canada's independence. Mr King, at first, was also impressed by the economic argument. There were two main reasons, however, why the matter was not proceeded with. First, the dangers of postwar recession and high unemployment were avoided; second, Mr King concluded, I think rightly, that the political risks, short-range and long-range, for the country and for his government, were too great. So no formal and governmental consideration followed. I have always believed that if the question had ever reached higher political levels on the American side, it would also have been rejected. It was, however, a useful exercise if, as it turned out, only an academic one. It made me even more aware than I was before of the importance and complexity of our economic relations with our neighbour. It confirmed my feeling that from now on we would have to consider these relations much more carefully and seriously than before. All the more because the US was not withdrawing into isolation as she did after 1918, but was taking on world responsibilities for peace and security as the leader and by far the strongest of the western powers. This policy of international commitment and leadership by Washington which I, for one, thought should be encouraged and supported involved Canada in many conferences and discussions with our American friends with a view to working out arrangements for collective security, particularly through the UN, and subsequently through an Atlantic Alliance when the 'cold war' paralysed the UN. In the circumstances of those early postwar years, this seemed a hopeful and constructive development, which I will be discussing later in detail.

Not long after the end of the war there were indications that I might be asked to leave the civil service for politics. The Prime Minister referred to this possibility more than once in his diary, before it was ever mentioned to me or indeed before I knew it was in his mind. The first indication that he was considering me as his successor as Minister of External Affairs, when he decided to separate that portfolio from the office of the Prime Minister, was on 3 August 1946 during our meeting in Paris. We were having a summer night's drive together through the Bois de Boulogne in a horse-drawn carriage when he told me I would be going back to the department and the question of entering politics came up. He mentioned this in his diary for that day:

I spoke to Pearson about the possibilities which the post [in External Affairs] might offer of his entering politics which I think he would like to do, but he wisely states that he is not letting that enter his mind at all. Will concentrate wholly on External Affairs regardless of party altogether and will be quite happy to stay on in that field and later perhaps return to some post of representation abroad.

I was, of course, flattered that the Prime Minister should be thinking of me as a possible Minister for External Affairs. I had no desire to leave the civil service, however, and thought that I made this clear to him on that rustic ride around the Bois.

That was, I thought, the last I would hear from Mr King about a transfer to politics. I was wrong. On 19 September 1947, after I had been happily at work for some months as Deputy Minister under Mr St Laurent, the matter came up again. I was discussing with Mr King an offer I had received of a very attractive position in the United States about which I knew he had been told. He urged me to turn it down and remain in Canada. He told me that Mr St Laurent, who wished to return to private life, had agreed to remain in the government for another year. Mr King felt, however, that, on his own retirement which, he said, would soon take place, Mr St Laurent would be chosen as his successor and would carry on for a few more years. The PM felt that if I would now enter politics as Minister for External Affairs, I could in all possibility look forward to succeeding Mr St Laurent. I was not really interested but said nothing. A month later, Mr King was kind enough to give me a ride home from a dinner at Rideau Hall when I told him I had decided not to become President of the Rockefeller Foundation but to remain in External Affairs. He expressed some pleasure and assured me I was right not to leave. He may have linked this decision with a possible entry into Canadian politics, though that had nothing to do with it.

The fact is that I really was not tempted by the offer of the External Affairs portfolio in Mr King's government. Quite apart from the question of leaving the civil service for politics, which made no great appeal to me, I knew that Mr King, as long as he was Prime Minister, would continue to direct and dominate External Affairs and even as a Minister I would, after so many years as one of his officials, remain essentially in that category. This might not have mattered if I had had political ambitions, which I did not; or if Mr King was certain to retire in a few months, which in 1947 was not all that clear; or, most important of all, if I was sure I could whole-heartedly support his views about Canada's foreign policy. I was very doubtful whether I could do this. I had become a strong believer in an activist policy for Canada in the development of strong international organizations for collective security and economic progress. I still hoped that the UN might become the instrument for this, though disappointed at the setbacks and frustrations which the Cold War had already brought to the world organization. Mr King, in his heart of hearts, was looking back to the cautious, non-committal policies of the twenties while I, as he would put it, continued to look for the parliament of man. He was even opposed to the expansion of the Commonwealth and was particularly irritated that he should be asked to take any responsibility for admitting India, as a Republic, to that association. In short, I would be unhappy in Mr King's government as the Minister technically responsible for a foreign policy which would be determined by him. I have often wondered why he wanted me for the post. I knew that, although he seemed to like me personally and was always very kind to me, he thought many of my ideas on foreign affairs rash and adventurous, which would lead Canada into trouble. I suppose he thought that political pressures and responsibilities would settle me down.

The whole situation changed, however, when Mr King retired and Mr St Laurent, on 8 August 1948, was chosen by a Liberal Convention to succeed him. Quite apart from my high regard for Mr St Laurent as a man, our views on the principles that should guide Canada's postwar foreign policy were very similar. We were both convinced that our country should play its full part in the international organization of peace and security. Our relations as Minister and Deputy Minister had for me been perfect. He gave me maximum freedom in carrying out the policies that the government had agreed on, and did not interefere in details. In return, I gave him complete loyalty and the best service I could. Thus when Mr St Laurent, now the chosen leader of the Liberal party and soon to be the Prime Minister, asked me in late August 1948 to become his Secretary of State for External Affairs, thereby continuing on a higher level the relationship which had become for me such a happy and rewarding one, I was bound to reconsider the whole position.

I knew that Mr St Laurent had already discussed with Mr King his intention of inviting me to join the government and that Mr King had strongly urged him to do so. A few days after Mr St Laurent's offer, Mr King urged me to accept it.

I was now faced with the most difficult decision that I had ever had to make. Acceptance meant leaving the security and satisfaction of the civil service for the hurly-burly, controversies, and uncertainties of politics, of which I knew little. Indeed, if I had known more, I might have made a different decision. It meant becoming a member of the Liberal party with which, of course, I had had previously no formal association of any kind. My academic duties had earlier discouraged such partisan association and my civil service status subsequently had prevented it. There was, however, no difficulty for me in accepting the general principles and policies of the party.

On the positive side, there was the honour of becoming a Cabinet minister with such an enviable and sought-after portfolio. I was certainly human enough to be impressed by that, while so ignorant of the nature of politics as to be unaware of the feeling that was bound to exist among Liberal Cabinet Ministers and Members of Parliament that this honour was being conferred on one who had done nothing to deserve it by service to Parliament and party. I would be working, as I have said, under a leader whom I admired, and who put the invitation to me in terms which were certainly designed to make the greatest possible appeal to me. When, thinking aloud, I asked Mr St Laurent why I should make the change with all the risks involved, his reply was 'For the same reason that I did in 1940, service to your country.'

There was truth in that. As a Minister of External Affairs, I would have far greater responsibility and authority to help determine that Canada's foreign policies were the right ones for the postwar years than I could ever hope to have as a civil servant, however senior I was and however much freedom I was given. We were in the midst of the negotiations leading up to the North Atlantic Pact. I was by now committed to Atlantic collective security and the development of an Atlantic Community and I confess that the possibility of playing a political role under Mr St Laurent in this and related matters made a strong appeal to me.

Naturally, I discussed all the pros and cons with my wife. She knew that my mind was moving toward one decision. She did not disagree with it, though she would have preferred the other one. In any event, the matter was put with characteristic clarity by our son at a family conference. After I had been engaged in 'on the one hand' and 'on the other hand' exercise for some time, he broke in: 'Why are you wasting so much time, Dad? You know that by now you have made up your mind and all you want is for the three of us to tell you that this is the right decision and to confirm your judgment. It's OK.' So I told Mr King and Mr St Laurent that I was available for new duties.

I recall so well Mr King's remark on hearing this. 'Now, St Laurent, we're going to have to get him elected.' I suddenly realized, almost with a shock, that there was more to politics than being made Secretary of State for External Affairs. A few constituencies were mentioned and discarded as a possible political home. Then Mr King decided that the member for Algoma East, who was marked for elevation to the Senate before the next election, should be given that honour at once. This would mean a vacancy in the Commons. Mr King asked me whether I had any connection with Algoma East. My reply was so negative that he had to show me where it was on the electoral map. I did, however, agree to take my chances there if a constituency convention would accept me. It was a choice I never regretted, either politically or personally.

On 10 September Mr King told his Cabinet that they were to have a new colleague. He then had the necessary Order-in-Council passed, took me to be sworn in, presented me with the Bible on which this was done, and, finally, with Mr St Laurent, exposed me for the first time as a Minister and a politician to the gentlemen of the press. This one was an easy and friendly conference, only slightly marred by my quip in reply to the question: 'How long, Mr Pearson, have you been a member of the Liberal party?' 'Since I was sworn in as a Minister a couple of hours ago.' I should have learned by now that, while quips can get a politician headlines, they can also get him more easily into trouble than more serious observations.

At the end of the day, one so momentous for me, I called my aged mother in Toronto to tell her that I was now the Minister for External Affairs in the government of Canada. She had once hoped that I would be a Minister of the Gospel, so could not refrain from sending me her congratulations, her love and best wishes in these words: 'Well, I am glad you have at last become a Minister, if only a second-class one.'

INDEX